Thunder in the West

The Oklahoma Western Biographies
Richard W. Etulain, General Editor

Also by Richard W. Etulain *(a selective listing)*

AUTHOR
Owen Wister
Ernest Haycox
Re-imagining the Modern American West: A Century of Fiction, History, and Art
Telling Western Stories: From Buffalo Bill to Larry McMurtry
Beyond the Missouri: The Story of the American West
Seeking First the Kingdom: Northwest Nazarene University, A Centennial History
Abraham Lincoln and Oregon Country Politics in the Civil War Era
The Life and Legends of Calamity Jane
Calamity Jane: A Reader's Guide
Ernest Haycox and the Western
Billy the Kid: A Reader's Guide

COAUTHOR
Conversations with Wallace Stegner on Western History and Literature
The American West: A Twentieth-Century History
Presidents Who Shaped the American West

EDITOR
Jack London on the Road: The Tramp Diary and Other Hobo Writings
Writing Western History: Essays on Major Western Historians
Basques of the Pacific Northwest: A Collection of Essays
Contemporary New Mexico, 1940–1990
Does the Frontier Experience Make America Exceptional?
César Chávez: A Brief Biography with Documents
New Mexican Lives: Profiles and Historical Stories
Western Lives: A Biographical History of the American West
Lincoln Looks West: From the Mississippi to the Pacific

COEDITOR
The Popular Western: Essays toward a Definition
The Idaho Heritage
The Frontier and American West
Basque Americans
Fifty Western Writers: A Bio-Bibliographical Guide
A Bibliographical Guide to the Study of Western American Literature
Faith and Imagination: Essays on Evangelicals and Literature
The Twentieth-Century West: Historical Interpretations
Religion and Culture
The American West in the Twentieth Century: A Bibliography
Researching Western History: Topics in the Twentieth Century
Religion in Modern New Mexico
By Grit and Grace: Eleven Women Who Shaped the American West
Portraits of Basques in the New World
With Badges and Bullets: Lawmen and Outlaws in the Old West
The Hollywood West
The American West in 2000: Essays in Honor of Gerald D. Nash
Wild Women of the Old West
Chiefs and Generals

Thunder in the West
The Life and Legends of Billy the Kid

Richard W. Etulain

University of Oklahoma Press : Norman

Publication of this book is made possible through the generosity of Edith Kinney Gaylord.

Library of Congress Cataloging-in-Publication Data

Names: Etulain, Richard W., author.
Title: Thunder in the West : the life and legends of Billy the Kid / Richard W. Etulain.
Other titles: Life and legends of Billy the Kid
Description: Norman : University of Oklahoma Press, [2020] I Series: Oklahoma western biographies ; volume 32 I Includes bibliographical references and index. I Summary: "Biography of the notorious westerner William H. Bonney, better known as Billy the Kid, and evaluates more than a century of interpretations of him by biographers and historians, novelists, and film-makers"—Provided by publisher.
Identifiers: LCCN 2019057916 I ISBN 978-0-8061-6625-4 (hardcover)
Subjects: LCSH: Billy, the Kid. I Outlaws—Southwest, New—Biography—History and criticism. I Billy, the Kid—In literature. I Legends—Southwest, New. I Southwest, New—In popular culture. I Southwest, New—History—1848—Historiography. I Lincoln County (N.M.)—History—19th century—Historiography.
Classification: LCC F786.B54 E88 2020 I DDC 364.15/52092 [B]—dc23
LC record available at https://lccn.loc.gov/2019057916

Thunder in the West: The Life and Legends of Billy the Kid is Volume 32 in the Oklahoma Western Biographies.

The paper in this book meets the guidelines for permanence and durability of the Committee on Production Guidelines for Book Longevity of the Council on Library Resources, Inc. ∞

1 2 3 4 5 6 7 8 9 10

For Fred Nolan and Bob Utley
the authorities
on Billy the Kid and Lincoln County
and for
Chuck Rankin
diligent and supportive editor

Contents

Contents

Illustrations

Illustrations

Series Editor's Preface

Stories of heroes and heroines have intrigued many generations of readers and viewers. Americans, like people everywhere, have been captivated by the lives of military, political, and religious figures as well as intrepid explorers, pioneers, and rebels. The Oklahoma Western Biographies build on this fascination with biography and link it with two other abiding interests of Americans: the frontier and the American West. Although volumes in the series carry no notes, they are prepared by leading scholars, are soundly researched, and include extended discussions of sources used. Each volume is a lively synthesis based on thorough examination of pertinent primary and secondary sources.

Above all, the Oklahoma Western Biographies aim at two goals: to provide readable life stories of significant westerners; and to show how their lives illuminate a notable topic, an influential movement, or a series of important events in the history and culture of the American West.

This volume on the famous Billy the Kid moves in two directions. The first, most extensive part provides an overview of Billy's frenetic life from 1859 to 1881. The second section examines the shifting legends circulating around the Kid from his closing years to the present. A connecting chapter,

Series Editor's Preface

"Who and What Was Billy the Kid?" evaluates the contours of Billy's character and career and prepares the way for a discussion and analysis of the biographical, historical, fictional, and cinematic interpretations of the infamous outlaw. The author especially aims his life-and-legends approach at two groups of readers: those who relish a lively story of a notorious Old West figure; and those who are convinced that what writers and readers think about facts (interpretations) are often as important as the facts themselves. In marrying biography and interpretation, this volume moves in a new direction for understanding Billy the Kid.

This book breaks from earlier interpretations of Billy. In the half-century from the Kid's death to the mid-1920s, journalists and dime novelists usually portrayed him as dangerous desperado, a violent gunman. But after the publication of Walter Noble Burns's romantic, sympathetic biography, *The Saga of Billy the Kid* (1926), biographers and moviemakers produced more positive accounts of the southwestern outlaw. This study follows neither of these competing interpretations. Instead, it presents a more complex figure, a Billy the Kid who was both dark and uplifting in his actions. Describing the outlaw as a "bifurcated Billy," the author depicts the Kid as a Dr. Jekyll and Mr. Hyde figure, who was a thief and murderer but also a charming companion and sometime opponent of crooked politicians, entrepreneurs, and legal authorities. This more complicated characterization of Billy the Kid deserves close attention.

These pages are based on careful research. The author provides extensive, wide-reaching coverage by drawing systematically on hundreds of published books and essays. The volume likewise thoroughly examines major manuscript collections. This volume, when combined with the author's companion work, *Billy the Kid: A Reader's Guide* (2020), provides the fullest account thus far of the life and legends of Billy the Kid.

Richard W. Etulain

———

Preface

I was in the Southwest teaching history at the University of New Mexico when the questions began. What did I think about Billy the Kid? Was he an evil villain or a warm companion? Had I read about him or seen a movie in which he was featured? Even my students were posing the questions. It took a while for me to realize that Señor Billy was the most written-about New Mexican and challenged Jesse James and General George Armstrong Custer as the leading attention-getter of the Old West. And here I was a specialist in the history of the American West.

It took a while, too, for me to realize that the Southwest (especially Texas, New Mexico, and Arizona), like the northern Rockies and the western Great Plains, had experienced a Wild West different from the frontier of my native Pacific Northwest. The Far West of the Pacific coast states certainly was also part of the frontier movement, but it had not hosted dramatic, controversial characters such as Billy the Kid, Wild Bill Hickok, Wyatt Earp, and Calamity Jane, or even charismatic Native heroes such as Sitting Bull, Crazy Horse, Chief Joseph, and Geronimo. Billy the

Kid and his legends lived in a romantic Old West I had to become acquainted with.

In the 1980s, I began researching and writing on Billy. That work led to several published essays, the introduction to a reprint of Walter Noble Burns's dramatic biography *The Saga of Billy the Kid* (1926), and parts of two other books. Then I got sidetracked on several other projects, including books on the recent American West, two volumes on Calamity Jane, a book entitled *Ernest Haycox and the West* (2017), and a volume entitled *Presidents Who Shaped the American West* (2018), coauthored with Glenda Riley. But Billy lurked in the stables and corrals.

A few years ago I decided that rather than do a large volume on Abraham Lincoln and the American West, I would undertake a long-delayed book on Billy the Kid. Soon the project ballooned into two volumes. This biography would be the first; *Billy the Kid: A Reader's Guide* would be the second.. Endless days of examining manuscript collections, reading all the major books and essays on Billy, perusing newspaper stories, and viewing the major films on the Kid followed. The Old West of Billy the Kid was being resurrected.

I have two specific purposes in mind for this volume. Part 1 provides a brief and balanced biographical account of Billy the Kid. Part 2 traces the interpretations of Billy, including multiple legends, that have taken root, sprouted, flowered, and matured in the nearly 140 years since his death in 1881. Although many accounts have been more sympathetic to than negative about Billy, this treatment in both sections avoids taking sides. I attempt to portray instead what I call a "bifurcated Billy," part villain and part generous companion.

This book summarizes the major twists and turns of Billy the Kid's life and surveys the flood of interpretations about him—stressing a few topics that previous biographers have underemphasized or overlooked. For example, the following pages deal explicitly with key women in Billy's life, including his mother, Catherine McCarty Antrim; Susan McSween; and the señoritas and señoras who played important roles in his life. The same is true for Mexican- or Hispanic-heritage peoples. Most residents in Lincoln County during Billy's years there were Hispanics, or Mexicans as they were then called by Anglos or whites. This book examines their clear contributions to the life and times of Billy the Kid. Finally and perhaps most importantly, at the end of the biographical section, a brief overview chapter addresses the large, significant question, "Who and what was Billy the Kid?" This chapter is purposely placed after the biographical section as something of a summation of part 1 of this volume. But I also place the pen portrait of Billy before the second section on popular and historical interpretations to aid readers in comprehending how the myths that congregated around his life after his death both followed facts and widely diverged from them.

As I prepared to write this overview volume, I moved in two directions. Over time, I visited all the major manuscript collections of documents on Billy the Kid and the Lincoln County War. Some I visited twice, including the Haley Library in Midland, Texas; the University of Arizona Library in Tucson; the collections in Lincoln, New Mexico; and, of course, multiple times, the libraries and archives in Santa Fe and Albuquerque. I also conducted research in Silver City, Roswell, Las Cruces, and Fort Sumner, New Mexico, and in several other libraries as well.

For part 2 of this volume, I read through all the major books and essays on Billy the Kid and the Lincoln County War. I particularly devoured the writings of Frederick Nolan and Robert Utley and gladly admit my heavy indebtedness to their research and writing. I also plowed through the earlier writings of Pat Garrett, Walter Noble Burns, William

Keleher, Maurice Garland Fulton, and later works authored by Jerry (Richard) Weddle, Kathleen Chamberlain, Mark Lee Gardner, and John Wilson.

Something needs to be said about the positions this book takes on the multiple controversies and unsolved mysteries that cluster around the life and death of Billy the Kid. Many of the first journalists and dime novelists pictured Billy as a dark and demonic desperado. I do not. Many historians and novelists writing after the appearance of Burns's influential *Saga of Billy the Kid* in 1926 began to see the Kid as a hero. I do not follow their view either.

Beginning in the 1960s and beyond, a majority of writers began to see—and have continued to see—Billy as part hero, part villain. That bifurcation of Billy is the point of view taken in these pages. I fashion him as a divided Billy, I try to show that the Kid combined positive and negative characteristics. Sometimes he was a friendly, gregarious, and helpful companion, especially to women and Hispanics but also to John Tunstall, Alex McSween, and pals such as Tom O. Folliard, Charlie Bowdre, and more than a few others.

On other occasions, the Kid was a violent, murderous villain. These untoward actions show up in his participation in the killings of Sheriff William Brady and the Tunstall assassins, William Morton and Frank Baker. Nor can I see that the Kid's first killing of Windy Cahill in Arizona in August 1877 should be considered an act of self-defense.

This back and forth view of Billy may lead some readers to wrongly conclude that I am waffling. Not so, the both-and view—rather than either-or conclusions—retains the ambiguity that lurks in Billy's character and actions. Complexity, not the simplicity of villain or hero, is central to a more probing view of the Kid.

Still other comment is necessary for a larger understanding of the organization of this book. Some writers and scholars are satisfied to produce the most factually correct biography of the Kid possible—and stop at that point. I try to move on to a second stage without overlooking the first. I am convinced that the most complete comprehension of Billy the Kid comes from combining a thoroughly dependable biography with a summation and evaluation of the changing interpretations of the Kid, including the legends about him that have evolved through time. If we are to truly understand the mysterious Kid, it is most likely to come from a marriage of biographical and historical facts to an understanding of shifting cultural and historical interpretations of him.

In two ways, then, this is a middle-of-the-road book. It balances or blends the greatly diverging portraits of Billy as villain and hero, and it steers a course between a solely factual biography of the Kid and a journey through the interpretive fields that have flowered over time. I am convinced that these two positions, mediating the biographical, historical, and cultural extremes, will lead readers to a larger, more complex picture of the famous Billy the Kid.

Following the guidelines for the Oklahoma Western Biographies series in which this volume appears, this book carries no annotations, but it is based on wide-ranging, thorough research, including reliance on all the major books and essays published on Billy as well as letters and other documents in the most-important manuscript collections. These published and unpublished sources are discussed in the essay on sources and listed in the bibliography at the back of the present volume. I have also drawn on my own previous writings; they too are listed in the bibliography. Extensive summaries and evaluations of these sources, especially in the discussions of biographies, historical novels, and some films about the Kid, also appear in a forthcoming companion volume, *Billy the Kid: A Reader's Guide* (2020).

Over the years, I have benefitted from several sources of support that I wish to acknowledge. When I began my work on Billy the Kid in the 1980s and 1990s, the University of New Mexico provided funding for my research and travel. The university also granted me several sabbatical leaves and supported my work through its Center of the American West in the History Department.

There was also the encouragement and help from several scholars. I wish again to salute the aid of Frederick Nolan and Robert Utley. They answered my questions, read and commented on my work, and made helpful suggestions for the future. Wonderfully supportive friends. Paul Andrew Hutton also encouraged my research dealing with Billy the Kid and other Wild West topics. His sense of humor and enthusiasm were—and are—buoying. In addition, Charles Rankin has been a diligent, supportive editor; Durwood Ball, a thorough copyeditor; Steven Baker, a dependable editor.

More recently Kathleen Chamberlain, Richard (Jerry) Weddle, John Wilson, Joel Jacobson, and Steve Tatum were helpful through their writings and in answers to my questions.

A host of librarians and archivists have been invaluable helpers. I especially want to thank Cathy Smith at the Haley Library; Nancy Brown-Martinez and Tomas Jaehn at the Center for Southwest Research in the Zimmerman Library at the University of New Mexico. Librarians at Boise State University, New Mexico State University, the New York Historical Society, the New Mexico State Records Center and Archives, and the Happy Valley Library in Clackamas, Oregon, have paved the way for my research on numerous occasions. I heartily salute them.

Richard W. Etulain

PART I

THE LIFE

Billy the Kid, 1859?–1881. This tintype, the only authenticated photograph of Henry McCarty Antrim (alias Billy Bonney; alias Billy the Kid) was
probably taken in Fort Sumner, New Mexico, in 1879–1880. The surviving
tintype was one of four produced at that time and cut from the same plate.
The other three are lost. Many of the early reproductions of this photograph
were reversed, leading some to conclude falsely that Billy was a "left hand
gun." Photograph courtesy of Richard Weddle.

1

Mysterious Origins

Henry McCarty to William Bonney

No larger, more enduring mystery surrounds Billy the Kid than the multiple missing details of his early years. Despite diligent, continuous research for several decades, most information about the first years of his life remains hidden. Not until 1873, when Billy was about fourteen, did his name first appear in print. Anyone interested in the life of Billy the Kid must be ready for a flood of maybes, perhapses, and unclears in accounts of his early childhood.

Most of the known fragments of information pertain to Billy's mother, Catherine McCarty. Born about 1829, she probably came from Ireland, perhaps pushed out by the Irish potato famine and drawn to the United States by the American dream. Residing in New York City—historians think—she gave birth to two boys, Henry and Joe. Which was the older of the two is not entirely clear, although most Kid biographers list Billy as the older. The identity of Catherine's husband, if she had one, is also unknown, even though some researchers list her husband as Michael McCarty, a Union soldier killed in the Civil War. Researchers have located other McCarty men, including a Patrick McCarty, but none of these McCarty families include a named husband, a Catherine, and two sons named Henry and Joe and born in the 1855 to 1865 period. In addition, no evidence proves the same man was the father of both boys.

Catherine McCarty Antrim, 1829–1874. This image is a drawing based on a widely circulated original photograph. Many, if not most, writers on Billy the Kid question the authenticity of the photograph said to be of Billy's mother, Catherine. Unfortunately there is no fully authenticated photograph of her. Perhaps the image has become part of the legend surrounding Billy's much-loved mother. Photograph courtesy of Bob Boze Bell.

To complicate things further, in 1880 a federal census taker in Fort Sumner, New Mexico, knocked at the door of the residence of Charlie and Manuela Bowdre, where a young man then called William H. or Billy Bonney, or the Kid, was staying or living next door. He or one of the Bowdres stated he had been born in Missouri. The census entry indicated that both his parents were Missourians and that he had been born in 1855 (making him now twenty-five). We do not know whether Billy, Charlie, or Manuela told this story to the census taker, but a search of the 1860 U.S. Census in Missouri turned up no boy with any of his names.

Eventually most Billy biographers have come to accept, hesitantly, 23 November 1859 as his birthdate. They do so because insufficient evidence exists to dismiss it or to advance other more defensible dates. In 1882, one year after the Kid's death, his killer, Pat Garrett, published his biography, *The Authentic Life of Billy, the Kid*, with most of the first chapters—if not the whole book—ghostwritten by journalist and friend Marshall Ashmun "Ash" Upson. The journalist, whose birthday was also 23 November, claimed he had lived for a few weeks with the McCarty family in Silver City, New Mexico (and perhaps even earlier in Santa Fe), from whom he had learned about Billy's birthdate in New York City. Skeptical scholars usually dismiss or clearly question the birthdate, perhaps as they should. Unfortunately, we have no evidence to disprove 23 November as the correct birthday or to replace it with another more believable date of birth. As a result most historians, biographers, and other writers about Billy, including this writer, accept the date as an uncomfortable compromise. We will haltingly accept it until something more persuasive or definitive is uncovered in the future.

Up to the present day, researchers continue to turn up new information about Billy's origins. In 2015–2016, for example, two writers discovered facts that both enlarge and perhaps help explain the McCartys' origins on the East Coast. In 2015 Frederick Nolan, a noted Billy the Kid specialist working with new evidence, speculated about Billy's first years in an online essay entitled "The Birth of an Outlaw." Nolan was convinced, after closely examining the backgrounds of witnesses to the Catherine McCarty–William Antrim marriage in Santa Fe in 1873, that he had discovered the birthplace of Billy in Utica, New York. He had found in the U.S. Census of 1860 a Catherine McCarty residing in Utica, who perhaps was the mother of a one-year-old Billy McCarty also living there in 1861. Nolan likewise concluded that the marriage witness in Santa Fe named "Josie" was not Billy's brother but Josephine McCarty, a relative (perhaps sister) of Catherine's. Braiding together these loose ends and re-reading the 1873 marriage record, Nolan deduced that Billy was born in Utica about 1860 rather than in New York City in 1859.

One year later journalist Wayne Sanderson added still another gloss on Billy's origins in his piece, "The Kid and the McCarty Name." Beginning with details in an 1872

Marriage record for Catherine McCarty and William Antrim. This record of the marriage of Billy's mother to William Antrim on 3 April 1873 in Santa Fe is the first published reference to the Kid. The document refers to him as "Henry McCarty" and his brother as "Josie McCarty." The report of ceremony appears in the records of the First Presbyterian Church of Santa Fe. Illustration in Peter Hertzog, *Little Known Facts about Billy, the Kid* (Santa Fe, N.Mex.: Press of the Territorian,1963), 4.

letter written by a Catherine McCarty in the mining town of Nevadaville, Colorado, and published in the New York newspaper *Pomeroy's Democrat*, Sanderson traced Catherine's family history to New Jersey. He surmised that Catherine, unmarried and pregnant, left newly born Billy with her sister Margaret McCarty for as long as ten years before taking him with her to Indiana and Kansas—hence the family rumor that Margaret was the mother and Catherine the aunt of Billy. Sanderson concludes that this "Willy" McCarty, making his way eventually to New Mexico, was our Billy the Kid.

These two provocative—and speculative—online essays indicate just how much is still unknown about Billy's birth and first decade. Both brief pieces also raise as many questions as those they try to answer. Still, their authors identify the additional factual information needed before we truly know and understand the early childhood years of Billy the Kid.

In the 1950s, more dependable accumulation of facts about Billy's early years began to emerge from historical records of the mid- to late-1860s. That more trustworthy evidence revolves around mother Catherine in Indianapolis, Indiana. In 1868 she was listed as the widow of one Michael McCarty in an Indianapolis city directory. Her two sons were not entered. In the mid-1860s she met William Antrim, a Civil War veteran and a hack driver. Born in 1842, Antrim was about a dozen years younger than Catherine. He delivered packages for an express company and may have met Catherine in that way. Her place of residence was not too far from the Antrim home and the company for which he worked.

By 1870 Catherine McCarty, her two boys, and William Antrim were living in Wichita, Kansas. Whether they came from Indiana separately or as a couple is not known. Wichita was just beginning to rise from the flat, treeless plains of south-central Kansas at the confluence of the Little Arkansas and Arkansas Rivers. Founded in 1868 and incorporated in 1870, Wichita was located in Sedgwick County, home to about six hundred residents in the census of 1870.

Unfortunately, the three McCartys and William Antrim left too early for the Indianapolis census of 1870 and arrived too late for the census in Wichita. But the amount of revealing information available about Catherine McCarty and William Antrim during the 1870–1871 period in Wichita is enough to bring a shout of joy to fact-hungry Billy the Kid researchers. The sparse and contradictory reports from New York and Indiana about Catherine McCarty are replaced with dependable details in Wichita.

Most of all, these sources picture Catherine as a spunky, ambitious widow, not a penniless, desperate woman. She was an American willing to speculate on the future of her family and herself in a raw frontier town. When a group of 124 residents signed a petition favoring the incorporation of Wichita in July 1870, Catherine was the only woman on the list. She was going to be part of the new, optimistic community. Even more confirmation of Catherine's ambitious character was revealed in several land acquisitions.

On 12 September 1870, she purchased a lot on Chisholm Street, followed by other lot acquisitions.

These were modest buys in Wichita's business district. Later, after receiving downtown lots from Antrim, Catherine opened a laundry, possibly with living quarters upstairs. In the first issue of the new Wichita *Tribune* on 15 March 1871, the newspaper editor saluted Catherine's work: "The City Laundry is kept by Mrs. McCarty, to whom we recommend those who wish to have their linen made clean."

Catherine also acquired a quarter section of farm land northeast of Wichita, paying two hundred dollars for the 160 acres. Antrim built a small, twelve-by-fourteen-foot house on the property, and Catherine and her two sons moved in on 4 March 1871. She cultivated about seven acres of land and made other improvements valued at two hundred to three hundred dollars. The diligent work and aid of William Antrim suggests he was not entirely a dreamy, wandering prospector, as his critics suggest after the family moved to New Mexico. What the exact relationship was between Antrim and Catherine remains a mystery. In an affidavit supporting Catherine's purchase of the quarter section, Antrim testified he had known her for six years, back to about 1865. Whether their contact was platonic is not clear, but they did not marry until 1873, about eight years after they first met.

One can only guess what the year or so in Wichita meant to Henry McCarty and his brother, Joe. It was clearly a cattle town, with thousands of Texas longhorn cattle tramping through the area to railroad depots that had opened— and were opening nearby—to the north and northeast. In 1881, soon after Billy's death one editor, describing the young man who became Billy the Kid, said that "many of the early settlers [of Wichita] remember him as a street gamin in the days of the longhorns." Obviously Henry would have seen much of the cattle business close at hand and undoubtedly witnessed some of the gunfire and violence that spilled out of saloons onto the town streets while he was there. More than one writer speculates that Catherine moved out to her quarter section to get her boys away from the unruly, dangerous streets of Wichita.

Change charged onto the scene in spring 1871. Catherine began selling off her land and lots. On 16 June she sold her farm claim. Later, in August she sold her town lots. Why? Some conclude that Catherine had now been diagnosed with the deadly tuberculosis that would take her life three years later and was urged to go farther west to higher, drier climates. By August she had relinquished her hold on her earlier land purchases. Scanty evidence suggests that Catherine, her boys, and Antrim left soon thereafter.

Where would they go? The paucity of evidence is frustrating, but two bits of information point in one direction. In 1928 Billy's brother, Joe McCarty, now a near-indigent, colorless old man in Denver, told an interviewer that he had arrived there in 1871 "with his father, a Wells-Fargo Express agent." And Billy Bonney also spoke once of being in Denver. According to Frank Coe, a friend in Lincoln County, Billy told him that Henry, his mother, and brother had lived for a few months in Denver. Then, in 2016 journalist Wayne Sanderson discovered the 1872 letter from Catherine McCarty residing in Nevadaville, Colorado, about thirty miles west of Denver and adjacent to Central City, a major mining area. This Catherine McCarty was trying to locate her sister Margaret McCarty and her two brothers Matthew and Barnard, perhaps now living in New Jersey. If this is *the* Catherine McCarty—and perhaps she is—the McCarty-Antrim contingent was residing in a climate said to be better for Catherine's TB than that of Indiana or Kansas and in just the kind of location William Antrim had dreamed of to find his mineral stake.

Where the McCarty-Antrim group went next was unknown until bits of information, hidden for nearly eighty years, were discovered in the early 1950s. Resourceful researchers turned up the record of a marriage ceremony uniting Catherine McCarty and William H. Antrim at the First Presbyterian Church in Santa Fe on 1 March 1873. Officiating these nuptials was the Reverend David F. McFarland; witnesses included the minister's wife, Amanda R. McFarland, and their daughter, Katie McFarland, Harvey Edmunds, a resident of Santa Fe, and the two McCarty boys, Henry and Joe (or Josie). Catherine and Antrim were listed as "of Santa Fe," which suggests they had been in the city for at least a month to fulfill local guidelines on residence and marriage. Some thought Antrim and the McCartys may have stayed with his sister, Mary Ann Hollinger, a resident of Santa Fe. Local rumors also suggested the newlyweds and boys stayed in Santa Fe for a short time, with Henry even working in a local hotel.

Before long, however, the family was on the move, going south. Perhaps they relocated for Catherine's health, perhaps for Antrim to pursue his prospecting dream, possibly for both. For Henry McCarty Antrim, during the next eight years, save for a two-year hiatus in Arizona, New Mexico would be his home. The historical contours of Henry's new home merit explanation, helping us to understand the sociocultural settings that surrounded and shaped the young man.

2

Entering Territorial New Mexico

Setting the Scene

New Mexico Territory, during the thirty-year period stretching from the end of the U.S.-Mexican War in 1848 to the high point of the Lincoln County War in 1878, was awash in continual change, transformation, and sometimes virtual chaos. Socioeconomic and cultural trends shifted so frequently and markedly that coherent, persistent patterns failed to emerge and solidify. The numerous conflicts among racial or ethnic groups, economic battles among merchants, cattlemen, miners, and landowners, and deadly contests between political factions were as prologue to the explosive conflicts that embroiled Billy the Kid in southern New Mexico. No one can understand Billy's life after he first came with his family to New Mexico in 1873–1874 without a clear view of the ever-changing times that surrounded him in the final eight years of his life. As we shall see in the subsequent chapters, these changes would transform New Mexico from the late 1840s until the early 1870s, thus shaping the territory for the McCarty-Antrim entry in 1873. The life of famous westerner Billy the Kid would be molded by the milieu that had come into focus—but would continue to change—during his New Mexico years.

Two powerful relationships did most to shape events in New Mexico in the three decades following 1850. They would greatly impact political, economic, and social affairs

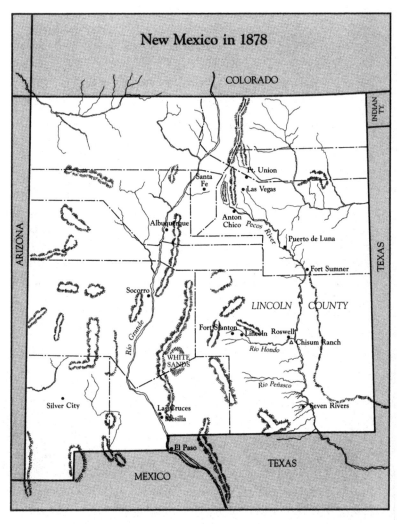

New Mexico in the 1870s. This map shows the major towns, settlements, and army posts in New Mexico Territory at the time of Billy the Kid. He either lived in, visited, or passed through nearly all of them. Map in Robert M. Utley, *High Noon in Lincoln* (Albuquerque: University of New Mexico, 1987), 50, reproduced courtesy of the author.

in the territory. The first was New Mexico's role as an emerging—and then aging—territory in the Union. In the American system of government, a territory was a halfway political house, standing midway between the acquisition of a new area and its eventual statehood. In the territorial system, the federal government largely retained control through its appointive power of the territory's executive officers, the governor, secretary, and supreme court justices, and paying their salaries. That meant, effectively, that territories lacked major levers to control their own destinies.

Unfortunately the men selected for territorial offices were too often political appointees—or even hacks—who knew little about the faraway places to which they were sent. Although New Mexicans, after receiving territorial status in 1850, could elect a nonvoting territorial delegate to the U.S. Congress and members to their own territorial legislature, they still remained, in many ways, under the lion's paw of Washington, D. C. In his classic study *The Territories and the United States, 1861–1890* (1947), historian Earl Pomeroy concludes that the "chief significance" of the territorial system was "being weak: it allowed a freer play of other influence, personal, economic, physiographic, spiritual." Other scholars see a Deistic design: the federal government created the territories and then allowed them to run, willy-nilly, on their own.

The laissez faire character of this governmental organization allowed local traditions, power-hungry newcomers, and others to move into and occupy the power vacuum in New Mexico Territory. In the 1850s and 1860s, its first generation as a territory, New Mexico was ruled by a group of wealthy Hispanic families, known as *ricos*, that gained prominence through their land grants, mercantile activities, or political connections dating to the Mexican period (1821–1848) of New Mexican history. By the early 1860s, about fifteen to twenty well-to-do Hispanic families dominated the territorial legislature, opposing the governors appointed by Washington, D.C., and pushing for the extension and expansion of what historian Howard Lamar calls "a conservative and tradition-minded society." Because Americans were slower in coming to New Mexico than to Texas and California in the 1850s, the native New Mexicans (Hispanics) retained control of the territory.

New Mexico was a massive territory that included nearly all of present-day Arizona and a piece of southern Colorado, In the years following the Treaty of Guadalupe Hidalgo signed in 1848, domination of the southern half of New Mexico gradually transferred from Indian to Hispanic and then to Anglo control. By the end of the 1870s, Native American power was almost entirely eliminated, with most tribal groups residing on reservations, save for scattered groups of Apaches in southwest New Mexico. But in the 1850s and 1860s, while Anglos and Hispanics clashed on legislative policies, both had to face a more urgent problem—what to do about Indian tribes in the territory. The Pueblos, scattered up and down the Rio Grande Valley and spilling out west and east, probably numbered between 5,000 and 10,000 people. In the north were the overlapping and competing Southern Utes and Navajos. To the southwest, stretching into what would become Arizona, were the Gila Apaches; in the southeast extending as far north as Las Vegas were the Mescaleros and the Jicarillas, sometimes competing with the Comanches and Kiowas raiding from farther east. In 1850, perhaps as many as 40,000–50,000 Native Americans controlled as much as 80 percent of New Mexico Territory. How to handle these large groups of Indians remained a major challenge for much of the next two decades.

The impact of the Civil War in the first half of the 1860s added markedly to the confusion that characterized New Mexico Territory in Billy's time. Historians from the east often underestimate how much the sectional war impacted the West and, in reverse, play down the influence of the

West on the entire country during the Civil War years. This misunderstanding results from two oversights. First, the Civil War was much more than simply an all-consuming military engagement; it was also a clash between opposing ways of life, competing economic systems, and clashing sociocultural trends. Second, it is true that conflict over slavery was the major reason for the outbreak of war in spring 1861, but no one should overlook the huge collision between the North and South, Republicans and Democrats, about the possibilities of expanding slavery into the trans-Mississippi West. The Civil War was brought on by both the controversies surrounding slavery in the South as well as its expansion into the West. As historian Elliott West has argued in one of the most important recent writings about the American West, historians must see and understand the need for a "Greater Reconstruction" in writing about the mid-nineteenth century, showing how U.S. expansion into the American West and events leading to the Civil War were linked, not separate, in the 1850s and 1860s.

When viewed from this perspective combining the Civil War and western America, the 1860s and 1870s in New Mexico, the backdrop for Billy the Kid's life in the territory, take on larger, more complex meanings. The war notably changed the status of the U.S. Army in the frontier West. Many—if not most—of the regular U.S. soldiers were recalled to fight in the theaters of conflict east of the Mississippi River. That movement of troops reduced the number of soldiers available to hold the forts established to control Indians and protect established and incoming settlers. In New Mexico, unlike many other parts of the West, the Civil War had another far-reaching impact; the territory became the site of battles between Union and Confederate armies. The encroaching war meant that most army posts in the West had two purposes: (1) to deal with Indian challenges; and (2) to protect populations sympathetic to the Union. In New Mexico Forts Union and Garland in the north, Fort

Craig in the center, Fort Sumner in the east, Fort Stanton in the southeast, Fort Fillmore in the south, and several other posts faced these challenges, with their presence and operations obviously influencing New Mexico's economic and social landscapes.

The shaping influences of the Civil War were illustrated in two important series of events in the early to mid-1860s. Eager to push to the West Coast to secure ports on the Pacific and to seize and control mineral riches in California and other parts of the interior West, the Confederacy sent an army from Texas to conquer New Mexico in 1861–1862. After defeating General Edward R. S. Canby's Union forces at the Battle of Valverde in February 1862, the Confederates under General Henry Hopkins Sibley, pushed north and easily took Albuquerque and Santa Fe. Finally, with the help of the southward-moving Colorado Volunteers, New Mexican forces met the Rebel invaders at Glorieta Pass, located between Santa Fe and Fort Union. The battle proved to be the tipping point in the Confederate invasion of the Far Southwest. In a surprise flanking move, a contingent of Union forces discovered and destroyed the southerners' wagon train. Losing their supplies forced Sibley's men to retreat back to Texas.

If this series of military events ending at Glorieta was one notable influence of the Civil War on New Mexico Territory, another dealt more specifically with Indian policy. After the stubborn, hard-nosed General James H. Carleton took command of the Department of New Mexico, he first cleared out Confederate sympathizers in the Mesilla area and then quickly moved against Indian tribes. Arrogant, arbitrary, and unfriendly toward Indians, Carleton went after them. First, he dispatched Union volunteers under Colonel Christopher "Kit" Carson to drive the Mescalero Apaches to their knees and sent them to the Bosque Redondo, a newly established reservation located near Fort Sumner. Next in 1863, he ordered Carson to round up the Navajos in western New Mexico, who had refused Carleton's directive to give up and relocate to Bosque Redondo. With his soldiers, Carson, following Carleton's orders with which he disagreed, destroyed Navajo crops and animals. Over two years, they rounded up as many as eight thousand members of the tribe and marched them on the deadly Long Walk to the Bosque Redondo. It was in all ways a horrendous decision, with hundreds dying on the trail and in their new cramped, infertile, and suffocating reservation. Finally relenting before waves of criticism and the pitiful facts of Navajo disease and death, the federal government removed Carleton and, relenting in 1868, allowed the Navajos to return to a reservation carved out of their old homeland in the Four Corners area and mostly in northeastern Arizona.

The sudden shifts in policy and actions dealing with Indian policy and the declining numbers and strength of Natives is revealing in that when Billy the Kid came into the Fort Sumner area a decade later, the Navajos were gone and the Mescaleros were living on a separate reservation near Fort Stanton. Fort Sumner had been deactivated and sold to Lucien Maxwell, the territory's largest landowner. When Billy arrived, Fort Sumner was a small village, mainly of Hispanics, nestled among surrounding small farms and ranches. Once most of the Indians were removed from the area, Hispanic farmers and Anglo cattlemen, especially those from Texas, found abundant open grassland and fertile areas in what later became Lincoln County of southeastern New Mexico.

Alongside the fractious conflicts over military engagements and Indian policies, New Mexico Territory experienced other changes during the 1860s and 1870s. In politics, two shifts were of note: one an act of separation; and the other a gradual, coalescing of special interests.

In 1863, Arizona was taken from New Mexico Territory and made a separate territory. Many of the same problems that had perplexed New Mexico in the previous dozen years now vexed Arizona. Coming later, these were perhaps more challenging. During the war, anti-Unionism surfaced in western New Mexico, the area that became Arizona, for a number of reasons. A few southerners had settled in the area and agitated for Southern and Confederate expansion there. Miners also felt they were being overlooked by the territorial government in Santa Fe. Especially going unaddressed was their need for protection from the western Apaches. And gathering near Mesilla in southern New Mexico, which had active transportation connections through Texas to the South, were Southern sympathizers. Some were long-term Anglo merchants, others incoming settlers, and still others ambitious Mexican-heritage peoples hoping for something better.

In the late 1850s and early 1860s, pro-southern supporters gathered strength and were better organized. Encouraged by Texans in nearby El Paso, some residents of Mesilla and pioneers in Tucson called for secession from New Mexico and for the establishment of the separate territory Arizona. In some ways Arizona owed its eventual territorial status to the ongoing conflict between southern and northern supporters in western and southern New Mexico. When Confederate forces invaded and captured the lower Rio Grande valley in 1861–1862, southern supporters immediately moved to establish a Confederate territory encompassing southern and western New Mexico. Several moves were made in that direction, with Arizona becoming an official southern territory in January 1862. But conflicts among Confederate supporters, the defeat at Glorieta Pass, and retreat of Sibley's army back to Texas undermined the Southern-organized Arizona Territory. Then when Carleton led the California Column across the desert to New Mexico, he swiftly and thoroughly drove out the pro-Southern leadership in 1862, and those in the Southwest and in the nation's capital advocating Arizona as a Union territory renewed their political efforts. With the strong support of leaders of the new Republican Party, the enabling act of Arizona passed the U.S. Congress in February 1863 and was quickly signed by President Lincoln.

New territorial status did little to address—let alone solve—Arizona's major problems. The most pressing issue was trying to control the diverse western Apache tribes and to make what is now southern Arizona safe for incoming settlers, chiefly miners, ranchers, and farmers. Several forts, including Fort Bowie, Fort Crittenden, Fort Lowell, and Camp Grant, were established in hopes of stopping the never-ending conflicts with the Apaches. In these early years of its existence, Arizona remained a "beleaguered territory" in the words of historian Howard Lamar. Relationships between New Mexico and Arizona Territories remained distant, thus allowing, for example, a young Henry Antrim or Billy Bonney freedom from apprehension once he broke the law in one territory and bounded into the safety of the other.

Meanwhile, in Santa Fe an informal movement toward political and economic coalescence was taking place among powerful men. It too would eventually have powerful impact on the last years of Billy the Kid's life. By the end of the 1860s, politics in New Mexico Territory were shifting away from the domination of elite Hispanic families. Although the federal government continued to appoint, by and large, ineffectual executive leaders, new local political leaders were emerging. None were more important than Thomas B. Catron and Stephen B. Elkins. Both graduates of the University of Missouri, the two friends served in the Civil War (Catron with the Confederacy, Elkins with the Union) and then came to New Mexico. By 1869, after less than five years in the territory, Elkins was the U.S. attorney and Catron, the territorial attorney general. In the next decade, working from their powerful legal firm in Santa Fe with branches in Albuquerque and Las Vegas, the duo became the most important lawyers in New Mexico. Adjudicating land grants was their specialty.

Thomas Catron, 1840–1921. Catron is often singled out as the leader of the much-criticized Santa Fe Ring. The most powerful figure in New Mexico in the 1870s and 1880s, he sided with The House, the Murphy-Dolan clique in Lincoln County, which bitterly opposed the Tunstall-McSween group Billy the Kid followed. Photograph in the Robert N. Mullin Collection courtesy of the Haley Memorial Library & History Center, Midland, Texas.

Before Elkins abandoned New Mexico for a brighter future in the East in 1877, he and Catron, especially through Republican Party circles, placed their large fingerprints on numerous political decisions in the territory. Catron and Elkins, wily and sometimes outside the law, fluent in Spanish and wise to the complicated Spanish, Mexican, and Anglo legal traditions operating in New Mexico, manipulated measures dealing with cattle ranching, mining, railroads, and statehood, and, above all else, with contested Spanish and Mexican land grants. Often the two lawyers helped

20

William Antrim, 1842?–1922. Antrim, the stepfather of Billy the Kid (Henry McCarty Antrim), is often depicted in negative terms, but the strongest evidence indicates that he was not a violent, cruel man but that he was uninterested in serving as a father to Henry and Joe after their mother, Catherine, died and most interested in "making it big" in mining. Later on William did not refer to Billy as his stepson. Photograph in the Robert N. Mullin Collection courtesy of the Haley Memorial Library & History Center at Midland, Texas.

Hispanic families gain clear title to their early, sometimes shaky land grants—but at a steep price. Catron particularly asked for large parcels from the land grants he defended. Caught in the web of legal uncertainties in New Mexico and of equally vague federal guidelines, the land grantees compromised with their challengers, giving up huge acreages to secure court approval for their grants. Toward the end of the century, building on dozens of these land grant settlements, Catron became the richest man in New Mexico and the largest landowner in the entire country. He owned seventy-five land grants totaling more than two million acres and owned parts of or served as legal counsel for another four million acres.

Catron was also the pivotal figure in what became known as the Santa Fe Ring. Informally working together as a network of lawyers, politicians, and developers, the Ring served like a Tammany Hall boss system transplanted to the

West. So powerful were Catron and other Ring participants that political and economic measures had little chance of passing in the territorial legislature or of being adopted at county levels unless they had Ring support. As we shall see, Catron's long arms of influence reached into Lincoln County and shaped much of its economy and politics in the 1870s through his connections with businessmen Lawrence G. Murphy and later James J. Dolan and his political links with District Attorney W. L. Rynerson and Judge Warren Bristol. These men, united by their Republican politics and their membership in the Masons, were determined foes of cowman John Chisum, Lincoln attorney Alex McSween, English rancher John Tunstall—and Billy the Kid.

By the early 1870s, and increasingly in the following decade, these historical trends, and the men who initiated or acted on them, set the scene into which the McCarty-Antrim family moved in 1873.

3

Negotiating Silver City and Arizona

The new settlement at Silver City must have seemed ideal for Catherine and William Antrim. Catherine needed a high, dry—and hopefully warm—climate to help combat her advancing tuberculosis. Santa Fe might have worked but Silver City would be better. Maybe she was willing to give way to another move because Silver City, the mining boom-town to the southwest, was pulling at her new husband, William. Even before their move west, Antrim had been interested in mining. All the rumored promises of "hitting it big" in Silver City were tugging at him.

After their wedding in March 1873, Catherine, William, and their two boys, Henry (Billy) and Joe (Josie), headed down the Rio Grande in late spring or early summer. It was a stagecoach trip of about 250 miles. Proceeding west from the river, they arrived in Silver City after a rumored but perhaps unsatisfying stop in Georgetown, a nearby mining boomtown. William evidently wished to try out mining claims near Georgetown, but Catherine upset by what she saw in the camp, wanted something more stable for her boys. On to Silver City they went.

The years in Silver City from 1873 to 1875, abbreviated and tragedy-filled though they proved to be, provide the fullest, if limited, picture we have of the Antrim family. It was the only time the parents, now married, and the two

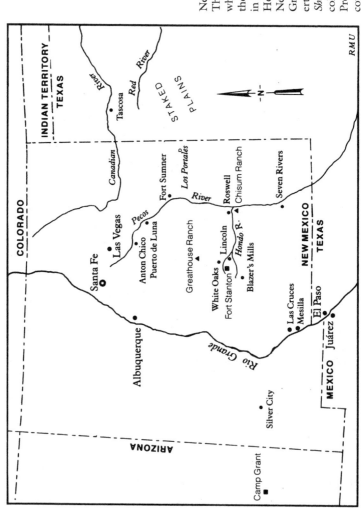

New Mexico and Arizona. This map includes the sites where Billy the Kid lived in the years from 1873 to 1877 in New Mexico and Arizona. He resided in Silver City, New Mexico, and near Camp Grant, Arizona. Map in Robert M. Utley, *Billy the Kid: A Short and Violent Life* (Lincoln: University of Nebraska Press, 1989), 2, reproduced courtesy of the author.

Antrim house in Silver City. Historians and biographers disagree over whether this building was the house where the Antrim family resided when Henry McCarty Antrim lived in Silver City from 1873 to 1875. But some view the back portions of the building—those to the right—as the Antrim home with sections to the left added later. Photograph by Alfred S. Addis courtesy of the Palace of the Governor Photo Archives, New Mexico History Museum, Santa Fe, negative no. 099054.

boys were together as a family, united for more than a few months. But the togetherness was exceptionally brief. The family quickly spiraled downward.

The Silver City stay is particularly helpful in trying to understand Billy's short life. Historians see in Billy during these two years bits and pieces of a teenage boy living with his family, going to school, traipsing around town with his chums, and taking part in musical and drama productions. These twenty-four months were his transition from boyhood to the first acts of criminality that would capture the rest of his life.

Silver City was booming. The discovery of rich silver strikes in spring 1870 set off a rush of incoming miners hoping to make it rich. About a hundred buildings, mostly adobe, were thrown up, but a surprising number of brick structures were erected later, giving Silver City a more modern and eastern look than most other New Mexico towns. Like other mining boom towns, Silver City soon experienced an influx of saloons and brothels. Gambling establishments and street violence quickly followed.

The town grew so rapidly that in 1871 it was named the county seat of Grant County. A census in 1873 enumerated 826 citizens, most of whom were Hispanics. Despite the influx of families and the paucity of available homes, the Antrim family was able to locate a small two-or three-room wood frame building near the center of the new town. The small home soon became a haven for Henry and a place his friends liked to visit.

Billy's boyhood friends in Silver City were unanimously positive in their glowing praise for his mother, Catherine McCarty Antrim. None was more effusive—and extensive—in his reactions than Louis Abraham, one of Billy's closest buddies. Mrs. Antrim, Louis recalled more than sixty years later, "was a jolly Irish lady, full of life, and her fun and mischief." She "always welcomed the boys [of Silver City] with a smile and a joke. The cookie jar was never empty. . . . From school each afternoon we made straight for the Antrim home to play." Catherine's open-arms spirit remained central to Louis: "she was as good as she could be, and she made every one welcome in her home." Catherine's health was increasingly precarious, but Louis recalled that she "could dance the Highland Fling as well as the best dancers."

Another friend, Dick Clark, had similar remembrances of Billy's mother. She "helped support the family," Clark recalled, "by baking pastries that were sold very easily in town." Still another acquaintance recalled that Catherine "lived in a log house and ran a boarding house for the early traveler through this part of the country." More than a few others remarked that Catherine took in visitors for room and board, even though her home was of the smallest dimensions.

Most notable of Catherine's boarders may have been the nomadic journalist Ash Upson, who later ghostwrote Sheriff Pat Garrett's biography of Billy published in 1882. Upson claimed, with but a few bits of evidence, to have boarded with Catherine in both Santa Fe and Silver City. The Garrett-Upson biography describes Catherine as of "medium height, straight, and graceful in form, with regular features, light blue eyes, and luxuriant golden hair." She may not have been "a beauty, but what the world calls a fine-looking woman." Travelers, including "many a hungry 'tenderfoot,'" found their way to Catherine's house for room and board. In all her activities, she "exhibited the unmistakable characteristics of a lady—a lady by instinct and education." There is no reason to doubt any of these salutes to Catherine; others remembered her similarly.

Catherine's energy, attendance at Mexican *bailes* (dances), and care-taking of boarders remain all the more remarkable because she was gradually weakening. Attempting to stave off advancing health problems, Catherine traveled the twenty-five miles to Hudson's Hot Springs, where she hoped the hot, sulfurous baths would help fight off her tuberculosis, but they did not. Still, Mary Stevens Hudson, who helped operate the hot springs, became Catherine's good friend and described her as "a sweet gentle little lady . . . as fond of her sons as any mother could be."

By May 1874 the creeping malady had taken over Catherine's life. Some thought the heavy smoke and fumes emanating from nearby smelters exacerbated her respiratory problems. About one year after the Antrims arrived in Silver City, her heath had declined to the point that she took to her bed. For four months, Catherine struggled to breath, unable to stem the tide sweeping her toward the cliff. Death came on 16 September 1874, nearly a year and a half after the Antrims arrived in Silver City. Three days later the Silver City *Mining Life* carried an obituary, telling readers that

Catherine, aged forty-five, had died from "an affection of the lungs." A funeral service had been conducted at the Antrim home.

In the closing weeks of her life, Catherine continually worried about what would happen to her two sons. True, her husband could take care of them, but she wanted a maternal influence on the scene. To fulfill that need, she turned to Clara Louisa Truesdell, the caring mother of one of Billy's best friends, Chauncey Truesdell. Clara, a trained nurse, promised to look after the boys, which she did for a brief time after Catherine's death. It was Clara who prepared Catherine's body for burial.

Catherine's two sons and a handful of friends attended the memorial service, but husband William Antrim did not. Even though Catherine's health was precipitously declining, William was out on another mining quest. He was absent at both her death and funeral.

If observers unanimously praised Catherine as a mother, friend, and hostess, they were more divided—and reserved—in their assessment of William Antrim. The Garrett-Upson account was critical of William Antrim, setting the precedent of clouding his reputation for later writers. According to the duo, Billy had "often declared that the tyranny and cruelty of his step-father drove him from home and a mother's influence, and that Antrim was responsible for his going to the bad." Billy did not leave home until after Catherine's death, and no other person acquainted with Billy tarred-and-feathered William Antrim as Upson and Garrett did. Others spoke well of "Uncle Billy" Antrim's work as a butcher and carpenter. Harvey H. Whitehill, the former county sheriff, who could be critical of Billy the Kid and others, asserted that Antrim "lavished upon them [his two stepsons] almost a mother's care." Another of Billy's acquaintances, Dick Clark, also opined that Uncle Billy "was good to his step-children." Still another friend of Billy's, Louis Abraham, added that Antrim "was a man of good character," and Abraham's wife added that after Catherine's death, the stepfather was "both father and mother to the boys [Billy and Joe] doing all he could for them."

Antrim might have been a good man, but he also gradually became, at best, a distant parent. After his wife's death, he placed the two boys in other Silver City households, a choice suggesting that he would not be keeping a home for his stepsons. Dick Clark thought that Uncle Billy liked "his liquor too well" (an accusation no one else ventured), and Agnes Meader Snider called him a penny-pincher. But a more likely explanation was that after Catherine's passing Uncle Billy's most cherished mistresses were prospecting and gambling, which he was drawn to in hope of scoring "big finds" or "big deals." Antrim seemed unable or unwilling to keep at his butchery and carpentry in town, and gambling and mining ventures wooed him away. When Billy fled from Silver City in early fall 1875 after a brush with the law, Antrim lost contact with him but less so with Joe. In later years Antrim remained, for the most part, in Silver City, El Paso, and the community of Mogollon, New Mexico. He mined, owned small mines, and invested in properties. Although never a major owner or player, Antrim was comfortable, later adding a Civil War pension of forty dollars a month. When aging and poor health crept up on him, he moved to California to live with a relative. Death came in December 1922. During these post–Silver City days, Antrim did not speak of his stepson Henry Antrim.

The family member least on stage during the Silver City days was Billy's brother, Joe. He and Billy attended school for a few months, rambled about town with a group of early teenage boys and took part in town festivities. Some acquaintances thought that Joe, bigger than Billy, was also older. His death notice in Colorado indicated he had been born in 1854, making him perhaps five years older than Henry/Billy. Other, stronger, and more widely accepted evidence indicates that Joe was born in 1863, thus making him younger than Billy. Some wondered whether Billy and Joe were half-brothers with different fathers. After Billy skedaddled, Joe remained for a few years, at first boarding with other Silver City families, then moving out on his own. He left for Colorado, where he lived most of his adult life, marrying and skimming by on gambling and odd jobs. Through the years, he seemed to get lost, with no one ever asking him about his notorious brother, Billy the Kid. He had cut his ties to Silver City and his stepfather. Joe died nearly penniless in Denver in November 1930.

Not surprisingly, we know more about Billy in Silver City than about other members of his family. Except for a brief contemporary newspaper story or two, most of what has been uncovered about Billy in these years, 1875 to 1877, comes from remembrances gathered after more than a half-century. Still, taken together these fragments of contemporary and later evidence provide inklings of what Billy was like as a young teenager, before he went out on his own in Arizona for two years, then on to Lincoln County in New Mexico.

According to nearly all these memories of the early teenager then known as Henry McCarty, he lived a normal boyhood in his first year or so in Silver City. When his mother was still healthy, Henry and his chums—"American boys" all, as one acquaintance put it—often gathered for fun at the Antrim home. Henry was "a good boy," Louis Abraham recalled. He might have been "a little mischievous at times" and showed "a little more nerve," but Dick Clark remembered Henry as "full of fun and deviltry." Running with his small group, sometimes dubbed the "Village Arabs," Henry struck still another contact as an "always courteous" young man, who "respected his elders."

Anthony Conner furnished one of the few physical descriptions of the youthful Henry. Conner thought that even though Henry was in early adolescence, he looked younger and seemed small for his age. Slender with small feet, Henry also spoke with a soft voice. He "was under-sized, and really girlish looking," Conner added. "I don't think he weighed over 75 pounds." Others remembered Henry as skinny, with a wiry build.

In the first few months the Antrim-McCarty family was in Silver City, Henry accompanied his mother to town dances, which occurred more than once a week. Mother and son frequented American dance floors located near the town's saloons and may also have walked to nearby Spanish bailes. Billy was said to love those lively Mexican dances especially. We know that he spoke Spanish fluently a few years later and flirted with the Mexican señoras and señoritas. His attraction to Mexican culture probably began in Silver City, where school-age Hispanics outnumbered Anglo students seven to one.

Billy's friends also spoke of his interests in songs and sing-ing. The songs included the then-popular "Silver Threads among the Gold," "The Irish Washerwoman," and espe-cially "Turkey in the Straw." Later in the town of Lincoln, Billy told Mary Ealy, the wife of a missionary-doctor, that when younger he attended church and sang hymns with his mother. Ealy spoke fondly of Billy's beautiful tenor voice.

Billy also took part in some of the town's theatrical presen-tations and his school's festivities. He may have participated in productions of *Uncle Tom's Cabin* and *Ten Nights in a Barroom,* then-popular dramas. We know that he acted in a minstrel show, in which he was "the Head Man in the show," meaning that he had a significant role in that perfor-mance. Several of the dramatic presentations raised funds for the Silver City public school, which opened after the Antrim family arrived in town.

Revealingly, Tony Conner also remembered Billy as an enthusiastic lover of books and magazines. Billy "got to be quite a reader," Conner recalled. As soon as he finished his chores or his work at the butcher shop, Billy "would be sprawled out reading a book." His major interests were dime novels and the *Police Gazette*. Within the decade, he would become a subject in both forms of print media.

Most of all, in his first year and well into his second in Silver City, Billy attended school. Boyhood friends such as Chauncey Truesdell, Tony Connor, Louis Abraham, Dick Clark, and several others all remembered Billy as a student. Once a public school opened in early 1874, Billy and Joe began attending in January and continued in subsequent school terms through the summer and fall and well into the next year. Even after his mother died and his stepfather farmed out the boys to other homes, they attended school.

Mary P. Richards, a single, English-born, slim young woman of twenty-eight, began teaching in fall 1874. Competent and pleasant, Richards proved to be a strong teacher, much better than her two predecessors in winter, spring, and summer 1874. The town's newspaper editor, acerbic O. L. Scott, touted Richards as the kind of teacher the town needed. She knew how to motivate students.

Miss Richards and Billy became friends. She captured his attention, remarking later that Billy was "no more of a problem in school than any other boy growing up in a mining camp." Richards also recalled his appearance and demeanor. He was "a scrawny little fellow with delicate hands and an artistic nature" and "always willing to help with the chores around the school house." Billy noticed that his teacher was ambidextrous, writing with either hand, just like he could. As Richards later told her daughter, Billy thought he and the teacher must be related because she was the only person he knew with dexterity equal in both hands.

Family and school provided anchors of stability for Billy, but after his mother's declining health and death and his stepfather's lack of close supervision, he lost much of his mooring and quickly began a downward slide into instability and petty thievery. Not surprisingly, his friends, the Village Arabs, were rambunctious boys pulling the usual adolescent pranks. Those pranks included rock-throwing, harassing the town's Chinese, and breaking windows. And perhaps, they engaged in petty larceny. Alongside the marble shooting, footracing, and roughhousing were actions clearly outside the town's laws.

On one occasion, Billy tried to get his friend Charley Stevens to join him in breaking into and robbing the Derbyshire store, a furniture business that carried candy and books. The Derbyshire also displayed jewelry in its front window. Billy cajoled Charley into thinking about sneaking into the store, stealing the jewelry, and selling it elsewhere—maybe even down south in nearby Mexico. But Charley, restrained by an active conscience apparently absent in Billy, fessed up to his father about the planned break-in. Charlie's father informed Derbyshire of the plot, and the two grownups, hoping to ward off other such future misadventures, gave the boys a vigorous talking-to, warning them of the consequences of such reckless behavior. When asked about the untoward plan, Charley explained, "The Kid had me hypnotized." Historian Jerry (Richard) Weddle wonders whether this episode, when discovered, led the bed-ridden Catherine to admonish her son that he would "hang before you're 21" if he did not shape up. Billy repeated his mother's warning to authorities when he was captured about a half-dozen years later in 1880.

By spring 1875, with his mother now gone Billy was staying with the Truesdell family when he became a pilferer. As newly elected sheriff Harvey H. Whitehill recalled, Billy stole a few pounds of butter from a Silver City–area farmer and peddled the purloined commodity to a local seller. "His guilt was easily established," Whitehill remarked, "but upon promise of good behavior, he was released."

Then came a career-changing event, a tipping point, in Billy's life. Had Catherine still been alive to provide him a stable home, the missteps leading to the event might not have happened. But the avenue to trouble was wide open, with no impediments to block his dash outside the law.

The turning point came when an upset arose in the Truesdell home, and Billy had to find a new place to live. He moved into the boardinghouse operated by Sarah Brown. About this time he began to take a larger interest in gambling and hanging out at the saloons. He quickly developed into an adept cardplayer. As friend Charley Stevens noted, Henry "was a very fine card player . . . and had picked up many card sharp tricks." On more than a few occasions, Henry's small frame, soft voice, and youthful looks lulled other gamblers into overlooking his talents and mistakenly thinking they could beat him easily and badly. In card playing, as he would prove in several facets of his life, Henry was much more skillful and cunning than his innocent appearance suggested.

If these card competitors were blind to Billy's cardsharping, he was, in turn, blind to the downside of a rascally companion who entered his life and led him down a disastrous path. George Schaefer, nicknamed Sombrero Jack after his outlandish head wear, and a stonemason, also lodged with Mrs. Brown. He and Henry quickly became fast friends, an act that would be replicated frequently in the coming years: Billy's falling in with and following older men.

Schaefer, something of a heartless man, had two weaknesses: he was addicted to alcohol, often getting drunk on the weekends; and, according to Sheriff Whitehill, he "liked to steal. He had a mania to steal and he was always stealing."

Billy followed Schaefer like a moonstruck disciple and soon became embroiled in an unfortunate incident that abruptly ended his stay in Silver City. On 4 September 1875, a Saturday evening, Sombrero Jack, maybe enjoying an alcoholic binge, and his henchmen broke into the home of Chinese laundrymen Charlie Sun and Sam Chung, and stole a gun, blankets, and a bundle of clothes belonging to several customers, property worth about $150 to

$200. Henry probably did not participate in the break-in but nonetheless agreed to hide some of the goods at the Brown house—for a cut of the proceeds. Sarah Brown, eventually turning up the stolen items in Henry's room, informed Sheriff Whitehill, who promptly arrested Henry on 23 September and lodged him in the town's jail.

Three days later, the *Grant County Herald,* in one of the first newspaper accounts about Henry or Billy, in Silver City told the story of his jailing and escape: "Henry McCarty, who was arrested on Thursday and committed to jail to await the action of the grand jury, upon the charge of stealing clothes from Charley Sun and Sam Chung, celestials sans cue, sans joss sticks, escaped from prison yesterday through the chimney. It is believed Henry was simply the tool of 'Sombrero Jack' who done the actual stealing whilst Henry done the hiding. Jack has skinned out."

Acquaintances later gave their version of Henry's petty crime. Anthony Connor thought the arrest "did not amount to anything . . . and Mr. Whitehill only wished to scare" Henry. Sheriff Whitehill's own son, Henry, agreed: His father "didn't want to put him in a cell. He was just a boy who had stolen some clothes. . . . He did not want to be mean." Louis Abraham's mother likewise believed the sheriff "just wanted to scare" young Antrim.

Perhaps Henry had no idea that Whitehill wanted only to teach him a lesson about staying away from men of disrepute such as Sombrero Jack and stop stealing. What young Henry did have in that jail cell, however, was a powerful desire to escape, to be free. And in the next few days he proved just how adept he would be in escaping constraints of all kinds in the future. Complaining to Sheriff Whitehill that the jailer was mistreating him and not permitting any space or time for exercise, Henry talked the sheriff into giving him run of the hallway to exercise for a short time each morning. "Right there is where we fell down," Whitehill later confessed. Left alone for a few minutes, Henry headed to the narrow chimney—which seemed no larger than his arm, the sheriff thought—and squeezed up and out the flue. "When we returned . . . the 'Kid' was nowhere to be seen," Whitehill reported.

What happened next is told in several versions. Of note, revealing Henry-Billy's life attachments, nearly all the accounts came from women. Sarah Brown, Henry's land-lady, claimed she and a female companion got a stagecoach to take Henry toward Arizona. Others wondered if that really happened given that she had earlier sent the sheriff after Henry. Henry's teacher, Mary Richards (Casey), also alleged that she and another woman hid Henry in a barn, fed him, and loaned him a horse after he promised to return to Silver City and face the consequences of his crimes. But the most acceptable version of the to-Arizona stories origi-nated with Clara Truesdell. In her account, she took Henry into her home, cleaned him up from the chimney soot, gave him some of her son Chauncey's clothes, and then asked him to stay out of sight at Ed Moulton's sawmill while she tried to reason with Sheriff Whitehill. Clara's hope foun-dered. The sheriff refused to budge, so Henry headed west to Arizona.

In the fertile twilight zone between fact and fiction, several other baseless stories about Henry's life in Silver City surfaced after his death. In one such account Billy viciously decapitated a cat with his knife. In another, he participated in killing a Chinese laundryman. But the most widely trav-eled and influential distorted tale asserted that Henry-Billy by himself committed a murder. This yarn first appeared in the Garrett-Upson biography of Billy, *The Authentic Life of Billy, the Kid* (1882), falsely accusing Henry of knifing and killing a man in a saloon brawl. Although those persons close at hand dismissed this gory tale and others like it as "poppy-cock," the fictional story stayed in vogue for more than a half-century until the diligent research of historians Maurice Garland Fulton and Philip J. Rasch proved it wrong in every way. Through the years, those who wished to portray Billy as a vicious killer—as a young man who killed twenty-one men in his twenty-one years—embraced this trumped-up story as Billy's first murder in a long line of homicides.

Billy's decision to flee the authorities in Silver City meant that he was crossing his personal Rubicon and making a profound life's decision while still only in his mid-teens. At most about sixteen or perhaps as young as fourteen, Billy was now on his own, without family, community, or a single person he had known and trusted previously. He was making a solo dash into an uncertain, strange, and potentially dangerous future. This dramatic choice suggests more than a little about Billy's character, revealing impulsiveness and courage that acts and events in his remaining half-dozen years would substantiate.

He was a risk-taker to the point of foolhardiness. He was self-confident enough to believe he could work out a future for himself, when he had little or no past to follow and carry over the horizon. He was a pragmatist, trying one thing and then another until something emerged he could pursue, even if he could barely exist while doing so. The Henry McCarty of 1875 was already displaying the traits and patterns that came to light in Billy the Kid's final years from 1877 to 1881.

Skipping out of Silver City was half the challenge for Henry Antrim. The escape would keep him out of jail. But the other half he had no answer for: What would he do in Arizona? Where would he go? How would he find a way to support himself while still in his mid-teens? He had no family, no friends, or even casual acquaintances to call or count on. In the next two years he would learn much about life's challenges—all on his own.

There was one person to the west in eastern Arizona, however, whom Henry wanted to see. His stepfather, William Antrim, was working as a miner near Clifton. Some way or another Henry found William and explained his dilemma. What happened next travels several conflicting paths in Billy the Kid narratives. One story says that when Henry explained what had happened to him, William gave him what cash he had and urged his stepson to avoid future problems. The counterstory, based on Harry Whitehill's unflattering memories of Antrim as a hardhearted tightwad, says the angry stepfather told Henry, "If that's the kind of boy you are, get out." However distant and perhaps indifferent William Antrim was toward his sons, the best evidence suggests he was not totally insensitive and unfeeling.

For the most part, despite the diligent efforts of researcher Jerry (Richard) Weddle to uncover valuable information about Henry's two years in Arizona, reliable facts remain elusive and small in number. Other than the meeting with William, nothing else specific is known about Henry from his arrival in Arizona, probably in October 1875, until about five months later in the following March. Unsubstantiated stories depict Henry as something of an itinerant worker, trying his hand at gambling, farm and ranch labor, and odd jobs to eke out a living. He was without family, home, horse, or ongoing employment.

Without money to buy a badly needed horse for transportation, Henry—he was now beginning to be called Kid or Kid Antrim—stole a U.S. soldier's mount near Camp Goodwin, south and west of Clifton and directly north of Camp Grant. One month later Henry surfaced in Camp Grant, searching for a job.

Founded by famed Indian fighter George Crook in 1872, Camp Grant was situated in the Sulphur Springs Valley south of the Pinaleño Mountains. Intended as a strategic location from which to watch and control the nearby Apache Indians, the military reservation already hosted several military companies and boasted hastily erected buildings. About three miles to the south was McDowell's store, a cluster of saloons, dance halls, brothels, and other stores. It was an

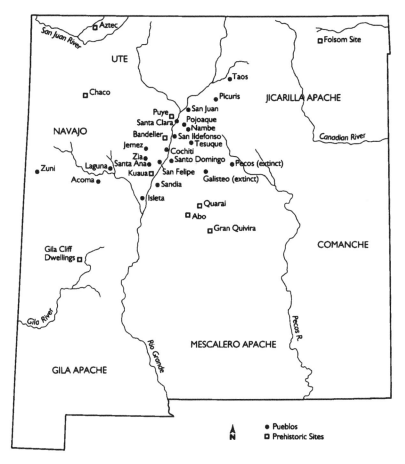

Indian tribes in New Mexico. This map pinpoints the early locations of the major Native American groups in New Mexico Territory. Map courtesy of Marc Simmons.

ideal environment for a gambler to practice his card arts with soldiers and ranch workers and a place to find some social solace or regeneration away from dull or physical labor.

Besides dealing games of faro and monte, Kid Antrim also tried his hand at ranch work. One of the ranchers he worked for was Henry C. Hooker, owner of the Sierra Bonita Ranch in Sulphur Springs Valley. A federal beef contractor supplying meat to soldiers and reservation Indians in the area, Hooker worked harmoniously with both the Apaches and soldiers. He needed workers for his expanding ranch and hired Antrim. The Kid's short career as a ranch hand revealed a good deal about him then and later. From the beginning, the Kid's small, slight physique disadvantaged him in physically demanding ranch work. He lacked the heft and strength to perform the arduous labor, and in an occupation that required initiative and drive, Antrim seemed unmotivated to others. Hooker's foreman, sizing up Antrim and his faltering work ethic, declared the Kid a "lightweight" and sent him down the road.

Although the evidence is slim and inconclusive, Antrim may have worked on one of John Chisum's ranches in southeastern Arizona. The southwestern cattle king's ranges and cattle herds fanned out from west Texas, through eastern New Mexico, and into southeastern Arizona. The Kid worked sporadically on several ranches from 1875 to 1877, and he may have hired on for a short time at Chisum's Eureka Springs spread. The cattle baron would play a large, increasingly negative role in the Kid's life after the teenager moved to New Mexico.

Like so many of the western legends such as Wild Bill Hickok, Wyatt Earp, and Calamity Jane, Kid Antrim rarely left behind much information about his daily life or routines. Those common happenings were not the stuff of sensational newspaper stories or retrospective memoirs. Instead, it was their rowdy behavior, illegal deeds, personal missteps that became widely known to the public.

So it was for the Kid. For a brief period, he was hired on as a cook at the Hotel de Luna, one of the few civilian establishments allowed on the Camp Grant military grounds. The Kid's culinary experiences were less than limited, however, and his inexperience may have undermined his kitchen work from the beginning. Whatever the case, rancher Henry Hooker, who operated the hotel, quickly sent Henry away, not because of his kitchen disasters but because "he got to running with a gang of rustlers," and the hotel had become "a headquarters of the gang."

Off and on the Kid had traveled on the right side of the law as a farm worker, ranch roustabout, and hotel cook. He soon moved to the dark side, however, when he hooked up with another young man who helped him steal horses. Just as Sombrero Jack had in Silver City, John R. Mackie (or McAckey) took Antrim under his more experienced wing and schooled him in making money in the dangerous enterprise of horse-stealing. A former soldier in his late twenties, Mackie was already a veteran horse thief in the area, especially making off with the army's horses.

During the period from March 1876 to August 1877, when Henry galloped hastily out of Arizona and headed east to New Mexico, nearly all his traceable tracks are tied to lawbreaking activities. His horse-stealing tricks, usually following Mackie's lead, were the stories later communicated to readers, political leaders, and local residents. Antrim and his companions often took horses picketed out front of saloons or bawdy houses while the horsemen were occupied inside. Even though the soldiers knew about the horse thieves and tried several dodges to keep their horses safe, Antrim and Mackie made off with several army mounts. In late 1876, soldiers followed and captured Kid Antrim after one horse-stealing incident, although strangely, they did not arrest him, instead leaving him afoot in very dangerous country. Three months later in February 1877, Mackie and Antrim stole horses from soldiers at nearby Camp Thomas. Following this escapade, the military roundly castigated Miles Wood, now a justice of peace, for not vigorously pursuing the rustlers. That criticism pushed Wood to act. He issued a warrant after complaints were filed against, among others, "Henry Antrim alias Kid," for horse-stealing. Again Antrim was captured—twice in fact—and both times he wiggled free. Although Henry tried to square himself with the army by returning stolen horses, his growing reputation as a horse rustler may have been too discomfiting or embarrassing for his stepfather William Antrim, who abandoned his prospecting in eastern Arizona and returned to Silver City.

Even though the army might have forgiven Henry for his thievery, Miles Wood did not. One month later on 25 March, Wood tried once more to capture and keep Henry and his sidekick, Mackie, under arrest. When they, like foolhardy twins, showed up at the Hotel de Luna and ordered breakfast, Wood played a trick on them. Hiding a six-gun under a platter piled with food that he took to serve the duo, he quickly pulled the gun from under the lid, placed the young men under arrest, and took them off to the Camp Grant guardhouse. But Antrim, already an experienced escape artist, somehow obtained salt, threw it in the guard's eyes, and bounded away. Within hours the Kid was back in the guardhouse. This time blacksmith Windy Cahill shackled Henry. Yet, spotting a very narrow space between the roof and walls of the guardhouse, Henry had Mackie boost him up, and he squeezed through the hole—shackles and all. Wood complained later that the Kid "was a small fellow not weighing over ninety pounds . . . and it was almost an impossibility to keep him imprisoned or hand-cuffed."

For a few weeks Henry behaved himself—or at least stayed out of sight, working at a hay camp that provided fodder for the military. H. F. "Sorghum" Smith, the boss, provided a valuable description of the Kid and his actions. "He said he was seventeen," a friend recalled Smith saying, "though he didn't look to be fourteen." After Antrim had worked for a short time, perhaps as long as two months, he asked for an advance of forty dollars, a surprisingly large amount. But the Kid bought himself a "whole outfit": gun, belt, cartridges, and other clothing items. When he headed into town, he was dressed "like a 'county jake,' with 'store pants' on and shoes instead of boots," reported Gus Gildea, a ranch hand who would play an important role in Antrim's life later in Lincoln County. His six-gun was stuffed into his belt.

On 17 August 1877, a Friday, the Kid rode into the Bonita settlement just down the road from Camp Grant and went into the Atkins cantina. What followed that evening was an unexpected explosion that dramatically shaped the arc of the Kid's career. In the days leading up to that traumatic day, Antrim had quarreled with Francis (Frank) P. Cahill. The burley ex-soldier and blacksmith had bullied the Kid on several occasions. Known as "Windy" because of his boisterous, assertive ways, Cahill was a short, stocky man, who relished lording it over the young, wiry Kid Antrim.

On this occasion, the ongoing conflict quickly escalated. Cahill had thrown the Kid to the floor repeatedly. The Kid cried out, "You are hurting me. Let me up"; Windy retorted, "I want to hurt you. That's why I got you down." Piling on the humiliation, Cahill called the Kid a "pimp," and the Kid spat back "son-of-a-bitch." As Cahill kept at pummeling him on the floor, the Kid reached around his own waist, grabbed his six-gun, jabbed it into Windy's ample belly, and fired a round. Windy rolled off in agony, and the Kid popped up, dashed from the cantina, "borrowed" the nearest horse, and galloped eastward.

The next day, when Windy knew he was dying, he gave a brief version of the previous day's drama. He and "Henry Antrem [sic], otherwise known as the Kid . . . had some trouble." Then "we took hold of each other. I did not hit him, I think; saw him go for his pistol and tried to get hold of it, but could not, and he shot me in the belly."

Now in flight, the Kid would not have known that two days after the incident, Miles Wood gathered an inquest to hear evidence and render an opinion. Its conclusion: "The shooting was criminal and unjustifiable, and Henry Antrim

43

alias Kid, is guilty thereof." Gus Gildea, often exhibiting sympathy toward the Kid, had a different version: he thought Henry had acted in self-defense. "He had no choice," Gildea said of Henry; "he had to use his equalizer [six-gun]." But no one—eyewitness or other—speaks of Windy Cahill's carrying a gun that day.

For the second time in two years, Henry "The Kid" Antrim had suddenly changed direction. Reared inside the law by his mother, he had taken, after her passing, a giant stride away from his conventional upbringing and toward a life outside the law. He had killed a man.

Where might Henry go? He had to move quickly because the sheriffs, posses, and other officials might be nipping at his heels in a short time. Not surprisingly, the Kid headed for the only other place he knew in that region, the Silver City area. Henry's absence from there for two years meant, perhaps, that the sheriff might not be lurking for him. Besides, if Henry stayed out of town, he might be able to gain a bit of time to decide what he would do and where he would go. Henry, about to rename himself William H. (Billy) Bonney, left no account of his thinking in fall 1877. But a long-standing rumor suggests that he had heard cattle baron John Chisum was hiring cowboys at three dollars a day, with no questions asked about backgrounds. If true, that prospect was undoubtedly enticing for a seventeen-year-old boy on the run without family, friends, or a job. Two years earlier he had jumped into the fire of uncertainty; now he faced a new conflagration. Something of a devil-may-care outlook was beginning to form in the youth's character. That unfolding attitude would shape his succeeding years.

4

Entering Lincoln County

Setting the Scene

When Billy Bonney arrived in Lincoln County, New Mexico, in fall 1877, the county had already gone through years of competitions, battles, and seemingly never-ending violence. Those incessant clashes had continued for nearly thirty years and would carry on past Billy's death into the 1880s.

Historians who tell the story of the Lincoln County War often speak of it lasting for a few months, from February to July 1878. They open accounts of the war with the murder of English rancher John Tunstall and end it in the town of Lincoln with the Five-Day Battle that included the shooting of lawyer Alexander McSween. Unfortunately, that compact chronology leads readers astray. Instead, the war passed through three stages. The competitions and conflicts had begun soon after the area moved from Mexican to American control in 1848 and reached an especially violent pitch in the 1860s and 1870s. True enough, the peak of conflict was achieved in the five-month period of early 1878. But the warring continued even after July 1878. In fact, Billy Bonney occupied center stage following—rather than preceding—the death of McSween and on to his own demise three years later in Fort Sumner. This three-stage chronology provides a larger and more complex picture of conditions in Lincoln County, the tumultuous and dangerous world in which Billy would rise to notoriety.

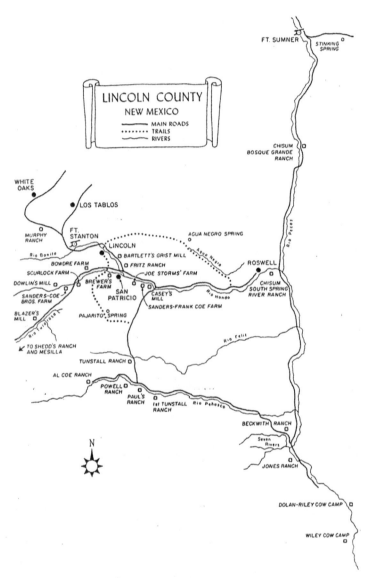

Lincoln County, New Mexico. This map shows the layout of Lincoln County and its environs at the time of Billy the Kid. Map in the Robert N. Mullin Collection courtesy of the Haley Memorial Library & History Center, Midland, Texas.

Town of Lincoln, New Mexico. The layout and appearance of the small town of Lincoln has changed little since the 1870s and 1880s when Billy the Kid rode its main street. In this photograph the Murphy-Dolan building, The House, occupies the center, with the Wortley eatery across the street. The Tunstall store stands to the right of the Wortley on the same side of the street. Later The House building became the county courthouse, where Billy was jailed in spring 1881. Photograph courtesy of the Lincoln Heritage Trust.

Another enlargement is necessary to set the scene for Billy the Kid's rise. Most biographies of Billy offer thorough, fact-filled portraits of his life and actions in the Lincoln County area of New Mexico from 1877 to 1881. Those pinpointed facts are the vital center of his story. At the same time, however, biographers often overlook or skip by the national and territorial histories that shaped the area into which Billy rode in 1877. Lincoln County, and Billy the Kid as well, was often outside the frameworks the U. S. government and the territory of New Mexico had established by 1877, but those frameworks were nonetheless in play and influenced Lincoln County in the 1870s. These historical contexts are necessary for a fuller, more revealing picture of Billy the Kid and the Lincoln County War. The scene for the drama that followed Billy's arrival requires a larger background and a view of the major characters who populated the historical drama. More than minor scene-setting is necessary to understand what Lincoln County had become in 1877.

In the immediate aftermath of the U.S.-Mexican War, southeastern New Mexico changed much less rapidly than most central and northern areas of the new territory. Distance and isolation kept out most newcomers. The centers of New Mexico population were to the north in Albuquerque, Santa Fe, and Las Vegas, and to the south in Mesilla. No major settlements were located in or near to Lincoln County. As of 1870, no major wagon roads or overland trails, much less railroads (none had come to New Mexico), linked Lincoln County directly to the outside world. Communication with Mesilla or Albuquerque, for instance, demanded several days of travel on horseback or in a bouncing stagecoach.

Perhaps even more important, southeastern New Mexico was still the homeland of Mescalero Apaches in the 1850s and early 1860s. Indeed early maps of that area designated the region "Mescalero Apache Country." The Mescaleros, a nomadic people, roamed through the Sacramento Mountains, ranged eastward toward the Llano Estacado, and southeastward into the Guadalupe Mountains shared with Texas. They also camped along the Rio Bonito, Rio Ruidoso, and Rio Hondo, attracted by the opportunities for hunting, gathering, raiding, and some trading with settlers and other tribes. Raids on farms and settlements brought military campaigns to quell the Mescaleros in the 1850s. Although the Mescaleros, among several other Indian groups in New Mexico, had initially welcomed the American takeover from the hated Mexicans, their dreams were soon dashed. Upset with the independence and raiding of the Mescaleros in the far southeastern reaches of the

Fort Stanton, New Mexico. Located about nine miles to the west of the town of Lincoln, Fort Stanton served as the major military post in Lincoln County. From here Lieutenant Colonel Nathan Dudley marched his soldiers to Lincoln and dramatically changed the scene of the Big Kill on 19 July 1878. Photograph courtesy of the New Mexico State University Library Archives, Las Cruces, image RG80–102–006.

new territory, the U.S. government established Fort Stanton on the Rio Bonito in the center of Mescalero country in 1855. Within days of founding Fort Stanton, the Americans pressured a peace treaty with the Mescaleros. Following the signing, a few settlers trekked into the area without much upset until the Civil War.

Although most of the Civil War took place east of the Mississippi, the horrendous four-year fratricidal conflict impacted the trans-Mississippi American West as well. Some of the same events and trends that influenced the American West elsewhere were also at work in territorial New Mexico. Those powerful influences came in two interrelated forms. When the war broke out in spring and summer 1861, hundreds of U.S. regular troops stationed in the West were sent east to fight the Confederate Army. Dozens of

Southern officers also left to join Confederate armies. The dual and connected impacts on the West, including New Mexico Territory, were first that fewer federal forces were available to protect frontier forts from Confederate invaders and second that the troop reductions meant weakened defenses against Indian raiding.

In southeastern New Mexico these two interrelated trends led to several years of disruption in the early 1860s. The absence of a sufficient military force to defend New Mexico against outside invaders became clear in 1861–1862 when a Confederate army from Texas rapidly took control of large swatches of the territory by early in 1862. Union defenders lacked the numbers to hold on to newly established forts in southern New Mexico, including Fort Stanton, which was abandoned and burned. The Confederates soon took over the ruins and revived the garrison, occupying it for a few weeks. The Texas invaders then realized they faced the same dilemma vexing Union commanders: both forces, reduced in size and strength by the numbers sent east, were unable to hold off opponents. For the Confederates, the major problem was the Mescaleros, who attacked Stanton and forced the Southerners to abandon the fort. If troops sent east weakened Union defenses, those actions also made it more difficult for both Union and Confederate forces to move against marauding Indians.

Once the Confederates gave up on Fort Stanton, Union forces, New Mexico volunteers in this case, returned under the leadership of Colonel Christopher "Kit" Carson. Waging war to pressure the Mescaleros for peace, Carson and other military leaders in the winter of 1862–1863 established the Bosque Redondo on the Rio Pecos and placed about five hundred Mescaleros there, with Fort Sumner established nearby to watch over them. Soon, the Navajos, defeated by Carson's volunteers and suffering through the nearly four-hundred-mile Long Walk from their homeland in northwestern New Mexico, were also resettled at Bosque

Redondo, near the Mescaleros, their traditional enemies. Attempting to resolve "the Indian Problem" by removing tribes to these dry, infertile, and cramped quarters was clearly a failure. The Mescaleros fled Bosque Redondo in 1865. In 1867, Lieutenant General William Tecumseh Sherman, never a warm-hearted advocate for Indians, nonetheless saw the catastrophic living conditions at the Bosque and engineered the Navajos' return to a new reservation formed from portions of their previous homelands.

Meanwhile, the Mescaleros had also been corralled onto a new reservation in the Sacramento Mountains in 1873. When the Comanche empire on the southern plains, crowding the Apache and other Indian groups in eastern New Mexico, began to crumble in the late 1860s, most of the nomadic Indian threats to settlers were greatly lessened, if not entirely ended.

Following the U.S.-Mexican War, the gradual reduction of size and strength of Plains Indian tribes slowly opened new areas of what became Lincoln County to incoming ranchers and farmers. By 1860, the Rio Bonito country hosted both Hispanic and Anglo families. Although it is not known for certain, the Hispanic newcomers had probably come from other areas of Hispanic-dominated New Mexico. The U.S. Census of 1860 listed the fifty-four families totaling 276 men, women, and children. Sixteen were Anglo, and the rest Hispanic. Most of the Anglo residents had come from the American South. Forty-nine houses were listed in the Rio Bonito precinct, not counting Fort Stanton.

Most of the residents were farm families. Early accounts reveal that farmers were raising corn especially, with an eye to selling it for food and fodder at Fort Stanton and later to the Mescalero Reservation, once it was established. More than a few whiskey-producers were also ready customers for their corn crops. Other farmers raised potatoes, beans, and wheat for the resident families themselves or for the military and Indians.

Other incoming settlers were not so much farmers as contractors providing supplies for the nearby fort or reservation. The contractors purchased crops and cattle, which they then sold to the Indian agent serving the Mescaleros or to the commissary and quartermaster officers supplying Fort Stanton. These early contracts and deadly competitions over them were forerunners of the violent clashes that broke out in the 1870s between the Murphy-Dolan-Riley faction (The House) and its major challenger, the Tunstall-McSween-Chisum combination. Mounting economic competition, beginning in the late 1860s, exploded in the next decade, providing the major cause for the ruinous Lincoln County War.

If mining rushes drew newcomers like the McCarty-Antrim family to southwestern New Mexico, the rich, open grazing lands of the High Plains beckoned Texas cattlemen to the southeastern quadrant of the territory. As early as the 1860s, more than a few Texas stockmen drove their herds west across the border into New Mexico, where they grazed their cattle and horses on lands for which there was no clear title. The incoming Texas cattlemen soon ran into conflicts with the Hispanic farmers already settled in the region, particularly along its valuable streams. The contention over land, water, and grass, already simmering in the 1860s, flashed into violent clashes in the 1870s.

These persistent conflicts, particularly the worst ones, created an atmosphere of violence that defined southeastern New Mexico beginning in the late 1860s. Contributing to the ongoing social upheaval was the lack of strong, local political and civil organization. When it was carved from Socorro County and organized as a separate jurisdiction in 1869, Lincoln County was far removed from the territorial capital as well as from other large settlements such as Mesilla, Las Cruces, Socorro, and Albuquerque. The settlement of La Placita (renamed Lincoln in 1873) was also distant from any political or civil control. Illegal whiskey production and violent incidents, even murders, seemed to carry on without legal prosecution. The turmoil during the Civil War years added to the already-chaotic civic life of the Rio Bonito region. Even though attempts were made to restrict the Indians to isolated locations such as Bosque Redondo, conflicts between Indians and Hispanic farmers continued, with little institutional stability to stop the on-and-off conflicts.

Yet the end of the Civil War and the partial removal of Indians brought some courageous and ambitious farm families to join those already settled in the Rio Bonito area. Lawrence G. Murphy, a central figure in later Lincoln County imbroglios, reported in 1866 that roughly five Anglos and three hundred Hispanics resided along the Rio Bonito. Another well-known Lincoln Count resident, Lily Casey Klasner, recalled years later that in 1868 La Placita "was predominantly Mexican" and that farmers lived up and down the Rio Bonito because of its "abundant water for irrigation." By the end of the 1860s, perhaps as many as three hundred persons resided in the town of La Placita.

When the settlement was renamed Lincoln three years later, in 1873, it was given a post office. Meanwhile, Lincoln County had been organized in 1869. At its largest in 1878, Lincoln County sprawled over almost one quarter of the entire New Mexico Territory.

In 1873 a conflict similar to others before and after those events erupted in nearby Tularosa Canyon. When incoming Anglo ranchers dammed Tularosa Creek to impound irrigation waters for their fields, nearby Hispanic farmers formed a vigilante group to destroy the dams and insure the flow of creek waters for their crops farther downstream. In May, after the warring camps had begun shooting at each other, federal troops from Fort Stanton tried to quell the deadly fire. Rancher George W. Nesmith reported after the first exchanges, "What the result will be we know not as yet." His predictions proved correct. Ongoing battles over these competing land and water needs divided Anglo and Hispanic ranchers and farmers for years to come.

Even more violent was the so-called Horrell (also Harrell) War, which broke out in 1873–1874 up and down the Rio Bonito valley. Here was an early, brief high point to the upheavals that led to the Lincoln County War. The Horrell conflict repeated earlier regional competitions and fore-shadowed those that would vex county residents in years to come. This earlier "war" came before Billy the Kid appeared in Lincoln County, but it prepared the ground for subse-quent events in which he would participate.

Five Horrell brothers, their families, and about a dozen supporters, all Texas ranchers and cowboys, left Lampasas County, Texas, in spring 1873 and rode into southeastern New Mexico. Repeating what other Texans had already done and would do for decades, the Horrells invaded New Mexico, somewhat on the run from Texas authorities, and were intent on making their presence obvious in the new setting. Buying land on the Rio Ruidoso south and west of Lincoln, they obviously hated Mexicans and soon swag-gered into communities in the Rio Bonito country.

In late 1873 and early 1874 the Horrells rode into Lincoln and other nearby areas, shooting up the town and killing "Mexicans." In the early days of 1874 a virtual civil war had erupted, with the Horrells pitted against local Hispan-ics and their supporters. Some of the Horrell opponents were also men from Texas, ranchers, farmers, and merchants who had moved to New Mexico and the Rio Bonito areas in the 1860s and married Hispanic women. These later well-known residents included George Peppin, William Brady, Hugh Beckwith, and "Ham" Mills. Their unions with Mexicanas made them targets of the Horrells too.

In the opening weeks of 1874, gunfights punctuated Lincoln and nearby areas. By late January, however, it was clear to the Horrells that they could not win the gun wars and dominate Lincoln County, so they sold their cattle to Murphy and Company and rode out of New Mexico. The brief, vicious conflict illustrated the anarchy, the lack of strong local law enforcement, and murderous racial and regional conflicts that stirred Lincoln County in the years immediately preceding Billy the Kid's arrival there.

Meanwhile, the leading men of the Lincoln County War were gradually making their way onto the contested stage of southeastern New Mexico.

5

Peopling the Battleground

Dramatis Personae

In the fifteen or so years stretching from the early 1860s to the late 1870s, nearly a dozen men and women, later to be major figures in shaping Billy the Kid's life and events involved in the Lincoln County War, were making their way into southeastern New Mexico. Among these major arrivals were Lawrence Murphy and Jimmy Dolan at Fort Stanton, John Chisum in the Rio Bonito region, and Thomas Catron in Santa Fe. A string of men and women staked their claims to the Lincoln County region, either in residence or through influence. Not long afterward came Alexander and Sue McSween and John Tunstall to the Lincoln area. To the south and west, and less central to Billy's story, were legal authorities Warren Bristol and William Rynerson. The lives and careers of those individuals are prologue to understanding the tense, violent setting that Billy Bonney rode into in 1877.

In the 1860s and 1870s Lawrence G. Murphy rose rapidly as business leader in what became the Lincoln Country area. Like thousands of other Irish immigrants, the ambitious and active Murphy had fled Ireland to escape the potato famine. Dreaming of a much better life (after studying for the priesthood, it is rumored), Murphy came to the United States and joined the army, seeing military life as a passageway to his larger goals. During the Civil War he came to New Mexico, where he served under Kit Carson in the New Mexico volunteers. Carson praised Murphy as a man of "zeal and intelligence," a "most efficient and energetic officer." Murphy won the admiration of fellow officers in moving the Navajos to Bosque Redondo and quelling the Mescalero Apaches. Shortly before he was mustered out of the army, he briefly served as commander at Fort Stanton.

Murphy's stint as a soldier provided valuable leadership experience and furnished him important connections, both of which served him well in the next dozen years in the Fort Stanton–Lincoln–Rio Bonito areas. While still at Fort Stanton, Murphy, along with army veteran Emil Fritz, established the L. G. Murphy & Co. at the fort. Over time the new company worked as something of a post trader contracted to supply beef, corn, and other foodstuffs to the soldiers. The company also gained a foothold in providing meat, corn, and other commodities to the Mescalero Reservation. As historian Frederick Nolan puts it, the Murphy company quickly "had a stranglehold on the economy." The operation was "the mercantile axis of Lincoln County."

Murphy and Fritz seemed to grow their business overnight. They built a large store and brewery near Fort Stanton and established a branch nine miles away at La Placita. In the decade following its founding in 1866, L. G. Murphy & Co. became so dominant that residents were forced to deal with what became known as "The House" and were at the mercy of its coercive economic policies.

Most Billy the Kid partisans have been critical—sometimes markedly so—of The House and "Major" Murphy. They accuse him of dishonesty, harassment, and even murder. But historian John Wilson counters these censorious images of Murphy and The House in his thoroughly and richly detailed book, *Merchants, Guns, and Money: The Story of Lincoln County and Its Wars* (1987). As businessmen, Murphy and his associates, concludes Wilson, were not entirely crooked. The ledgers of Murphy & Co., the

The House leaders. Standing (*left to right*), Jimmy Dolan and William Martin; seated (*left to right*), Emil Fritz and L. G. Murphy. Dolan and Murphy were the major opponents of the men who rode with Billy the Kid. Photograph courtesy of Lincoln Heritage Trust.

"mercantile capitalists," prove the firm was not a gang of swindlers, and "allegations that the House charged exorbitant prices would seem to have little basis."

But there were problems, some lying obviously at the feet of Murphy and his assistants, and other challenges arising from circumstances beyond his control. Dolan, said to be Murphy's bookkeeper early on, was a fiery Irishman in several ways. Murphy gained admiration for his sociability and convivial ways, but Dolan was prone to conflict and violence. In 1873, when Dolan and Captain James F. Randlett locked themselves into an escalating argument at Fort Stanton, Dolan threatened to shoot the captain. That outburst, plus other mounting criticisms and controversies surrounding the Murphy company's actions, led to its ouster from the fort "as post trader in 1870."

In supplying the Mescaleros, Murphy clearly operated beyond legal bounds. As the major supplier of food and commodities to the Mescalero Indians on the reservation, Murphy played with numbers, often inflating the Indian population well beyond the actual number present in order to maximize the profits from his government contracts. If the company's records indicate that Murphy was not a conniving rascal in his business with soldiers and Rio Bonito residents, his vouchers for Indian contracts reveal that Murphy lied about the aggregate of reservation Mescaleros, defrauded the federal government, and obviously profited from his machinations.

Murphy moved his headquarters to Lincoln after being thrown out of Fort Stanton. In 1873–1874 he erected an imposing two-story store and residence (the largest building in Lincoln County save for Fort Stanton), which cost about seven thousand dollars. He also negotiated a new agreement that made Jimmy Dolan the junior partner in the company, and they resumed their attempt to win all beef contracts for the fort and, to a lesser extent, for the Mescalero Indian reservation. But the nationwide Panic of 1873, competition from other bidders, and Murphy's faltering health and gradual withdrawal from the business drove the company deeper into debt. Mounting loans from Santa Fe merchants and bankers and inadequate cash flow in a barter-dominated economy added to the mounting burdens of the Murphy-Dolan firm.

Faced with possible financial collapse, the Murphy-Dolan partnership reacted like a nearly defeated but stubborn competitor that would rather bring on its own demise

John Chisum, 1824–1884. Chisum, the "Cattle King of New Mexico," owned or squatted on vast swatches of grazing lands up and down the Pecos valley and ran up to eighty thousand cattle on these sprawling pastures. He was largely a reluctant, distant participant in the Lincoln County War, a man whom Billy the Kid increasingly disliked. Photograph courtesy New Mexico State University Library Archives, Las Cruces, image 00150052.

than cave in to a rising opponent. When John Tunstall and Alex McSween, with the possible support of rancher John Chisum, let it be known they would do battle with The House, Murphy and Dolan did not back down an inch or rethink their policies. They would take on the newly announced competitor in a fight to the end. For a region already frequently involved in conflict, the announcement of the new business rival seemed like throwing a new supply of explosive fuel on an already-burning fire.

Dolan played an increasingly larger role in the Lincoln County story in the late 1870s. Like Murphy, he was an Irishman, an immigrant to the United States, and a former military man, but Dolan was much more temperamental. Small-boned and short—about five feet three—he was extremely pugnacious, much like a firecracker ready to explode. He most often set himself off.

Dolan was also ambitious and hard working. Arriving in the United States at age five, he was already clerking in a New York City store at age twelve. Three years later he joined the Union Army and fought in the Civil War. In

1866 he reenlisted for three more years, mustering out in 1869 at Fort Stanton. Soon, he was working at the fort for the Murphy-Fritz firm.

Jimmy Dolan and Lawrence Murphy were simpatico. Observers thought Murphy treated Jimmy like the son he never had. For nearly a decade Dolan served as Murphy's right-hand man, then his partner. Although the circumstances remain unclear, it is possible that Murphy, trying to avoid stress, sent Jimmy into negotiations fraught with conflict, but if compromises were impossible to reach, he was to push on—never to give in against all obstacles and odds.

Dolan's assertiveness, which often illustrated his hotheaded personality, came into play in the 1870s. After the company's expulsion from Fort Stanton, Dolan increasingly became Murphy's henchman, the ambitious associate who helped establish, then enforce the company's economic dominance of Lincoln County. Realizing the danger of some company missions, Dolan took out a life insurance policy for ten thousand dollars in 1873, a year before he formally became Murphy's partner.

In the mid-1870s, Dolan increasingly became the face of the Murphy-Dolan firm. Dolan also threw himself into community affairs. In 1874, he led a posse against the Horrell brothers and burned their ranch. And three years later, he became the Lincoln postmaster, keeping the post office in The House building.

That same year, suffering from the effects of alcoholism and bad health, Murphy willed the company to Dolan. It became J. J. Dolan & Co., with two new partners, John H. Riley and Jacob B. Mathews. Dolan still tried to land beef contracts for Fort Stanton and the Indian reservation but ran into mounting problems from competitors, falling prices, and a cashless economy.

Then in May 1877 Dolan's proclivity for lethal acts became public when he shot twenty-two-year-old Hiraldo Jaramillo. Dolan claimed the act was self-defense against

61

the young Mexican's attack. But more than a few Lincoln residents wondered whether the short-tempered Dolan had been the attacker rather than the defender. Whatever the exact circumstances, the dramatic event was but one instance in a long train of such episodes in Dolan's erratic, often violent early life.

When Emil Fritz, Murphy's previous partner, died in Germany in June 1874, the controversy over the provisions of his ten-thousand-dollar life insurance policy came on scene in Lincoln. Dolan leapt into the contretemps. He claimed that most of the sum was owed to the Murphy-Dolan business to settle Fritz's debts. When lawyer Alex McSween, handling the Fritz estate, refused to accede to his demands, the combustible Jimmy talked Fritz's siblings, Emilie Fritz Scholand and Charles Fritz, into suing McSween. The charge was absconding with the Fritz estate. The controversy surrounding the Fritz settlement gradually displayed Dolan's unscrupulousness and heightened the factional conflict in Lincoln County.

Just before the armed conflict broke out in February 1878, Dolan's actions turned more sinister. Twice, in January and February 1878, Dolan tried to egg John Tunstall, an Englishman, into a gun fight, but Tunstall, often carrying no gun in public, refused to take the bait and get into a shooting match. When McSween declined to budge on the Fritz estate, Dolan talked the local courts and his good friend, Lincoln County sheriff William Brady, into attaching McSween and Tunstall's holdings—calling them partners, which they were not legally—to cover the value of the Fritz inheritance, to which he believed J. J. Dolan & Co. was entitled. At the same time, Dolan's financial status became increasingly precarious, and in January 1878 he was forced to mortgage his crumbling company to Thomas B. Catron in Santa Fe.

During the next three years, no one occupied a stronger position of opposition to Billy the Kid and his supporters than Jimmy Dolan. Dolan, often arrogant and boastful, relished the dogfight that broke out between The House and the Tunstall- McSween faction, which Billy Bonney fought for and John Chisum sometimes sided with. Although Billy also claimed Irish heritage, Dolan thought of him as an underling, to be treated as such. If the Lincoln County War produced no heroes, Jimmy Dolan was closest to a villain in the conflict.

Most accounts of Billy the Kid and the Lincoln County War focus on his activities within the county, but these accounts overlook important ingredients of the larger story, particularly influences flooding in from outside the county. For example, Murphy and Dolan were the most significant opponents of Billy and his supporters, but in turn forces outside Lincoln County were helping to shape the actions and destiny of the county, particularly with regard to The House's interests. The person outside Lincoln County wielding the most power was Catron. His major influences on Lincoln County are evident in his singular personal deeds as well as those as chieftain of New Mexico's most powerful political coterie, the Santa Fe Ring.

Catron was New Mexico's most conspicuous representative of the Robber Barons, the fabulously wealthy men who dominated U.S. business, banking, and politics in the Gilded Age, essentially the 1870s through the 1890s. In New Mexico Catron and his law partner, Stephen Elkins, were soon pulling the strings of the Santa Fe Ring. Reminiscent of other Gilded Age "rings" such as Tammany Hall in New York, the loosely connected group of politicians, businessmen, and lawyers in Santa Fe were powerful enough to control elections, investments, and other economic endeavors throughout much of the territory. The ring's pivot was Catron. As New Mexico lawyer and historian William A. Keleher succinctly states in *The Fabulous Frontier* (1945), Catron was "the one man, who more than any other, dominated New Mexico political and business affairs for fifty years."

Catron's hand was already at work in Lincoln County before the Kid arrived in 1877, but the Santa Fe leader's reach was even longer and his influence more explicit and powerful during the next few years. Catron's machinations were exerted in several ways; some were indirect and seemingly minor, while others were major and especially significant. Catron's membership in the Masons fostered connection with fellow members Murphy, Dolan, and Sheriff Brady. Links to Governor Samuel Axtell, who in turn had strong ties with the Ring, also influenced Catron's sway in Lincoln County. Indeed, from the late 1860s to the mid-1880s most of New Mexico's governors were implicated in the Ring and, in the latter half of the period, too often compliant with Catron's political hegemony. Catron's military background likewise ingratiated him with Murphy, Dolan, Rynerson, and Brady. Even as a U. S. attorney, Catron had power over and beyond the territorial courts, possibly exercising influence over judicial decisions. Catron also invested in a cattle-raising firm in southeastern New Mexico.

But Catron's most important linkage to Lincoln County came through his growing ties to the Murphy-Dolan firm. As the business increasingly fell on bad times, Catron stepped up his support—and control—of the firm. By January 1878, he controlled all the Dolan company's assets, and, after funding the mortgage, sent his brother-in-law, Edgar Walz, to look after Catron's interests in the Dolan company.

In all these areas—the Masons, Civil War military experience, and legal, political, and economic agendas—Thomas Catron was at odds with the McSween, Tunstall, and, to a lesser extent, Chisum interests. When Billy Bonney arrived in Lincoln in fall 1877, he very soon fell in with men opposed to Catron, the Santa Fe Ring, and Murphy and Dolan. That meant in the next three to four years, the most powerful man in New Mexico Territory traveled a road at odds with the paths of Billy the Kid and his supporters.

If Dolan and Catron proved to be Billy's strongest and most dangerous opponents, his clearest supporter in late 1877 and early 1878 was John Henry Tunstall. More than any other person during that time, Tunstall accepted Billy and encouraged him with a job and gifts. Billy's connections with the Englishman were brief but warm and strong.

Tunstall came to Lincoln by way of an unusual route. He was born in 1853 into an upper-middle-class English family; his father was a successful international businessman. John immigrated to Victoria, Canada, as a nineteen-year-old anxious to make his own mark. Three years later in 1876, he traveled to California, looking for grazing land for a possible sheep ranch. Unable to locate what he wanted, Tunstall next came to New Mexico, again hoping to invest in a livestock ranch. After hearing of the beckoning possibilities of a wide-open Lincoln County, especially from lawyer Alex McSween, Tunstall arrived in the Rio Bonito country near the end of the year.

Tunstall lost little time in moving ahead with his dreams after coming to Lincoln. In early 1877 he wrote to his father, illustrating his grandiose—as well as perhaps dangerous—ambitions. Everything in New Mexico, he said, was part of a "ring," including networks controlling army contracts, politics, legal affairs, land, and other institutions, resources, and enterprises. So, to work his way forcefully into Lincoln County, he would have to establish his own ring. He reported, "I am work[ing] at present [on] making a ring. . . ." In Lincoln County, he intended "to handle it [the ring] in such a way as to get half of every dollar that is made in the county by *anyone,* and with our means we could get things in shape in three years. . . ." Although clearly naïve and certainly dangerous, Tunstall's goal was a bit community-minded—at least he thought so. His rise as a competitor would rescue residents from the destructive clutches of Dolan by bringing about the reduction, if not destruction, of The House. Obviously, more than a few residents of Lincoln would relish that change, but at first they did not realize that Tunstall's plan was to replace Dolan with his own controlling "ring."

To achieve his large dream, Tunstall needed help. Besides his father's funding, he had to find supporters in Lincoln County. Fortunately, an equally ambitious newcomer, Alex McSween, was willing to aid Tunstall. McSween and his vivacious wife, Susan, had arrived in March 1875, a year and half before the Englishman and were seriously working to establish themselves in the Rio Bonito area. Building on their original contact in Santa Fe and soon thereafter in Lincoln, Tunstall and McSween were, within months, driving ahead together with their plans. But McSween, cash-poor at the moment, would have to rely on Tunstall's money, or at least the promise of the funds, from his family in England.

The Tunstall-McSween agreements would eventually include several parts. First, Tunstall secured land for a cattle ranch about twenty miles south of Lincoln on the Rio Feliz. Taking advantage of several land acts, sheriff's sales, squatters rights, and other provisions, Tunstall obtained necessary grazing lands and a small herd of cattle to establish his ranch. Then he moved into the business field, opening a store that competed directly with the Murphy-Dolan enterprise. Not yet satisfied, Tunstall also founded a bank that included McSween, Chisum, and himself as executives. In August 1877, both the mercantile store and bank opened for business.

How McSween and Tunstall were exactly involved in the two firms is not entirely clear, particularly the financial arrangements of the agreements. But McSween obviously helped Tunstall with the legal instruments needed to found the businesses, even if his own financial contributions might have been minimal. And crafty old Chisum might lend his name and signature to the endeavors, but he rarely put his dollars into anything but his own bank account.

Alexander McSween, 1843?–1878, and Susan McSween, 1845–1931. Alex and Sue McSween were central figures in the rising Lincoln County conflicts. Alex, a lawyer, was shot dead in the Big Kill of 19 July 1878. Sue later remarried and gained the label Cattle Queen of New Mexico. Although the McSweens sided with Billy the Kid, they were not his major supporters. Photograph of Alex McSween courtesy of the Lincoln Heritage Trust; photograph of Susan McSween in the Robert N. Mullin Collection courtesy of the Haley Memorial Library & History Center, Midland, Texas.

Tunstall's efforts were not long in creating competition—and sparks. As the Englishman's plans unfolded and brought about clashes with Dolan's firm, the two sides took several verbal shots at one another. Later in an interview, Dolan asserted he would not "hesitate to declare that they [McSween, Chisum, and Tunstall] would be guilty of any crime, even murder, to accomplish their ends." In turn McSween, always more inclined than Tunstall to respond, nonetheless reflected his partner's views, charging that Dolan and his cronies were guilty of "fearful villainy" in all their doings.

By early 1878, Tunstall had fully launched his ambitious agenda. As historian John P. Wilson concludes, "Tunstall's plans were simply the old Murphy formula repackaged and, it was hoped, shorn of economic liabilities." The tinderbox was stoked with explosive materials; all that was needed was some kind of ignition. The spark was not long in coming.

Alex and Susan McSween were on the same side of the Lincoln County divide as Billy the Kid, but they never cared much for the young gunman. They came together in 1877–1878 more through necessity than from friendship; Billy's relationship with the McSween's was unlike the warmer connection he enjoyed with Tunstall. Still, Alex and Susan were the most important married couple in the Lincoln County War and interacted more with Billy than any other couple in the area.

The McSweens arrived in Lincoln in March 1875, bearing grandiose dreams similar to those Tunstall harbored. Probably of Canadian Scottish birth, Alex had studied for the ministry but changed to law and entered law school in the United States in 1871. Later he taught school and became a lawyer in Kansas. In Illinois, he met Susan Hummer, and three years later they were married. Dissatisfied with their prospects in Kansas and possibly compelled by Alex's health problems, the newly married couple left for climes farther West, pulling up in Lincoln in early 1875.

The town of Lincoln drew the McSweens because it lacked a lawyer, and they had heard of bright prospects in the area. Alex soon became the legal advisor and debt collector for the Murphy-Dolan business and learned the inner workings of The House. He also represented cattle baron John Chisum in other cases. But theaggressive and rapier-tongued lawyer could alienate clients with his high fees. In a short time McSween fell out with Murphy and Dolan, then attached himself to equally idealistic Tunstall after he came in late 1876. Before long McSween was deeply committed to agreements and plans made with the Englishman.

The string of contests that did most to anger Dolan were the increasingly fractious debates surrounding the Fritz insurance policy and attempts to settle it. Maurice Garland

Fulton, surely one of the best researchers on the Lincoln County upheavals, or his editor Robert N. Mullin wrote: "Scratch beneath the surface and you will find one thing as the prime mover in most of the Lincoln County troubles—money." The explosive issues surrounding the Fritz insurance policy brought money conflicts to the surface—rapidly, dramatically, and violently.

When Emil Fritz died, the company holding his life insurance policy failed to make a payment, so Lawrence Murphy, Fritz's surviving partner, placed the collection in the hands of McSween. Following the instructions of Emilie Fritz Scholand and Charles Fritz, the administrators of their brother's estate, McSween traveled east to New York City to collect the policy settlement. Even though the company holding the policy claimed insolvency, $7,148 of the original $10,000 policy was paid by another firm, after that company deducted its commission and expenses. After two months of working assiduously to collect the settlement, McSween was notified the remainder, $2,852, had been placed in his personal account.

Things quickly exploded into controversy. Desperate to get his hands on the Fritz settlement, Dolan demanded the total amount, asserting that Fritz owed the $7,148 and more to The House. But McSween put him off, refusing to accept Dolan's claim as little more than self-aggrandizement and waiting to make sure any other possible Fritz claimants, especially those in Germany, received their due. Dolan speedily executed a counter move, talking Emilie Scholand and Charles Fritz into filing suit against McSween for embezzlement and asking Thomas Catron to get McSween jailed for absconding with the Fritz funds. Both of Dolan's desires were accomplished, and the Lincoln County–Santa Fe Ring connection solidified even further when the courts attached the McSween-Tunstall holdings (even though they were not legally partners) until the Fritz monies were obtained.

Dolan publically attacked McSween as a shameless embezzler, who used the Fritz funds for his own designs, among them the building a commodious house in Lincoln and stocking the Tunstall store with goods. How accurate were Dolan's accusations? McSween claimed the charges as trumped up. But in the only fully researched, academically sound book-length study of Susan McSween, *In the Shadow of Billy the Kid: Susan McSween and the Lincoln County War* (2013), author Kathleen Chamberlain reveals that years later Sue McSween "admitted to the Dolan family . . . that the insurance money indeed paid for her home and helped buy stock for the Tunstall store." Others dismiss this story as a fabricated, unsubstantiated rumor.

If the story is true, however, Alex made a terrible blunder. Perhaps he thought he could use the Fritz money as something of a loan that he would repay from revenue generated through his work with Tunstall. Historians and biographers often point to the assassination of Tunstall in February 1878 as the opening shot of the Lincoln County War, but rocking Lincoln before that tragic killing was the bitter controversy surrounding the Fritz settlement.

Even before Tunstall's violent erasure from the scene, the Lincoln area's leaders were locked in an impending battle that led to protracted and angry exchanges—and to murder. One might well argue that prior to Tunstall's demise the controversy over the Fritz estate had launched the war.

In these explosive stumbles toward battle, Susan McSween played roles both similar to and different from those of her husband. Her family upbringing, largely unknown until the recent Chamberlain biography, remains obscure. But now historians know some of her origins. She was born Susannah into the Hummer family in Pennsylvania and reared in the conservative German Baptist or Church of the Brethren. In two marriages Peter, Susannah's father, produced sixteen children, with the first wife, Elizabeth, dying when

Susannah (or Susan) was only five. The girl and later young woman was increasingly alienated from her strict father, her distant step-mother, and perhaps an overbearing church. At age seventeen or eighteen, about 1863, she fled home.

Where she lived out the next ten years is not clear in the historical record. Family traditions place her with a married sister, Elizabeth Shield, in Ohio, or with Elizabeth and her husband, David, in Missouri. But Susan clearly surfaced in Kansas in 1873. After meeting Alex McSween in Illinois, they had begun to correspond, becoming engaged, and he too moved to Kansas. She now went by Susan or Sue Homer, had abandoned her plain dress, and had become more stylish. In August 1873, Susan and Alex married in his Presbyterian Church in Atchison, Kansas.

Not much has been uncovered about Susan's personality before she came to Lincoln with Alex in March 1875. But it is obvious that Sue shared with her husband a strong, persistent drive for success, to gain wealth and status. Their desire for upward mobility put Susan and Alex on the same social track. Observers in Lincoln spoke of her as "vivacious" and "lively" but also as "not very large." Actually, she was an inch or two taller than the five foot, five Alex. Several observers commented on her personal beauty and stylish dress. One stated, "Mrs. McSween always looked like a big doll." Appropriately corseted (which enhanced her attractive figure) with well-styled hair and eye-catching clothes, Susan attracted attention in the remote hamlet of Lincoln, New Mexico.

Over time some Lincoln residents expressed their distaste for Susan. She was, they said, much too outspoken and betrayed a sharp temper. Others thought her a bit forward, maybe flirtatious, and not as retiring or traditional as they expected a frontier woman to be. In general Susan was more outgoing than her reticent, religious, and reflective husband. Those differences were grounds for whispers and comments comparing the two McSweens.

Susan's life in Lincoln kept her aloof from much of what went on in the town. She was one of only a handful or less of Anglo women in Lincoln, and without children she seemed to some observers to be traveling a personal path radically divergent from that of other women in the community. The differences were palpable. Most women in the region were Hispana, uneducated, and Catholic. They were also mothers. Susan was none of these; she stood out. Bystanders often commented critically about her uniqueness in Lincoln County. But not all took to grumbling about Susan. John Tunstall, for example, wrote glowing words about her. She had explained much about Lincoln and the ways of its people to the Englishman, and he responded with gratitude, telling his parents that Susan told him "as much about the place as any man could have." Although others might be critical of Sue's actions, behavior, and dress, Tunstall never criticized her as bold, assertive, or unwomanly. To him, she was in every way proper and helpful.

Susan did worry, nonetheless, about the mushrooming dreams of Alex McSween and John Tunstall. Although she trusted Tunstall and obviously wanted her husband to push ahead financially, she greatly feared head-to-head competition with Murphy and Dolan. Nearly forty years later Susan told a friend that in 1877 she had warned Tunstall and her husband that "they would be murdered if they went into the store business." But Alex did not listen to her. Although she had done her "best" to keep him "from entering the business," she recalled, "he went in against my will." She fretted, too, that Tunstall was too much of a cajoling agent, talking nonsense about how he and McSween would push Murphy and Dolan off track. Clearly, Susan was more rational and realistic than Tunstall and Alex about the murderous competition that would arise in Lincoln if they took on The House.

Gradually the grudges, threats, and shootings were too much for Susan. At the end of 1877, the McSweens left

Lincoln for an extended trip to St. Louis and maybe points farther east. Their plan was that Alex would carry out legal business and Susan would get some respite from her mounting worries. They did not get very far until the nets of the Dolan-Catron–influenced courts ensnared them just north of Las Vegas and threw Alex into jail, along with John Chisum also traveling east. Manifestly upset and worried about what to do, Susan finally decided to go on to St. Louis, staying away from New Mexico while Alex, something like a fugitive, moved in and out of Lincoln. (McSween had been placed under house arrest but was allowed extraordinary freedom as long as Deputy Adolph P. Barrier was on the scene.) By the time Susan arrived home at the end of March 1878, Lincoln had exploded into chaos, Tunstall had been murdered, and Alex and his supporters, thrown into confusion, were groping for a way forward in the conflict.

In slightly less than three years, Susan McSween had been introduced to territorial New Mexico. Her new home, with its Hispanic-dominated population, its cattle country surroundings, and its unrelenting threats of violence and actual violence, scared more than calmed or reassured her. She was motivated to succeed, wanted to impress others with her sophisticated dress and hosting, and hoped to garner a respectable reputation. Some of those goals seemed in sight, but the frustrations, insecurities, and dangers were even more evident in her daily life. And conditions got worse. Some challenges were brought on by her husband's imprudent plans and unwise decisions, others by the Murphy-Dolan interests, and still others perhaps augmented by the actions of newcomer William "Billy" Bonney. For the next six months—from January to the end of July 1878—Susan McSween and her Lincoln neighbors lived in a maelstrom of escalating violence.

In some ways, John Chisum, although a central figure in the development of Lincoln County, remained a mysterious sideliner in the rising conflicts leading to the Lincoln

County War. Chisum may have been the most enigmatic figure among the major contacts Billy made from 1877 onward. At first their relationship seemed cordial, but after the Big Killing, the violent last day of the Five-Day Battle in Lincoln on 19 July 1878, Billy was increasingly upset with the cattle king and preyed on his livestock. According to the Kid, Chisum had promised but failed to pay Billy and his fellow riders a handsome daily wage for protecting his cattle and other interests.

Chisum was likely the richest man in Lincoln County. Born in 1824 and reared in Tennessee, then Texas, he turned to cattle raising at the age of thirty and soon expanded into north and west Texas. By 1872, he had moved his expanding cattle herds into New Mexico and as far west as Arizona. In the mid-1870s, his cattle holdings had mushroomed to eighty thousand head. His Long Rail and Jinglebob (a cutting procedure allowing more than half of a cow's ear to dangle down) brands sprawled dozens of miles along the Pecos River, from the Bosque Grande area in the north to far below Roswell in the south.

Chisum did not so much buy land or legally settle on thousands of acres of rich grazing lands; he mainly squatted on these vast, fertile ranges. His tendency to aggressively expand and control his lands upset smaller ranchers, particularly those in the Seven Rivers area to the south from Lincoln. Rustling Chisum's cattle was a way to redistribute the wealth and get even with the baron.

These anti-Chisum tensions were swirling in the air when Billy arrived in early fall 1877. Although Chisum did not offer the Kid a job when he needed one (why is not clear), he did side with the McSween and Tunstall contingent in their escalating competition and tensions with House leaders Murphy and Dolan. At best the cattle baron would be a reluctant and unreliable combatant in the looming war.

So Lincoln County was a region of old and new arrivals, an area of rising economic tensions, and a place on the verge of violent conflict when Henry Antrim arrived, in flight from the murder of Windy Cahill, rode into Lincoln County under his new name, William "Billy" Bonney. Both the place and the people would provide the tumultuous context for the nearly four remaining years of his galloping life.

6

Billy Comes to Lincoln County

The daily or weekly activities of William Bonney from the time he galloped out of Arizona in August 1877 until he settled in Lincoln County that fall are difficult to trace. Yet we have for these few months as many details as for his two years in Silver City or the following two years in Arizona. Once Billy came in contact with several people well known in New Mexico territorial history, his life and theirs became entangled, thereby enlarging and thickening the Kid's story.

As Billy dashed eastward from Arizona, running away from a murder charge, he undoubtedly thought more about the chase and pursuit of law enforcement officials than about where he would go. Still, he had to venture someplace, so the familiar beckoned him.

Billy's first stays were with previous acquaintances from Silver City. These brief stopovers may have allowed the Kid a few days to decide what to do next. The first one was at Knight's Station, located about forty miles south and east of Silver City. Richard and Sara Conner Knight, whom Billy had known earlier, welcomed him. Sara's younger brother Anthony Conner, one of Billy's buddies in Silver City, recalled many years later that the Kid stopped "about two weeks" and "told folks what he had done." But now, at the end of August or early September, "fearing that officers from Arizona might show up any time[,] he left." The Knights urged him to pick out a horse from their corral, which he did, and move on to Ed Moulton's nearby sawmill. Moulton, who had earlier aided Billy and now heard what the young man had done in Arizona, encouraged him to relocate, "not to stay too long around his place if he was running from the law."

Perhaps the most upsetting stop came when Billy rode to Georgetown, about fourteen miles east of Silver City, to see his brother, Joe. Another Silver City friend of Billy's, Chauncey Truesdell, and Joe had abandoned Silver City to avoid a smallpox outbreak. The contact with Joe brought tears to Billy, especially when the brothers realized it might be their final meeting. This brief sojourn was, Truesdell remembered, "the last I ever saw of Henry Antrim." In Georgetown, Billy may also have reunited with his former teacher, Mary Richards Chase. Long afterwards in 1960, Chase's daughter recalled her mother relating the visit. Billy explained his difficulties to Mary Chase and asked her for money. "My mother gave him all the cash she had in the house," the daughter remembered. Billy also spun a yarn, probably untrue, that he had killed an Apache to get his fine horse. "Toward evening," Billy "took off."

The next three to four months of Billy's complex life—from October 1877 to January 1878—are a jumble of competing stories. Newspapers, friends, and opponents tell a variety of tales, usually with a "I was there and I know all about it" tone. Not all the stories can be entirely true, however, because they conflict, indicating the difficulty of sorting out the truth from falsehoods and tall tales. A hundred and forty years later, the best one can do is to rely on what seems the best, most reliable evidence.

Events taking place at the beginning of October clearly impacted Billy as he galloped away from Arizona toward Lincoln County. On 13 October, the *Mesilla Valley Independent* reported that Samuel P. Carpenter, a contractor from Silver City, had spotted Kid Antrim eleven days earlier with a gang of rustlers in Cooke's Canyon in southwestern New Mexico. Although some writers doubt this story, the strongest reports indicate that Billy was indeed riding with the lawless Jessie (or Jesse) Evans and his outlaw gang known as The Boys or The Banditti.

Jessie Evans, who connected with the Kid several times in the next two years or so in Lincoln County, was a genuinely bad man. From Texas, he was about twenty-five when Billy met him in 1877. Evans struck observers as the epitome of arrogance, callousness, and disregard for humanity. He had worked briefly for John Chisum and then fallen into livestock rustling, gathering a gang of rascals who stole or pillaged their way across southern New Mexico. For a time, Evans hooked up with John Kinney, another thief and cutthroat, who had established a ranch where rustling was the major activity.

However shadowy and brief, Billy's connections with Evans and Kinney nonetheless illustrated his uncertainty about the future. He had just stayed a few days, or perhaps longer, with solid, dependable persons he had known in Silver City. Now he was riding with a pack of rustlers and killers who lived brazenly outside the law.

Beginning to call himself Billy Bonney, the Kid may have spent as long as a month with the Evans gang as it cut a destructive path toward the southeastern corner of New Mexico. The reasons for Henry's name change during this time are unclear, although some historians have speculated, on good grounds, that the new name allowed separation from the McCarty or Antrim names linked to his previous unlawful actions and granted some protection from legal authorities. Others wonder whether perhaps Catherine McCarty might have been married to or lived with a man named Bonney in New York and who might have been Billy's biological father. Neither supposition is sufficiently grounded in solid fact to be entirely accepted.

Jessie Evans would be linked with the Kid in the coming few years. After this first contact and some riding together, the duo split up. Evans devoted his life to crime and mayhem, participating on both sides of the Lincoln County War and evidently hiring out to the highest bidder for his shooting skills. Sometimes he sided with Billy; on other occasions he was a deadly opponent. As writer Mark Lee Gardner succinctly puts it, Evans was "a cold-blooded killer and accomplished gunman . . . used to doing as he planned with little fear of the law or anyone else." Later, after taking part in the Lincoln shootouts Evans headed off to Arizona, then to Texas, where he was sentenced to a ten-year term or more for second-degree murder. That story, however, has not been entirely substantiated, in part because Evans broke out of jail and disappeared to history.

On 10 October, Billy was with the Evans gang when it met with John Riley, a junior partner in J. J. Dolan & Co. Newspaper accounts tell of the gang organizing into something resembling a military unit, with Evans elected "colonel"; drinking and debauching; and even performing an impromptu skit for Riley and his companion. How and when Billy separated from the Evans riders is a mystery. Some think he rode into Lincoln County with the gang. But even stronger evidence places him with the Jones family near Roswell, during his initial stop in Lincoln County.

The Joneses, residing in the Seven Rivers settlement south of Lincoln in the lower Rio Pecos valley, told a story that Billy had left the Evans gang, struck out on his own, and nearly headed into disaster. As Ma'am Jones argued for many years, the Kid staggered into the Jones's house—he was hungry, exhausted, and destitute. Earlier Billy and another young man, Tom O'Keefe, ignoring sound advice to avoid troublesome areas, had taken a shorter but dangerous route through the Guadalupe Mountains in southern New Mexico, where the Mescaleros attacked them, chased away O'Keefe, stole their horses, and left the Kid alone without food, water, and a horse. For three days, the Kid hid out in daytime and tripped along at night, before he arrived near collapse at the Jones's welcoming home.

If the Ma'am Jones story is to be entirely believed, she mothered and revived an exhausted Billy. He spent the next few days with Ma'am, her husband, Heiskell, and their large family, including a son, John, with whom Billy may have practiced backyard shooting. Even though the Jones tribe and Billy were frequently on opposing sides in the Lincoln County shootouts, he retained warm feelings and gratitude for the family that had accepted him with open arms and shelter and without questions and judgments.

The next few weeks displayed the challenges Billy faced as a young man pushing toward the end of his teens. Between November 1877 and the following January, he made a number of stops, clearly looking for a place to stay and work of any kind. Billy did not have much to sell himself with. He had worked a few months as a cowboy, in hotels, and perhaps as a go-between for ranchers and tradesmen. But by now what he seemed to know best was riding, shooting, and stealing. The latter two would not open many doors—unless gunmen were needed. After a few false leads, Billy finally located a place, in a few weeks, to display his gun skills, courage, and stubbornness.

After leaving the Jones home near Seven Rivers, Billy made his way north up the Pecos, then gradually a bit west. Undoubtedly the Kid rode through the vast grasslands near the Pecos that fed thousands of Chisum's cattle. Some thought the baron's ranges, which stretched from Texas into eastern New Mexico and into eastern Arizona, may have occupied almost sixty miles of the Pecos valley from south to north. Riders were nearly always welcomed at the Chisum ranch houses, where Billy probably pulled up; but it is revealing that the Kid was not offered a job riding the rough string even though he was searching for a grubstake.

George Coe, 1856–1941. Coe and his cousin, Frank Coe, were Lincoln County ranchers. They immediately became friends and later strong supporters of Billy the Kid. The Coes rode with the Kid and others as the Regulators, opponents of The House forces of L. G. Murphy and Jimmy Dolan. Photograph courtesy of the New Mexico State University Library Archives, Las Cruces, image 00180314.

Moving on, Billy wandered farther west, going up the Rio Hondo, then the Rio Ruidoso, where he arrived at the ranch of George Coe. Over the next few days, or perhaps even weeks, Billy became fast friends with George, his cousin Frank Coe, and several others. Much later in the 1920s, the Coes, particularly Frank, had much to say about their friendship with the Kid, which remained strong to the end of Billy's life.

Frank Coe provided one of the most extensive and probing descriptions of Billy and evaluated his personality and development. He told Miguel Antonio Otero Jr., who had served as territorial governor of New Mexico and who published *The Real Billy the Kid* (1936):

I found Billy different from most boys of his age. He had been thrown on his own resources from early boyhood. From his own statement to me, he hadn't known what it meant to be a boy; at

81

the age of twelve he was associated with men of twenty-five and older. Billy was eager to learn everything and had a most active and fertile mind.

Coe, especially struck by Billy's sense of humor, added that although the Kid could be "serious in emergencies, his humor was often apparent even in these situations." Not many participants in the Lincoln County battles provided comments about Billy Bonney as revealing as this one shared by Frank Coe.

In late 1877 and early 1878, Billy became acquainted with several other men who became close friends. Like his cousin, George Coe pointed to the Kid's good sense of humor and sunny personality, characteristics that endeared him to many acquaintances in the Lincoln area. Another of the new friends was Charlie Bowdre, a neighbor of George Coe, and his Hispanic wife, Manuela, who were eking out a living on a farm on the Ruidoso. Although Bowdre had purchased the small farm from The House, he became Billy's dependable companion in later shootouts with Jimmy Dolan and his cronies. Living nearby was Doc Scurlock (Josiah Gordon Scurlock), a friend of Bowdre's also trying his hand at farming.

Scurlock had married Manuela Bowdre's half-sister, Antonia Herrera, making Charlie and Doc brothers-in-law. Undoubtedly, the Kid's fluency in Spanish helped cement his friendship with the two families. But most of all, like the Kid, Charlie and Doc loved to ride and hunt and would sometimes claim for themselves the horses and cattle of other ranchers. They would become central figures in the group known as the Regulators that Billy also joined when it formed and eventually led by the end of 1878.

Other men and women claimed to have met Billy in fall and winter of 1877–1878. In the common phenomenon that grows up around legendary characters, several Lincoln County residents, displaying what might be termed the

I-Knew-Billy syndrome, revealed in later years their connections with the Kid. The family of William Brady, the Lincoln County sheriff and House friend, with whom Billy would have a violent encounter the following April, claimed that the Kid worked a few days for them. Lilly Casey Klasner, a perky, assertive, and half-educated young woman, recalled Billy in stories brimming with vitriol and animosity. She and her brother thought the Kid nothing but a "bum" unwilling to work; all he wished to do was fire off his guns and showoff. Klasner claimed in her memoir, *My Girlhood among Outlaws* (1972) edited by Eve Ball, that she encountered Billy at the Jones's ranch when she and her widowed mother, trying to trail to a cow herd to Texas, had failed and returned to the Pecos valley.

Billy Bonney's behavior in fall and early winter of 1877 showed him trying to figure out what direction his life should take in Lincoln County. In mid-October a posse under the leadership of Richard Brewer, Tunstall's able foreman, caught up with Jessie Evans and members of his gang and hauled them into Lincoln's inadequate underground jail. Nearly a month later, the Kid joined nearly thirty of The Boys, rode to Lincoln, and released Evans and others of his gang. After the breakout, Evans and his followers galloped south to Brewer's ranch and stole some of Tunstall's horses. Leaving their apologies because Tunstall had visited the Evans gang in jail with a bottle of whiskey, The Boys turned toward the Seven Rivers country farther south. Whether this lawless episode came before or after Billy's contacts with the Jones family and the Coe cousins is not clear, but all these contacts, new friendships, and back-and-forth connections between opposing groups in Lincoln County revealed that by the end of November 1877 Billy had not yet made up his mind which faction he would join.

But Billy's most important connection was with Englishman John Tunstall. As the conflict between The House and the McSween-Tunstall combine heated up, Tunstall

John Tunstall, 1853–1878. The ambitious young English-man appeared in Lincoln County in late 1876 and quickly vowed to challenge The House leaders as a rancher, businessman, and banker. He and Alex McSween worked together to oppose and challenge the Murphy-Dolan interests. Tragically Tunstall was murdered on 18 February 1878. Some historians see that killing as the beginning of the Lincoln County War. Photograph courtesy of the Lincoln Heritage Trust.

commenced looking for men handy with guns to protect his interests. His needs described Billy, a courageous if not yet daring young man handy with several kinds of guns. Perhaps by the end of November but certainly by December 1877 Billy was an employee of the Englishman. It is rumored that Tunstall gave Billy a horse, a gun, and, most important, a job and security. During the next month or two Billy's loyalty to and admiration for Tunstall grew and deepened. The relationship featured Tunstall as the more stable, older brother looking out for a needy younger brother. It was not something entirely new for Billy since his bonds with Sombrero Jack and John Mackie were similar. But Tunstall was different from any man important to Billy's life thus far: he was English, well educated, well off, and a symbol of security.

Historians narrating the Lincoln County War and biographers telling Billy's story often picture the Murphy-Dolan contingent, aided by the Santa Fe Ring and regional court justices, as the villains of these stories. In several respects they were. Not a saint or hero among the bunch. But these anti-House accounts, realistic in the treatment of clear villains, often absolve the Tunstall-McSween opponents of any skullduggery. Not so. Their hands were dirty, too.

When Tunstall realized the difficulty of competing with and winning out over The House, he turned to violence. He dug in to push on with his "ring," as he had promised his parents he would do. Like The House partisans, Tunstall was plenty willing to hire gunmen, more skilled with their pistols than with their cowboying. He told his family that these hires had "cost a lot of money, for men expect to be well paid for going on the war part." Rumor had it that Tunstall laid out five dollars a day for gunmen to put their lives on the line. Among those added to his string of toughs was Billy Bonney, probably brought onboard by Dick Brewer, Tunstall's courageous foreman.

The hired gunmen may not have known all that was expected of them, as historian Frederick Nolan correctly notes. But as the conflicts over the Fritz insurance imbroglio and the court and county legal authorities burned even hotter, the pistoleers must have realized that their job was to protect Tunstall's ranch, cattle, and store against all variety of rascally opponents. Among those riding with Brewer and Billy were Fred Waite, a part-Chickasaw, college-educated young man from Indian Territory. He would become Billy's close friend for a short period.

Also serving with Tunstall's riders were John Middleton, whom the Englishman described as "about the most desperate-looking man" he had ever seen. Another was Henry Brown, whom George Coe judged "to be a good warrior" but whom Frank Coe characterized as "just a kid . . . and not half as smart as Billy." Also coming on the scene was Rob Widenmann, a refugee from the Midwest, to whom Tunstall took a liking. Although blustery and assertive, Widenmann turned out to be a rather uncourageous soldier in the conflict.

So stabilizing to Billy's unsettled life were the weeks with Tunstall that he even thought of looking for a place of his own. He and Fred Waite talked of partnering in a small ranch and farm on the Rio Peñasco, a valley lying about forty miles south of Lincoln. Maybe the eighteen-year-old could reach a new tipping point in his turbulent young life—stop drifting like an aimless vagabond. Tragically, that life would not be his.

When Billy began riding for Tunstall, the tensions mounted in Lincoln. Most pressures were linked to the ongoing dispute over the Fritz insurance settlement, but there were other disruptions emanating from the bitter acrimony between The House and the McSween-Tunstall partnership and now simmering for more than a year. Billy was more a bystander than a participant from December 1877 through January 1878. But he fell into the fire that broke out in February.

Contentious, complex, and lengthy at the time, the Fritz insurance settlement baffles most writers and readers. As Billy biographer Robert Utley asserts, the "insurance policy turned out to be the explosive charge that set off the Lincoln County War." Few settlers on the American frontier took out a ten-thousand-dollar life insurance policy, and New Mexico lacked the agents and banks to deal with the details after Fritz's death. Eventually, after missteps by others, Alex McSween was asked to represent the beneficiaries and to help settle the troublesome case. As noted earlier, McSween traveled to New York, worked through the aftereffects of company's bankruptcy, and finally began to settle the inheritance, minus the fees of New York lawyers and bankers. But McSween made a mistake—or maybe not—in depositing the remaining funds in his St. Louis bank rather than transferring them to Santa Fe. He also held off settling the case because he thought two major heirs, Charles Fritz and Emilie Fritz Scholand, Emil Fritz's brother and sister residing in New Mexico, clearly under the lion's paw of Jimmy Dolan, were not the only legal heirs. Others could have resided in Germany. McSween might have wondered, too, whether he would receive his negotiated fees if he deposited the funds in an account outside his and under Dolan's or Catron's control.

What McSween testified to under oath and what he wrote in several personal letters helps explain the complicated Fritz case that caused so much friction in Lincoln County. While in the East, McSween obtained $7,148.46 of the original $10,000 sum after paying off the New York bankers and the Spiegelberg Bros., an earlier agent for the policy. McSween received $1,500 (10 percent of the original sum plus a retainer of $500); $3.076.90 for commissions the estate owed him; and $538.60 as reimbursement for his expenses in traveling to New York. Other necessary reimbursements brought the original $10,000 down to about $2,000, the amount that should have gone to the Fritz heirs. But both Murphy and Dolan claimed that Fritz owed them a large sum, when, in fact, they owed sizable amounts to the Fritz estate.

Then the louder, more destructive fireworks exploded. The contested territory where McSween feared to tread— legal suit—Dolan suddenly entered. Overnight, he talked Emilie Scholand into charging McSween with embezzlement because the Lincoln lawyer had not paid off the American claimants. Also, applying to the House-friendly courts in Mesilla, Dolan persuaded Judge Warren Bristol to issue a warrant for McSween's arrest on the charge of absconding with the Fritz funds. When Dolan next heard that McSween was traveling east, he thought Bristol had more than enough cause to immediately arrest McSween, with the aid of U.S. Attorney Catron in Santa Fe. Utilizing the territory's new telegraph lines effectively, officials arrested and jailed Alex and Susan McSween and rancher John Chisum, who was also going east on business, in Las Vegas. After complicated negotiations, Chisum remained in jail, as historian Frederick Nolan writes, "to tough it out in his own way." Sue McSween continued on toward Missouri, and Alex, under guard, returned to Lincoln. All this happened in the days leading up to and shortly through Christmas of 1877.

McSween then went to Mesilla to clear himself of the embezzlement accusations. Judge Bristol commenced the case by not jailing McSween but demanding that he raise eight thousand dollars in bail money. Not satisfied with that decision, Dolan also worked with Charles Fritz, Emilie Scholand, and District Attorney Rynerson to bring a civil suit against McSween, this time for ten thousand dollars. Once the case had been written up and filed, Dolan and his cronies sent a fast-galloping courier to Lincoln to begin attaching McSween and Tunstall's holdings. While on the way back from Mesilla to Lincoln, the McSween-Tunstall and Dolan parties happened to meet at Shedd's Ranch near the Organ Mountains. Dolan was outraged by a recent Tunstall letter to the *Mesilla Independent* accusing him and Sheriff Brady with the misuse of Lincoln County tax monies (which proved, for the most part, untrue). Fired with legal suits filed in Mesilla, Dolan challenged Tunstall to a gunfight. When Tunstall refused, Dolan labeled him a "damned coward" and threatened to get him in the near future.

When the McSween-Tunstall party arrived back in Lincoln, they discovered Sheriff Brady and his cronies already inventorying the contents of McSween's home and Tunstall's store. Conforming to instructions issued by the courts in Mesilla and strongly supported by the irresponsible Dolan, Brady incorrectly assumed that McSween and Tunstall were partners and thus that all their assets were fair game for attachment to the value of ten thousand dollars, the figure claimed in the suit. McSween verbally protested the sheriff's actions, but Tunstall brought Billy Bonney and other shootists back on scene. As would become clear in the next weeks, Billy had grown close to his English boss.

Dolan's forceful moves from December 1877 to early February 1878 pushed Lincoln County to the precipice of civil war. Although the conflict was already on in the courts, it turned particularly ugly and violent in the second half of February. And Billy Bonney would be a combatant in some of these clashes after 10 February.

From that time until the murder of Tunstall eight days later, Billy and the other fighters tried to protect their boss' merchandise at his store in Lincoln and his livestock at his ranch south of town on the Rio Feliz. On 11 February a skirmish almost broke out when Tunstall, backed by some of his men, including Billy, confronted Sheriff Brady and his troops as they inventoried the goods imported from the East to stock his store. Words flew, guns bristled, and violence seemed imminent. But on some unknown grounds, the two gangs worked out a minor compromise, staving off a gunfight.

Brady then turned to examining the livestock at Tunstall's Feliz ranch, sending one of his lieutenants, Jacob B. "Billy" Mathews, to carry out the legal process. While on their way they were joined by Jessie Evans and other Boys, who stated they wanted to reclaim a horse that Bonney had "borrowed." Uniting forces, Brady's posse led by Mathews and three of The Boys rode on to the Tunstall ranch.

The ranch house at the Feliz place was a small, two-room adobe that housed several of Tunstall's men. When Mathews, Evans, and their followers trotted up, foreman Dick Brewer and several other Tunstall cowboys, Bonney among them, stepped out of the house to confront them. Mathews explained that he had come to attach McSween's cattle, but Brewer responded that McSween kept no cattle at the Feliz ranch. Uncertain about what to do next, Mathews replied he would return to Lincoln for additional instructions from Sheriff Brady.

Mathews's response did not end the confrontation. Among Tunstall's men on the Feliz ranch was the erratic, sharp-tongued Rob Widenmann. Previously appointed a deputy U.S. marshal, Widenmann declared that he held arrest warrants for Evans and his men and summoned Bonney and the others to help him serve the papers. But the defiant Evans menaced the marshal with his rifle, and all the Tunstall men refused to assist, convinced that their efforts would draw gunfire and bring on certain death from the sheriff's posse, especially Evans and his men.

After breakfast Mathews, his posse, Billy Bonney, and Fred Waite rode back north. When the group reined in at Lincoln, Brady pushed Mathews to gather a new, larger posse, return to Tunstall's ranch, and attach all his livestock. Simultaneously, a galloping rider dispatched south to Dolan's cattle holdings also carried instructions to collect additional men and move rapidly on the Tunstall ranch. Dolan was part of the expanded group. So were Evans and his men, although Brady had instructed Mathews not to include the outlaws in his posse.

On the morning of 16 February, Widenmann, Waite, Bonney, and two others rode back to the Rio Feliz to prepare defenses. But after the Tunstall gunmen had punched portholes in the adobe walls of the ranch house to take on the Mathews-Dolan posse, Tunstall changed his mind and told the challengers they could attach the ranch cattle and would not be opposed. He likely realized that opposing the posse would bring on a gunfight he hoped to avoid.

On the fateful morning of 18 February, Tunstall rode off with Brewer, Bonney, Widenmann, and Middleton, with Fred Waite driving a wagon. Widenmann later told federal investigator Frank Angel that they were driving nine horses toward Lincoln. At approximately 5 P.M., after nearly twenty miles of steady but not frantic riding. Tunstall and his four lieutenants were about ten miles south of Lincoln, had topped a ridge, and were now beginning to descend into a narrow, small valley. A flock of wild turkeys fluttered to the left, and Brewer and Widenmann scampered in that direction up a rocky slope to see if they could bag some of the turkeys. Bonney and Middleton, following Tunstall by about three or four hundred yards and now on the ridge, spotted behind them a group of the Dolan-Evans riders thundering onward.

The two Tunstall riders hustled forward, Middleton racing toward Tunstall with a warning and Bonney galloping toward Brewer and Widenmann. When Tunstall, confused, did not heed the warning and turned toward the pursuers, Middleton scrambled up the slope toward his fellow riders, leaving Tunstall in the draw with the horses.

What happened next is still contested through competing stories after more than a century of research and writing. Tunstall's men later testified that their boss, uncertain about what was unfolding, did not ride to safety. Instead he looked toward the Dolan riders and may have started in their direction. This was a fatal error. William (Buck) Morton, Dolan's foreman from the Pecos cow camp, fired at Tunstall, the slug hitting him in the chest and throwing him off his horse. In an instant, another rider Tom Hill dashed forward, snatched up Tunstall's own pistol and shot the still-struggling Englishman in the back of the head. Hill also fired the same pistol to kill Tunstall's horse and, sadistically, laid the head of the dead animal on Tunstall's hat. Evans was also involved in the murder of Tunstall, although his exact role is unclear.

An alternative story told by members of the posse was later repeated to listeners in Lincoln and in the courts. Tunstall had shot first, they claimed, hence the two spent cartridges in his pistol. The pursuers had merely fired back, protecting themselves from Tunstall. The narrative the Dolan followers told, although they had few facts to substantiate it, convinced some legal authorities, particularly those already inclined toward Dolan. After the killing of Tunstall, his riders hastened away to avoid the posse. Later that evening, about 10 P.M., Widenmann and Bonney arrived in Lincoln with the sad news of Tunstall's murder. A few hours later a man living near the murder site brought Tunstall's body to Lincoln.

The killing of John Tunstall—senseless and traumatic—changed the life of Billy Bonney. First, the murder ignited (or reignited) the youth's tendencies toward vengeance. Shortly after Tunstall's death and after viewing the rancher's lifeless body, Billy reportedly told one group, "I'll get some of them [the posse] before I die." Over the next months he made good on this threat of retribution. Second, the death of Tunstall suddenly and dramatically removed from his life a symbol of stability. So few had surfaced in Billy's life.

Tunstall had given Bonney a job, a horse, and a gun and had trusted and relied on him. As Frederick Nolan has put it, "The Kid had grown up fast, no longer Tunstall's frightened rabbit but now his trusted warrior."

7

A War Heats Up in New Battles

In the five increasingly turbulent months stretching from Tunstall's murder on 18 February 1878 to a giant shootout in mid-July in Lincoln, Billy Bonney gradually emerged as a more important figure in the Lincoln County War. His step-by-step rise owed as much to the loss of in-place leaders as to Billy's ambition. During these months, not only Tunstall but Dick Brewer and Frank MacNab (McNab), key leaders in a newly organized group, the Regulators, were killed. And then McSween in the Big Killing, as it was called, on 19 July. That meant major spokesmen for the Regulators had been removed, leaving a vacuum in leadership. Those writers who place Billy at the front of the Regulators early on are reading history backwards; they are exaggerating his leadership too early in the story. But neither should it be overlooked that Billy in the spring and early summer of 1878 was not the same young man who had arrived in Lincoln County in the early fall of 1877. He was riding from the margin toward the center of its affairs.

Billy was on the scene in the days immediately following Tunstall's murder. After the victim's remains were brought into Lincoln, Bonney, Brewer, and Middleton told the coroner's jury their version of the murder. Billy was also among those Tunstall men threatening reprisals against Sheriff Brady and the Dolan forces. Securing a warrant

William Brady, 1829–1878. Sheriff Brady, supporting The House contingent and backed by local legal officials, opposed Billy the Kid and his fellow riders. The Regulators, including Billy, ambushed and killed Brady on the main street of Lincoln on 1 April 1878. Photograph in the Robert N. Mullin Collection courtesy of the Haley Memorial Library & History Center, Midland, Texas.

against Brady from Lincoln justice of the peace John B. Wilson, Constable Atanacio Martínez, the Kid, and Fred Waite walked to Dolan's store to serve the warrant. When Martínez balked at serving the paper—saying it might lead to his death—the Kid threatened him: "You better take that chance because if you don't, I'll kill you myself."

But when the warrant-servers came to the entrance of the Dolan store, they found themselves immediately covered by several gunman and their threatening weapons. Brady quickly arrested the trio but soon released Martínez. The sheriff kept Billy and Waite under arrest, however, and that meant they were unable to attend Tunstall's funeral. As Frederick Nolan notes, these events from Tunstall's murder through the jailing were actions that "exacerbate[d] . . . [the] already animosity between the Kid and Brady . . . to hatred." The hatred flared in front of the Dolan store, as Billy's friend George Coe describes the confrontation. Brady "threw down on the Kid, saying 'You little sonofa-

94

bitch, give me your gun,'" and Billy fired back "'Take it, you old sonofabitch!" That fiery face-off and the resultant accelerating hatred would lead to another murderous incident about six weeks later.

In March 1878 Dick Brewer, working at his small ranch on the Rio Ruidoso and serving as Tunstall's foreman, was named a deputy constable, deputized a posse including the Kid, and called them the Regulators. Their task was to go after Tunstall's murderers and bring them in for justice. On 6 March, the Regulators with the Kid, rode down the Pecos. They found and chased down three men, William "Buck" Morton, Frank Baker, and Dick Lloyd, all thought to be involved in Tunstall's murder or at least in the posse that pursued him. It is rumored that the Kid, showing his spite and desire for vengeance, wanted to kill Morton outright for his part in Tunstall's murder, but Brewer reined him in. Staying put overnight, the Regulators and their captives began to ride back to Lincoln. What happened next remains shadowy, contested, and inconclusive.

The story is that Morton and Baker, who had clearly been present in the posse that shot down Tunstall, thought they would never reach Lincoln alive. They were right. Along the way, Bill McCloskey, a friend of Morton and a rider among the Tunstall killers, joined the group and promised a bystander in Roswell that "they will have to kill me first" if the Brewer posse attempted violence against Morton and Baker. Frank Coe later reported that on their way to Lincoln on 9 March Morton, who had hidden a pistol that no one discovered, and Baker, who grabbed McCloskey's pistol, made a break to get away. The two men shot McCloskey (why is unclear) but were gunned down themselves. One contemporary writer asserted that Billy galloped forward to get ahead of Morton and Baker and shot both of them—a story that has never been confirmed. But Billy certainly was one of the Tunstall agents now trying to gain revenge on his killers. Within a month the murder of the Englishman, Billy showed his vengeful side, which would flare from time to time until the end of his life.

On the same day that Morton and Baker were killed, Governor Samuel B. Axtell was in Lincoln to issue a proclamation that would dramatically change the scene in the county. Axtell, a supporter of the Santa Fe Ring, had requested and received from President Rutherford B. Hayes permission to use federal troops to quell upheavals like the one convulsing Lincoln County. With the support of the president and U.S. Attorney Thomas Catron in Santa Fe, Axtell traveled to Lincoln, staying only three hours, most of which he spent with Murphy and Dolan. Claiming he had all the information he needed—none from McSween supporters—Axtell announced a multifaceted proclamation. First, he declared illegal and void the Lincoln County commissioners' appointment of John B. Wilson to justice of the peace,. That also meant that all decisions made by Wilson were no longer in effect. Second, the proclamation ended Rob Widenmann's commission as a deputy U. S. marshal. Conversely, the legal decisions that Wilson had rendered and Widenmann had been carrying out were now put in the hands of county judge Warren Bristol, with Sheriff Brady and his deputies empowered to enforce them. Clearly, the McSween side had lost a good deal of legal and political leverage while the Murphy-Dolan contingent gained additional power.

While these events were taking place, the Lincoln County story began connecting with national and foreign governments. Just after Tunstall's killing, McSween and Widenmann had sent letters to Carl Schurz, the secretary of the interior; Sir Edward Thornton, the British ambassador in Washington; the Tunstall family in London; and other federal officials in Washington, D.C. In response Montague Richard Leverson, an enthusiastic, opinionated British citizen living in the United States and perhaps associated with John Chisum interests, began to flood the mails with

strongly worded letters calling for the federal government
to investigate the Tunstall murder, quell the ongoing dis-
turbances in Lincoln County, and examine the blatant
partisanship of New Mexico's legal authorities and political leaders. Sending his demanding letters to a number of
leaders and authorities, including U.S. Marshal John Sherman in Santa Fe, Ambassador Thornton, President Hayes,
and cabinet members, Leverson instructed them on what
they should do now. Upon receiving copies of the Leverson
missives, U.S. Attorney General Charles Devens instructed
U.S. Attorney Catron of New Mexico Territory to launch
an investigation into the charges leveled in Leverson's letters
and in other reports about Lincoln County then arriving in
Washington from New Mexico. Not surprisingly, Catron
dragged his feet on Devens's request, but additional letters
from McSween, Widenmann, Leverson, and Ambassador
Thornton spurred Washington officials to action. When Secretary of State William Evarts received Thornton's charges
that District Attorney Rynerson and Governor Axtell were
likely involved in the events surrounding Tunstall's murder
and the coverups, Evarts sent Thornton's letter to Attorney General Devens. This time Devens not only pushed
Catron to investigate the accuracy of the damning charges
but promised to launch a federal investigation of the sordid
happenings. A few weeks later Frank Warner Angel, a special
investigator from the U.S. Justice Department, arrived in
New Mexico. His instructions were to look into the Tunstall murder, possible fraud committed by the territory's
political and judicial leaders, and corruption in the federal
Indian service and land holdings.

Billy Bonney, of course, was not involved in any of this
letter writing, but the impact of the letters and the subsequent connections between national and international enti-
ties, influenced his life in Lincoln County. Local historians,
focusing on the sensational story unfolding in southeastern New Mexico, often overlook or underemphasize how

Warren Bristol, 1823–1890, and William Rynerson, 1828–1893. These engravings show Judge Bristol and District Attorney Rynerson, who closely sided with the Murphy-Dolan group in the Lincoln County War. They were also strongly linked to the Santa Fe Ring. Illustrations in the Robert N. Mullin Collection courtesy of the Haley Memorial Library & History Center, Midland, Texas.

much the Lincoln County War expanded in influence during 1878. By the end of the year, news of the frontier conflict had spread across the country to Washington, D.C., and in some respects across the Atlantic to Great Britain. That expansion and subsequent national attention paid to the Lincoln County affairs clearly influenced the next three years of Billy's life.

The alternating pattern of explosive and quiet times between February and July 1878 repeated itself after the killing of Morton and Baker and the pronouncements of Governor Axtell on 9 March. For the most part, things were quiet in the environs of Lincoln, and Billy seemed off the scene. But in the first week of April two explosive events destroyed the short peace.

After chasing McSween and the Regulators for several days Sheriff Brady, some of his men, and a detachment of federal troops from Fort Stanton returned to Lincoln on

30 March. McSween, remaining out of town to avoid gunfire and to meet his wife returning from the East, arrived
in Lincoln on 1 April about 11 A.M. He soon learned that
about an hour earlier Brady and Deputy George Hindman
had been shot down on Lincoln's main street.

The details behind the shooting of Brady and Hindman
are vague and unspecific, but a few facts are clear. A band of
the Regulators, including John Middleton, Henry Brown,
Jim French, Frank MacNab, and the Kid, had gathered at
a corral gate on the eastern end of the Tunstall store. As
Brady, Hindman, George Peppin (later sheriff of Lincoln),
Billy Mathews, and Jack Long walked the street, the five
shootists opened fire. Brady went down immediately, cried
out "Oh Lord," and struggled to get up. Hindman was also
struck and fell in the street, begging for water. A second
barrage finished both. The other deputies fled for cover.

With Brady and Hindman dead, the Kid and French
dashed out to the two bodies. French's intentions remain
unclear, but some contend that Billy wanted to confiscate
the warrant Brady probably carried for McSween's arrest;
others more convincingly argue that Billy was after his Winchester rifle, which the sheriff had taken from him back in
February and was now lying near his body. Shots rang out
from across the street. Billy Mathews, now safely hidden,
opened fire on the Kid and French. One round seriously
injured French, who had to be hauled to safety and hidden
away the next few days. A few writers say the same bullet
glanced off Billy's leg, but Dr. Taylor F. Ealy, who tended
to the wounded French, later recorded that Billy was "not
hit." The assassins grabbed their horses and dashed down
the street but not before Middleton dismounted and coolly
fired away at Brady supporters who had come into the street
and were firing at the dashing riders.

Involvement in the killing of Sheriff Brady was Billy's
most despicable act. Nothing he did before or later equaled
that coldblooded deed on a frigid April Fool's morning.

Why did the Regulators murder the county sheriff? That violent, irrational act turned most of the town's residents decisively against them. Was the lethal ambush merely an act of retribution, getting even for Tunstall's murder and with Brady for his opposition to Tunstall and McSween? Was it a deed intended to rebalance power in Lincoln, taking from The House and giving back to McSween and the Regulators? Or was it a senseless, opportunistic, spur-of-the-moment act of rage? Perhaps all answers furnish some illumination.

The Regulators gave reasons for their actions. Brady, they claimed, was going after McSween; the warrant for McSween's arrest, the handcuffs he carried, and the accompaniment by four well-armed deputies, they argued, were proofs for their claims. Brady supporters asserted, conversely, that Brady was on his way to explain a delay in a court session to deal with the McSween accusations. Knowing that, the Brady proponents continued, the Regulators went after him to keep McSween safe and, indirectly, to attack The House. A better explanation, although not an excuse, comes in considering what might happen in the frenzy of war. In the weeks before and just after Tunstall's murder, House advocates and McSween supporters and Regulators increasingly became violent opponents in an escalating war. When the Dolan posse shot down Tunstall, it was killing an enemy leader; when the Regulators shot Brady, they were doing the same, wiping out one of their opponents' leaders. The same explanation, when extended into the coming months, helps explain—but again does not excuse—the events taking place through the summer of 1878. In outright war, enemies kill enemies by whatever means.

The Brady killing was a turning point in Billy's shifting reputation. He might be seen as a young tough who had killed a man in a saloon fight in Arizona seven to eight months earlier, but there were extenuating circumstances in the shooting of Windy Cahill that gave polite society reason to forgive him. Billy might also be viewed as a dangerous and foolish gunslinger in his deeds committed alongside Jessie Evans and The Boys. He could be criticized, too, for his vindictive actions following Tunstall's killing. But the shooting of Brady put Billy beyond the pale. As Robert Utley has bluntly written in *Billy the Kid: A Short and Violent Life,* Billy and his partners "were willing to take human life in circumstances that violated even the lax ethical code of the time and place. Even more than the killing of Morton, Baker, and McCloskey, even more indeed than the slaying of Tunstall, Brady's death was cold-blooded murder." For that deed Billy was eventually sentenced to death on the gallows. He was the only perpetrator condemned to hang for the premeditated murder of Brady and Hindman.

Four days later the violence exploded, with Billy again a central figure in the action. The Kid, with Dick Brewer and more than a dozen Regulators, had ridden west to Blazer's Mill just two days after Brady's murder. The sawmill stood along the small Rio Tularosa on the western slope of the Sacramento Mountains. Surrounded by the Mescalero Reservation, the mill site had been—and would be—the site of dramatic conflict, although the owner Dr. Joseph Blazer had worked out a workable agreement with Frederick Godfroy, the Indian agent for the Mescalero. In fact, Blazer had rented his large two-story adobe to the Godfroys, who took in travelers and served meals. A post office was also located at the mill.

On the morning of 4 April Andrew L. "Buckshot" Roberts rode to the post office at Blazer's Mill. He had worked for Jimmy Dolan and been in Mathews's posse but not the band that killed Tunstall six weeks earlier. Now tiring of the tensions and violence spreading across Lincoln County, Roberts decided to pull out and relocate to Las Cruces. He had sold his small ranch and was coming to the post office hoping that the buyer's check had arrived. His ride led to surprise—and tragedy.

Blazer's Mill. On 4 April 1878 several members of the Regulators cornered and killed Buckshot Roberts at Blazer's Mill near Tularosa, New Mexico, and southwest of the town of Lincoln. Regulator leader, Dick Brewer, was killed by Roberts. The shooting of Roberts, just three days after the murder of Sheriff Brady in Lincoln, added to community opposition to Billy and his fellow riders. Photograph in the Robert N. Mullin Collection courtesy of the Haley Memorial Library & History Center, Midland, Texas.

Roberts rode down into the Mill area because he had not seen the Regulators' horses tied up out of sight in the corral. John Middleton, posted as a guard against any surprises, including the possibility of Roberts's appearance, spotted him and informed the others. (It was rumored that Roberts was a bounty hunter aiming to bring in a Regulator or two for two hundred dollars a head.) After securing his packhorse to a tree some distance away, Roberts pointed his mule toward the post office. When Brewer learned that Roberts was approaching, the Regulator chief replied, "I've got a warrant for him." Hearing those words, Frank Coe, a neighbor and acquaintance of Roberts, offered to talk to him, perhaps advise him to surrender. To Billy and the Regulators, Roberts was a marked man in his support for Dolan and his presence with the posse. Coe later reported in an interview that he tried to talk Roberts into giving up and ward off what would likely be a shootout in which Buckshot was outnumbered more than a dozen to one. "No way, Mary Ann," Roberts shot back stubbornly. He may have recalled that just a few weeks before Morton and Baker had surrendered to a similar gang and were cut down "while attempting to escape." Looking toward a new life in Las Cruces, the proud Roberts was determined to avoid that ignominious ending.

Losing patience, several other Regulators rounded the corner where Coe and Roberts were conversing and called on him to surrender. No, Roberts emphatically replied; he was convinced that the Kid would want to kill him on sight. A gunfight erupted. Charlie Bowdre and Roberts fired almost simultaneously. Bowdre's shot plowed through Roberts's lower stomach, mortally wounding him. But Roberts, who could fire only from the hip because of a previous shoulder injury, sprayed the Regulators with shots from his Winchester rifle. One round bounced off Bowdre's belt buckle into George Coe's shooting hand, shearing off one finger and dangerously injuring another. Another shot plowed into Middleton's chest near his heart, and still another shot ricocheted off Doc Scurlock's holster and pistol. A fourth bullet nearly hit the Kid, grazing his arm and chasing him away, "as if it was too hot in there for him."

Billy turned around when he realized Roberts was out of shells, shoving his rifle into Buckshot's belly. Roberts, in turn, jammed his Winchester into the Kid's midriff, causing Billy's shot to go astray and the boy to lose his wind. Again, Billy backed out.

Roberts proved to be a valiant opponent and lethal marksman despite his wound. Backing into Dr. Blazer's adobe house, Roberts discovered Blazer's single-shot Springfield rifle, grabbed a mattress, and threw it up as a barrier near the front door. Brewer, meanwhile, scouting for a better angle of fire on the severely injured Buckshot, had circled around to crouch behind nearby logs, from where he could view the front entry. Seeing what he thought to be Roberts in the doorway, Brewer snapped off a shot that missed. Recognizing where Brewer's shot came from, Roberts waited, then fired a deadly response when Brewer's head appeared above the logs. The bullet caught Brewer just above the eyes, crashed through his head, and broke off the back of his skull. The chief of the Regulators died instantly.

The murderous gunplay, lasting but a few minutes, took two lives (Roberts died the next day) and injured others. The Regulators decided to abandon the mill, found help for their wounded companions, and went on their way. Billy never said much about these events of 4 April, but he may have thought he had proven his daring and courage in front of his fellow fighters. Interestingly, most of the contemporaries who did speak about the dramatic incident generally sided more with Roberts, whom they saw as unfairly gunned down, than with the Regulators. In a four-day period the Regulators had dramatically undercut their support in Lincoln County with the killing of Sheriff Brady and Buckshot Roberts. Billy, a known Regulator, became infamous as well.

The Regulators felt the need to recuperate after the shootout at Blazer's Mill. Dr. Ealy removed George Coe's trigger finger and part of another finger. John Middleton, thought to be on the verge of death, gradually recovered. Soon after the firefight on 4 April and the loss of their captain, Dick Brewer, the Regulators named Frank MacNab their new leader. A Texan from the panhandle, MacNab had come to New Mexico as a cattle detective, hoping to lasso the thieves stealing John Chisum's beef, and later to do the same with Hunter, Evans and Co., who had purchased Chisum's cattle. Most of the rustlers were working out of Seven Rivers, and their theft of stock from the cattlemen made them anathema to the Regulators, at least at this point. As the Regulators' chief, MacNab now became the top man of the McSween faction. He was also named deputy constable by José Gregorio Trujillo, justice of the peace in San Patricio, adding a new badge of legality to his leadership.

Meanwhile, events were bruising Jimmy Dolan and his henchmen. When the district court met on 13 April, the grand jury failed to return all the indictments Dolanites hungered for. Most importantly for McSween, the grand jury refused to charge him with embezzlement. Adding insult to injury in Dolan's mind, the body concluded, "We fully exonerate him [McSween] of the charge . . . and, regret that a spirit of persecution has been shown in the matter." This was a particularly courageous decision because Judge Bristol, setting aside the neutrality expected of his office, had urged the jury to declare McSween an embezzler. But the Kid did not escape indictments. He was charged, along with John Middleton and Henry Brown, with the murder of Sheriff Brady. Conversely, he somehow escaped indictment for the murders of Morton, Baker, and McCloskey. In fact, those killings led to no charges. Nor was Billy indicted in the death of Buckshot Roberts at Blazer's Mill; only Charlie Bowdre was charged.

Jimmy Dolan experienced other disappointments as well. Because business in Lincoln County had fallen off dramatically, he was forced to declare bankruptcy, dissolve J. J. Dolan & Co., and deed his firm to Catron. With the Dolan store closed, Jimmy had to look for other ways to challenge the McSween faction.

One day after the Brady murder and two days before the shootout at Blazer's Mill, a new person—Lieutenant Colonel Nathan A. M. Dudley—appeared on the scene. Dudley, an experienced regular soldier, assumed command at Fort Stanton and would rearrange the balance of power in the Lincoln County War the next summer. Blustery, opinionated, and sometimes whiskey-driven, he would become, in the next four months, a central figure in the region, and may have, on the momentous day of 19 July, played the decisive role in the entire war. Dudley, though urged to be nonpartisan in his decisions and actions, clearly sided with Dolan's forces. He was no friend of McSween, the Kid, and the rest of the Regulators.

The tenuous peace between the two warring factions in Lincoln County broke apart on 30 April and threatened to erupt into a full-scale battle. Gathering a large group of backers, including nearly two dozen Seven Rivers riders, a Dolan contingent rode into Lincoln. Having just killed Frank MacNab, severely injured his brother-in-law, Ab Saunders (he soon died from the shot), and captured Frank Coe at the Fritz ranch, the so-called posse surrounded parts of Lincoln and even sneaked into the now-shuttered Dolan store. The men wanted to force the hand of the new sheriff, John Copeland, a former butcher from Fort Stanton. They aimed to push Copeland into serving warrants on the Kid and other killers of Brady and Roberts. Instead, the sheriff and Regulators greeted the invasion with gunfire. For several hours the two sides exchanged lead, with few injuries. Befuddled with the chaos, Sheriff Copeland called for the army, and a detail of two dozen black soldiers under Lieutenant George W. Smith, arrived in midafternoon. Asked by Smith what he wanted, an exasperated Copeland told the lieutenant to take "the whole damn business." About thirty men, slightly more than half Dolan supporters and the rest McSween followers, were led off to Fort Stanton. Although listed as taken into custody by the regulars, Billy skipped out of town, escaping another legal net.

What followed was both ludicrous and revealing about the legal disorganization of Lincoln County. Puzzled beyond reason, Sheriff Copeland pushed the responsibility of the serving warrants he held onto the shoulders of Colonel Dudley at Fort Stanton, who, in turn, shrugged off the duty of holding the Dolan men. Copeland had secured arrest warrants for Dolan's gunmen from a justice of the peace at San Patricio, accusing them of murdering MacNab. To further the case, McSween added his legal support to keep the Dolan supporters jailed.

But, in turn, the Dolanites gained the support of Dudley, who received affidavits from Jimmy's men charging their opponents with riotous behavior. Warrants for the arrest of the McSween supporters came from a justice of the peace in Blazer's Mill. These warrants included one for the Kid. Dudley nearly forced Copeland to serve the warrants, with McSween but not Billy ending up in jail.

The exchange of charges, warrants, and arrests proved that the Lincoln County legal system was little more than a charade. Each side had found a justice of the peace to side with it and charge opponents with crimes. The house of legal cards totally fell over when Sheriff Copeland, unable to manage the disorganization, allowed all those arrested — on both sides — to skip out.

Hoping to reorganize themselves and move forward, the Regulators elected Joseph G. "Doc" Scurlock as their new leader. In the last month, they had lost Dick Brewer, then Frank MacNab; now they needed a new captain. Hanging around the McSweens in Lincoln, the Regulators also benefitted from the sympathies of Sheriff Copeland, who had won the support of the county commissioners. They were convinced that Copeland, unlike Sheriff Brady, would be neutral in his decisions and actions. Surprisingly, the McSween faction so won over Copeland that he did not serve warrants on the Kid, Middleton, Waite, and Bowdre, Regulators whom the grand jury had indicted for murder in its spring session.

In May and June, the violent McSween-Dolan contest continued sporadically but persistently. Rarely a week passed without some kind of shooting tussle. Billy was involved in several of these affairs.

The Regulators were beginning a new kind of organization. If Billy and others followed the new party chief, Doc
Scurlock, a contingent of Hispanics under the leadership of
Josefita Chávez also backed their efforts. Their combined
force numbered as many as two dozen shooters. In mid-
May the Regulators invaded a Dolan cattle ranch near Seven
Rivers. Scattering the cattle and taking horses and mules,
the Scurlock-led riders also captured Manuel Segovia,
known as the "Indian." Since he had ridden in the past with
the Mathews posse, he realized his chances of survival were
slim. He tried to get Francisco Trujillo, a rider with the
Regulators, to protect him, but once Trujillo rode away, the
Indian was soon shot down by the Regulators, with Billy
and Josefita Chávez among the possible shooters.

The county conflict then moved in a new direction.
Stirred to action by letters from Lincoln writers supporting Tunstall and McSween and from the British Foreign
Office, the Hayes administration had decided to investigate
the violent turmoil in Lincoln County. Dispatched by the
U. S. Departments of Justice, the Interior, and War, Angel
traveled to New Mexico in late May and began interviewing many residents of Lincoln County, including the Kid,
McSween, others linked earlier to Tunstall as well as Dolan
and other members of The House faction. Angel stayed in
New Mexico until the end of August, gathering testimony
given under oath and collecting other information. His
report, which he submitted in October 1878, proved to be
a major—if not *the* major—source for understanding the
violent explosions that racked Lincoln County in the mid-
to late-1870s. The Kid's deposition, taken by Angel on
8 June, substantiated what the Tunstall riders had told Lincoln residents on 18–19 February—and afterward. Dolan
men had ridden down and killed Tunstall. None of the Tunstall men had fired or returned fire at the pursuers.

Billy also revealed in his matter-of-fact testimony that he
and Fred Waite, with the support of Tunstall, had dreamed

of establishing a small ranch on the Rio Peñasco. In the late spring and early summer of 1878, Billy and the other Regulators often stayed at the expansive McSween home in Lincoln. In those weeks they became better acquainted with Alex and Sue McSween. The contact between the Kid and the McSweens is all the more extraordinary because their temperaments, life goals, and actions were so at odds. Alex was a religious, well-educated, rather phlegmatic, and contemplative man. Almost none of these characteristics were evident in the secular, spontaneous, action-oriented Kid. While McSween was a trained lawyer conversant with legal guidelines and practice and ambitious to push ahead with his career, the Kid lacked much knowledge or interest in the law beyond the power of his six-shooter and rifle, and there are only small bits of evidence that Billy thought about the future and what his life might entail.

Although more realistic and assertive and perhaps more driven than her husband, Sue McSween also had little in common with the Kid. As Kathleen Chamberlain makes clear in her recent biography of Susan, the lawyer's wife had mixed reactions to Billy. She might have liked his willingness to stand up to their death-dealing opponents in the Big Killing, something her husband was not able to do, but she also thought Billy was too much like Jimmy Dolan, too inclined to use violence to get his way. Sue never exhibited toward the Kid the warmth that more than a few other adult women did.

The death of Tunstall thrust more leadership responsibilities on McSween, particularly in opposing Dolan and his supporters and the county legal officials siding with The House. Despite his legal training, the lawyer did show some inclination to fight his opponents' riders with his own gunmen. Although the claim by some biographers that McSween urged his sympathizers to gun down Sheriff Brady is probably untrue, he was undoubtedly happy to see the sheriff, who had repeatedly threatened him, out of the way, even if he did not support the assassination. In addition, the Kid and McSween both detested Dolan and his leading lieutenants. In that shared animosity, the lawyer and gunman found more than enough common ground to remain clearly on the same side.

The bond between the Kid, the other Regulators, and Alex McSween became stronger in the weeks leading up to the mid-July shootout in Lincoln.

8

The Five-Day Battle

Nearly every major history of Lincoln County and biography of Billy the Kid defines the Lincoln County War as beginning with the murder of John Tunstall on 18 February 1878 and ending with the killing of Alex McSween the following 19 July. But this biography of the Kid reveals that the five-month period, although the most explosive period of the Lincoln County War and the "high noon" of the vicious conflict, was the second stage of the local civil war and followed at least two or three years of additional tension and conflict. In fact, the five-month period ushered in a third and final stage in which the major issues were finally settled and high-profile participants in the war were gradually driven off the scene. Most importantly, the conclusion of the war was the killing of Billy the Kid in July 1881 and the rise of Pat Garrett as the new sheriff of the Lincoln County.

The Five-Day Battle fought from 15–19 July 1878 was probably inevitable then or later. Begun two or three years earlier, the competition and hatred between the Murphy-Dolan and Tunstall-McSween groups had evolved into a series of heated, murderous confrontations. Not only did the two major factions battle in the shootout, a new protagonist, Colonel Dudley with his regulars and big guns from Fort Stanton, decisively entered the fray and probably was the determining factor in the Big Killing of 19 July, the last day of the battle.

The inexorable steps toward deadly conflict became increasingly apparent in early summer. As historian Mark Lee Gardner has phrased it, the days after the Blazer's Mill shootout "were a blur of shooting scrapes, *bailes,* and hard riding." Week by week, then day by day, the shootings and killings went on, with neither side able to achieve victory. Then in mid-July having chased one another around the surrounding mountains and valleys and in town, both sides moved toward Lincoln, perhaps expecting a coup d'état and victory.

On 14 July, Sunday evening, a group of Regulators, reinforced by another contingent of Hispanics under Martin Chávez, rode down into the Rio Bonito valley. Numbering nearly sixty men, the riders quietly but directly invaded and took over Lincoln. They greatly outnumbered the gunmen serving Sheriff George Peppin (he had been appointed sheriff in May 1878) and scattered through the town. The Kid and about a dozen others were posted in the McSween house to protect Alex and Susan from threats recently voiced against the lawyer. Chávez and maybe as many as two dozen of his fellow Hispanics were positioned in the Patrón house and the Montaño house and store, and other Regulators including Scurlock, Bowdre, and about ten others were occupying the Ellis store. At the moment, the Regulators seemed to be in charge of Lincoln, keeping Dolan, Peppin, and their men at bay.

In fact, the Dolanites were in an untenable situation. They were surrounded and separated by the heavily armed McSween supporters. At that point Billy and the other Regulators had good reason to feel confident about victory, should a horrendous gunfight take place in Lincoln. With his forces in control of the town, McSween was likely reassured about his decision to gather between fifty and sixty parti-

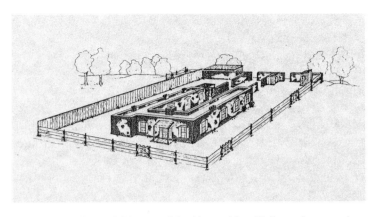

The McSween house. This map of the Alex and Sue McSween house and
the environs in the town of Lincoln was drawn by Robert N. Mullin, a Billy
the Kid collector and historian, and based on the information of Sheriff
George W. Peppin. Map in the Robert N. Mullin Collection, courtesy of the
Haley Memorial Library & History Center at Midland, Texas.

sans. In case of a showdown, odds were that the numerically
superior McSween forces would be able to chase the Dolan
men out of town.

The battle lines began to shift on Monday morning,
15 July. The notorious John Kinney and his riders, some of
them from the Seven Rivers area, had been out looking for
the "Modocs," their name for the McSween band. (One of
the Kinney men had taken part in the recent Modoc War,
where the opponents were the Modoc Indians; hence the
reason for "Modocs" in the New Mexico conflict.) Finding
no Modocs in the countryside, the Kinney men rode into
Lincoln from the direction of Fort Stanton. Soon gunshots
were sounding in town. The Five-Day Battle had begun.

Even though the odds had begun to shift on Monday
morning with the arrival of Kinney's gang, the McSween
supporters still outnumbered the Dolan-Peppin forces. The
highest estimates were up to sixty McSween fighters and
forty or a few more for the Dolan side. But other advantages

and disadvantages, not yet clear on 15 July, would emerge in the next four days. In most of those shifts, Jimmy's side benefitted more than the lawyer's partisans.

The first obvious advantage for Dolanites was the determination and stubbornness of their leaders. Dolan himself needed little convincing that his side was the "law and order" party, with the backing of the legal officials such as Judge Bristol and District Attorney Rynerson. And through them Dolan's faction had the support of U.S. Attorney Catron and other influential federal authorities and political leaders in Santa Fe.

No less significant—and even more important for the street battles in Lincoln—was the support of shootists John Kinney and Jessie Evans. In Lincoln County and southern New Mexico during the previous ten years, these two gunmen had shown they were skilled guerrilla fighters and even coldblooded killers. In fact Kinney and Evans may have been even more trigger happy than the Kid. Rumor had it that the two gunmen had been promised five hundred dollars if they shot down Alex McSween.

McSween lacked nearly all the cussed belligerence and decisiveness of Dolan. Although persuaded that his path had taken the legal and moral high roads, McSween also exuded indecision and sometimes foreboding. The urge to stop running away from his opponents and his conviction that he might not win the battle clouded his decision-making. His wife was more inclined to push ahead and make decisions, although she had not approved of his ventures with Tunstall or his other actions that stirred up lethal opposition.

On Tuesday, 16 July, the shooting spontaneously begun the day before popped and sputtered all day. Neither side at this point was inclined to chance a full-scale shootout. But McSween and Dolan gunmen skittered around and skirmished, hoping to find a path to eventual victory. Thinking the Dolanites might gain the upper hand through additional men or augmented firepower, Sheriff Peppin wrote

Lieutenant Colonel Nathan A. M. Dudley, 1825–1910. Colonel Dudley, a blustery, opinionated U.S. Army officer, single handedly changed the balance of power toward The House supporters on the fateful final day of the Five-Day Battle in Lincoln New Mexico, on 19 July 1878. Photograph courtesy New Mexico State University Library Archives, Las Cruces, image 00140632.

Colonel Dudley to ask for the loan of a howitzer, which he believed might convince those enemies under warrant to "surrender without a shot being fired." And if Dudley granted the request of the Dolan-Peppin party, he would confer "a good favor on the majority of the people of this country, who are being persecuted by a lawless mob."

Given Dudley's sympathy for the sheriff's side in the unfolding battle, he might have agreed to send the howitzer—and maybe to have intervened with a squadron of federal troops. But the previous month the U.S. Congress had passed the *Posse Comitatus Act,* which forebade the use of soldiers as a posse to assist the legal process, such as serving arrest warrants, and to keep the peace in civilian society. In other words federal troops could enter civil disputes only in the direst circumstances. At this point Dudley would be disobeying orders and defying Congressional legislation if he intervened in the fray escalating in Lincoln.

The first two days of sporadic shooting especially frightened mothers in Lincoln. Mary Ealy, the wife of missionary
doctor Taylor Ealy, later wrote that the bullets smacking
against the McSween home and the Tunstall store, where
the Ealys were housed, particularly scared her and her children. Mary described the horrendous days of the big battle
as intense, nonstop shooting. Similar fears frightened Elizabeth Shield, Sue McSween's sister, as she tried to protect her
brood of five children. Later in the 1920s, Sue McSween
Barber told historian Maurice Garland Fulton that dreadful
worries seized all the inhabitants of the McSween house,
where the Shields and other noncombatants were housed
alongside the Kid and other gunmen.

Alex McSween seemed insensitive to most of these maternal fears. Indeed, when he learned that Captain Saturnino
Baca, a Dolan partisan, was utilizing the *torreon* (a cone
like rock fortress) in the center of Lincoln as a refuge for
McSween opponents, he threatened to burn Baca out of
the house that McSween claimed to own and in which the
Baca family resided. This warning came even though Baca's
wife had just given birth to a son and needed recovery time.
Many other good people in Lincoln, trying to be nonpartisan and stay out of the battle, so feared for their lives and
families that they fled Lincoln for safety. Some wrote territorial officials to ask for aid in settling the issues causing
the war and for protection merely to live in their homes and
walk the streets, where getting water and food was now a
life-threatening act.

At this point the McSween partisans made a major mistake. Toward evening a soldier, bringing Peppin a message
from Dudley that his hands were legally tied and that he
could not send a howitzer or troops, came under fire as he
entered Lincoln. Evidence suggests that several McSween
supporters on the roof of his house had fired on the black
soldier, Private Berry Robinson, and in doing so were guilty
of breaking the law against shooting at—supposedly—non-

partisan soldiers. That unwise act opened the door to Colonel Dudley's subsequent intervention in the shootout.

Wednesday, 17 July, the third day of the Five-Day Battle, saw the continuation of what had happened on the two previous days. As Mary Ealy recalled, "shooting, yelling, and screaming kept up incessantly," and "Wednesday night was worse and worse." Indeed Wednesday was a day of terror for the entire Ealy family. After the doctor had gone to bed, a knock at the door brought two men asking for his help with a badly injured Ben Ellis, the son of the store owner. Quickly rousing himself, dressing, and grabbing his medical bag, he followed the men out the back of the store. Hoping to avoid the shooting on main street, they attempted to move east by a backyard route. But the moonlight allowed the shooting opponents to see the men, who were on an errand of mercy. No matter, the gunshots rang out, with bullets whizzing very close to the doctor's head. Rather than risk his life, Dr. Ealy returned to the safety of his bedroom in the Tunstall store. The next morning, Ealy ventured out again—this time with his wife and his two young daughters as possible "protection"! He made his way to the Ellis store and sewed up the badly injured Ben Ellis. Then the doctor quickly returned to the safety of the Tunstall store and stayed inside.

Neither side made a major new move on Thursday, 18 July, but both armies, especially the Dolanites, were moving in directions that would prepare the way for the next day's drama. Jimmy decided he needed help to balance the odds against him, so he traveled the nine miles to Fort Stanton to seek the army's help. His pretext, although never clarified, might have been the protection of women and children. One bystander reported that he overheard Colonel Dudley's response. He urged Dolan to return to Lincoln and "stand them [McSween's faction] off," and the colonel would come to Lincoln the next day.

Earlier on Thursday, in an official message, Dudley reported that reinforcements might be headed to Lincoln.

They were rumored to be coming to protect McSween's endangerment from the sheriff's posse. The colonel did not think these rumors were valid or that any changes made would end the war; indeed, anyone who thought so, he asserted, was "seriously mistaken."

Then, new requests that may have changed Dudley's mind came into Fort Stanton. When McSween again threatened to expel the Baca family from its rented house, the captain renewed his fervent request to Dudley to protect his family. Perhaps even more compelling was another event. Risking her life, a Lincoln woman walked to the fort and begged the soldiers to stop the fighting. She could not leave her house for wood or water; her children cowered in their house, afraid to go outside; shooting endangered their lives in nearly every moment. Her emotional request, and the entreaties of the Baca family and others trapped in Lincoln—these heartfelt and authentic pleas got the attention of the fort's officers.

Other historians are convinced that another incident drove Dudley more than these humanitarian requests. When it was reported to him that shots had been fired at the soldier he sent into Lincoln, and when information he received the next day confirmed the firing on his man, Dudley seemed satisfied there were sufficient reasons to change his mind, to do something specific in Lincoln.

On Thursday evening Dudley made a crucial decision. Gathering his officers in council, the colonel presented the dilemmas with the mounting crisis in Lincoln and asked them to think about intervening, even going beyond the recent congressional legislation forbidding them to do so. Whether Dudley pressured his officers into voting for intervention in the Lincoln shootout and whether they were convinced on their own reflection that something must be done to protect the innocent, particularly women and children, remains a mystery. But they all signed an agreement backing his balance-changing move to enter Lincoln the next day. It was a fateful decision.

As Friday morning dawned, the mood was tense yet seemingly no worse than the previous four days. Despite the unease, no one could have predicted that events in Lincoln on 19 July would rival the Battle of Little Bighorn, the Shootout at the OK Corral, or the assassination of Wild Bill Hickok as one of the most memorable events of the Old West. Before the day was over, High Noon had occurred, and the violent landscape of Lincoln and the Lincoln County War would rapidly move in new directions.

On the climactic fifth day, events by mid-morning were shifting the balance of power in Lincoln in rapid, dramatic ways. The most important of these transitions came when Colonel Dudley led a column of four officers, eleven African American cavalrymen, and twenty-four white infantrymen down the beleaguered town's main street. Horses pulled a lethal Gatling gun and an even more deadly twelve-pound howitzer. The first of the step-by-step events that suddenly and decisively reached a violent apex at the end of the day was under way.

Dudley warned both sides—Sheriff Peppin and the Dolan forces first and then the McSween supporters—that he would not take sides in the civil war. Rather, he had come to keep harm from descending on women and children. After conversing with Peppin and telling him to keep his men from firing on the soldiers—if they did he would "blow you above the clouds"—he marched his column to an open area farther east in town, across from the Montaño store.

During Friday morning, McSween seemed to sense that the balance of control was clearly shifting, but he did not see the change at first. In fact, early in the day McSween wrote Postmaster Ash Upson in Roswell, asking for stamps and making no mention of the mounting conflict in his threatened community. Perhaps McSween, sheltered in his protected home, missed the first steps. Quite possibly he did not see Sheriff Peppin standing next to Dudley, their stance clearly signaling where military support was the strongest. Dudley, after setting up camp, pointed his threatening howitzer toward the Montaño store, which for several days had lodged Martin Chávez and his nearly twenty Mexican lieutenants. The howitzer, which could blow apart an adobe building with a murderous shot or two, was too much fire-power for the men to face. They abandoned the store and the nearby Patrón house and fled into the adjacent hills. Their leaving quickly reduced the McSween superior num-bers from about sixty to less than twenty men, all remaining in the Tunstall store or McSween house. In no more than a few minutes, Dudley's intervention with regular troops and heavy weapons had decisively rearranged the balance of strength in Lincoln.

Seeing what was happening and understanding now was the time to move, Sheriff Peppin sent one of his men to the McSween house and called on the lawyer and his men to surrender. Some of "the boys," as Sue McSween called her husband's younger partisans, profanely refused. They also told the Peppin man that they too had arrest warrants for his and other Dolan supports and would use their guns to serve them. The vituperative exchange was but the first of several that undercut any hope of compromise.

Much of the accelerating violence on Friday swirled around the McSween house. A dozen people, perhaps nearly twice that many (including women and children), were crammed into the lawyer's home. The expansive u-shaped building fronted on the main street but faced toward the Rio Bonito. At the northern end of each wing was a kitchen, with the McSweens in the western and Elizabeth Shield and her five children in the eastern wing. (Elizabeth's husband, David, had gone to Las Vegas to flee the violence that he thought was aimed at him.) Dr. Ealy, Mary, and their two young daughters had left the crowded home to stay in the back of the nearby Tunstall store. Susan Gates, the assistant to Dr. Ealy, was also in the McSween house. Finally, more than ten Regulators, including the Kid, were packed into the home. About half of the McSween men in the house were Hispanic supporters of the lawyer.

Once most of the other Regulators had fled Lincoln, Peppin's men took aim at the McSween house. A steady stream of bullets destroyed the windows, and even dislodged some of the bricks placed inside the windows to deflect any rife or pistol shots. Furniture was also moved around to accommodate other defensive measures. Fear mounted in the house as the taunting and shooting intensified, and the number of Dolan gunmen increased. Susan McSween uttered her fears: "They are going to kill Alex. . . . They intend to kill us all."

Gradually seeing what was happening, Alex McSween tried to reason with Colonel Dudley. The lawyer addressed him a note, handing it to Billy to read before the Shields' young daughter took the message to the commander. It read: "Would you have the kindness to let me know why soldiers surround my house. Before blowing up my property I would like to know the reason." Taking advantage of McSween's dangling construction, Dudley sarcastically replied that no soldiers surrounded the McSween house (those were Peppin's men) and that if McSween wanted to blow up his own house, that was all right with Dudley as long as the explosion did not harm any soldiers.

Susan became convinced that she must speak to Dudley, something Alex seemed unable to do. Bravely she made her way down to the encampment of soldiers, and after a bit of delay she began a spirited conversation with the colonel. Their exchange was a verbal duel of emotional intensity, and the soldier got the better of the contest. Susan unloaded her fury on the colonel, attacking him for siding with Sheriff Peppin but also begging him to do something to protect her husband.

Dudley, blustery and opinionated as usual, said he would not interfere with the sheriff's legal duties. Denigrating Alex McSween to Susan, he would do nothing to help her and her husband as long as they sheltered outlaws such as Billy Bonney and the other Regulators in their house. Then the colonel raised his misogynist colors, berating Susan for being the wife of Alex McSween and for abandoning all respectability. The shouting match reached an apex of emotion before Dudley ordered Susan out of his camp. Frustrated and maybe despondent, she retreated to her besieged home. No help was coming from the U.S. Army.

The Peppin men tried a new offensive maneuver, which eventually brought down the McSween house. Three of the sheriff's force poured oil on the floor near the Shields' kitchen and tried to light it. The first attempt fizzled, but the tactic later succeeded. The McSween men inside the house blasted away at the arsonists, forcing them to race away. Running to the nearest building, a nearby privy, the men jumped into its pit and were forced to stay in that aromatic site until the end of the gunfight that night.

About two o'clock that afternoon Andy Boyle, another Peppin partisan, tried a different technique to fire the McSween house. Gathering shavings, chips, and small bits of lumber, he piled them near the back entrance and lit the kindling. The fire took hold, and in the succeeding hours, the fire slowly but steadily ate its way around the adobe house. Feeding on *vigas* (rafters), door frames, window frames, and flooring—the only wood in the McSween home—the flames forced the inhabitants to relocate carefully into smaller and smaller areas of the house.

The expanding fire and engulfing smoke spreading throughout the house sent the McSween contingent in new directions. The gutsy Suzy Gates walked to Dudley's encampment and requested protection and safety for the women and children. Even though Dudley had announced the security of innocent women as his purpose for coming to Lincoln, he had done nothing to carry out that mission. Dudley listened to Gates, provided exits for the Shield and Ealy families, and even helped Susan McSween when she reluctantly joined the other women at about five o'clock.

Susan had tried to rally Alex in the defense of his home and in planning how to abandon it, if needed. But Alex seemed frozen in indecision. As Susan put it, "The Kid was lively and McSwain [*sic*] was sad." Billy had encouraged Susan to leave. When the men burst out of the burning house and dashed to possible freedom and safety, he told her, "dresses ain't made for running."

By dark, the fire had burned its way to the other side of the McSween house, leaving only the northeastern kitchen inhabitable. In the meantime Billy had hatched a plan. He and the first batch of men would race out of the kitchen, across what was thought a darkened open space, turn east behind the Tunstall store, and head northeast to the Rio Bonito. If the strategy worked, the Kid's contingent would attract the Dolanites' attention and gunfire and allow McSween and a second group to sneak out in another direction.

Approaching nine o'clock, Billy and four others, including Jim French, Tom Folliard, José Chávez y Chávez, and Harvey Morris, a law student working with McSween, raced out of the kitchen and across the open spot. But the light from the fire and moonlight partially illuminated the runners. The Kid, French, Folliard, and Chávez y Chávez escaped through the hail of gunfire but not Morris; a bullet to the head brought almost-instant death.

The second part of the plan failed under McSween's indecision. At first irresolute, the lawyer then blurted out he would surrender, but when some of Peppin's men approached, he shouted, "I'll never surrender." A volley of bullets, as many as five, brought down McSween and, at the same time, Francisco Zamora and Vicente Romero. Fifteen-year-old Yginio Salazar was also seriously injured in the fusillade and left for dead, but during the night he revived

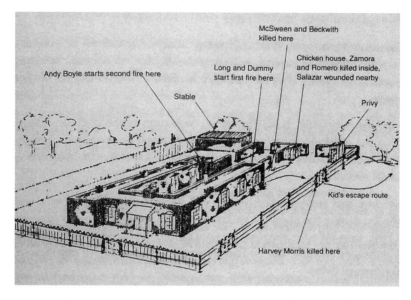

The Great Escape. Late evening on 19 July 1878, Billy the Kid, assuming leadership of the Regulators from Alex McSween, engineered the escape of several of his men from the burning McSween house. A few minutes later McSween was shot down Murphy-Dolan besiegers. Illustration courtesy of Human Systems Research, Las Cruces, New Mexico.

and dragged his body as much as a half-mile to safety while the shooters celebrated. In the horrendous melee, Ygnacio González, Florencio Chávez, and José María Sánchez got away. About one-third of the McSween's forces in his house were slaughtered, and two-thirds escaped.

Billy Bonney's experiences in the Five-Day Battle and especially in the Big Killing on Friday forced a turning point. His dramatic dash to freedom not only saved his life but put him on a new path. In the next three years, he traveled a route different from the previous three years, even though actions in those two segments of life had commonalities.

At the beginning of his tension-filled five-day stay in Lincoln Billy was a follower. He was not making decisions for the McSween group as the men opened their defense in the lawyer's home. By time he raced out of the burning McSween home, he was displaying leadership qualities that came to the fore in the next months. Survival under desperate conditions changed him for good.

On the final day, things moved in a new direction. Doc Scurlock, then the chief of the Regulators, had left town, chased out by Dudley's menacing gestures with the howitzer. On the spot McSween, the accepted leader of his force and the provider of financial support for the gang and of refuge in his house, could not shoulder the needed leadership role. His wife, an eyewitness to events taking place in their home, described the need: "McSween sat with his head down, and the Kid shook him and told him to get up, that they were going to make a break." Here was the change, the symbol and demonstration of shifting leadership. But Billy did not *take on* the leadership; he was *forced* into that role because the Regulators had to escape the burning house. Since McSween could not engineer the necessary moves to save the group, Billy took over. Someone had to assume the role of decision-maker, so Billy moved into that slot. In the next three years, he increasingly moved to the front of the pack, but not, as too many historians have suggested, because he wanted to lead. A vacuum brought him toward the front.

9

A New Kind of Journey

Billy biographers make much of his rise to captaincy in the months after the fiery shootout on 19 July. And they should. In the next few weeks Billy gradually became a leader more than a follower, directing most of the activities of his much smaller gang rather than trailing after the orders of others. His rise to bandit chief became increasingly apparent in the next three years.

From midsummer 1878 onward, Billy entered an open place. In the short five months from February to July, the Regulators had lost four leaders: John Tunstall in February; Dick Brewer and Frank MacNab in April; and Alex McSween in July. Equally important for Billy was that the financial contributions of Tunstall and McSween were gone. As well-funded as anyone in the Lincoln area save for rancher John Chisum, Tunstall had hired Billy and given him a horse, saddle, gun, and salary. He provided Billy security that the wanderer previously lacked. McSween did the same after the death of Tunstall. It is said that the Lincoln lawyer paid Billy and other followers four dollars a day, when average wages for a New Mexico farm laborer in the 1870–1880s were two dollars per day, for protecting McSween, his wife, and his property, although admittedly the details are vague. Again, if true, this meant that Billy had again enjoyed financial security in riding for McSween.

Now in late summer 1878 both providers were gone, along with the good wages they had been paying Billy. What would he do, looking ahead? He had to find a grubstake to replace the support of Tunstall and McSween.

Billy's elevation to leadership must be linked to two other developments: (1) the loss of four previous leaders, and especially the financial support of Tunstall and McSween; and (2) Billy's need to find food, a horse, ammunition, and sundries. Billy's response was to become a leader to replace others now gone and to find a new way of supporting himself. Many speak of the Lincoln County War as ending after the death of McSween. It did not.

The cast of characters and the war's central issues changed, however. Tunstall and McSween were gone; so were Brewer and MacNab. Now Doc Scurlock and the Kid, as well as Charlie Bowdre, Fred Waite, Henry Brown, and Tom Folliard, were the core of the Regulators. That organization would soon shift again, with the Kid gradually moving to the front of a much-reduced group.

Similar transitions were taking place in The House before and after midsummer 1878. In May of that year, Murphy left Lincoln and moved to Santa Fe, where alcoholism, then cancer led to his death in October. Dolan had assumed control of The House, but he had lost the Murphy-Dolan firm, deeply in debt, to Catron in April. In Santa Fe during early October, Catron was allowed to resign the office of U.S. district attorney in New Mexico Territory; and soon after Angel's damaging report reached Washington officials, Governor Axtell was removed from office. Although Warren Bristol remained district judge and would impose the death penalty on Billy in 1881, increasing pressure was placed on William Rynerson over his role in the Lincoln County War, and he was removed as district attorney in 1880. All these men were opponents of the Kid, but real enmity toward him mounted as he became a bandit leader in southeastern New Mexico.

In the days after the Lincoln blowup in July 1878, Colonel Dudley well understood the tensions and participants who kept the Lincoln County War going. Within hours of returning to Fort Stanton following the shootout in Lincoln, he wrote a formal report revealing his insight into Lincoln present and future.

"One thing is sure," Dudley began, "both parties are still determined, [and] the fearful sacrifice of the McSween clique on the 19th inst[ant] does not seem to satisfy either side. A deep revenge will [also] be sought by the sheriff's posse . . . and a still stronger spirit exists on the part of the McSween men to retaliate for the death of their headman, McSween." Endorsing Dudley's insights, Billy specialist Frederick Nolan adds, "The fire had not gone out; it would flare into life all too soon." No one has figured out, with any certainty, how the Kid dealt with daily necessities. Where did he stay? How and what did he eat? And perhaps most importantly, how did he make a living that allowed the purchase of scanty bed and board at least?

Even before the Big Killing, Billy had been involved in rustling. But in the coming months, he increasingly turned to livestock theft. Or as he put it, he would "steal for a living." His rustling operation usually involved cattle and horses in Lincoln County, then driving them to the Texas panhandle, where Billy and his gang found buyers who asked few or no questions about brands or bills of sale. Always opportunists, the gang likewise found in west Texas horses and cattle it delivered to buyers in New Mexico. Billy and his bunch particularly targeted John Chisum and his vast herds; the Kid was convinced that the cattle king had not kept his earlier promise of wages for protecting Chisum's Jinglebob livestock. In the weeks and months following the Five-Day Battle, Billy remained an outlaw under indictment, but he also became a nearly full-time rustler.

The rustling pattern began to harden in fall 1878. In the tense hours and days following the 19 July blowout, Billy seems to have abandoned Lincoln. He was not in town when the Peppin-named coroner's jury declared that McSween and his followers had been killed while resisting arrest. Nor was he involved in the burial of McSween and his dead followers or in the protection of the Patrón house, where Sue McSween was staying. Instead, like the other Regulators the Kid moved in and out of the Lincoln area, stealing horses to replace those they had lost in the Big Killing, threatening their enemies, and terrorizing Sheriff Peppin. Generally the former McSween partisans were searching, during the next few weeks, for a new path to follow.

About three weeks later Billy and most of the Regulators were nearby when another killing took place. On 5 August Doc Scurlock led nearly twenty gunmen to the Mescalero Indian agency southwest of Lincoln on the South Fork of the Rio Bonito. About half the group were Hispanics, including Atanacio Martínez, the former town constable in Lincoln. Frank Coe stated that they went to visit Dick Brewer's grave at Blazer's Mill, but better evidence suggests they coveted some of the horse herd at the Indian agency.

The Hispanics and Anglos divided as they approached the agency. The Hispanics rode straight ahead, while Billy and his group turned toward the creek. While watering their horses, the Anglos heard shots up ahead. At the agency, Frederick C. Godfroy, the U.S. agent for the Mescaleros, and Morris Bernstein, his clerk, were handing out goods to Apache women when they too heard the shots. Grabbing their horses, the two agents dashed toward the shooting. Bernstein galloped ahead, even though Godfroy urged him to be cautious. When the chief agent arrived, Bernstein was dead, perhaps shot down by Martínez. The Hispanics had encountered an Indian group and exchanged shots. Martínez evidently fired on Bernstein. Why he did so is still unclear.

Revealingly, when news of Bernstein's death reached Fort Stanton and Lincoln, many assumed that Billy was the killer.

By fall 1878 Billy's reputation as a trigger-happy gunman was already fostering rumors that he would take lives without much reason. In this case he was accused of the murder even though he was hundreds of yards away watering his horse.

In the meantime, the trauma and other fallout from the Five-Day Battle led to large changes among the Regulators. In the late summer and fall of 1878 the group transformed from the Regulators under the chieftainship of Doc Scurlock to a band, a much smaller group, under the direction of Billy Bonney.

The transition began with the Coes, cousins Frank and George. In a decision-making gathering in Anton Chico, Frank informed Billy and the others that he and George were dropping out and heading north to Colorado. But Billy spoke up to say, "It's not all over with me. . . . I'm going to get revenged. . . . Who wants to go with me?" In August only the Coes left, but the "iron clad" loyalty that had united the Regulators was beginning to fall apart. Early in September Doc Scurlock and Charlie Bowdre, tiring of the daily stresses surrounding Lincoln, moved their families to Fort Sumner, a mostly Hispanic enclave that struck them as a less dangerous place for their wives and children, who were also Hispanic. The Regulators dwindled further in numbers when Scurlock, left New Mexico altogether and headed back to Texas toward the end of 1879. After these changes, Bowdre and Folliard became Billy's chief partners and followed him loyally for the next two years, until their violent deaths in December 1880.

Another change gradually reshaped Billy's reputation in Lincoln County in fall 1878 and thereafter. Although The House opponents and legal officials such as Bristol and Rynerson disliked—even hated—competitors like Tunstall and McSween, they could not deny the considerable high social status of these men in the region. Billy lacked their respectability. Although he was already viewed by his

Regulators Tom O. Folliard, 1858–1880, and Charlie Bowdre, 1848–1880, with Manuela Bowdre. Folliard and Bowdre were enthusiastic supporters of Billy the Kid. Both fell before the guns of Pat Garrett in December 1880. Folliard photograph in the Robert N. Mullin Collection courtesy of the Haley Memorial Library & History Center, Midland, Texas; photograph of the Bowdres courtesy of the New Mexico State University Library Archives, Las Cruces, image 0110081.

opponents as an adolescent, gun-happy drifter, Billy's bad reputation expanded. He was becoming known as an outlaw, even a desperado. By the end of 1878, the Regulators had become, in the eyes of their foes, a small band of violent troublemakers, bad men bent on little more than stealing and robbing from the "best sorts" of the community.

Yet Billy's band was not the worst of the Lincoln County desperados. War continued in Lincoln County, with ingredients dramatically shifting. Within the county itself, a new gang of murderers galloped on scene. In the late summer and early fall, gunman John Selman fled authorities and vigilantes in Texas pursuing him on cattle-stealing charges and ran to Lincoln County. Once there, he and perhaps as many as ten violent gunmen, known as Selman's Scouts, terrorized the southern reaches of the county. Also dubbed the Rustlers (or Wrestlers), Selman's outlaws indiscriminately killed Hispanics and other residents, robbed others, burned down houses, and used women "for their own pleasure." Although not part of the earlier House-Regulator civil war in Lincoln County, the Selman bunch were even more violent and murderous than the men serving Dolan and McSween. On one or two occasions there were minor confrontations between the Rustlers and Regulators. Eventually, in 1880 Lincoln County residents banded together to chase Selman and his gang out of New Mexico Territory. He relocated to west Texas and gained a small foothold in Old West history by killing noted gunman John Wesley Hardin in an El Paso saloon in August 1895.

If Billy and the Selman hard cases stirred up Lincoln Country from within the region, another shift emanating from outside also impacted the area in 1878–1879. These cross-continental influences, beginning with complaints and pleas from New Mexicans to federal and other authorities in Washington, D.C., sparked a special investigation, then leadership changes and policy shifts in the territory.

These eastern forces brought to bear on New Mexico impacted Billy in 1878—and the remainder of his life. The links between New Mexico and the federal government and the policies that moved from east to west are another substantiation of what western historian Elliott West calls "the greater reconstruction" demonstrating how East Coast happenings shaped events, people, and society in the American West.

Soon after the killing of John Tunstall in February 1878, residents of New Mexico began writing to political leaders and their well-connected friends on the national scene.

The correspondents begged the easterners to do something about the violent chaos that had descended on New Mexico. They often singled out Lincoln County, but other correspondents also described the dramatic disruptions in Colfax County northeast of Santa Fe.

Some letters sent east went to officials high up in the federal government; others were no more than wild shots in the dark. The first letters came soon after the killing of Tunstall. Alex McSween detailed the horrendous event to Sir Edward Thornton, the British ambassador to Washington. Robert Widenmann sent another letter to Thornton the next day, with Thornton then forwarding both letters, along with one of his own, to Secretary of State William M. Evarts, who transmitted the correspondence to U.S. Attorney General Charles Devens. The Attorney General's Office sent all the information to Thomas B. Catron, the U. S. District Attorney for New Mexico, and instructed him to investigate. Catron, a friend of Governor Samuel Axtell, the judges, district attorneys, and sheriffs in southeastern New Mexico, and some of The House leaders, did nothing. More letters begging for further investigation flooded east to Washington, D.C., including several from Montague R. Leverson, a nosy British citizen who detested Axtell, Catron, and their cronies and hungered and thirsted for political office in New Mexico. Finally, the pressure on federal government officials and the failure of Catron to act compelled the Hayes administration to do something. In April 1878 Frank Warner Angel was named a special agent of the U. S. Departments of Interior, Justice, and War and sent to New Mexico to investigate the death of Tunstall, the violent uprisings in Lincoln and Colfax counties, and the possible wrongful leadership of territorial officials.

After arriving in Santa Fe in early May, Angel traveled first to Lincoln County, where he interviewed persons on both sides of the territorial civil war raging there. Throughout May and June he gathered information in the

Lincoln area, then moved to Colfax County, and finally came back to Santa Fe to put pressing questions to Axtell and Catron. Both the governor and U.S. attorney asked for more time, and Catron eventually did not answer Angel. By August Angel had returned to his home in New York, but before he finished his written report, he was instructed to report orally to President Rutherford B. Hayes in Washington, D.C., about his findings. Angel's negative conclusions about Axtell, Catron, and others soon led to their replacement or resignation. Within days, Civil War hero Lew Wallace was named to replace Axtell as New Mexico's territorial governor. By the end of September, Wallace was in Santa Fe and soon launched new ways to quell the violence in Lincoln County. His policies would clearly impact Billy the Kid in the next two to three years. The governor and the Kid would even meet personally to work out a blueprint for the future.

Days after Wallace arrived in Santa Fe and realized more clearly what was going on in Lincoln County, he encouraged President Hayes to declare martial law in the troubled county. Wallace did not get what he wanted. Reluctant to transgress the Posse Comitatus Act that denied the use of troops to quell civilian unrest—save in the most dire situations—Hayes instead issued a proclamation. On 7 October, the president ordered "all good citizens of the United States and especially of the Territory of New Mexico" to cease their illegal actions and "disperse and return peaceably to their respective abodes on or before noon of the thirteenth day of October." The proclamation had almost no effect; Wallace needed to find something stronger to deal with Lincoln County.

Other transitions in Lincoln County and New Mexico shaped the Kid's journey in the fall of 1878 and later. His fellow McSween partisan Rob Widenmann fled from Mesilla to Las Vegas and then back to his family in Michigan, never to return. Jimmy Dolan also departed Fort Stanton for Santa

Fe, where Lawrence Murphy died in mid-October. But Sue McSween, previously abandoning Lincoln to protect herself and to secure needed medical attention, returned to Lincoln with outspoken attorney Huston Chapman in tow to look after her interests and to fight back against The House and Colonel Dudley. She and Chapman arrived in Lincoln toward the end of November. Chapman's energetic I'll-stand-up-to-you-guys attitude supported Sue in the aftermath of Alex's death but roiled Lincoln in the next few weeks.

These shifts in personnel and polices impacted Billy and his reduced band of followers in the late summer and fall of 1878. The Regulators had to find a way to feed themselves. Their wandering and stealing started in August and September of 1878. After the Bernstein killing at the Mescalero Agency in early August, Billy and his gang rode north and east to Fort Sumner. In mid-August they stopped for rest and relaxation at the old fort now headquarters of the Peter Maxwell holdings. Bowdre and Scurlock secured jobs working for Maxwell, although Bowdre did not entirely sever his ties to Billy. Frank Coe remarked many years later that "The Kid and others had a baile for us" in Fort Sumner.

Billy and his gang next moved north up the Pecos toward Puerto de Luna, where they ran headlong into a posse hunting for them. Hearing that Billy and his sidekicks were coming to Anton Chico, Sheriff Desiderio Romero of San Miguel County rode into town to confront the "Lincoln County War party." Frank and George Coe, in later interviews and written accounts, some appearing a half century afterwards, recalled what happened next. "Let's go down and see what they look like," the take-charge Billy asserted, "and not have them hunting us all over town." In a nearby saloon, Billy and his shootists stood up to Sheriff Romero, with the Kid straightforwardly telling the posse, a group of "about eight big burly Mexicans . . . [with] all the guns and pistols you ever saw," they were "the Lincoln County War party I guess you are looking for right here." "What do you want to do about it?"

The stick-it-in-their-face manner of the Kid threw off Sheriff Romero. After a moment or two of hesitation, the posse leader backed off and his men took up Billy's offer of a drink, then meekly slunk out of town. Billy, "always in the lead" as Frank Coe remembered, had challenged the group head-on with "Now is the time and you'll never get us in a better place to settle it right here." Nothing better illustrated how Billy, still in the last months of his teen years, had clearly stepped into the leadership of the remaining Regulators.

After carousing a day or two at Anton Chico, Billy's small group returned to Lincoln. After controlling the town for a few days, the Kid and his riders then rode out, stealing a few horses to sell in the Texas panhandle. Ten miles south of Lincoln at the Fritz ranch Billy's gang made off with fifteen horses and more than a hundred cattle. Driving the animals up the Pecos, the gang moved north through the Bosque Grande and to a point about fifty miles east of Fort Bascom. There, they encountered the Chisums near Red River Springs, also on their way to Texas. Sallie Chisum, cowman John's niece, wrote in her diary, "Regulators came up with us . . . on 25 Sept 1878." Billy and Sallie were acquainted; she had spoken of candy he had given her, and he had even written her in the midst of the violent Five-Day Battle. Some thought they may have been sweethearts, but this chance meeting was the last time they saw one another.

Billy's decision to run his stolen stock to the Texas panhandle proved to be a financially sound idea. He headed for the new town of Tascosa. Huge, sprawling open-range cattle ranches were springing up in west Texas only a few years after Indian tribes had been pushed out of the country, specifically the Llano Estacado. Tascosa, just two years in existence and little more than a cluster of a half-

Tascosa, Texas. This new, small cowtown in the Texas panhandle attracted Billy the Kid and his riders as a place to sell their livestock rustled in New Mexico. Nearby the town were ranches and ranges with abundant livestock that the Kid stole on the return trip and sold in New Mexico. Billy and his riders spent time in saloons like this one in Tascosa. Photograph in the J. Evetts Haley Collection courtesy of the Haley Memorial Library & History Center, Midland, Texas.

dozen jerry-built structures, including two stores, a saloon, but no church, had become a negotiating site for nearby cattlemen. Needing horses for their expanding cattle holdings, ranchers were willing to buy sturdy horses and ask few questions about their origins. The same was the case for those cowmen needing stock for their ranges or buyers wanting animals to butcher. No one asked for bills of sale. These loose standards were a boon for Billy and others bent on purloining horses or cattle from elsewhere and driving them to west Texas.

While near Tascosa, Billy met Dr. Henry F. Hoyt. The twenty-four-year-old doctor had ridden into west Texas in

137

1877 to help with a smallpox epidemic and had taken up cowboying and mail delivery to fill in after the epidemic subsided. In the next few days, Billy and his comrades questioned Hoyt about Tascosa, the nearby ranches, and the cattle business. The eighteen-year-old Billy and the young doctor became fast friends, hanging out in Tascosa and its saloon, although neither was a drinker.

The warm friendship led to an exchange of gifts. Hoyt gave Billy a woman's gold watch he had won in a card game, thinking that Billy might present it to a New Mexican girl he was enamored with. (Was it Paulita Maxwell?) In turn, before Hoyt left the panhandle, Billy gifted him Dandy Dick, a handsome race horse and the best of Billy's mounts, which he had taken from Sheriff Brady after his death. Billy, realizing he needed to protect Hoyt from charges he might have stolen the horse, wrote a bill of sale for seventy-five dollars but actually presented the horse as a gift. The extant bill of sale remains a revealing, early example of Billy's penmanship.

When Hoyt published *A Frontier Doctor*, in 1929, he furnished a snapshot description of Billy. His memoir is one of the few accounts from a first-hand source:

> [Billy was] a handsome youth with smooth face, wavy brown hair, an athletic and symmetrical figure, and clear blue eyes that could look one through and through. Unless angry he always seemed to have a pleasant expression with a ready smile. His head was well shaped, his features regular, his nose aquiline, his most noticeable characteristic a slight projection of his two upper front teeth. . . . [And] he spoke Spanish like a native . . . and although only a beardless boy, was nevertheless a natural leader of men.

Billy had to be more circumspect with other residents living near Tascosa—certainly more cautious than with Hoyt. Cattle ranchers had heard of Billy and warned him how things would go well with both of them if he maintained a cool head, fomented no violence, and kept his promises.

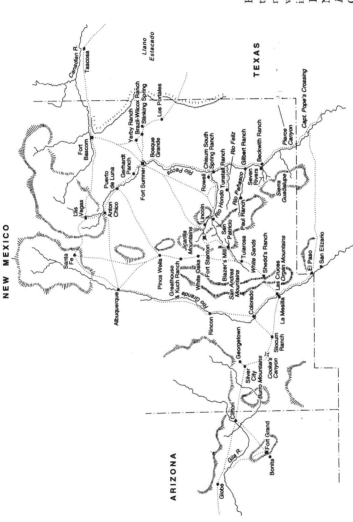

Eastern New Mexico and the Texas Panhandle. This map of the Southwest shows where Billy the Kid roamed in the years from 1878 to 1880. Map in Frederick Nolan, *The West of Billy the Kid* (Norman: University of Oklahoma Press, 1998). 50.

He did, and they responded agreeably to Billy and his four partners. Ironically some of the same ranchers who agreed to keep the peace with Billy in the fall of 1878 were among those who helped organized a posse of rangers from Texas to capture Billy in New Mexico in 1880–1881. In the intervening two years, Billy had been guilty of stealing west Texas cattle and selling them to butcher Pat Coghlan in Tularosa and to other folks in White Oaks, New Mexico.

While in Tascosa, Billy suffered other losses from his dwindling Regulator bunch. John Middleton, Fred Waite, and Henry Brown decided they had enough of the rustling, wandering, and death threats; they were signing off. They urged Billy and Folliard to do the same. But Billy refused, perhaps because he could not leave the life that he knew and hesitated to face what he did not, the new. He and Tom returned to Fort Sumner in late 1878.

Another, often-unmentioned wrinkle helps explain the decisions of the threesome to abandon Billy. As observers noted later, Billy was a stern leader, demanding unquestioned loyalty and obedience to his decisions. Middleton, then in his mid-twenties, for example, might have been reluctant to trust and follow a demanding teenager. When Billy and Tom returned to Fort. Summer, they were the only original Regulators remaining.

10

Looking for a Path

Returning to New Mexico in late 1878, Billy again faced the dilemmas of the post–Five-Day Battle. Would he continue to wander, looking for a place to stay, remaining a nomad without a home or employment? He and Tom Folliard landed in Fort Sumner for a time, then in Lincoln in December. The Kid told a friend he was tired of wandering and hoped to find a place, maybe a small piece of land, where he could settle down. He had expressed the same wish a year before, but the killing of John Tunstall had turned that dream into a nightmare. Yet, even when Billy and his opponents seemed on the verge of making peace a few weeks later and opening the way to tranquility and stability, untoward events intervened and again threw things off-track.

In Billy's absence during early fall 1878 the scenes of his earlier haunts in Lincoln County were beginning to change. Or perhaps better said, they were transitioning out of the false peace of late summer and early fall to another kind of warfare.

In late November when Susan McSween returned to Lincoln after a two-month sojourn in Las Vegas, she immediately indicated that she would not walk away from her earlier dream to "make it" in Lincoln. She brought with her the firebrand lawyer Huston I. Chapman, who intended

Fort Sumner, New Mexico. Fort Sumner and the nearby Bosque Redondo had been utilized to intern the Navajo and Mescalero tribes but was closed in 1868 and sold to the Maxwell family. After the shootout in the town of Lincoln in summer 1878, Billy the Kid moved on to Fort Sumner. He liked the predominantly Hispanic town, which would be his principal hangout during his last years. Photograph courtesy of the New Mexico State University Library Archives, Las Cruces, image 00150180.

to protect McSween's interests but soon riled the people of Lincoln and its environs. Even before McSween with Chapman returned to Lincoln, they had verbally attacked Colonel Dudley, accusing him of being "criminally responsible for the killing of [Alex] McSween," threatening Sue, and other "actions [that] have been offensive in the extreme to a large number of the best citizens of Lincoln County."

Not surprisingly, the colonel fired back—immediately, explosively, and scandalously. He went after Sue's character, accusing her, as Tunstall biographer Frederick Nolan writes, of being "a scandalous, immoral, lewd, licentious, dishonest, and ruthless woman." Bitterly defending his honor, which Susan and Chapman had impugned, Dudley and his supporters castigated her as an adulteress who more than likely had slept with Tunstall and Chapman. Saturnino Baca, still upset that the McSweens had tried to evict him, his family, and their new-born child, vilified Sue as a "profane, lewd, and unreliable woman." Sheriff Peppin, another Dudley partisan, claimed he had seen Sue commit adultery. Worst of all, Francisco Gómes, just past twenty, testified that he and Sue had enjoyed "sexual intercourse" several times in the grass near the Pecos. None of these vicious attacks was based on the testimony of reliable witnesses with verifiable information and may have come primarily from Dudley's campaign to smear Sue's reputation. Whatever the truth of the damaging allegations, they achieved much of their purpose: Sue McSween failed to reestablish her reputation as a loyal wife and virtuous woman.

The new governor, Lew Wallace, also made moves that changed the legal terrain surrounding Billy. After his assumption of the governor's chair in the last week of September 1878, Wallace pushed for a presidential declaration of martial law in Lincoln County, but President Hayes declined his request, instead merely issuing a toothless proclamation "admonishing" the lawless depredators in southeastern New Mexico to "disperse and return peaceably" to their homes and farms by 13 October 1878. Not satisfied, Wallace published in mid-November his own amnesty proclamation because, as he wrote idealistically (and incorrectly), "the [recent] disorders . . . have been happily brought to an end." His office would grant amnesty to the soldiers at Fort Stanton for their illegal actions and to residents of Lincoln County because after the violence and tumult they had "kept the peace, and conducted themselves in all respects as becomes good citizens."

The amnesty did not help or please Billy and Colonel Dudley. First, amnesty did not apply to those citizens already under indictment, who included Billy. He would remain a wanted man in Lincoln County, charged with the killing of Sheriff Brady and Buckshot Roberts. Second, upset by Wallace's suggestion that his soldiers needed amnesty, Dudley

Lew Wallace, 1827–1905. A Union Civil War veteran, Wallace was named governor of New Mexico Territory in September 1878. He promised to pardon Billy Bonney in exchange for the Kid's testimony in the killing of lawyer Huston Chapman. Billy kept his promise; Wallace did not. Photograph courtesy of the Lincoln Heritage Trust.

insulted the governor in a letter that accused Wallace of making "a false and unjust accusation" against "the gallant officers of my command." Dudley refused the offered amnesty because the governor, he thought, had outraged the loyal troops of the U.S. Army.

The threats and disruptions arising from Selman's Scouts, Sue McSween and lawyer Chapman's return and declaration of war, and the ongoing tensions between Dudley and Wallace—let alone the ongoing frictions with Dolan supporters—were too much for Billy. And the daily threats that local officials would try to capture or shoot him down were another pressure. Sometime in late 1878 or early 1879, he decided on an unusual route forward, one toward peace and stability in his life. He would attempt to foster a no-shooting agreement with Dolan and his backers by offering to put away his guns, if they would do likewise. His gesture, so at odds with harsh critics who dismiss Billy as little more than a violence-prone kid, was an offer to try something that no one else in the vortex of the Tunstall and McSween killings had attempted.

In a letter lost to historians and biographers, Billy wrote Jessie Evans with an offer to meet and parley, to see whether both sides could work out an agreement. On 18 February 1879, exactly one year after John Tunstall was shot down, the Kid and Dolan bands met in Lincoln, first behind opposite adobe walls. With Billy were the faithful Folliard, Yginio Salazar (the young Hispanic left for dead in the Big Killing at McSween's house), perhaps Doc Scurlock, and Joe Bowers. With Dolan were Jessie Evans, Billy Mathews, Edgar Walz (Catron's brother-in-law now overseeing the former Murphy-Dolan interests), and a mysterious newcomer, Billy Campbell. The possible peacemaking almost fell apart when the indomitable Evans threatened to kill Billy. In turn, the Kid replied that they had come to parley, not to fight. Besides, if the Dolan tribe came at him three at a time, he would wipe them all out.

Cooler heads prevailed, handshakes of agreement followed, and a written compromise was drafted. Both sides agreed not to kill their opponents or to testify against them in court. And anyone breaking these promises would be executed. After signing the document, men on both sides celebrated their good fortunes and took to serious drinking, save for Billy in the imbibing.

Just as the celebrants, now half-drunk, returned to Lincoln's main street, they encountered Chapman, recently returned from Las Vegas. Campbell confronted the lawyer, brusquely requesting his name and business. Chapman did not respond. Jabbing his pistol into Chapman's belly, the gunman commanded him to dance a jig. The lawyer refused and talked back. Standing several feet behind Chapman, Dolan then shot off his pistol, probably into the street, but Campbell triggered a pistol round into Chapman's stomach, not only killing the lawyer but setting his clothes on

145

fire. Turning away from the murder scene, Dolan realized he had to cover up Campbell's drunken, violent act. He urged Walz to place a pistol in Chapman's hand to make it look as though Campbell had shot him in self-defense. When Walz refused, Billy said he would plant the weapon. The Kid took the pistol, but he did not return to Chapman's body, instead riding out of town with Folliard.

The inexcusable killing of Chapman greatly upset residents of Lincoln. The uneasy peace of the past few weeks vanished literally in a flash. Was another violent war coming?

The Chapman incident prodded Governor Lew Wallace into action. Early in fall 1878 he had written to Washington, D.C., to brag that his efforts had brought peace to Lincoln County. The troublemakers and the upheavals they engineered had ended, Wallace erroneously claimed. The killing of Chapman proved that the governor's earlier optimism was clearly wrongheaded. Now he would need to go to Lincoln (a visit he had put off), deploy the army to bring real and lasting peace to Lincoln County, and uncover the causes of the Chapman murder.

Hearing that the governor was seeking information about Chapman's killing and knowing that Wallace's earlier pardon did not cover him, Billy embarked on an illuminating act of self-definition. Lacking any Santa Fe connections or political leverage, the Kid had the sand to write to Wallace, offering to reveal who was involved in the shooting of Chapman. Identifying the perpetrators would put his life in danger because of the "iron clad" agreement with the Dolan group, but Billy hinted he was willing to talk in exchange for a pardon or at least the withdrawal of the indictments against him. He could give "the desired information" and wanted "a chance to explain" the Chapman affair. He confessed to Wallace that he had "no Wish to fight any more"; in fact, he had "not raised an arm since Your proclamation." Plus, if the governor checked with Lincoln residents, he would discover their testaments "to my Character . . . for a majority of them are my friends."

Two days later, wishing to capitalize on this unexpected opportunity, Wallace quickly responded. He requested that Billy come alone to Squire Wilson's house in Lincoln for a meeting. "I have authority to exempt you from prosecution, if you will testify to what you know." (Lincoln County officials disagreed; Wallace lacked the legal power to pardon a federal crime, if Billy were accused of one.) "The purpose of the meeting," Wallace added, "is to arrange the matter in a way to make your life safe." This was exactly what Billy wanted to hear.

Billy was putting his life in jeopardy when he agreed to the meeting. In the months that lay ahead, he kept most of his part of the bargain, but the governor mostly failed to fulfill his promises to the Kid. Billy biographer Frederick Nolan concludes that Wallace "never had any real intention of fulfilling any of the promises he made." Perhaps this is true, although hard evidence for that conclusion is lacking.

The meeting went off well. Hesitant and arriving well-armed, Billy quickly warmed to the governor, a man in all ways different from the wandering Kid. Billy agreed to surrender in a contrived arrest and to testify against Chapman's murderers. In exchange Wallace promised, "I will let you go free, with a pardon in your pocket for all your misdeeds." Even after Jessie Evans, a violent, vengeful man, escaped from Fort Stanton where he had been jailed, Billy went ahead with fulfilling his promise to Wallace. On 21 March 1879 he and Folliard surrendered to Sheriff George Kimbrell and were jailed in Lincoln.

Ten days later, in a letter from his place in Lincoln to Secretary of the Interior Carl Schurz, Wallace revealed his supercilious condescension toward Billy. "A precious specimen named 'The Kid' whom the Sheriff is holding here in the Plaza," Wallace wrote, "is an object of tender regard. I heard singing and music the other night; going to the door I found the minstrels of the village actually serenading the fellow in his prison." A larger than life Billy was already beginning to emerge but not in the way Wallace and like-minded others wanted.

In the next two months Billy participated in two hearings that would shape his future. Neither turned out as he hoped. When the spring court session opened in Lincoln in mid-April, Billy kept his side of the bargain with Wallace, but the governor's promise was not upheld, although not entirely his fault. Billy's testimony before the grand jury helped lead to the indictments of Dolan and Campbell for Chapman's murder. In addition, these citizens considered nearly two hundred other indictments, including those for the murder of McSween, the burning of his house, the killing of Frank MacNab, and the numerous killings of John Selman and his Rustlers in fall 1878. Many of those indicted applied for pardon under Wallace's amnesty, and others asked for a change of venue to the fall court in La Mesilla.

Billy had hoped and probably expected that his agreement with Wallace the previous month in Lincoln would free or protect him from indictment for the murder of Sheriff Brady. It did not. Governor Wallace, remaining in Lincoln for nearly six weeks, eventually returned to Santa Fe and was not on scene to advocate for Billy's case and to remind regional legal officials of his promise of a pardon to the Kid. Instead William Rynerson, district attorney for Doña Ana, Grant, and Lincoln Counties and a prosecutor in Billy's case, refused to allow or honor Wallace's promise, arguing that the governor did not have the legal power to grant Billy a pardon for a federal crime. Ira Leonard, Billy's lawyer in La Mesilla two years later, told the governor that Rynerson was "no friend of law enforcement. He is bent on going after the Kid . . . bent on pushing him to the wall. He is a Dolan man and is defending him in every manner possible." Rynerson asked for and got a change of venue to Doña Ana County for Billy's trial on the Brady murder charge. Although Judge Warren Bristol, showing blatant legal partisanship, pushed for decisions supporting the Dolan interests, the grand jury had refused to indict many of the other pro-McSween men. Support for that group, however, did not include Billy.

One week later, a court of inquiry investigating charges against Colonel Dudley opened at Fort Stanton. The object of the hearing was to determine whether there were grounds for court-martialing Dudley over his one-sided intervention in the violence in Lincoln on 19 July. Removed from post command, the colonel was charged with conduct unbecoming an officer among other misdeeds. The judges, clearly favoring Dudley, turned the inquiry into a mutual admiration society for the colonel. And Dudley's strong, assertive lawyer, Henry Waldo, a law partner of Thomas Catron in Santa Fe, made mincemeat of Dudley's critics. Very soon, Sue McSween, who had initiated some of the charges against Dudley and served as a central agent in bringing about the hearing, realized the court was stacked against her and gave up.

On 28 May 1879, riding over from Lincoln to Fort Stanton, Billy appeared before the court to testify about Dudley's actions in Lincoln the previous July. Not the least bit overawed or rattled, Billy appeared "as cool and self-controlled as if it were attending a cockfight or horse race," one observer recalled. But Billy's testimony, Waldo asserted, was little more than hearsay since he had neither spoken to Dudley nor seen much of what the colonel did on 19 July. Most of Billy's testimony dealt with details of his escape from Alex and Sue McSween's burning house and the deaths of several persons at the back (east) end of the house. A major point Billy made was that Dudley's soldiers actually participated in the fight. Billy supporters have emphasized this part of the Kid's testimony, but his critics have pointed to the lack of corroborating evidence to confirm Billy's criticism of the soldiers. In his closing argument, Waldo viciously attacked Billy. "Then was brought forward," Waldo wrote, "William Bonney, alias Antrim, alias 'the Kid,' a precocious criminal of the worst type." Waldo went farther: Billy was guilty of the "cowardly and atrocious assassinations" of Brady and Roberts. So many warrants were out for the Kid's arrest that they would "have plastered him from his head to his feet."

Even before the Dudley court of inquiry was finished, Billy decided to abandon ship. Increasingly apparent to him was that the tide of events was running counter to his interests. The grand jury, it was true, had not followed Judge Bristol's admonition to rule in a pro-Dolan direction. Still, what Billy wanted and needed most—the pardon promised from Governor Wallace—had not come through. And now the court of inquiry was obviously marching toward a dismissal of the charges or complaints against Dudley.

Another decision may have driven Billy out his jail door. In early June, Judge Bristol opened the U.S. District Court in La Mesilla and demanded the Kid and Doc Scurlock be brought to Mesilla to face charges of murdering Buckshot Roberts on federal land. If Billy remained incarcerated in Lincoln, he would be easily transported by county officials to Mesilla. On 17 June, even before the Dudley inquiry was completed, Billy simply walked out of whatever room or building he was held in and rode away from Lincoln. Billy later summarized his actions: "I went up to Lincoln to stand trial on the warrant that was out for me, but the territory took a change of venue to Doña Ana, and I knew that I had no show, and so I skinned out." What Billy left in mid-June was clear, what he aimed toward much less certain.

Abandoning Lincoln and his attempts to clear his name there, he rode north to Las Vegas, where he stayed for several weeks. On 4 July, the trains of the Santa Fe Railroad arrived in Las Vegas for the first time, setting off a raucous celebration lasting for nearly a month. The festivities undoubtedly appealed to Billy. He may even have done a bit of gambling while in Las Vegas, for a person known as the "Kid" was arrested at the beginning of July for illegally operating a monte table. Billy was an expert dealer. In an equally vague incident, where the evidence is just as shaky and incomplete, Billy was said to have met legendary train robber Jesse James at a hot springs near Las Vegas. One reliable source, Dr. Hoyt, claimed that Billy introduced a "Mr. Howard," a name James often used, at a card game. But other sources assert no such meeting occurred.

Billy was soon back in his familiar haunts. His activities and movements in late summer and fall of 1879 illustrate one of Billy's characteristics: he was unable to leave familiar places and people to set himself up in new places. Las Vegas or another place away from Lincoln and southeastern New Mexico would have offered the possibilities for a fresh start. The frenetic days following the arrival of a new railroad were an ideal time for Billy to put down new roots. After all, Las Vegas was overflowing with new opportunities and people, such as Slapjack Bill, the Pockmarked Kid, and Bullshit Jack, who were available as new comrades.

Instead, Billy retreated to his familiar stomping grounds. He was back in the Lincoln area by early August. A confrontation with a soldier at a dance in Sue McSween's home in Lincoln and his near-capture at the hands of Sheriff Kimbrell and his henchmen brought home to Billy just how unsafe Lincoln and nearby Fort Stanton were for him. When Frank Coe, visiting from Colorado, reminded Billy about the pursuing county lawmen and Fort Stanton regulars, he told Coe that he knew about the pursuers "but [that] he was tired of dodging and had run from them about enough."

Yet very shortly Billy did "run," although not far, to a safer place. Isolated and often beyond the easy reach of distant law, Fort Sumner was located about eighty miles northeast of Lincoln. Sumner seemed an ideal spot for Billy to lie low beyond the reach of Lincoln and Fort Stanton officials. Heavily Hispanic and ruled by the Maxwell family, with the oldest son, Pedro or Pete, in charge of the family holdings, Fort Sumner became an enjoyable place for Billy for much of the next two years. The old army fort, originally established to guard the Apache and Navajo Indians relocated at nearby Bosque Redondo Reservation, was now a small town that hosted weekly (or more frequent) bailes, with attractive, colorfully dressed señoritas and señoras in attendance. These gatherings greatly appealed to Billy. He loved to dance, he was attracted to the women, and they, to him. Decades later, Paulita Maxwell Jaramillo, Pete's young sister and one of Billy's *novias* (girlfriends or sweethearts), spoke of Fort Sumner as "a gay little place."

In fall 1879 Billy drifted back to his earlier hangouts. He gambled frequently at Beaver Smith's saloon in Fort Sumner, but more often he was rustling cattle and horses. Over the next few months he established and followed a pattern connecting eastern New Mexico and the western panhandle of Texas for his criminal deeds. Knowing about the sprawling cattle ranches in west Texas and how their unherded cattle often wandered toward the New Mexico border, particularly during winter storms, Billy and his riders repeatedly went after these straying animals.

Billy was accompanied by old partners and a few new ones. Folliard remained beside the Kid, and on a few occasions Doc Scurlock and Charley Bowdre showed up for his escapades. Three fresh faces also came on board: badman Dave Rudabaugh, a cattle rustler, a bank robber, and, most recently, the murderer of a Las Vegas policemen; Tom Pickett, a former Texas Ranger; and Billy Wilson, who had gradually moved west from Ohio and was a bit younger than the Kid. These veterans and newcomers brought a wide range of experience to Billy's criminal enterprises.

After riding off with the Texas cattle, Billy and his rustlers kept them in his holding "ranch," no more than a few acres in a declivity near Los Portales. Then most of the cattle were delivered to butchers. Nearby White Oaks was booming with a gold rush, so that area became a beckoning market for stolen beef sold to butchers, who in turn fed the hunger miners. Chief among these buyers-butchers was notorious Pat Coghlan of Tularosa, who catered to the gold miners and also had signed a recent contract to supply beef to Fort Stanton. Other outlets for the Kid's stolen cattle were the Dedrick brothers, who now ran the old Chisum ranch and operated a butcher shop and other businesses in White Oaks.

The other half of Billy's criminal pattern, although undertaken less often, included purloining livestock in eastern New Mexico and selling the animals—cattle and horses—in Texas. The two routines meant that Billy and his gang were rustling and selling in both New Mexico and Texas. By the end of 1879, he was an increasingly unpopular rustler in both places.

In a less-authenticated story, Billy also stole cattle from Jim and Pitzer Chisum, brothers of John. The Chisums lost a considerable number of livestock, but whether most of those stolen animals could be chalked up to the Kid and company is not entirely clear.

Another Billy Bonney–John Chisum story, if true, illustrates Billy's bravado. According to Will Chisum, John's nephew, the Kid was convinced that John Chisum was not fulfilling his promise to pay Billy for supporting the Tunstall-McSween contingent. Cornering the old rancher in Fort Sumner, Billy threatened to kill Chisum if he did not pay up. Unarmed as usual, Chisum tried to calm the Kid but also told him, "Billy, you know as well as I do I never hired you to fight in the Lincoln County War," and continued: "I always pay my honest debts. I don't owe you anything, and you can kill me but you won't knock me out of many years. I'm an old man." Hesitating, Billy responded, "Aw . . . you aren't worth killing," and turned away. But, according to more than one source, Billy stole enough Chisum stock to compensate himself for whatever sum he thought the cattleman owed him.

Some think that a violent incident involving Billy in Fort Sumner in early 1880 may have been linked to his ongoing conflict with Chisum. Whether connected to Chisum or not, the shooting casts further light on Billy's character. In January, when Billy and his followers, along with some Chisum cowboys, entered Bob Hargrove's saloon, one of the two popular hangouts in the small town, they encountered Texan Joe Grant, also dubbed "Texas Red." The rousing, half-drunk Grant pestered the Kid and boasted, "I bet $25 I kill a man today before you do." Wobbling over to one of Chisum's riders, Texas Red snatched the man's pistol out of its holster and began smashing bottles across the saloon. Then he turned the gun on Jim Chisum and threatened to shoot him. Wise to what was unfolding, Billy had asked to see the pistol, saw that three shells had been fired, and rolled the cylinder until the next two shots would misfire on empty chambers. When Grant moved toward Jim Chisum, Billy told him, "Hold on. . . . You got the wrong sow by the ear." "That's a lie," Texas Red bellowed, twisting to aim at Billy, who turned away. But when the Kid, with his back to Grant, heard the hammer click on a spent shell, he whirled around and fired three shots, tightly patterned, into the drunken bully's chin. Down went Grant, dead immediately.

Billy's reaction to the shooting revealed his attitudes. Looking down at Grant's body, he said, "Joe . . . I've been there too often for you." Later in Sunnyside, a small town near Fort Sumner, Milnor Rudulph, postmaster of the settlement, asked Billy about the shooting. The Kid replied: "Oh, nothing. . . . It was a game of two and I got there first."

Billy and his riders continued to ply their thievery trading in spring months of 1880. The movement between New Mexico and Texas persisted, but there were some manipulations of that plan. The Rustlers, as they were sometimes labeled, also stole horses from the Mescalero Apache Reservation and sold them up and down the Pecos valley. And thriving White Oaks and its miners provided an expanding market for rustled beef whether from east or west of the Pecos.

These and succeeding raids outraged ranchers on both sides of the New Mexico–Texas boundary. Billy's heists were keeping stockmen, soldiers, and town residents on edge. Someone or something needed to take strong measures to lock up the Kid and his partners. Emerging by fall 1880 were plans to bring more law and order to southeastern New Mexico and west Texas. These plans, once put into effect in late 1880 and led by Pat Garrett, began to put Billy on the run. One group of pursuers sprang to action in west Texas, the other in Lincoln County, with financial support coming from outside the Southwest. In Texas, cattlemen in the Llano Estacado, or Staked Plains, area gathered; this group of a few riders, scouting west to Fort Sumner, found evidence that cattle stolen in Texas had been driven to and butchered and sold in eastern New Mexico. Based on evidence of changed brands and other suspicions, the Texas stockmen moved to raise financial support and courageous riders to hunt Billy and his gang and to drive them out of Texas or perhaps to capture them there or in New Mexico.

The public sentiment rising against the Kid in Lincoln County was complex and involved other issues besides rustling. J. C. Lea, a stalwart leader in the new town of Roswell, Jimmy Dolan, and other merchants and ranchers in New Mexico had begun complaining to the U.S. Treasury Department about counterfeit bills being circulated in Lincoln County. Acting on these complaints, the Treasury Department sent Azariah F. Wild of the U.S. Secret Service to investigate. By October, Wild was sleuthing in White Oaks, where much of the actual counterfeiting seemed to be taking place.

In the next few weeks, Wild's numerous reports to Director James Brooks of the Secret Service and other federal officials traced some of Billy's activities. Although the agent's assertions were often incorrect, his correspondence to Washington, D.C., also revealed he was accurate in other conclusions. He found residents of Lincoln County often reluctant to talk because they were afraid of Billy and his confederates. After a few days of investigation and interviews, however, Wild concluded that the other Billy—Billie Wilson—was the major counterfeiting culprit, passing bogus hundred-dollar bills in the county, especially in White Oaks and Fort Sumner. Wild also discovered that the phony printing plates were probably stashed in White Oaks. Although Wild did not finger the Kid as a major counterfeiter, it is likely Billy supported Wilson and the other counterfeiters since the two of them were riding together throughout the fall and early winter of 1880.

Other revelations from Wild's reports included explicit comments about Bonney's other activities. First, there were the numerous errors the agent sent on to Washington: he referred to Billy as "William Antrom," who came from Kansas to Lincoln County; he told his superiors that Billy had killed men on the nearby Indian reservation. Both claims were wrong. Second, other information was new to most readers—and still is. Wild claimed that he had seen a letter from Lew Wallace to Ira Leonard, now serving as the Kid's lawyer, indicating that the governor was willing to free Billy from pending charges, but Leonard told Wild that Wallace had "failed to put it [the pardon] in shape that satisfied . . . Leonard." Wild also informed U.S. officials that "we can use Antrom [sic] in these cases [counterfeiting prosecutions] provided Gov. Wallace will make good on his written promises." These were possibilities full of hope for Billy, but never came to fruition.

Other Wild observations, if true, provide glimpses into Billy's feelings in fall 1880. The agent told his director that he had seen still another Kid letter to Leonard "in which he [Billy] expressed himself as being tired of dodging the officers." Wild also pointed to an unusual crime committed by the Kid and his associates. Billie Wilson and the "Kid gang" had twice robbed the U. S. mails in Fort Sumner, and letters in the stolen mail, if the thefts actually occurred, would likely have exposed to the Kid Wild's investigations in Lincoln County.

Aggravated by the inefficient law enforcement in Lincoln County, Wild organized local officials to capture Billy and his cohorts—or at least to chase them out of the area. Without explicit instructions to do so, he helped organized a posse to go after the counterfeiters, thieves, and mail robbers. But the Kid's gang paid little attention to or exhibited no fear of the new posse. In late October, the gang stole nearly seventy cattle from one ranch, almost four hundred from another, and seven horses from John Chisum.

These persistent and costly depredations finally pushed Lincoln County residents, especially John Chisum and J. C. Lea, to adopt a more decisive action. Entirely dissatisfied with the service of Lincoln County sheriff Kimbrell, who winked at Billy's thievery and even played cards with him, they turned to Pat Garrett as a new kind of sheriff who would bring stability and safety to the area. A Texan and former buffalo hunter, Garrett arrived in Fort Sumner in fall 1878, where he did ranch work and served as a bartender at Beaver Smith's saloon. He brought no experience to the sheriff's office. But at more than six feet, six, he towered over other men. Hispanics called him Juan Largo, or Long John, and Garrett had earned the reputation as a quiet, no-nonsense physical specimen whom no one tried to buffalo. He and the Kid were acquainted and had played cards together, but they were not close friends, as some writers and filmmakers have wrongly asserted.

Chisum and Lea talked the thirty-year-old Garrett into running for sheriff of Lincoln County in fall 1880. He

Pat Garrett, 1850–1908. Elected sheriff of Lincoln County in November 1880, Garrett immediately went after, captured, and jailed Billy the Kid. When Billy shot two of his deputies and escaped jail the following April, Garrett pursued and killed him in July 1881. Garrett was a diligent, courageous, and effective lawman. Photograph courtesy Lincoln Heritage Trust.

moved to Roswell with his Hispanic wife and stood for election against Kimbrell. The Kid, of course, favored his "pal" Kimbrell and, as he told one acquaintance, doubted Garrett could win. Billy's political prognostications were dead wrong. Garrett defeated Kimbrell 320 votes to 179. Kimbrell acknowledged and accepted the results, and never enamored with the tricky role of county sheriff, he named Garrett a deputy sheriff and essentially turned over the reins of sheriffing to him.

While these events unfolded, the Kid busied himself and a small band in stealing horses and selling them in the northern areas of the Pecos valley. In late November, hearing that Billy and his gang of thieves were at the Greathouse Ranch a few miles north of White Oaks, Sheriff Will Hudgens and his posse of thirteen men rode north through the bitter weather and surrounded the Greathouse home. "Whiskey Jim" Greathouse, a rancher, thief, and friend of Billy, was reluctant to obey the posse, which called for the Kid's surrender. Billy refused. What happened next comes in several versions. Evidently, in something of a two-way negotiation, Greathouse walked out to the posse to serve as its hostage while Jim Carlyle, a member of the posse, went into the house to parley with Billy. After a standoff and a warning from the posse that Greathouse must be released soon, a shot was heard outside the house. Thinking the posse had killed Greathouse, as it had threatened to do, Carlyle burst through the house's front window to get away. He was shot several times and fell dead on the snowy ground. Was he shot by those inside the house? The posse argued that line—it asserted that Billy stepped out the window and shot down Carlyle.

Dave Rudabaugh, one of Billy's gang, said that he, Billy, and Billy Watson had shot Carlyle and that others in the house maybe shot him too. But historians and biographers have argued that Carlyle was killed by the friendly fire from fellow possemen.

Billy's version of the firefight appeared in the *Las Vegas Daily Optic* the next February. As Billy put it, when the shot outside was fired and Carlyle thought "Greathouse was Killed [he] Jumped through the window, breaking the Sash as he went and was killed by his own Party they thinking it was me trying to make my Escape." Billy's version was undoubtedly self-serving, but posse members later admitted they too had fired at the fleeing Carlyle. Perhaps several had hit the unfortunate Carlyle.

After the chaotic gun fight, Billy and his horsemen rode away in the cold. Where they would go and what they would do were unclear. The Kid seemed bent only on staying out of the clutches of the law, which he had successfully done thus far. But he did not know that the changes then underway in Lincoln County would dramatically change his life in the next month.

11

Days of Decline and Death

Pat Garrett was a man of his word, as his actions in December 1880 soon proved. About six weeks after he was elected sheriff of Lincoln County on 2 November but before he officially became sheriff on 1 January 1881, he worked out a plan to hunt Billy.

Garrett acted as both sheriff of Lincoln County and a deputy U.S. marshal in the next few weeks. This dual position allowed Garrett to pursue Billy in and beyond Lincoln County. In the early days of December, about two weeks after the shootout at the Greathouse ranch, three groups of Kid hunters met in Las Vegas to plot their chase of the much-talked-about young outlaw. One outfit under the leadership of cowboy Charlie Siringo had ridden over from the LX Ranch in the Texas panhandle. Serving with him were riders such as Big-Foot Wallace (Frank Clifford), Jim East, and Lee Hall, among others. A second group rode in under Frank Stewart, another Texan and a deputy U.S. marshal for Azariah F. Wild of the Secret Service. Stewart, representing the Canadian River cattlemen of Texas, traveled with a party of ten men. Hearing about the two other groups of Kid pursuers besides his own, Garrett called them to Las Vegas.

The three posses decided to ride under the leadership of Garrett, with Frank Stewart assisting him. Moving quickly south to White Oaks, the combined posse, after contacts with Siringo, slimmed down to Garrett, Stewart, Hall, East, and three or four others. Garrett warned his new posse that the men faced a cunning, valiant, and dangerous gang in Billy and his lieutenants. They should expect deadly gunfights if they caught up with the Kid's gunmen.

Moving south to Puerto de Luna, Garrett's riders heard stories that Billy, Folliard, Bowdre, Rudabaugh, Billie Wilson, and newcomer Tom Pickett had returned to Fort Sumner. Garrett's troop moved on to Fort Sumner.

The sheriff quickly set a trap for Billy's gang. He forced a Hispanic boy to take a false note to the Kid's gang indicating that Garrett and his men had left Fort Sumner and that Billy was safe to return. Billy's riders bought the ruse and that night rode toward Fort Sumner for a night of partying.

On the night of 19 December, Garrett was ready for Billy. Thinking the Kid would ride by the former post hospital, where Bowdre's wife Manuela lived, Garrett scattered his men in the shadows around the rambling building. On the cold, snowy evening Billy's riders sauntered toward town. The Kid was perhaps wary of something unusual about to happen. Riding at the front of his group, he dropped back to pull a chaw of tobacco. Whether a deliberate or a chance decision, Billy's dropping to the rear probably saved his life.

As the riders neared the hospital building, Garrett shouted "Halt." Folliard reached for his pistol, but Garrett beat him to the draw, firing a deadly shot into Tom's chest. Only the blinding flash of another rifle kept Garrett from also killing Wilson. Billy and the others spun their horses around and galloped out of town. Within an hour or two, Folliard was dead. Less than ten days after Garrett launched his pursuit of Billy and his gang, he killed the Kid's closest companion. Folliard's death was a grim warning to the outlaws they would receive no respite from Sheriff Pat Garrett.

Within days Garrett was again in hot pursuit of the Kid. Even though Billy knew Garrett was close at hand and still coming, the Kid did not leave his home country. Perhaps the numbing weather and the lack of a warm place to go kept the rustlers nearby in their familiar haunts. Within a week, remaining near at hand proved to be wrong-headed. In this case, as before, Billy had difficulty deciding on a newer, safer future. He chose instead to keep to the familiar, thus the dangerous.

Billy's men returned to the Wilcox Ranch, where they had begun their ride into Fort Summer on the previous day and evening. What to do? Billy decided to turn the tide on Garrett by sending Manuel Brazil, a friend of Billie Wilson, into Fort Sumner as a spy to watch the lawmen and report back on their doings. Brazil, however, sided with the lawmen rather than with Billy and, once in Fort Sumner, informed Garrett of his mission. The sheriff instructed Brazil to return and stay at the Wilcox Ranch, then report back when Billy's cohort made a move. On the bitterly cold evening of 20 December Brazil rode back to Fort Sumner and told Garrett that the Kid and his riders, after ransacking the ranch, had gone on, although their destination was unclear to Brazil.

Despite the inclement weather Garrett and his posse rode quickly to the Wilcox Ranch, easily spotted the outlaws' tracks in the snow, and followed them. Knowing the territory and seeing the direction of the footprints of Billy's riders, Garrett concluded the rustlers were headed for a rock-built building, the only edifice of that sort in the area, known as Stinking Spring.

Garrett's surmise proved entirely correct. Billy's band once again underestimated Garrett's tenacity. He clearly understood the Kid and would do whatever was necessary to bring Billy down, capturing him or, if need be, shooting him. It seems that Billy's gang thought Garrett would not know where they had gone or would postpone his pursuit until the bitter cold ended. Neither was the case. When Garrett's posse approached the abandoned rock house, which had served as a way station for cattle and sheep men, they saw some of the rustlers' horses tethered outside and assumed rightly that others were inside. Arriving in the dark, they decided, after considerable discussion, not to attack but to wait until morning, spreading their blankets in the snow as they waited.

Garrett's plan again produced results. The sheriff, the only man among the pursuers who knew and recognized Billy, had told his men they might have to shoot the Kid because he would probably fight to the death. As a signal, when Billy emerged from the building, Garrett would raise his rifle, indicating they should shoot down the Kid. When a figure looking like the Kid in his familiar sombrero came out, Garrett raised his rife and a fusillade of bullets tore into the man.

But he was not Billy. Charlie Bowdre, Billy's boon companion, had emerged to feed the horses and now absorbed the posse's deadly slugs. Screaming in agony, Bowdre staggered back into the building. Billie Wilson called out to Garrett's men that Charlie wanted to surrender. Hearing agreement, Charlie tried to walk out of the rock house. Before he did, however, Billy pushed a pistol into his friend's hand and told him: "They've murdered you Charlie, but you can get revenge. Kill some of the sonsofbitches before you die." Charlie tottered out and toward the posse, uttering his dying words, "I wish—I wish—I wish." Bowdre received death at the hands of Garrett, whom he had met with just days before, expressing his wish to leave rustling and go straight.

When an occupant of the rock house attempted to pull one of the tethered horses inside, Garrett wisely shot down the animal, effectively blocking an escape route through the only doorway. He next expertly shot through the reins of the other tethered horses, and they scampered away. All day the captives and posse bantered back and forth. Garrett called out, "How're you doing?" and Billy responded, "Pretty well . . . but we have no wood to get breakfast." Garrett answered, "Come on out and get some. . . . Be a little sociable." Later in the day, without food or the promise of any forthcoming the outlaws finally, after considerable disagreement (Billy did not want to surrender), sent out Rudabaugh with a white flag. Garrett told Billy and his men to lay down their guns, and he promised to protect their lives. A few minutes later the rest of the outlaws, including Billy, crawled out over the dead horse in the doorway.

The events at Stinking Spring changed the direction of Billy's final months. From December 1880 to July 1881, he was either in jail or trying to avoid being recaptured. In Pat Garrett, Billy had met another kind of opponent, one who was more courageous and forceful than any person who had pursued him previously.

A second series of events, occurring concurrently, launched Billy from a follower and two-bit outlaw into something much greater, more powerful, more significant. The Kid would become a legend in his own time during the last months of his life. And the legendary Billy the Kid emerging in these months would remain vibrant and relevant for nearly the next century and a half to the present day.

The legend-making began in and around the eastern New Mexico so familiar to Billy in early December 1880. The first segments of the legend were quite modest but nonetheless attention-getting. Like many others, journalist J. H. Koogler, having just returned from a trip down the Pecos valley, was appalled by the rampant rustling and violence continually disrupting eastern New Mexico. On 3 December 1880, in a fiery, assertive article in his newspaper, the *Las Vegas Gazette*, Koogler ripped off multiple verbal shots at the problems in the region and was sharply critical of those he thought were the trouble-makers. Filling two-columns, his detailed story called on residents of San Miguel County, where Las Vegas was located, to "immediately discharge" their duties "to arrest a powerful gang of outlaws harassing" stockmen and "terrorizing" people up and down the Pecos and over in the Texas panhandle. "The gang . . . [were] all bad characters . . . fugitives from justice, and desperados by profession," Koogler declared.

In one of the first full references anywhere to "Billy the Kid," Koogler signaled that the young man was no longer Henry McCarty, Kid Antrim, Billy Bonney, or alias Billy, the Kid. He was now and would ever be Billy the Kid. Koogler stated that Billy, the leader of an outlaw gang of forty or fifty cutthroats, was "a desperate cuss . . . eligible for the post of captain of any crowd, no matter how mean and lawless." Here was the devilish Billy who would ride through the pages of dozens of newspapers, potboiler biographies, and dime novels until the mid-1920s. He and his gang had to be captured, for they were plundering the Pecos country, stealing stock from White Oaks to the Texas panhandle, and upending the lives of residents in those areas. Koogler ended his extensive article summoning "resolute men" to go after Billy and his riders, "this horde of outcasts and the scum of society."

The content and tone of Koogler's bombastic, accusatory piece rapidly spread across New Mexico. The sensational description of Billy the Kid even traveled to the East Coast. On 22 December the New York *Sun* published a long piece on Billy in the Pecos country entitled "Outlaws of New Mexico: The Exploits of a Band Headed by a New York Youth." The story in the *Sun* was less reliable on facts than the *Gazette* piece, although it followed the account in the Las Vegas newspaper. The *Sun* article might not have been a "dime-novel fabrication," as one writer claimed, but it played up the size and dramatic activities of the outlaws. "William Bonney, alias the Kid," the New York journalist wrote, "the leader of the band, is scarcely over 20 years of age. He is handsome and dresses well . . . He is about six feet tall and deceptively handsome."

The journalist closed his story by warning, "It is not expected that the Kid or [Dave] Rudabaugh will be taken alive, as they will fight to the last." The New Mexico, and

165

now the New York, newspapers indicated that Billy was no more just the Kid, but Billy the Kid, well on his way to becoming the most-talked-about western outlaw in the United States.

Not surprisingly, Billy read and reacted to Koogler's story. Instead of replying to the Las Vegas newspaperman, however, he wrote to Governor Lew Wallace, perhaps hoping to renew his plea for clemency. Billy's letter, the first of several to the governor in the next four months, was a string of explanations, defenses, and dodges. In his letter dated 12 December, Billy told the governor he was not the captain of a hard-bitten group of rustlers and cutthroats in eastern New Mexico. "There is no such Organization in Existence," he explained. Besides laying out his views of the Carlyle incident ("killed by his own Party"), Billy declared that he was not an outlaw but made his "living Gambling." True, "a great deal of Stealing [was] going on in the Territory," but as for his "being at the head of a Band there is nothing of it." In fact, on some occasions he had "recovered Stolen Property when there was no chance to get an Officer to do it." In a parting shot, Billy asserted that "if Some Impartial Party were to investigate this matter they would find it far Different from the impression put out by Chisum and his Tools."

Wallace forwarded Billy's letter to Koogler, who published it in the *Gazette* on 22 December. Even before the letter appeared, Wallace wrote out, one week earlier, his offer of a $500 reward for the capture of Billy the Kid. Billy's legend was building even as his chance for freedom from charges was disappearing.

Once Garrett had Billy and his three riders in custody, he rode toward Las Vegas. With no dependable jails for the gang in Lincoln, Fort Sumner, or White Oaks, Garrett headed for the jails that could hold the outlaws. On the morning of 24 December, the posse and their four captives rode west to Fort Sumner, arriving shortly before noon, and soon faced two emotional meetings. When they met Manuela Bowdre to deliver her husband's body, she lost control and "kicked and pummeled Garrett until she had to be pulled away." Manuela "was crazy with grief," one eyewitness reported. It was a difficult scene for the sheriff, who tried to assuage some of the outburst by promising the new widow a new suit of clothes for Charlie's burial.

The other emotional scene played out much differently. While Garrett, his riders, and Billy and his trio were at a blacksmith shop having handcuffs placed on the outlaws, Deluvina Maxwell, the Native American servant of the Maxwell family and a devoted fan of Billy, appeared to ask whether doña Luz Maxwell and her daughter Paulita, probably Billy's closest novia, could see him for a warm goodbye. With some reluctance, Garrett agreed, but the sheriff nixed allowing Billy's handcuffs to be removed so he and Paulita could enjoy whispering their goodbyes in an adjoining room. Disappointed, Billy and Paulita embraced in front of the men. According to the truthful James East, one of Garrett's riders, Paulita, "gave 'Billy' one of those soul kisses the novelists tell us about . . . We had to pull them apart. . . ."

It was Christmas Eve. That night the travelers stayed at Los Ojitos on their way north. On Christmas day they arrived at the store of Alexander Grzelachowski, known as "Padre Poloco," in Puerto de Luna, forty miles up the Pecos from Fort Sumner. They enjoyed a "splendid dinner" and, by the next evening, were riding into Las Vegas.

News of the capture and the coming of Billy and his men to Las Vegas proceeded their arrival. The town was agog with anticipation. A special issue of the Las Vegas *Gazette* had been printed, and streets crowded with spectators waiting to see the now-famous Billy the Kid. When the Garrett wagon rumbled into town, the crowd's "astonishment gave way to joy."

The attention paid to Billy in the next few days in Las Vegas and Santa Fe revealed how much he was coming on scene as

Paulita Maxwell, 1864–1929. Historians and biographers differ widely on whether Paulita Maxwell, the younger sister of family leader Pete Maxwell, became Billy the Kid's favorite sweetheart. The strongest evidence suggests a possible romance between them, a relationship that drew Billy back to Fort Sumner and Paulita after his jail break. His unwise decision led to his death a few months later. Photograph courtesy of the History Colorado.

Sallie Chisum, 1858–1934. Niece of cowman John Chisum, the vivacious Sallie caught Billy the Kid's eye. They met on a few occasions, exchanged gifts, and were attracted to one another. No intense romance occurred, however. Photograph in the Robert N. Mullin Collection courtesy of the Haley Memorial Library & History Center, Midland, Texas.

a larger-than-life figure. More column inches of newspaper coverage appeared on Billy and his recent escapades than in all the months since his first appearance in a Silver City *Grant County Herald* in 1875. Equally revealing was how little factual information seemed available on the Kid.

More than one of the late December stories depicted Billy as a rascal who needed to be captured. The same articles praised Pat Garrett for his diligent, courageous work to bring in the Kid. On 27 December editor Koogler or one of his staff filed a particularly lengthy story about Billy for the *Las Vegas Gazette*. After reviewing the events since the Greathouse shootout in late November and up to the Stinking Spring capture, the journalist stated his views about Billy. The Kid was a "notorious outlaw" with a gang of three followers. Drawing on information gathered from M. S. Brazil

169

(Brasil) rather than from Garrett, the writer stated that Billy "had repeatedly given out that he would never surrender," even if a gun were put to his head. Billy had also branded his riders "as cowards"—a charge Billy later vociferously denied—when they called on him to surrender. Billy might facetiously say, "Life is sweet if it is behind prison bars," but the journalist thought Billy would soon "have enough of it" and turn sour on that fenced-in life. The story ended with explicit praise for Garrett and his "brave fellows" for "the successful issue of their round-up."

That same day, the *Las Vegas Daily Optic* printed a story similar in format and content entitled "A Big Haul" and subtitled "A Notorious Gang of Outlaws Broken Up, and the County Breathes Easier." This piece depicted Billy as the leader of a "gang of daring desperadoes" who "roamed over the county at will, placing no value upon human life, and appropriating the property of ranchmen and travelers without stint." After discussing events of the past month, the *Daily Optic* writer penned a capsule paragraph about Billy. The "Kid is about 24 years of age," the profile began. The young man fends off much of what is said about him: he was not the leader of a large band of rustlers, and he chuckled at the description of him as having "a reputation second only to that of Victorio," the Apache leader. The writer also touted Billy as a boastful opponent who would never be taken alive. Now, the outlaws were on their way to Santa Fe and its jail.

Before Billy completed his one-day visit to the jail and train station in Las Vegas, a *Gazette* reporter interviewed the Kid, labeling him "Billy Bonney, The Best Known Man in New Mexico." The interview included the most extensive comments to date from Billy himself. In his own words while locked in his cell and later guarded at the train station, the Kid defended himself and tried to correct earlier statements published about him. First of all, he was not the leader of a gang; instead, he "was for Billy all the time." Although he never identified the men who led him astray or harassed him, he asserted, "They wouldn't let me settle down . . . [or] wouldn't let me live in the country." He made his living by gambling because his enemies only allowed him that occupation. He had not "stolen stock." Billy admitted to no crimes.

Intriguingly, the two news stories and the interview, although primarily critical of Billy—or negative in their descriptions—also featured a few positive comments. The preponderance of negative comments but the simultaneous advance of a few positive statements about Billy illustrated the spread of diverse opinions about him in his final months and up to the 1920s.

The favorable notices dealt with the Kid's personality and cheerfulness. The interviewer, for example, opened his conversation with the statement, "You appear to take it easy," to which the Kid rejoined, "Yes! What's the use of looking on the gloomy side of everything. The laugh's on me this time." Yet he could be gloomy. At the train station, he told the journalist: "I don't blame you for writing of me as you have. You had to believe others stories; but then I don't know as any one would believe anything good of me anyway." Although Billy was not manly in appearance, the questioner thought, he nonetheless had "a schoolboy look" and "a frank open countenance." In fact, he was "quite a handsome looking fellow" and had "agreeable and winning ways." Here were the first divergent ingredients of the legendary Billy the Kid beginning to emerge.

Billy arrived in Santa Fe on 27 December and remained in the jail there until 29 March. He found the jail in the territorial as despicable as that in Las Vegas. The treatment of inmates was equally bad. On Billy's first day in his dark, cold cell the jailers ate up all the food meant for the new prisoners and gleefully kept secret their selfish actions.

Situated on Water Street, the jail was but a few blocks from the Palace of the Governors, where Governor Lew Wallace was ensconced.

In the next few weeks stretching to more than three months, Billy tried to renew contact with Governor Wallace. The governor had not responded to the Kid's letter of 12 December. Nor would he answer the Kid's later letters, despite the young outlaw's attempts to establish communication. On New Year's Day, Billy wrote a brief note to Wallace:

> Gov. Lew Wallace Dear Sir
> I would like to See You for a few minutes if You can Spare time.
>
> > Your Respect
> > W. H. Bonney

No response came from the territory's chief executive. After Billy penned the note, he heard that the governor was absent from his office on a leave of absence to go east. Billy was probably not aware of Wallace's increasing interest in furthering the sales of his romantic historical novel, *Ben Hur: A Tale of Christ,* published in 1880 and garnering respectable sales and literary headlines. The governor was becoming less interested in New Mexico, especially headaches such as Billy the Kid, and more involved in promoting his novel and gaining a more-promising appointment in the federal government.

Two months went by before Billy tried again. On 2 March, he wrote a two-sentence message that attempted, more forcefully, to capture the governor's attention and perhaps to spark action.

> Dear Sir
> I wish you would come down to the jail and see me. it will be to your interest to come and see me. I have Some letters, which date back two years. and there are Parties who are very anxious to get

them. but I shall not dispose of them until I see You. that is if you will come immediately.

Your Respect

W. H. Bonney

Was Billy trying to blackmail the governor with the letters they exchanged before the clandestine meeting in Lincoln in March 1879? Perhaps. Whatever Billy intended did not work; again Wallace did not respond. Beginning to worry that the governor was going to avoid contact altogether, the Kid tried another approach. Two days later in a much longer letter that tried to pull Wallace into a conversation, Billy pointed out his mistreatment and asked for the governor's sympathies and support. "I wrote you a little note the day before yesterday, but have received no answer," Billy began. Recalling Wallace's promise of a pardon if he provided damning evidence on Huston Chapman's murder, he wondered whether Wallace had "forgotten what you promised me." The Kid had done "Everything that I promised you I would, and You have done nothing that You promised me." Wallace hardly would have been drawn into a conversation with Billy's next statement: "I think when You think the matter over, You will come down and See me, and I can then Explain Everything to you."

Other things were also not working out for Billy. The lawyer Ira Leonard had promised to revisit Billy when he returned from a trip to the East, but he had not done so. Moreover, Billy wrote, U.S. Marshal John Sherman was letting in "Every Stranger . . . to See Me through Curiosity . . . but will not let a Single one of my friends in, not Even an Attorney." Billy was turning pessimistic, thinking he was "getting left in the Cold." And he ended on a low note: "I guess they mean to Send me up without giving me any Show. but they will have a nice time doing it I am not entirely without friends." He still "Expect[ed] to See you [Wallace] Sometime today." Here was vintage Billy:

reminders, complaints, and gloom but, in the end, warning and bravado.

Nothing happened, the governor did not come. Knowing he was headed down the Rio Grande the next day for his trial in Mesilla, Billy wrote his fourth and final letter to Wallace on 27 March. It was brief, direct—and commanding:

> Gov. Lew Wallace Dear Sir
> for the *last time* I ask. Will You keep Your promise. I start below tomorrow Send Annser [*sic*] by bearer
>
> > Yours Respt
> > WBonney

Billy's attempts to bring the governor back to his case had failed. Although Wallace kept the letters, he never responded to the Kid. A few weeks later, after Billy had been sentenced to hang, Wallace was asked about the Kid and a pardon and responded, "I can't see how a fellow like him should expect any clemency from me." The journalist went on to provide a probing evaluation of Wallace's position on Billy: "Although not committing himself, the general tenor of the governor's remarks indicated that he would resolutely refuse to grant 'the Kid' a pardon. It would seem as though 'the Kid' had undertaken to bulldoze the governor, which has not helped his chances in the slightest." This assessment was accurate: Billy had tried to pressure Wallace, and the tactic had failed. Still, what the journalist did not comment on should have been drawn to the attention of Las Vegas *Gazette* readers. Billy had kept his promise in the "deal" that he and the governor had made two years earlier in Lincoln, but Wallace had reneged.

Even though Billy groused about being treated as an amusement for curiosity-seekers, neither contemporary newspapers or later accounts confirmed the reasons for his complaints. In fact, once Billy was in his cell in Santa Fe, he seemed to receive little attention from anyone. True, Leonard, his lawyer, did come by to talk and promised a follow-up visit. When Leonard did not return, Billy tried to work with Rudabaugh's lawyer, Edward Caypless, but he wanted a retainer, and the Kid had no money. Their relationship went nowhere.

Newspapers were silent about Billy from the middle of January to late February, perhaps because he was busy. Sometime in February (possibly mid-month), Billy and his cellmates began to dig their way out to the street. They used their bed ticking to conceal the dirt and rocks they dug out of the tunnel, but an "informer," paid by the jailer to watch the inmates, squealed on them. On the last day of February, the sheriff barged into the cell, uncovered the tunneling evidence, and placed Billy in solitary confinement. The Kid was shackled and kept distant from other prisoners. His dream of escape was on hold.

On 28 March, one day after Billy wrote his last letter to Governor Wallace, he and Billy Wilson, three deputy marshals, and Ira Leonard boarded the train for their trip down the Rio Grande valley for Billy's murder trial in Mesilla. That night the train arrived in Rincon, where an unruly crowd had assembled and threatened the group, but when the onlookers were threatened with gunplay by the marshals, they dispersed. After arriving at the train route's most southern stop, Billy and his fellow travelers rode in an uncomfortable stagecoach to Mesilla, where the Kid would be tried. During the trip, Billy proved he had not lost his usual sense of humor, despite the gloomy prospect. In Las Cruces an inquisitive onlooker asked which one of the travelers was Billy the Kid. Slapping Ira Leonard on the back, he said, undoubtedly with a chuckle, "This is the man."

Some thought Billy had little chance of escaping the serious charges against him. The events in Mesilla more than proved them right. The trial judge was Warren Bristol, a Murphy-Dolan partisan with strong ties to the Santa Fe Ring. He had already demonstrated his intense dislike for the Kid. Now that distaste became even more apparent.

On the morning of 30 March, Billy was arraigned in federal court on the charge of murdering Buckshot Roberts on the Mescalero Reservation. Others such as Doc Scurlock, Charlie Bowdre, Fred Waite, and George Coe were also charged, but they were either dead or not present for trial. Billy had no money for a lawyer, so Bristol named Leonard his defense attorney. Billy pleaded not guilty, and Leonard argued, satisfactorily enough to win Bristol's support, that Blazer's Mill did not sit on the Mescalero Reservation and thus was not federal territory, so Billy could not be tried for murder in the U.S. court. Bristol agreed and quashed the charge. Bristol was undoubtedly amendable to throwing out the federal charge because he was convinced the territorial indictments, which he would also hear as a territorial justice, were so strong that Billy would obviously hang.

A few days later on 8 April, Billy was back in court to face charges for the murder of Sheriff Brady. Again, others besides the Kid were involved in the murder, but only he was brought before the judge. Bristol then dismissed Leonard as Billy's defense attorney; his reasons for doing so were not clear. Instead John D. Bail and Albert J. Fountain, good and able lawyers but not particularly Kid fans, were named as Billy's new defenders. A jury, all Hispanics who did not know Billy, was selected, and three Lincoln County residents, J. B. Mathews, Bonnie Baca, and Isaac Ellis, testified for the prosecution. Why Baca and Ellis, said to be friends of the Kid, testified is not known. Mathews, of course, another Dolan and Brady supporter, witnessed the killing and later shot at Billy when he rushed out to the middle of the street after the shooting.

What Bail and Fountain did to defend Billy remains unknown. Did they call anyone to testify in the Kid's behalf, and did they have Billy testify? No one can answer these and many other questions because the trial records mysteriously disappeared at some point and have never been found. But Bristol's instructions to the jury have survived, and he defined the charges and possible penalties against Billy in a way that made it very difficult for the jury to vote against hanging. The jury quickly returned a verdict of guilty in the first-degree.

On 13 April Billy was back in court for sentencing. Asked for a statement, Billy said he had nothing to say. Bristol then sentenced Billy to be executed one month later, 13 May, in Lincoln. The judge ordered that sometime between 9 A.M. and 3 P.M. "the said William Bonney, alias Kid, alias William Antrim, [shall] be hanged by the neck until his body be dead." As sheriff of Lincoln County, Pat Garrett would be in charge of the public hanging.

Twenty-five years later Arthur Chapman, journalist and poet, demonstrated how legends worked their way into the story of Billy the Kid. According to Chapman. when Bristol sentenced Billy, the judge almost taunted the Kid with the words that he was to be "hanged by the neck until you are dead, dead, dead!" Chapman also imagined, without any evidence at hand, that Billy retorted, "And you can go to hell, hell, hell!" Afterwards, too many unsuspecting writers, merely followed Chapman's made-up words without checking the sources. Nothing in the historical record supports what Chapman wrote.

Billy had not planned to say anything, but a reporter from the *Mesilla News* caught up with him and published his responses on 15 April. Billy told the reporter that he thought Simeon H. Newman, another Mesilla journalist, had given him a "rough deal." On 8 April Newman had labeled the Kid "a notoriously dangerous character . . . and has made his brags that he only wants to get free in order to kill three men—one of them being Governor Wallace." These unflattering comments, Billy added, "created prejudice against me" and tried "to incite a mob to lynch me."

The reporter then asked Billy whether he expected a pardon. "Considering the active part Governor Wallace took on our side and the friendly relations that existed between him and me, and the promise he made me," Billy responded, "I think he ought to pardon me." Billy had kept his promise to help the governor, but Wallace had reneged on his. "Think it hard I should be the only one to suffer the extreme penalty of the law," the Kid continued.

The wheels of justice, or injustice, thought Billy, moved on. Late in the evening of 16 April without fanfare to avoid any public uproar, Billy and his law enforcement watchdogs set out for Lincoln.

The Kid was under very close watch, with seven deputies, including Bob Olinger and former cattle rustler John Kinney, on the scene. Once back in Lincoln, Billy was handcuffed, his legs were shackled, and he was chained to the second-story floor in the northeast corner of The House, the old Murphy-Dolan store, which had been sold for a jail to the town of Lincoln. The Kid was separated from the other five prisoners, and Deputies Olinger and James W. Bell shared the twenty-four-hour watch over the Kid. Genial, kind, and well-liked, Bell tried to connect with Billy, even under these challenging circumstances. On the other hand, Olinger was an unremitting bully, harassing Billy, taunting him, and threatening to kill the Kid as soon as the opportunity arose. Olinger wanted to shoot down the Kid and, fingering one of his guns one day, dared Billy to try an escape. The deputy also told the Kid that he looked forward to watching Billy hang from the gallows on the Lincoln's main street. Knowing of Billy's previous escapes in Silver City, Camp Grant, Fort Stanton, and Lincoln itself, Sheriff Garrett warned his two deputies to be constantly vigilant; he knew the Kid, resourceful and cunning, would try to bust out.

The attempt came on the evening of 28 April, after Billy had been jailed in Lincoln for about a week. He had been watching the deputies to see when one was gone and he was left to the other. Plus, on that day Garrett had ridden to White Oaks to collect taxes, part of his duty as county sheriff. He may also have gone there to purchase the nec-

The Murphy-Dolan store and Lincoln County Courthouse. Built to house the store and serve as the home of L. G. Murphy, this building was sold to Lincoln County for a courthouse. Billy the Kid was jailed here briefly in April 1881. Photograph courtesy of the New Mexico State University Library Archives, Las Cruces, image 02230152.

essary materials to construct a gallows for Billy's hanging. When Olinger took the other prisoners across the road for a meal at Wortley's eatery, the Kid was left alone with Bell.

What happened next comes in multiple, conflicting versions, which is true of several major events in Billy's life. One account says that as Billy and Bell were playing a card game, Billy pushed a card off the table, as if by mistake. When Bell bent over to pick up the card, Billy lunged across the table to grab Bell's pistol at his belt. Securing the gun, Billy warned the deputy not to move. Another story indicates that Billy asked to visit the privy out back, and when they returned, Bell carelessly allowed Billy to get ahead of him on the steps and around the corner, out of sight. When Bell turned the corner, Billy, having wriggled out of one of his handcuffs, viciously hit Bell over the head with one handcuff, and when Bell was dazed, Billy grabbed his

179

side arm. Billy warned Bell not to move. Still another and the most persuasive version reveals that when Billy went to the outhouse, he secured a pistol hidden there by a friend. When Billy gained the top of the stairs as they returned toward his "cell," he turned, pointed the pistol at Bell, and warned him not to move.

All three versions suggest that Bell did not heed Billy's warning but fled down the stairs to escape out the back door. Whether Billy's pistol shots hit Bell in the back or ricocheted off the wall to lodge in his back, Bell was mortally wounded. He staggered out the back door, falling dead into the arms of Gottfried Gauss, an employee of the county and an old friend of Billy.

Hearing the shots, Olinger rushed out of Wortley's and dashed toward the jail. As he did, he heard Gauss yell out, "Bob, the Kid has killed Bell." Meanwhile, after shooting Bell, Billy quickly turned toward the armory with its stock of weapons, grabbed Olinger's loaded shotgun, and limped to the northeast corner window facing out toward the street. When Olinger heard Gauss's warning, he looked up to see Billy leaning out the window and covering him with his own shotgun. "Hello, old boy," Billy said, and blasted Olinger with both barrels. The thirty-six buckshot turned Olinger's upper torso and head into a bloody mess. His death was immediate.

What happened next demonstrated the cool calculation of Billy the Kid. After murdering Bell and Olinger, Billy told Gauss to throw up a pickax, which he used to break open one of his leg shackles, and then he strode onto the balcony overlooking the road and a gathering of wary townspeople. He told the listeners he had not wanted to kill Bell, or anyone else for that matter, but if they or anyone else tried to stop his getaway, he would shoot to kill. Gathering weapons, the Kid ordered Gauss to bring him a horse. As Billy left the jail, he smashed Olinger's shotgun and threw the pieces at the dead deputy's body, yelling out: "There is your gun, God damn you. . . . You won't follow me with it any longer." When Billy tried to climb on the secured horse, the animal spooked and pitched him off. Remounting, Billy rode out of town. Nearly mesmerized, the onlookers did nothing to stop Billy. Two men thought of pulling their guns to shoot at Billy but were persuaded not to try. The others were undoubtedly fearful of getting into a gunfight with the notorious young gunslinger, who had just murdered two of Garrett's deputies.

Writer Bob Boze Bell correctly identifies this extraordinary episode as pivotal point in the Kid's life. "Billy the Kid's defining moment," Bell states, "was when, against all odds, he escaped from the Lincoln County jail . . . That was the event that really catapulted him into history and legend."

In commenting on Billy's dramatic escape, newspapers in the spring of 1881 foreshadowed how he would soon be treated in print. On 2 May the Las Vegas *Daily Optic* reported that "the daring young desperado, the murderer of Bob Ollinger [*sic*] and J. W. Bell," had escaped. The next day the *Optic* added that Olinger and Bell were "victims of Kid's wiles" and were worthy "martyrs to their duties as peace officers." Again, on 4 May the *Optic* referred to Billy as "a notorious outlaw," as a "young demon" guilty of "ruthless murder." Then followed a string of the harshest criticisms: Billy was the worst of young men, "urged by a spirit as hideous as hell," with "a character possessing the attributes of the damned." The image of Billy as a devilish, murderous outlaw was already entrenched in many minds. The other more positive side—Billy buying, not stealing, a rope on his way out of town and his kind treatment of a young man on the street—did not appear in the contemporary newspapers. That description of the virtuous Billy would come later.

The story of where Billy hid and what he did in the next seven weeks is, at best, shadowy and incomplete. A few scattered, disjointed bits and pieces of information are known, however. Sauntering out of Lincoln, Billy turned north and west toward the Capitan Mountains. Stopping at the home of a Hispanic acquaintance, which he did regularly in the days to come, Billy got the man to help him remove his leg shackles, then moved on to the small settlement of Las Tablas, the home of his good friend Yginio Salazar, the young man who survived three gunshot wounds received during the Big Killing near McSween's home in Lincoln. The Kid's experiences with his amigo Salazar illustrated what we know about the Kid's perambulations in May and June 1881. The Salazar family fed Billy, provided him blankets to sleep away from the settlement, and probably helped him find another mount; his horse from Lincoln had broken lose and returned home. Most importantly, Salzar urged—in fact pleaded—with the Kid to leave New Mexico and head south into Mexico, where he would be safe from Garrett and other pursuers.

Billy seemed to have a hard time making a decision. He spoke of going to Texas, perhaps heading in that direction and then turning toward Mexico. On the Rio Peñasco some forty miles below Lincoln, Billy appeared at the cabin of John Meadows, whom he had met and befriended in Fort Sumner.

A conversation with Billy that Meadows recorded later and that seems accurate reflects Billy's decisions at that time. "Whatever you do," Meadows told the Kid, "don't go back to Fort Sumner. Garrett will get you sure as you do, or else you will have to kill him." But Billy responded: "I haven't any money. What could I do if I went to Mexico or some place else with no money? I'll have to go back and get a little before I can leave." Meadows repeated his warning about Garrett and Fort Sumner. "Don't you worry," the Kid told Meadows. "I've got too many friends up there. Anyhow I don't believe he will try to get me. I can stay there awhile and get enough to go to Mexico on." Then, Meadows gave a final warning: "You better go while the going is good. If you go back up there, you will either get killed or kill Garrett." The conversation overflowed with the Kid's naiveté, his excessive self-confidence, and his underestimation of Garrett. Meadows, on the other hand, was dead right with his clear warnings.

Billy's opponents were closing in on him, even if from afar. In Santa Fe on 30 April, Governor Wallace signed a death warrant for the Kid, following up on the sentence of hanging pronounced earlier that month in Mesilla. Later in the day, a telegram arrived in the governor's office informing Wallace about Billy's killing of the two deputies during his dramatic escape to freedom in Lincoln. Soon thereafter, Wallace republished his $500 reward notice in the *Santa Fe New Mexican* for the recapture of Billy the Kid.

If the governor was moving against the Kid from Santa Fe, so were several of the territory's newspapers. In the earliest report of Billy's flight from the Lincoln jail, a story datelined from Socorro but published in the Las Vegas *Daily Optic* on 2 May denounced Billy as a "murderer." Two days later the *Optic* declared that the "notorious outlaw," "this young demon," was "at once the terror and disgrace of New Mexico." His name was "synonymous of all that is malignant and cruel." In short, Billy was a man of "brutal murder" and one who "gloried in his shame."

Even more important to most residents of New Mexico was the question, "Where is Pat Garrett, and what will he do to recapture Billy the Kid?" Criticism of Garrett soon mounted, with naysayers convinced the sheriff was too lackadaisical in his pursuit of Billy. The next few weeks were especially challenging for Garrett. Praised earlier for his brave and courageous capture of Billy, he was now being condemned for his "unconcern and inactivity."

But as Garrett's most thorough biographer, Leon C. Metz, shows, Garrett had not abandoned his duty to roundup Billy. He would trail the outlaw but in his own way, not in a dangerous, headlong, unplanned pursuit. Besides, Garrett was not getting the support he needed. Hispanics in and around Lincoln and Fort Sumner were reluctant to provide information leading to the capture of their beloved El Chivato. Other Anglo citizens, fearing for their safety, chose to remain silent and uninvolved. Billy had claimed he was not out to kill Garrett, but the jail break and the murder of Bell and Olinger made clear that Billy would shoot anyone who stood in the way of his freedom. In going after Billy, Garrett would take his time, carefully plan his tracking to avoid a surprise encounter with the outlaw, and try to outwit the Kid rather than to fall victim to the outlaw's wiles.

Garrett began to hear rumors that Billy had been sighted in Fort Sumner. At first, he did not believe the stories, thinking that Billy would not be so foolish as to return to a place clearly unsafe for him. The rumors circulating through the region revealed that Billy was regularly visiting Paulita Maxwell, the young, vivacious sister of Pete Maxwell. Finally, convinced that all the rumors must have some validity, Garrett gathered a new deputy, John W. Poe, and another man, Thomas "Kip" McKinney, and rode to Fort Sumner on 13 July.

Garrett remained cautious. The next morning Poe, unknown in Fort Sumner, wandered into town to chat with townspeople. Maybe indirectly he could hear about Billy without arousing suspicion. But the town was suspicious of an Anglo newcomer, especially since nearly all the residents were Hispanics. They did not talk. Returning to chat with Garrett, Poe doubted whether the residents of Fort Sumner told all they knew. Still doubtful about Billy's presence in the area, Garrett nonetheless decided he would try another way to gain information about the Kid. He and his two deputies would ride into town under the cover of darkness to see whether Billy was around.

Garrett's decision, made reluctantly, would shape everything in the next fateful hours. Riding into town, the three lawmen dismounted and stopped in a nearby peach orchard to watch things, especially the residence of Celsa Gutiérrez, one of Billy's Hispanic girlfriends and, surprisingly, the younger sister of Garrett's wife, Apolinaria. Although Celsa was the sheriff's sister-in-law, she had not informed him about Billy's recent activities. As the three-man posse stood in the orchard, they overheard a couple nearby speaking in Spanish, but in the dark they could not be recognized. A young man arose from ground, vaulted over the surrounding fence, and walked away. Not until later did Garrett find out that he had probably seen and heard Billy the Kid in the orchard.

Thinking they had accomplished nothing, Garrett and his men decided to leave town, but before they did, Garrett elected to make one last call. He would talk to his acquaintance Pete Maxwell, the largest landowner and most important man in Fort Sumner. If anyone in town had information about Billy, surely Maxwell would know it.

About midnight, Garrett, Poe, and McKinney approached the Maxwell house, the large and impressively redone officer's quarters, of the old fort. Poe and McKinney remained outside Maxwell's bedroom door, left open during the warm New Mexico evening, while Garrett went inside to awaken and chat with Maxwell. None of them realized, of course, that a parallel train of events evolving near them would lead to another dramatic event of the Kid's life.

Staying at Celsa Gutiérrez's house—or, as some would claim, in another house nearby—less than a five-minute walk from the Maxwell residence, Billy became hungry. He was told that Pete Maxwell had just killed a beeve and that it was hanging near the house. If he went out to cut a slice or two from the critter, Celsa would cook the meat for him. Setting off in bare feet and only partially dressed, Billy cut across to the Maxwell house. As he approached the building, Poe and McKinney saw him, and he, they. Alarmed, Billy jumped back and whipped out his six-shooter, calling out in Spanish "*Quién es?*" or "Who is it?" then immediately

Maxwell home, Fort Sumner, New Mexico. When the U.S. Army sold
Fort Sumner to the Maxwell family in 1878, these former officers' quar-
ters became the home of Lucien Maxwell and his family. Pat Garrett shot
Billy the Kid in the bedroom of Pete Maxwell in this house late at night on
14 July 1881. Photograph courtesy of the New Mexico State University
Library Archives, Las Curces, image 00150174.

repeating the question. Billy set off no alarms in Poe and
McKinney, who had never met him. Trying to calm the
stranger, Poe said: "Don't be afraid . . . There is no one
here to hurt you." Dissatisfied with Poe's reassurances, Billy
retreated into Pete's bedroom.

It was dark, and most of what happened next occurred in
the heavy shadows. Just a minute or two earlier, Garrett had
entered the bedroom, walked to Maxwell's bed, and had
awaken the sleeping rancher. The sheriff asked Pete about
Billy, and Maxwell may have told him that although the Kid
was not in the Maxwell home, he might be nearby. At that
moment, Billy backed into the darkened bedroom.

Before Billy could make out who or what was in the darkness, he called out, "*Pedro, quiénes son esos hombres afuera?*"

(Who are those men outside?) Then, thinking someone else might be near Maxwell's bed, the Kid stepped back and called out again "*Quén es?*" and followed in English, "Who is it?" Maxwell, in a low voice, whispered to Garrett, "It's him."

Billy hesitated—an unusual but fatal indecision. Garrett quietly yanked out his pistol and rapidly fired two shots. One was the fatal round that punched into the Kid's breast just above his heart; the other ricocheted harmlessly off the wall.

Panic and confusion ruled. As soon as he squeezed the two rounds, Garrett rushed out of the bedroom, not certain about what had happened to the man he had shot. The terrified Maxwell untangled himself from his blankets and stumbled out the door and straight into the drawn six-gun of Deputy Poe, who, with McKinney, was alarmed and confused. As Garrett came racing out the door, he told Poe: "That was the kid that came in there and I think I got him."

Garrett probably saved Maxwell's life. Brushing aside Poe's gun, he yelled out, "Don't shoot Maxwell." No one knew for sure whether the stranger who entered was dead. Hesitant to return to the bedroom, Maxwell and Garrett secured a lighted candle and placed it on the windowsill outside, the light from the flame allowing them to see that the body on the floor was motionless. Once they recognized Billy, the sheriff and Pete went into the bedroom.

The shots awoke residents in nearby houses, and they soon crowded around the Maxwell home. It is often said that Deluvina Maxwell entered the darkened bedroom first, but she later told an interviewer that was not the case. She did not tell the interviewer, however, that when she realized the dead man was the Kid, she ran at Garrett, striking him on the chest and shouting out, "You pisspot . . . you sonofabitch." Others in the crowd tried to show their

187

sympathy for Paulita and other young women gathered nearby. Still other young men threatened the three lawmen, accusing them of shooting down their much-admired Billy. Feeling threatened and vulnerable, Garrett and his two deputies withdrew into the Maxwell house, barricading themselves against possible attacks.

Early the next morning a coroner's jury convened, although no official coroner was present, and wrote out a report in Spanish, later translated into English. Most of the jurymen were Hispanic. Those unable to read or write signed with their "x." They declared unanimously that Garrett had killed Billy, but it was their verdict "that the act of said Garrett was justifiable homicide." They also unanimously asserted "that the gratitude of the whole community is due to said Garrett for the act, and that he deserves to be rewarded." Did the jury, presided over by Milnor Rudulph and convened by San Miguel County justice of the peace Alejandro Seguro, in fact reflect the opinions of a majority of Fort Sumner residents? Some historians have suggested that an earlier coroner's report, now lost, did not include the words praising Garrett and that he forced the group to write the second document.

Later in the day, Billy's body, having been prepared and dressed by several women, was placed on display, with thirty or more eyewitnesses viewing his remains. After the viewing, Billy's body was placed in a newly made coffin, loaded onto a cart, and taken to the nearby cemetery. After a brief ceremony, the Kid was buried next to his pals Tom Folliard and Charlie Bowdre. Near his grave, a crude wooden cross with his name was planted. The large crowd that had followed the wagon to the burial stop gradually dispersed.

In the days after Billy's coffin was covered over, dozens of people—critics, aficionados, fence-sitters—attempted to discern who and what was Billy the Kid. That large, complex question deserves extended discussion.

12

Who and What Was Billy the Kid?

Fans as well as other interpreters of Billy the Kid wishing to embrace the widest-angle view of Billy may have to rearrange their mental furniture. Defenders of Billy usually label him a hero, freedom fighter, young man of courageous action. Detractors often harpoon him as a soulless murderer devoid of morality and stability. But a balanced interpretation shows he was both. Billy often demonstrated charity, companionship, and warmth but also displayed crass indifference to others and participated in acts of senseless violence and callous villainy. To gain a more complex view of Billy the Kid, we must see him as neither solely saint nor entirely unrepentant sinner. And by turns, over his lifetime he illustrated these conflicting characteristics. In full focus, Billy was an ever-shifting kaleidoscope, often changing direction under varying pressures and transformative leaders, events, policies, and ideas.

The beginning point for answering the question of who and what was Billy the Kid is to avoid *either-or* thinking that reduces him to hero or villain and to embrace *both-and* thinking that depicts him as a multifaceted character. This chapter attempts to view Billy whole, as a young man with a complex identity and one who obviously changed over time. In addition to changes through time in his personality, Billy faced shifting pressures from the outside. What he experienced from Santa Fe and Washington, D.C., in his Lincoln County days was much different from what he had faced in Silver City and Arizona.

Clearly then, the fullest outlines of personality and character that we can pull together on Billy the Kid must come from several directions. Not only did his personal journey and his personal reactions to that journey shift over time, but he also faced different circumstances through the years, in his march from a preteen boy to a man approaching age twenty-two. Combining these changes and shifts brings us closer to the complicated Billy the Kid the public deserves to know.

Biographers trying to depict this complex Billy face the same challenges that have become barriers to anyone interested in the Kid. Historians and biographers know so little about his first fourteen or fifteen years that it is difficult to see how his life might have been different in the final six or seven years of his life. There is safety only in sticking to the known or most dependable facts.

Even though Billy's childhood and boyhood remain largely in the shadows of uncertainly, a few discernable facts seem verifiable. He was originally Henry McCarty, then Henry Antrim. We know bits and pieces about his mother Catherine McCarty Antrim, step-father William Antrim, and his brother Joe. In about a half-dozen or more sources, Billy spoke warmly about his mother. He expressed his love and enduring affection for her. Although he did not say much specifically about Catherine, we know she helped with his education, encouraging him to read and write, which he did better than several of the men with whom he traveled later. Mary Ealy, the missionary's wife in Lincoln and elsewhere, also praised Billy's knowledge of hymns and his delightful voice. He told her he had attended church with his mother. Residents of Silver City also spoke approvingly about Catherine, celebrating her approachableness, kindness, and openness to Billy's young male friends. She accompanied

Billy to dances, made sure he went to school, and certainly shaped much of his life in their first year or so in Silver City. Even with her advancing tuberculosis, Catherine tried to be an attentive mother. When the disease drove her into bed in late spring 1874, she could no longer parent Henry as she had.

Parenting was of much less importance to Henry's stepfather, William Antrim, for he too was afflicted with a disease. Antrim increasingly dreamed of striking it rich as a prospector. Even when the dying Catherine was confined to bed, Antrim was out of town chasing the dreamed-of strike. He was not present in Silver City to attend Catherine's funeral or burial. It would be a mistake, however, to dismiss Antrim as an abusive parent, as a few historians have. Rather he was an inattentive parent, uninterested in serving as a father figure to Catherine's two boys, who needed male intervention and direction in a raucous mining boomtown. Once Catherine was gone, Antrim farmed out the two boys, hoping that another family or home would take care of them. When Antrim was faced with deciding between responsibilities of fatherhood and the prospect of mineral strikes, he went to the mines.

Historians know little about Henry's relationships with his brother, Joe, or Josie as some called him. Judging by the fragmentary knowledge of his life in Silver City, during a brief period a few years later, and at the end of his life, he too lived a drifter's life. He was sometimes a gambler, miner, room clerk, and day laborer. At some point he did father a child and then marry. A few rumors suggest Joe lived a bit on the shadowy side in the Southwest before moving to Denver, where he resided most of his life. Henry, now calling himself Billy Bonney, may have had a final, emotional meeting with his brother during his flight from Arizona to Lincoln County in 1877.

Several women in Silver City clearly impacted young Henry. Clara Louisa Truesdell, the mother of Henry's

Silver City, New Mexico. The boomtown of Silver City was the home of the Henry McCarty Antrim during his early to mid-teens from 1873 to 1875. This photograph is the view from the south looking north. Photograph courtesy of Richard Weddle.

buddy, Chauncey, not only looked after Catherine Antrim in her final days; she also took in Henry, and maybe Josie, for a short time. Sara Knight, older sister of Henry's chum, Anthony Connor, Jr., provided bits of encouragement. Still another woman, Mary Stevens Hudson, mother of Henry's companion, Charley Stevens, helped out by inviting Catherine Antrim to rest and attempt to regain her health at the nearby Hudson Hot Springs. Perhaps the woman most influential in Henry's life in Silver City—outside Catherine—was Mary P. Richards, Henry's teacher during his second year in Silver City schools. She connected well with Henry, encouraged his studies, and later helped him in his flight to and from Arizona. These stories are evidence of how adult women bonded with and influenced Henry (later Billy) and often readily helped him during stressful periods in his life.

Soon after the death of his mother and during his step-father's absence, Henry got into trouble, with another rabble rouser leading the way. First, Henry was involved in the theft of butter and then, much more importantly, in the clothes-stealing episode in 1875. The absence of parental supervision had left him to fall in with George Schafer, "Sombrero Jack," a drunk and thief. A twenty-something roustabout, Schafer became a pal to Henry, something of an older brother, replacing the parents and family now gone from Henry's life. The pilfering of the clothes, of course, led to Henry's jailing and his quick exit from Silver City and an equally sudden trip to Arizona.

Here was the first evidence of the bifurcated character that would define Henry or Billy the rest of his life. His friends, his teachers, and several adults in Silver City described him as a good guy, a boy not much different from other young men in the growing town. He might pull pranks, but he was not devilish in any way. But after the death of his mother and in the closing months of his life in Silver City, he became a thief, a troublemaker willing to break the law. In short he was now a likeable young man and companion who also stole from others for his own delight.

The months following Catherine's death, coupled with the absent stepfather Antrim and the eventual absence of his brother, Joe, signaled the end of the first stage of Henry's life and the beginning of the second. Parenting and family were now off scene, and days, weeks, and even months of independence or autonomy lay ahead. Into the vacuum rode men such as Sombrero Jack, surrogate parents and big brothers who would play major roles in the rest of Henry's life.

The roughly two years in Arizona from 1875–1877 solidified the emerging pattern of Billy's life, which had appeared even before he left Silver City. Most of what we know about Kid Antrim's life in Arizona stems from his misdeeds in the same way that the preponderance of information about the younger Henry in Silver City describes the behaviors and actions of a typical, if rowdy, boy. Now living on his own in Arizona and making decisions for himself about work, play, and other activities, the Kid unveiled more of his behavioral patterns that would dominate him to the end of his life.

Some undisputed evidence clearly reveals that Kid Antrim tried to walk a straight line in Arizona. He worked on ranches, in hotels, and in saloons and gambling halls. But cowboying and ranch work were physically too much for him, and he slid into illegal activities. The theft of horse blankets and saddles and of horses themselves became the most apparent Kid activity in Arizona. And he fell in with twenty-seven-old John Mackie, a former soldier with a criminal record. During his nearly two years in Arizona, Kid Antrim increasingly devoted himself to horse-stealing, even without Mackie. By summer 1877 the Kid was known as a thief and had been jailed for horse-stealing but stole more and more, particularly livestock, in the Camp Grant area.

Then Henry's dramatic confrontation with Francis P. "Windy" Cahill took place. Windy, also a former soldier and now a blacksmith, was a bully who loved to tease and taunt the Kid, a small, wiry, and, some thought, effeminate young man. But the Kid had also become something of a gunman. Often practicing with his weapon, he gained some reputation as a target shooter. Had he taken to guns and gun culture to offset his dubious masculinity and to protect himself against predators and competitors? Perhaps. When Cahill went beyond his usual bullying, throwing Antrim down and pummeling him, the Kid resorted to his ace in hand, his pistol, and shot the burly Windy in his belly.

Writers about the Kid often describe the killing of Windy Cahill as a lawful act of self-defense. But the incident was more complicated than the typical interpretation allows. Cahill's physical assault was not life threatening to the Kid. Windy had neither drawn a gun on the Kid nor threatened him with death or severe bodily harm. Windy's own response to Henry's assault—utter surprise and bafflement—suggested that the object of his bullying was at most to frighten and torment, not to kill or maim, Henry. The most revealing conclusion to draw from the shooting of Cahill is that Antrim would now use a gun as an equalizer when he thought his life or freedom was threatened. Henry, the Kid Antrim, not yet eighteen, had killed a man, his first.

In late summer and early fall of 1877, Billy Bonney, as he began to call himself after leaving Arizona, faced a future similar to but also different from his experiences in his first nearly eighteen years. With neither parents, family, nor friends to encourage and support him, Billy had to make his own decisions for the future based on his own thoughts and experiences. And judging from what happened during the coming months, Billy had no plans other than to escape Arizona, keep ahead of any law-enforcement officials who were after him, and find some kind of work to keep going.

Billy had been a mere petty thief when running to Arizona two years earlier, but he was now a murderer in flight back to New Mexico. By September 1877 regional newspapers were already trumpeting his killing of Windy Cahill. His escape from Arizona and his attempts to fit into New Mexico over the next year revealed a good deal about Bonney's developing character in a new kind of social, cultural, and political setting.

Billy had become a searcher and follower during his last year or two in Silver City and his two years in Arizona. Those paths continued to unroll before him as he rode across Arizona, through the southwestern and southcentral parts of New Mexico, and onward to the southeastern quadrant of the territory by fall 1877. On his journey to Lincoln County, Billy moved swiftly to and through the area of Silver City, his former home. But his series of stuttering steps depict a young man uncertain of what to do next.

Billy Bonney, the alias he adopted at least by the time he arrived in Lincoln County in October 1877, made a series of short stops mostly in September. Seen whole, the brief visits were illustrative of a young man not yet certain of what the future held for him, checking in with supporters and friends while he followed the uncharted road into adulthood and undertook decision-making for and by himself. First came as much as two weeks at the Knight ranch, the waystation operated by the sister and brother-in-law of Billy's buddy, Anthony Connor. They fed him and gave him some of Anthony's clothes and, most importantly, a horse. Although the order of subsequent stops is unclear, he evidently saw his brother, Joe, for the last time near Georgetown northeast of Silver City. It was an emotional visit, the final contact Billy had with any family. In Georgetown he may also have visited Mary Richards Chase, his former teacher in Silver City. During his brief sojourn there, he admitted he had no money; she gave him all the cash she had at the moment. Then Billy headed south toward Apache Tejoe.

It was at Apache Tejoe, a travelers' stop on the way from Silver City to the Rio Grande valley that Billy Bonney probably found a new cohort to join and follow. He could not have chosen a more fiendish set of outlaws, including two violent young men a bit older than Billy. They were Jessie Evans and John Kinney, both rustlers and violent killers. They made Billy's previous older role models, Sombrero Jack and John Mackie, seem like Sunday school boys. How long Billy rode with The Boys, as the Evans-Kinney gang was known, is unclear in the historical record, but he was in their company perhaps several weeks. The Kid was following a pattern now consolidated in his character: he chose to ride with young men who were older than he was; and he chose friends unwisely, again running with those who were a bad influence on him. Evans and Kinney were already despised desperados and rustlers; they were feared and hated by the people who knew them and whom they victimized. The Boys headed east through Mesilla, stealing as they went and telling saloon keepers "to chalk it up" when they left without paying their tabs. Billy went along with them, stealing the good horse of the sheriff's daughter in Mesilla. Before The Boys reached the Pecos valley, Billy had dropped out of the gang, deciding again to proceed in an uncertain direction.

In the next few weeks Billy's life was like a backyard robin hopping around to look for sustenance. Some of the bobbing worked fairly well; other actions were disappointments. The first act illustrated Billy's sometimes erratic thinking and decisions. He and his friend Tom O'Keefe had unwisely taken a dangerous shortcut through the Guadalupe Mountains, where Billy was separated from O'Keefe, lost his horse, and maybe nearly lost his life. Fortunately, after limping along for three days without food and then no shoes, he stumbled into the Jones ranch in the Seven Rivers area. There he met Ma'am Jones, who seemed cut from the same maternal cloth as his much-loved mother. Jones helped Billy recover from the mishap and go on his way. He tried to land work with the Brady family (according to that family's memories), at the L. G. Murphy ranch, and at the George Coe holdings. Nothing worked out. He also tried to work with the Casey family in trailing a herd of cattle to Texas, but they pushed him away, especially the widowed Ellen Casey and her daughter, Lily, who thought Billy was a dangerous horse thief they should avoid.

Billy's meandering journey took a new, positive turn toward the end of 1877, a turn that illustrated his need to find a place and to belong somewhere. Although cattle baron John Chisum could not find a place for Billy among his sprawling spreads, the newcomer Englishman John Tunstall did. Some writers have made too much of the Tunstall-Billy connection and, in doing so, distort the unfolding character of the Kid. Tunstall, only about six years older than the Kid, was not a father figure to him. If anything, an older brother

is more appropriate. And Tunstall, in all his full, voluminous letters to his family in London, never once mentioned
Billy. These writers also gush too much about this relationship considering how little Billy said about Tunstall. Crystal
clear, however, is that Billy saw the English rancher as a man
different from others he had known, especially the characters who crossed his path in Arizona and New Mexico, and
that he appreciated what Tunstall did for him. The Englishman, in his cultured, naïve, and mostly nonviolent ways,
stood apart from the cowboys, soldiers, and ex-soldiers Billy
encountered in the Southwest. Also, when Tunstall gave
Billy a good horse, saddle, and gun, he obviously won over
and made a follower of the young drifter.

Billy's time with Tunstall repeated his previous experiences and introduced new ones. Here again was a big
brother to follow and admire, and this time he had found
a man who had money, could hire Billy, and ensure some
of his future. Billy's connection with Tunstall promised
some measure of security and upward mobility. Tragically,
the Tunstall employment and security were short-lived. In
his ties to the Englishman, Billy soon learned another hard
lesson—how to be an enemy. Backing Tunstall and riding
with his cowboys and hired gunmen thrust Billy headlong
into what became the deadly Lincoln County War. Billy,
adhering to his need to belong somewhere and to someone,
easily became a partisan supporter of the John Tunstall–Alex
McSween contingent in its warfare against The House, the
Lawrence Murphy–James Dolan establishment that dominated Lincoln County.

His partisanship, an emotional as well as a labor bond,
made it all the more difficult for Billy when House gunmen
shot down Tunstall on 18 February 1878. After Tunstall's
murder, Billy's violent, vengeful proclivities swiftly surfaced,
and he promised he would "get" some of The House riders
who had killed Tunstall before he was finished. In the coming months, he sometimes followed and other times led the

violent actions that resulted in the killing of Morton and Baker, the assassination of Sheriff Brady, and the shooting of Buckshot Roberts. Once the Kid had fallen in with the Tunstall-McSween bunch, he became a violent adversary of The House, Sheriff Brady, and anyone else who fought against his beloved Regulators, the gang that served the Tunstall-McSween faction.

Two other men were leaders whom Billy chose to follow. They too were cut from a different cloth when compared to Sombrero Jack, John Mackie, Jessie Evans, and John Kinney. Dick Brewer, Tunstall's foreman and a rancher in his own right, was a sturdy, no-nonsense young man in his late twenties. In the months from late 1877 until his grisly death at Blazer's Mill in early April 1878, Brewer attempted to rein in Billy's tendency to shoot first and think later, as in the Morton-Baker and Sheriff Brady killings. Brewer was only partially successful in putting a lid on the untoward actions of the Kid, who seemed to respect Brewer's leadership and judgment.

Billy's relationship with Alex McSween was a more complicated affair. McSween stood apart from many of the men Billy knew and followed in the area. In his mid-thirties, McSween was a lawyer and an intensely religious man. Like Tunstall, he broke the mold of men whom Billy supported. Neither was McSween a gunman, nor did he carry a gun, and he hoped to avoid violence. But like Tunstall, he was willing to hire gunmen to fight against The House foes. Men such as the Kid and his pals were tools of violence in McSween's and Tunstall's war on the Murphy-Dolan faction.

In the weeks following Tunstall's death in February to the Five-Day Battle in Lincoln in July, one sees more of the Kid's character traits emerging. Unmistakable evidence of the bifurcated Billy was demonstrated in his actions as well as in the comments about and attitudes toward him from his friends and opponents. Some partisan observers then and later saw the Kid as a courageous hero, a young man willing to stand up against the villainy and treachery of The House. Enemies viewed Billy as a capricious killer willing to pull his pistol out and shoot down anyone who stood up to him. Accepting both sides as containing elements of truth and biases opens the way to important evidence of a complex Billy the Kid.

The two-sided Billy, the hero and villain, came to the fore in the months stretching from Tunstall's assassination in mid-February 1878 to the killing of McSween five months later. Not unlike other age-old political, religious, class, and racial-ethnic conflicts and wars, opposite sides spent nearly as much time and energy in attempting to blacken the reputations of their opponents as in trying to kill them. So it was in the Lincoln County War, with both praise and character assassination at work from the supporters and opponents of Billy Bonney. Revealingly, here were the roots of the conflicting images of Billy the Kid that emerged and persisted for nearly the next century and a half. Was he truly a hero or a villain—or both?

In the closing months of 1877 and the early months of 1878, more praise than denunciation rolled forth about Billy. Like many other women before and later, Ma'am Jones took to youthful Billy. As her son Sam recalled: "My mother loved him. . . . He was always courteous and deferential to her. She said he had the nicest manners of any young man in the country. She never could bear to hear anyone speak ill of him." Much later, Mary Ealy, wife of missionary-doctor Taylor Ealy, saluted Billy and his companions. Taylor thought of Billy as a "lost soul," but Mary, in a conversation with Sue McSween in the late 1920s, spoke of the Kid as handsome, intelligent, and particularly courteous to women. She wondered, too, what kind of life Billy might have lived if he had come to adulthood in the East or California.

The strongest recorded support for Billy came from the Coe cousins, Frank and George. Billy met the Coes in fall

1877 and was soon hanging out at their ranches, hunting with them, and becoming fast friends. Both Frank and George rode with Billy in some of the Regulator operations and supporting McSween and other leaders. But in late summer 1878, tiring of the violence and killing and the dangerous riding in Lincoln County, they moved north to other farms and stayed away from Billy for most of the next two to three years. But their relocation did not mean they had turned against Billy. Indeed, their memories of the Kid remained rich and warm well into the twentieth century.

In the 1920s and 1930s both Frank and George Coe gave strong, direct accounts of what they thought of Billy. In 1927, in an interview with Texas writer J. Evetts Haley, Frank portrayed Billy as a determined young man of vengeance. When the Kid saw Tunstall's body laid out on a bench in his store, Billy reportedly told Coe, he swore vengeance on the killers and enemies of Tunstall. Frank celebrated Billy's uncompromising drive to run the Murphy-Dolan crowd out of Lincoln County. To Frank, "all that was anybody on the river was for the Kid." He also delighted in Billy as a companion: "The first [hunting] trip out I saw that the Kid . . . was a fine shot with a rifle; he was handy in camp, a good cook and good-natured and jolly. He spent all his spare time cleaning his six-shooter and practicing shooting." Overall, Frank thought he had "never enjoyed better company" than Billy, who "had a touch of humor in everything, being naturally full of fun and jollity."

George Coe was even more upbeat in describing Billy. The Kid, George wrote in his memoir, *Frontier Fighter* (1934, 1951), "was the center of interest anywhere he went." "Though heavily armed . . . he seemed as gentlemanly as a college-bred youth." Over time, Billy "quickly became acquainted with everybody, and because of his humorous and pleasing personality grew to be a community favorite." After riding for several months with the Regulators, Coe was convinced that Billy and Charlie Bowdre were the group's "best fighters." Both were "cool and cautious," seemingly "not know[ing] what fear was." George also alleged that Tunstall, after getting acquainted with Billy, considered the Kid "the finest lad I ever met."

Other observers pointed to alternative facets of Billy's character. Mary Ealy was smitten with Billy's singing when he told her of his attending church as a boy, learning hymns, and singing them in a clear tenor voice. Still others were pleased with the respect Billy showed toward the *viejos* (old people), the *mamacitas* and their children, and, of course, the young, attractive women. And Frank Coe got in a large dig by declaring that "the Kid had twice as much principal [*sic*] as Pat Garrett and was more brainy."

Billy writers often overlook three other groups who did not comment on the Kid but who would likely have spoken favorably about him had they been able to leave or record their memories. The first group is the Hispanic community in southeastern New Mexico. Billy connected extremely well with Hispanic people. He spoke their language, befriended them, and engendered their admiration and warmth. But almost no Hispanics wrote about the Kid during the 1877 to 1881 period or in the years immediately thereafter. They probably lacked facility in written English and thus could not express their affection for Billy. A second group, including Tunstall, McSween, Brewer, MacNab, Folliard, and Bowdre, might have written about Billy in his last years, but their lives were also cut short, before any of them wrote much about the Lincoln County War, Billy, or other contemporary subjects, save in their personal letters. A third group is more difficult to understand. These include the young women who became enamored with Billy. A handful of Hispanic women in Lincoln and Fort Sumner were drawn to the Kid, but none wrote about him. Others, such as Paulita Maxwell, probably shied away from such comments because Billy's reputation as her sweetheart might have blemished the reputation of the Maxwells as an upper-class family of honorable men and virtuous women in southeastern New Mexico. Much later, Paulita did salute Billy's warmth and friendliness. Taken together, the silence of these three groups on Billy meant the diminution of first-person accounts that would likely have portrayed Billy the Kid in complimentary terms.

Of course, as the closing months of 1877 and the opening months of 1878 wore on and the conflict in Lincoln County escalated, other men and women in the area saw a very different Billy. One of the critics was Lily Casey (Klasner), whose pointed barbs jabbed Billy as well as more than a few others. She saw Billy as "a young and a poor orphan boy in bad company," who "played traitor" when he abandoned Jessie Evans and joined the "McLain Hunstad" (McSween-Tunstall) party. The Kid, she added, "was smart enough and crooked enough to change crowdes [*sic*], but he sure rued it in the end." Lily had no trouble agreeing with her mother, Ellen Casey, that Billy was essentially a lazy drifter, a young man who "was not addicted to regular work."

Jimmy Dolan, perhaps Billy's toughest and most relentless opponent in Lincoln County, completely dismissed the Kid. On 16 May 1878, he wrote a stinging letter to the Santa Fe *New Mexican* castigating the profound dishonesty of McSween and Chisum and exonerating the activities of the Murphy-Dolan-Riley contingent. Then he turned to the "regulators." First on his list was "William H. Antrim, alias 'the Kid,' a renegade from Arizona, where he killed a man in cold blood." And, Dolan continued, the Kid probably learned his criminal ways by keeping company with other outlaws and killers.

Along with Dolan, some of Billy's opponents reduced him to a dangerous, even despicable killer. Some spoke real authority with solid evidence on their side. Billy's roles in the murders of Morton and Baker and Sheriff Brady in March and April of 1878 made clear that he had become a brutal gunman willing to participate in vengeful, lawless shootings. By time the Regulators cornered Buckshot Roberts at Blazer's Mill on 4 April, Billy's reputation as a killer was already proven at least to some of his opponents. Frank Coe tried to get Roberts to surrender, but the veteran shootist refused to lay down his guns and declared, "The Kid is with you and he will kill me on sight." And when owner Doctor Blazer rejected Billy's command that the owner force the mortally wounded Roberts out of his house, the Kid threatened to shoot him. Blazer was a fool, Billy asserted, and if he did not do as the Kid demanded, he would burn down his house.

Even before the Big Killing in Lincoln in July 1878, Billy's detractors, including several members of the Murphy-Dolan combine, listed him among the worst of the gunmen aligned with the Tunstall-McSween partisans. They pointed to his threats against several opponents, his involvement in the Morton and Baker, Brady, and Roberts killings as indictments of his murderous character and actions. If many praised Billy as an upstanding, courageous hero, more than a few others, equally vociferous, condemned him as a villain and blackguard. Both sides had strong evidence for their conflicting depictions of Billy's character.

Interpretations of Billy rapidly shifted in the first half of 1878. During that time he was obviously moving through the end of the second period of his career and approaching the third stage. In the first stage, the Kid was something of an orphan; in the second, he became a footloose fellow, a wanderer, during his last year in Silver City, his two years in Arizona, and his first months in Lincoln County. And now he was galloping into a third stage, evolving into something new and different.

The clearest signs of this transition toward a new stage came during the deadly week of mid-July in Lincoln. There, a new kind of Billy was emerging. True enough, in the cases of Tunstall and McSween Billy was following men older than he, but in both situations he became more than just another follower. And within McSween's group at the time he was migrating toward the top of the hired gunmen. Historian Robert Utley succinctly summarizes this challenge. After Tunstall's death Billy gradually became another person. "For the first time," Utley writes, Billy "had a cause to which he could dedicate himself wholeheartedly—revenge for Tunstall." Through the Regulators, Billy left "anonymity" and "progress[ed] toward adulthood." Or, as close friend George Coe put it later, Billy was not yet known "as a warrior. . . . But he grew bigger and bigger."

In the final hours of the bloody five-day conflagration in Lincoln, Billy became something different. It was not that his character changed overnight but that in these new, ferocious circumstances he began to fill a new role he soon would assume for the rest of his life. The appearance of U.S. regulars in Lincoln under the command of Colonel Nathan Dudley had upset the balance of power between the Dolan and McSween forces, forcing many of the latter group to abandon town and leave the remaining McSween supporters huddled in Alex and Sue's house. And the house was on fire, burning toward the last crowded rooms. As one source notes, McSween "sat in a daze and the Kid slapped him and shook him and pulled his hair and told him to pull himself together and make a run for it."

McSween could not move, frozen in indecisiveness. "Boys," he told them, "I have lost my mind." So Billy took the reins of leadership and planned their escape route. Following the Kid's directions, the first group were to burst out of the fired McSween house and attempt a dash to freedom. Their precipitous actions, intended as both an escape and cover for the second group, including McSween, mostly worked for Billy and those with him, but the indecisive lawyer, unable to act, lost his life moments later in a blizzard of bullets. In those life-changing moments, Billy rose from loyal lieutenant to acting general. It was the position he would hold for the most of the next three years from his eighteenth to his twenty-first years.

In the next months after the gunfight in Lincoln, the Kid's circumstances revealed new developments in his character. Consider those circumstances: his sponsors—Tunstall and McSween—were now gone. Other leaders he had depended on—Brewer and, to a lesser extent, Frank MacNab—were also gone. Doc Scurlock had failed badly as the Regulator captain in Lincoln in July and had abandoned the "iron clad" group and returned to his family by early fall.

Billy also lost some of his closest friends in other changes. Frank and George Coe decided they had had more than enough danger and violence. Frank told the Kid that "things were all broken up and there was nothing in Lincoln" for him. Similarly, George added, "We are going the other way." Even though Billy tried to keep the Coes linked to his next activities, they refused to get involved and turned away. George stated they were not going to steal horses "for a living"; they were "through" with all that. All right, the Kid answered, "you may do exactly as you please," but, "as for me, I propose to stay in this country, [and] steal myself a living."

By the end of September, Billy had crossed his Rubicon. For the remainder of his life, he would be a rustler and a part-time gambler. Heading over to the panhandle of Texas with only four followers, Billy was now, in the words of Frederick Nolan, "the undisputed leader of what was left of the Regulator group."

A central question remains: did Billy exhibit a significantly different character in his few remaining years? This account posits that he did change noticeably over time—that character traits coming to fore in late 1878 were at odds with those framing his life when he arrived in Lincoln in fall 1877. Violence and loss did change him. But not entirely, for other parts of the Kid's personality persisted from his pre–Lincoln County days.

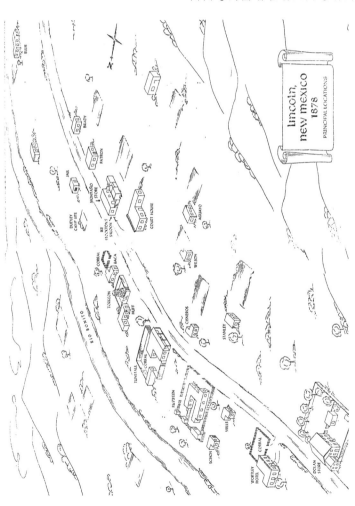

Lincoln, New Mexico, in 1878. Billy the Kid came to the town of Lincoln in southeastern New Mexico in fall 1877. It served as his major stopping place during much of 1877 to 1879. The town's layout and buildings remain much as they were in the 1870s and 1880s. Map in the Robert N. Mullin Collection courtesy of the Haley Memorial Library & History Center, Midland, Texas.

207

The Life

Several transitions beginning in 1878 clearly shaped Billy's life in the next three years. The civil war in Lincoln County, although not over, was less vicious and murderous than it had been in the first half of 1878. The actors in the regional drama were changing. Not only were Tunstall and McSween gone, but so was Lawrence Murphy. Sick from cancer and weakened by his rampant alcoholism, Murphy had gone to Santa Fe, where he died in October 1878. The Murphy-Dolan company, having gone bankrupt in May 1878, was now under the ownership of Santa Fe Ring leader Thomas Catron. The civil war of business interests between the Tunstall-McSween and Murphy-Dolan factions was moribund. Cattle baron John Chisum's interests were also shifting. Evidently, Chisum thought the Lincoln County War was not finished, and to avoid it, he left the area. He increasingly moved his large herds into the Texas panhandle to escape the Lincoln County upheaval and also sold off large numbers of cattle to Hunter, Evans & Co.

Some legal and political officials remained on the scene, but others new to the conflict were coming in to the picture. Although court justice Warren Bristol remained on the bench to harass Billy, by 1880 District Attorney William Rynerson was removed from office. Even more important for the Kid was that Lew Wallace replaced Samuel B. Axtell as territorial governor in September 1878. From fall 1878 to fall 1880, the new sheriffs and other legal authorities were seldom energetic and inspired in chasing rustlers and other lawbreakers, including Billy the Kid.

Once Billy decided to rustle livestock for a living, he himself etched some of the patterns practiced in Lincoln County. He found that stealing on one side of the New Mexico–Texas border and selling on the other was a financially rewarding pattern. And in his rustling, Billy was following traditions already underway. For several years, rustlers had been stealing cattle from Chisum's sprawling ranges in New Mexico. In west Texas near Tascosa, the lack of strong law enforcement was something of an inducement for thieves to steal cattle from those widely separated ranches.

Two other transitions were scene-shifting in their impact on Billy's life. The discovery of gold in nearby White Oaks, New Mexico, and its overnight rise as a market for stolen goods shaped events in 1879–1880. Also influential was the disappearance of Billy's old buddies and the appearance of newcomers. As we have seen, the Coe cousins exited the region in 1878 rather than join the rustling gang Billy was launching. Others, including Doc Scurlock, Henry Brown, and John Middleton, parted company in Texas in October 1878. Only loyalist Tom Folliard remained with the Kid.

But new recruits appeared. Billy always attracted at least a handful of followers. Those who joined Billy after 1878–1879 were not always good influences on him, and he was perhaps a poor role model for them. The least well-known of the new riders was Tom Pickett, a refugee from earlier skirmishes in Las Vegas, New Mexico, where had had been a policeman after a brief stint as a Texas Ranger. Billie Wilson, a couple years younger than the Kid, possibly led Bonney into counterfeiting activities in the White Oaks area, further complicating the Kid's journey in 1880. The most reprehensible of the newcomers was Dave Rudabaugh, a half-dozen years older than the Kid and already guilty of murder and other violence. As Robert Utley puts it, "for unadulterated evil, Rudabaugh outshone Billy."

The new face on the scene who could have made the most difference was Governor Lew Wallace, who was appointed the territorial executive in early fall 1878. An outsider from the Midwest and East, Wallace became an insider in New Mexico Territory for about two-and-a-half years. But the failure of Wallace to redirect the Kid's journey resulted from failures on both sides. After Billy wrote to Wallace and offered to provide eyewitness testimony about Huston Chapman's murder, they met secretly on 17 March 1879 and worked out a plan acceptable to both sides. But later, that agreement fell apart when, first, Wallace seemed not to fulfill his promises and Billy, unwilling to wait, "skinned out" and returned to thievery even more overt and outrageous than before.

The Billy-Wallace connection—or lack thereof—took on new dimensions once the Kid was captured at Stinking Spring in late 1879 and jailed in Santa Fe in early 1881. We have seen the four letters the Kid addressed to Governor Wallace between 1 January and 27 March 1881. The naïve Kid seemed to think he could capture the governor's attention after Wallace had ignored his letter of the previous December—and he thought again he could convince the governor to give him the pardon or to plead his case with the subsequent letters in the next three months. Some sentences or passages seemed like blackmail, some paragraphs overflowed with the Kid's ignorance of the law, and still others indicated Billy thought he could force Wallace into action. All this correspondence suggested Billy lacked any realistic appreciation of his legal situation.

One can, of course, point out that Wallace was focused on other activities. His newly published novel, *Ben-Hur,* was gaining traction in the book market and zooming up the best-seller list. He was also trying to land a new diplomatic position, a presidential appointment, that would release him from fractious New Mexico. In fact, he had already resigned from the governorship before Billy's fourth letter to him. Billy had kept his promises to Wallace for the most part, and the governor had not. But Billy's threatening letters, practicing a rough diplomacy, revealed the Kid's inability to deal with and cultivate an important person who might have helped him. Billy showed he was an innocent abroad in such chancy dealings in the real world.

So the conditions in Billy's life transformed the trail ahead of him. He was forced to support himself and to become a leader. And the new leadership role also pushed him fully into rustling and outlawry to make a living. It is clear that

Billy became a different kind of man after the events of midsummer 1878. One might argue that surrounding events more than a changed personality determined the Kid's direction, but the long view back to his last months in Silver City demonstrate that Henry McCarty, Kid Antrim, and Billy Bonney had always betrayed a wide streak of independence and bravado. Now he needed to follow these individualistic tendencies to make his way, or at least he was convinced that he must.

Events in the second half of 1878 illustrated the changes surrounding and within Billy. In late summer and early fall, Billy launched his rustling business, stealing cattle and horses primarily in New Mexico and attempting to sell them in west Texas. He was now the gang leader with loyal followers. The significance of this fundamental transition surfaced in Tascosa in the Texas panhandle in October 1878.

Dr. Henry Hoyt met Billy on his way to Texas in early fall 1878. Later in his memoir, *A Frontier Doctor,* Hoyt provided revealing sketches of Billy as a new rustler chieftain. The doctor wrote that Billy led "with a rod of iron" but that his followers "fairly worshipped him." Even though Billy was still a teenager and a "beardless boy," he "was nevertheless a natural leader of men."

An unusual occurrence in Tascosa illustrated the close bond between Billy and his lieutenants. In an enthusiastic footrace, Hoyt and Billy dashed toward a dance hall, but Billy tripped and fell forward, sliding onto the dance floor. Hoyt described what happened next: "Quick as a flash . . . [Billy's] prostrate body was surrounded by his four pals, back to back, with a Colt's forty-five in each hand and ready for business." Although guns were forbidden at the dances, Billy's followers were ready, at a flick of an eye, to defend their captain.

That kind of tight bond remained in the months to come. Even Rudabaugh, older and more calloused from violence and murder than Billy, followed the Kid. So did the earlier pal Tom Folliard and, for some time, Charlie Bowdre. The esprit de corps glued them together throughout 1878 into 1880, but the close bond did not keep Billy from making several mistakes.

Despite his fantasy of owning his own place, Billy was a drifter, easily wandering from one place and activity to others. Even though this knock-about lifestyle continued from 1878 to 1881, there were scattered evidences of Billy's desire to change his pattern of life. He spoke of trying to settle down, to get a piece of property and of taking up farming. And in 1879 he tried to bury the hatchet with Jimmy Dolan, his most-often-mentioned nemesis. The Kid did his part in contacting Dolan and his followers to parley and bring about peace—until a drunken celebration tragically led to the Dolan's party shooting down the obstreperous lawyer, Huston Chapman, the same day. Still other Kid overtures promised peaceful settlements, but Billy had trouble staying on track to see the overtures come to fruition.

Billy and his riders continued to ply their rustling trade in spring 1880. The New Mexico–Texas network persisted, but there were also adjustments to that customary pattern. The Rustlers, as they were now labeled, stole horses from the Mescalero Apache Reservation and got rid of them down the Rio Pecos. And thriving White Oaks gradually expanded as a lucrative market for the Rustlers' purloined beef, whether it originated east or west of the Pecos.

These and succeeding livestock raids enraged ranchers on both sides of the Texas–New Mexico border. After running off with Texas cattle, Billy kept them in his holding "ranch" near Los Portales or delivered them to regional butchers. Booming as the result of a gold rush, White Oaks became a beckoning market for beef consumed by hungry miners. Rustlers such as Billy often worked with Pat Coghlan, a shady merchant who fed the gold prospectors and supplied beef to Fort Stanton. Another outlet for the Kid's stolen cattle was the Dedrick brothers, who now ran the old

Chisum ranch and owned places in White Oaks in which they butchered beef.

Billy's thefts on both sides of the Texas–New Mexico border kept ranchers, soldiers, and town residents on edge. By the end of 1879, he was an unpopular rustler in both jurisdictions. Something needed to be done to eliminate the Kid and his henchmen from the cattle ranges.

In a less authenticated story, Billy also stole cattle from James and Pitzer Chisum, brothers of John. The Chisums lost a considerable number of livestock, but whether most of these animals were purloined by the Kid and company is not clear.

The final new face who did so much to realign south-eastern New Mexico's law-enforcement landscape in 1880–1881 was Pat Garrett. Billy knew Pat; they had played cards together. But they were not intimate friends. What Billy failed to understand was that Garrett would be a law officer unlike any other sheriff—Brady, Copeland, Peppin, Kimbrell—who had served in Lincoln County. Billy obviously underestimated Garrett's perseverance and overestimated his own talents for evading Garrett and other pursuers. Within a few weeks after his elevation to sheriff (not legally until 1881), Garrett had Billy in handcuffs and headed north to the Las Vegas and Santa Fe jails. Later, although several friends, including John Meadows, Yginio Salazar, and a handful of others, warned Billy about staying in the Fort Sumner area and urged him to flee to Mexico or elsewhere, he blithely replied that he had friends in the area and would stay ahead or aside of his pursuers. Billy overestimated what he could do.

Changes beyond Billy's control and ones he probably never recognized or understood also impacted the direction of his personal journey. He came on scene during the Gilded Age of the United States. His days were part of the continuing move from the Age of Jackson in pre-Civil War America to the that of the Robber Barons, industrial

Fort Sumner, New Mexico. Once the U.S. Army closed and sold Fort Sumner in 1868, it became the home of the Maxwell ranch family and a few dozen Hispanic families. The small town became a favorite stopping place and refuge for Billy the Kid. Photograph courtesy of the New Mexico State University Library Archives, Las Cruces, image 00150177.

capitalism, and political and economic rings, such as Tammany Hall, following the Civil War. That ongoing transformation obviously impacted Lincoln County, New Mexico, even if it was geographically far removed from the center of political and economic power in the East. Too often biographers and historians, so focused on the violence and turmoil of southeastern New Mexico, have overlooked these large, powerful contextual forces.

Lincoln County seemed, mistakenly, two giant steps removed from Washington, D.C., federal decision-making, and East Coast influences. Although a distant territory with little economic or political power, New Mexico was still under the lion's paw of the federal government. The president selected territorial governors and secretaries, Indian superintendents and agents, U.S. marshals, and the three federal justices. That meant these executive and judicial officials looked eastward for their political cues, not to the citizens of the territory where they served. As in all western territories at the time, conflicts between the presidential appointees and representatives of the elected territorial legislature dominated New Mexico. In the territorial capital, political power cohered even more tightly because the so-called Santa Fe Ring, an informal association of local power brokers, often worked hand in glove with federal appointees coming from Washington. Nowhere was that political bed sharing more apparent than in the ties of Governor Samuel B. Axtell and Secretary W. G. Ritch to Santa Fe Ring leaders Thomas B. Catron and Stephen B. Elkins. These powerbrokers and their cronies largely controlled the politics and economy of the territory.

If a Washington, D.C.–Santa Fe connection was an indirect but still molding force on Billy the Kid, an even-more-direct linkage existed between Santa Fe and Lincoln County. This complex relationship included Catron and other members of the Ring; regional legal officials such as District Attorney William L. Rynerson and District Judge Warren Bristol; and local entrepreneurs Lawrence G. Murphy and James J. Dolan. Together, the men at the federal, territorial, and county levels had a lock on the political, legal, and economic affairs of Lincoln County until John Tunstall and Alex McSween began to challenge the sources of power emanating from Washington, D.C., surging into Santa Fe, and spilling out onto Lincoln County. No one from Santa Fe, and few from Washington, if they cared at all, were friendly to Billy's interests in Lincoln County.

So anyone trying to understand who and what Billy the Kid was cannot overlook the cross-continental and territorial-wide sources of power and politics that shaped so much of Lincoln County in the last three years of Billy's life.

But Billy is still the most significant key to understanding Billy's personal character and development. Such was the case in comprehending his relationships with young women. Billy discovered young women—several of them—in his closing years. He said almost nothing about his sweethearts or sexual partners, and they, unsurprisingly, did not write or speak about their encounters with him. Most were Hispanic, and most resided in or near Fort Sumner.

No one has uncovered a close association between Billy and a young woman before he came to Lincoln County and previous to his eighteenth birthday. In fact, the first brief mention of a woman or girl who attracted Billy came a little before and just after the summer shootout in Lincoln. In August 1878, headed north and eventually east into the Texas panhandle, Billy and his handful of riders visited Chisum's Bosque Grande Ranch. John Chisum was not there, but his attractive teenage niece, Sallie Chisum, was present at the ranch. Sallie and Billy had met once before at another Chisum spread, but this time he paid specific attention to her. She recorded in her diary that in about a week's time "William Bonny" and "Willie Bonny" had given her gifts, including an Indian tobacco sack and "candi hearts." In September Billy and his pals again encountered the Chisums moving a herd—and Sallie. It was the last time the two adventurous young people met. Were they friends, sweethearts, lovers? No one seems to know, but the contact suggests Billy's rising interest in young women.

Later in the Fort Sumner area Billy's contacts with several young Hispanic women were even more intimate. Again, one has to rely on rumors, secondhand stories, and later innuendos to piece together the Kid's involvement with Hispanic women. The stories revolve around four young women. Two—Abrana García, married, and Nasaria Yerby, a common-law wife—were rumored to have conceived and borne children with Billy. No census or birth records, however, confirm these long-held stories.

The Kid's relationship with Celsa Gutiérrez, although more frequently mentioned, is equally difficult to trace. Married to an older man, Saval (or Sabal) Gutiérrez, and living in Fort Sumner close to the Maxwell family, Celsa was the sister-in-law of Pat Garrett. By nearly all accounts, Celsa was well acquainted with Billy. Whether they became lovers, however, remains unclear. More than a few old-timers in Fort Sumner thought Billy often visited Celsa's house and perhaps was visiting her the night he was killed.

The most complex of Billy's romances involved Paulita Maxwell (later Jaramillo), the daughter of Lucien Maxwell and the younger sister of Pete Maxwell, who looked after her. Paulita was the often-rumored novia of Billy. They saw one another frequently in the last year or two of his life, especially at the lively bailes at Fort Sumner. Some have vouched they were intimate, that Billy returned to the fort after his escape from the Lincoln jail because Paulita carried his child, and that a rushed marriage in early 1882, after Billy's death, was arranged to cover up the paternity of her child. The most recent research by Professor Robert Stahl proves that the marriage did not occur until January 1883 and that Paulita's first child was not born until January 1884. Still, these new revelations cannot scotch the hard evidence that Billy and Paulita were greatly attracted and warm toward one another. A dependable eyewitness account from deputy Jim East describes the parting kiss Billy and Paulita shared in December 1880 when he, captured by Pat Garrett, rode through Fort Sumner on his way north to Las Vegas and Santa Fe. The embrace and kiss, East wrote, were the kind novelists write about. "Much against our wishes," East continued—"for you know all the world loves a lover"—we had to separate the two.

These obvious attractions to young women, married and single, proved that Billy had come alive romantically in his final years. Whether these relationships led to sexual activity is not known and cannot be proven, but the likelihood of intimacy seems strong. Billy was clearly pulled in that direction after 1878.

Even though some evidence points to Billy's character moving down different paths after 1878, the strongest evidence substantiates a continuing bifurcated Billy. Several eyewitnesses testified to the conflicted personality of the young man.

One of these observers was John P. Meadows from Alabama and Texas whom Billy met and befriended in Fort Sumner in spring 1880. They encountered one another on several occasions; Meadows was warmed by the Kid's friendship. "He always treated me fairly," Meadows recalled. "The more I talked to him, the better I liked him." But Meadows also admitted that when Billy "was rough, he was as rough as men ever get to be." The contradictions in Billy's outlook and actions were still vivid in Meadows's recollections.

One married couple came to opposite conclusions about Billy's character. The Rev. Dr. Taylor Ealy did not like Billy, labeling him a dangerous, lawless young man. But his wife, Mary, spoke of the Kid as "a charming looking chap with splendid manners." She praised Billy's "intelligence, his courtesy, his love of beauty, his capacity for leadership . . . and his capacity for making friends." Perhaps as often was the case, Mary reflected the reactions of women to Billy, which generally were more positive than those of men, such as Doctor Ealy. A similar divided attitude characterized the responses of Alex and Sue McSween to the Kid. Although Alex never said much about Billy, he did hire the young gunman, rode with him, and invited him to protect his house. But Sue was repulsed by the Kid. He was too much influenced by the "foolhardy boys" he associated with. "I never liked the Kid," she told a friend much later; she "didn't approve of his career . . . because he was too much like Dolan," not thinking "it amounted to much to take a man's life."

Even Pat Garrett appreciated the conflicting sides of Billy. He acknowledged the Kid's danger as an opponent, his threat as a gunman, and his sometimes-murderous ways. As Garrett once stated, Billy was "a well-known violator of the law." Yet the sheriff also recognized the other, less negative side of the Kid too. In the second half of his *The Authentic Life of Billy, the Kid* (1882), the portion most likely written by or taken from Garrett, the sheriff noted that the Kid "expressed no enmity towards me for having been the instrument through which he was brought to justice." Billy, Garrett continued, was not angry or vindictive in his attitudes toward the sheriff. The Kid accepted that Garrett had only done his job and had not gone after him out of hatred or a thirst to kill. Garrett's description of the Kid's character, undoubtedly driven some by the need for self-appreciation, nonetheless provided a balanced account of Billy as an outlaw but also a fair-minded captive. And this character sketch came from the man who killed the young outlaw.

For well more than a century since Billy's death, biographers, historians, movie-makers, novelists, and other students of American popular culture have tried to answer the question, "Who and What Was Billy the Kid?" At first these interpreters generally depicted him as a murderous desperado through World War I, and then after the mid-1920s he became something of a romantic hero protecting himself and his interests. More recently, particularly since the 1960s and 1970s, other writers and film-makers have come to more complex, believable conclusions about the Kid's character. Who was the Kid? To these recent writers, he is an amalgam of negative and positive characteristics. He was guilty of numerous acts of violence and outlawry, which escalated in his final years, but he was also a cheerful, humorous, and respected companion, especially to a handful of riders, women, and Hispanics. Gradually, scholars and lay writers have realized that one-sided views of Billy as villain or hero fall far short of comprehensive understanding. Only portraits of him as a conflicted, complex, and bifurcated young man will provide the fullest, most revealing portrait. Perhaps novelist Ron Hansen has come closest to a succinct understanding of Billy's conflicted character. In his superb novel, *The Kid* (2016), Hansen is dead center when he imagines Billy answering the question of what he most wanted in life: "To belong. To be liked. To be famous. To be feared." These competing desires, both positive and less so, are illuminating representations of the conflicting forces that powered the Kid in his closing years.

PART II

THE LEGENDS

13

The Rise of a Legendary Billy the Kid, 1880–1926

When journalist Walter Noble Burns's creative biography, *The Saga of Billy the Kid*, appeared in 1926, it sent many Billy interpreters in new directions. From the final moments of the Kid's hectic life and for the next two generations, most biographers and historians depicted Billy as, at worst, a thieving, murdering outlaw and, at reluctant best, as a violent desperado of the Wild West. After the appearance of Burns's romantic work writers began, sometimes tentatively, to treat Billy as something of a hero righting wrongs and standing up for his own liberties. For another two generations and more this romantic, heroic Billy dominated books and movies about him. Then in the 1960s and stretching toward the present, a newer, more complex Billy appeared. Neither entirely villainous or wholly heroic as he had been portrayed, Billy became a New Grey protagonist, embodying simultaneously both negative and positive characteristics. These four time periods—the early 1880s to the mid-1920s, 1926 to 1960, 1960 to 1995, and 1995 to the present—illustrate the major stages in the development of the legendary Billy the Kid.

In the first stage of Billy's legendary career beginning in the early 1880s newspaper writers, dime novelists, and Pat Garrett's *The Authentic Life of Billy, the Kid* were the most significant forces shaping public opinion about the Kid.

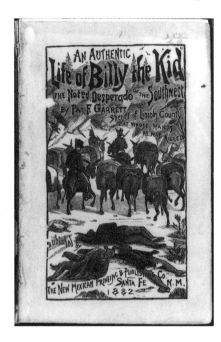

Cover of Pat Garrett's biography of Billy the Kid, 1882. Garrett's *The Authentic Life of Billy, the Kid*, published in spring 1882, became the principal early source on Billy despite its inaccuracies and otherwise shaky information. For the next forty years this brief biography, primarily ghostwritten by Garrett's journalist friend Marshall Ashmun Upson, served as the reservoir for facts on Billy's life and death for historians, biographers, and novelists, ultimately misleading most of them to write flawed portraits of the notorious outlaw. Courtesy National Archives.

Although a few dissenting voices would surface in the next forty plus years, the early treatments presented not only a clearly unflattering portrait of Billy the Kid but also introduced several legendary elements far distant from the facts of Billy's life and career.

Before Pat Garrett shot down the Kid in Pete Maxwell's bedroom and even more so after his violent death, journalists were placing Billy among the West's most desperate outlaws. He was a young man with abundantly bad, if not evil, ways. The newspaper accounts that appeared immediately after Billy's death and in the next few years by and large mimicked the characterizations of him that had grabbed headlines in his last years.

Within days of Billy's death, accounts of his demise appeared as headline stories in New Mexico and national newspaper. Not surprisingly the New Mexico newspaper stories continued the negative stories about Billy appearing in 1880–1881. Nearly all depicted him as the territory's chief "desperado." On 18 July 1881, the Las Vegas *Daily Optic* published a piece titled "'The Kid' Killed," building on three reports of the events in Fort Sumner four days earlier. One of those interviewed for the story was Pat Garrett. These "thoroughly reliable sources," the reporter wrote, confirmed the death of Billy the Kid, "the terror not only of Lincoln county, but of the whole Territory, a young desperado who has long been noted as a bold thief, a cold-blooded murderer, having perhaps killed more men than any man of his age in the world." Pat Garrett ought "to be well rewarded," the *Daily Optic* opined, for giving Billy his "just dues." In fact "all mankind rejoices" at the demise of Billy. Five days later *The New Southwest and Grant County Herald*, published in Silver City, was even more specific. That paper added that "despite the glamor of romance thrown around his dare-devil life by sensation writers, the fact is he was a low down vulgar cut-throat with probably not one redeeming quality."

Also reporting the death of Billy, the *Albuquerque Daily Journal* celebrated the demise of the Kid on 18 July. He was "the worst desperado that has ever infested the Territory of New Mexico." Now New Mexicans could relax, for the young, violent gunman "whose name had become a terror to every family in New Mexico was laid away." Three days later the *Santa Fe Weekly Democrat* dished up a more imaginative rendition of the moments immediately after Sheriff Garrett gunned down Billy. Once the Kid's comatose body hit the floor, "there was a strong odor of brimstone in the air, and a dark figure with the wings of a dragon, claws like a tiger, eyes like balls of fire, and horns like a bison, hovered over the corpse." Lest readers miss the devilish connection, the journalist added that the dark figure, "with a fiendish laugh, said 'Ha, Ha! this is my meat!' and sailed off through the window."

Across the country in the East, obituaries were particularly widespread in New York City where at least eight of the urban newspapers carried items about Billy's end. Interestingly, perhaps because earlier journalists had stated that the city was Billy's birthplace, some of the East Coast stories appeared there first, then were telegraphed west rather than arising in New Mexico and going east. Depictions of Billy in the eastern newspapers differed not at all from those in New Mexico.

Some of the New York newspapers, like the one appearing in the *Times*, did little more than announce Billy's death. The *Times* labeled the Kid a "notorious western desperado" who, "it is said," was a native of New York, but the *Sun* stated that the "former murderer" had vowed to kill John Chisum and Governor Wallace. He was born in Brooklyn, the *Sun* added, and "had slain twenty-one men and was twenty-one years old." The *Mail*, on the other hand, fabricated a story that Billy had broken into the Maxwell house in Fort Sumner, "terrorizing the family and threatening the women," and engaged in a running gunfight with Garrett before tripping, falling down, and being shot by the sheriff. The *Globe* had new facts of its own: Billy was born in Ireland, crossed the plains in a wagon at the age of twelve, and received his instruction in violence in the Lincoln County War.

The *Daily Graphic*, recognized then as a tabloid, printed the most outrageous of the New York yellow-journalism stories. "With fangs snarling and firing a revolver like a maniac," Billy had escaped capture at Stinking Spring only to be shot down later by Pat Garrett. The Kid was a "Robin Hood with no mercy, a Richard the Lion Hearted who feasted on blood" and who "stole, robbed, raped, and pillaged" his way across New Mexico. Only the courageous Pat Garrett "had the courage to capture this desperado" and "end [the] wild west lawlessness" by this "master criminal of the American Southwest." In these newspaper obituaries as in the dime novels of the 1880s, Billy the Kid is widely

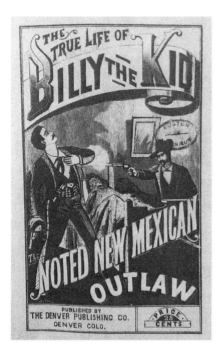

Dime novel *The True Life of Billy the Kid*, 1881. More than a dozen dime novels about Billy the Kid were published between 1881 and 1890. Nearly all, including this work, depicted Billy as a violent gunman. These predominately negative images of the Kid continued for at least the next forty years. Image in the author's collection.

portrayed as a fiendish desperado of the worst sort.Courage, supportive individualism, congeniality, and warm, supportive friendships—he had none. No one had come forward to speak for the Kid. One should not miss the strong continuities linking these newspaper stories with the soon-to-come dime novels. Indeed, more than a few facts—often false and negative facts—in the journalistic accounts reappear, clearly and thoroughly, in the subsequent dime novels.

From the opening of the Civil War to the early twentieth century, the United States was awash in dime novels. Millions of cheap, sensational, and usually quickly written novels were available for a nickel or dime. Modern advances in inexpensive printing, an escalating interest in a Wild West, and the reading public's clear desire to flee from a horrendous Civil War and its divisive aftermath were major reasons for the rising fascination with this new form of popular literature.

Building on earlier interest in the Leatherstocking Tales of James Fenimore Cooper, the writings of other authors such as Emerson Bennett and Edward S. Ellis, and the "story papers" and "penny dreadfuls" of the United States and England, dime novelists ransacked a faraway, romantic frontier for fresh settings and storylines. Other dime novelists depicted detectives standing up to thieves and corrupt police. Still others such as Edward L. Wheeler combined the two to send his hero, Deadwood Dick, and heroine, Calamity Jane, as detectives to ferret out and defeat evil-doers in the West.

In the three decades following the Civil War, several western demigods first appeared not in overnight biographies but in dime novels. For example, author Prentiss Ingraham churned out nearly seven hundred novels, about two hundred of which dealt with his friend, Buffalo Bill. Other dime novelists capitalized on widespread interest in Jesse James and Kit Carson for their quickly produced works. Billy the Kid dime novels numbered much fewer in number than those about Buffalo Bill, Jesse James, and fictional characters such as Deadwood Dick and Old King Brady. In his important book, *The Dime Novel Western* (1978), Daryl Jones suggests that the lesser number of Kid dime novels resulted from the widespread depictions of Billy as nothing but a "fiend incarnate" or "young monster." "Rather than introduce the persecution and revenge motif" to rationalize Billy's violent actions, as Wheeler had done in his very popular Deadwood Dick series, the Kid dime novels overflowed with his dastardly, repugnant behavior. "The public's refusal to condone unjustified violence," Jones adds, led to the limited number of Kid dime novels.

The first of what can be called a Billy the Kid dime novel was Thomas F. Daggett's *Billy LeRoy, the Colorado Bandit; or, the King of the American Highwaymen*. This most curious of the nearly dozen or so available dime novels about Billy the Kid appeared in 1881, then with a slightly altered title in 1882, and was reprinted again in 1883.

The unusual ingredient was the divergent content of the work. Said to be a "biography" of Billy LeRoy (Arthur Pond), an actual Colorado highwayman, the novel is also a fictionalized portrait of portions of the life of New Mexico's Billy the Kid. After tracing the violent and mindless exploits of LeRoy's dramatic life in Indiana and Colorado, Daggett conflates LeRoy's career with that of the Billy the Kid in New Mexico. Even more confusing, the Colorado outlaw is also known as Billy, or the Kid.

LeRoy is never identified as Billy Bonney, but he meets and travels with the New Mexican Kid's friends and partici-pates in events in which Bonney took part. While in south-ern Colorado, LeRoy encounters Tom O'Phallier (Tom O. Folliard), "one of the most notorious desperadoes in the West" and his fellow outlaw, Dave Rudabaugh. In a cave ritual, LeRoy is initiated into the O'Phallier gang and soon proves himself as a highwayman in holding up a stagecoach and robbing a man of his considerable cash. LeRoy does so well that the outlaws call for his elevation to captain of the gang.

When things get too hot in Colorado, LeRoy rides south to New Mexico. He rustles cattle and is involved in a red-hot shootout in Lincoln, and his extralegal activities bring pos-ses from Texas, White Oaks, and parts of Lincoln County in pursuit. He and his gang try to work out something with Governor Lew Wallace, but the New Mexico leader fails to keep his promises.

The New Mexico event treated most extensively is the shootout between Billy's gang and the White Oaks posse at the Greathouse Ranch. Some of the details are accurate, others are not, and Billy is singled out as the killer of Jim Carlyle. Soon thereafter Billy rides into a Chisum cow camp, shoots three of the four cowboys, and sends the fourth off to John Chisum himself, warning the cattle king that Billy will murder other cowboys because Chisum has not paid Billy for "riding shotgun" in earlier conflicts.

Billy LeRoy in Colorado and New Mexico is depicted throughout as a vicious, driven killer. Without much cause, Billy whips out his pistol and shoots down opponents; he seems immune to the bullets of others and always on target in his own shots. Assertive, desperate, his soul "dead to remorse," and never haunted by "the consequences of his deeds," Billy "stole, murdered, [and] ravished women" after arriving in New Mexico. Defiant to the end, Billy tells a gang of lynchers readying to hang him, "I am ready to meet the cashier. Go on with your cart."

This initial Billy the Kid dime novel features familiar facets of the genre. The West is a wild place ruled by the strongest and most desperate characters and boasting little law and order. Close families, sturdy farmers, and mushrooming cities are nearly nonexistent, with individualistic miners, outlaws, and cowboys dominating the scene. Still, women's virtue is protected even among bands of murderous outlaws. Indeed, sexual subjects overall are taboo. Plot tricks, including fantastic disguises, false identities, and strings of dramatic action, dominate the scene. Dimes novels were meant to entertain, titillate, and perhaps inform (often with false facts), and this work is no exception. Excessively sensational, unbelievable, and contrived, the story of Billy LeRoy (and some of Billy Bonney) evidently proved to be sufficiently entertaining and profitable to be reprinted twice. The novel also helped launch the legendary life of New Mexico's Billy the Kid, albeit in an imagined, altered form.

Also in 1881, the Las Vegas *Daily Optic* published an eleven-part serial entitled "The Dead Desperado, Adventures of Billy, the Kid, as Narrated by Himself." This brief account, more dime novel than biography (although it claimed to be the latter), does and does not follow the life story of Billy. The nameless author opens the story in

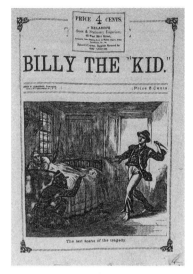

Billy the Kid, desperado. The early dime novels and the first newspaper accounts in the decades immediately after his death in 1881 pictured Billy in very dark terms, largely as a vicious desperado. Images in the author's collection.

a Santa Fe gambling establishment, where Billy threatens to kill a gambler who has tricked him in a card game. The narrator of the story, first called Charlie Fresh, then John Antrim, plays aimlessly with his names, but Billy takes a liking to him. They ride back to Billy's adobe castle to the south, where the Kid and his gang of a dozen or more outlaws hang out.

Billy then tells his history: his birth in Ireland; the poverty of his family; the death of his father; and the migration of his mother, his two sisters, and himself to Canada. Soon thereafter, his mother marries "an old reprobate named Antrim," who is depicted as a drunken dictatorial stepfather, and they move to Silver City. In short order, Billy gets into trouble, although he defends himself in arguing that if he had "received proper treatment from others," he would not have embarked on a career of violence and murder. Billy steals two or three items, and when a Chinese man "rats on him," he sneaks up on him and cuts his throat. Captured and jailed, Billy escapes through the chimney and heads off to Arizona, where he falls into the clutches of a bullying blacksmith. Unable to accept the blacksmith's abuse, Billy shoots him and dashes toward New Mexico. Then Billy kills the sheriff and a dozen others in the "tough tussle." Most of these stories are wrong historically.

Storyteller Billy zips through the last three years of his life in the eleventh and final installment of the series. His account spins a different version of the Lincoln jailbreak and the killing of two guards. The narrator, in the last four sentences, notes Billy's death but skips over the details.

Billy is depicted here as violent gunman always ready to take a life. But he is also painted as friendly, caring, and warm especially to the narrator. In all likelihood, the writer's pedestrian style, his lifeless story, and the numerous vague details kept the series from being published early on in book form. Plus publishers in the area already knew that Pat Garrett had completed a book on the Kid that would appear soon.

Neither of these two novels attracted much attention. Nor did Don Jenardo's (John Woodruff Lewis) *The True Life of Billy the Kid* (1881), but it was reprinted several decades later and attracted attention as one of the few available Kid dime novels. Jenardo-Lewis combines fact and fiction throughout his plot. Billy comes from New York to New Mexico, lives for a while in Silver City and Arizona, and then spends most of his days in Lincoln County, New Mexico. In the war Billy sides with John Chisum and Alex McSwain (McSween) and viciously opposes the Murphy-Dolan combine. He's involved in the killing of Sheriff Brady and posse members Morton and Baker and heads up a gang of thieves and shooters, after the firing of Lincoln. Pat Garret (Garrett) apprehends Billy, but the gunman breaks out by shooting deputies Bell and Ohlinger (Olinger). Garret catches up with Billy in Pete Maxwell's bedroom and shoots him—with Maxwell absent from the scene.

Most of these segments of Billy's story are mistakenly told or narrated from a different slant. Billy is a bloodthirsty killer, and John Chisum an equally barbaric cow thief. Lawrence Murphy, James Dolan, Sheriff Brady, and Pat Garrett are all good guys. Governments in Santa Fe and Washington, D.C., play almost no role, and Governor Wallace is portrayed as a weak-kneed, inconstant, deeply flawed leader.

The largest divergence from fact is the author's off-key treatment of Billy's character. The Kid is an unrepentant, pathological villain lacking any redeeming qualities. A diminutive, pale-faced killer, he murders dozens of people, even dipping his finger into the blood of some victims he has gunned down. His slight body lacks even one sympathetic or empathetic bone.

The other Billy dime novel reprinted in the twentieth century was Edmund Fable's *The True Life of Billy the Kid* (1881). In his preface. Fable argues that eastern readers have been led astray on Billy the Kid. These previous writers have portrayed Billy as rich, living in a castle, and armed with elegant, gentlemanly manners. These wrongheaded accounts, Fable tells us, were "made up of whole cloth"; if eastern readers believe these stories about Billy, they have as much understanding of the Kid "as a burro has of the beauties of Milton."

Fable states that William Bonny (Bonney) was born in New York in a "tenement house in the Fourth Ward of that city." After Billy's widowed mother failed to make a living on her own, she married Thomas Antrim (William Antrim) and moved west. Nearly all of this account is false or unconfirmed facts on names, place of marriage, and the role of William Antrim.

After being reared in Colorado, Billy sets off on his own and arrives in Silver City. On his first night there, he attends a dance, gets drunk, is robbed, and lands in jail on false charges. A pathbreaking point occurs, the author tells us, when Billy, suffering in jail under this trumped-up penalty, decides that thereafter "I'll hold my own with the best of them."

Escaping up the chimney, young Billy happens into a freighter's wagon and ends up in Lincoln County, New Mexico. Almost overnight, he kills a blacksmith threatening him and becomes embroiled in the Tontsill (Tunstall) and Chisom (Chisum) side of the county's civil war. When Chisom tries to cheat him, Billy kills his riders—killings, the author says, that show Billy as a "heartless Kid" guilty of "cold-blooded murder." The killings continue. Sometimes Billy thinks about his vicious actions but mostly gathers followers like Tom Phaller (Folliard) to help with rustling and killing.

None of the incidents Fable describes closely follows the actual events of Billy's final years. The murder of Sheriff Brady, the Lincoln shootout at the McSwain (McSween) house, the gunfight at the Muscalero (Mescalero) reservation, and finally Billy's death at the hands of Pat Garrett are wide of the historical mark. Fable's large promises of authenticity fail in nearly every aspect of the novel.

If readers expected to "get the facts" about Billy and the Lincoln Country War—and evidently some believed Fable's claim that he was telling the truth—they should have been disappointed with the novel's many distortions. Like nearly all the dime novels about the Kid, this one depicts Billy as a compulsive, pathological murderer. Fable's Billy lacks depth, warmth, or substance as a character; he enters numerous scenes in which he took no part; and he is kept from other events where he was a central figure. Those readers hungering and thirsting for a veracious, literary portrait of Billy the Kid would have to look elsewhere.

The Cowboy's Career; or, the Daredevil Deeds of Billy the Kid, the Noted New Mexico Desperado, by "One of the Kids"

(1881) exists with only three of its many chapters available to modern readers. It too presents the Kid as a merciless killer. He guns down McClusky (William McClosky), Morton (William), and Baker (Frank) without hesitation. Quickly thereafter, Billy also murders Sheriff William Brady and Deputy George Hindman at a Chisum ranch rather than on Lincoln's main street as it really happened. The shootout in Lincoln in July 1878 is almost entirely fanciful. Here was another portrait of Billy as a soulless murderer, with little veracious history.

Dime novelists sometimes played tricks on readers by reprinting earlier works under new titles, hoping to attract additional buyers. Such was the case with the novels of J. C. Cowdrick, who first published *Silver-Mask, the Man of Mystery; or, the Cross of the Golden Keys* in 1884. Then in 1890 the book was twice reprinted as *Billy the Kid from Texas; or, Silver Mask's Clew* and as *Billy, the Kid from Frisco.*

Most Billy the Kid dime novelists attempt to write parts of his actual biography and considerable historical context into their pages. But Cowdrick's work breaks from that usual mold. It is decidedly an imagined mystery story overflowing with action, adventure, and entertainment but with little emphasis on place, historical events, or known characters. The author spins a tale of drama and nonstop action.

Billy, the Kid makes sporadic, brief appearances. He is occasionally on scene, entering first to capture the story's heroine. In that episode and those that follow Billy is described as a "mighty chief," but is really "only a common cut-throat," as one character says. Another adds that Billy is "a man of great nerve and daring," and a third describes Billy as dressed something like a Mexican dandy.

On two different occasions, Billy escapes jailing even though closely guarded in a cabin. One of the desperado's opponents explains that the Kid is too strong and supported by too many followers to remain locked up. He "has got more friends right here in this very town than ye'd ever dream of." As predicted, Billy breaks out in a few hours. Later he will again break out of a lockup.

In the final sequence of events, Billy and his riders are caught up in the search for a Lost City and its hidden treasure. A mysterious figure, Silver-Mask, helps capture the Kid. Again Billy escapes. The final line, after the loose ends of other strands of the narrative have been braided, states: "How Billy, the Kid from 'Frisco ended his days, is known to all." Perhaps some readers understood this cryptic closing line. Most might have been puzzled since the novel never explains Billy's origins, the development of his character, his personal life, or what happened to him. Indeed, the novel's ending was but one more indication of how this Billy the Kid dime novel differs from others. Cowdrick had produced a mediocre dime novel that brought the Kid on scene but only as a minor background figure perhaps for interest's sake. In the end, he produced an enigmatic, mysterious story.

One of the last of the Billy the Kid dime novels, Francis Doughty's *Old King Brady and "Billy the Kid"* (1890), was published about a decade after the Kid's death in 1881. This work features a well-known New York detective, Old King Brady, pursuing Billy the Kid in a distant, lawless New Mexico. Like so many other dime novels, this one intersperses episodes of dramatic, violent conflict with scenes of adventure and travel. Dime novel authors kept readers engaged with gunfights and other horrendous clashes, then often followed with depictions of major characters traversing dramatic and also placid landscapes of a mysterious, scenic West.

Most memorable in this novel is the skewed depiction of Billy the Kid. He is the worst of human beings, a brutal murderer. He leads violent attacks, viciously assaults opponents, and kills on a whim. Early on, Billy shoots down a pious minister, who does nothing more than to try to protect his virtuous daughter from the Kid's rapacious actions. Later Billy kills several others, again without cause.

In the opening and closing scenes of the novel, Billy is described in the darkest of hues. As one acquaintance put it, Billy "is the blood thirstiest [*sic*] little cowpuncher whatever straddled a horse"; he "thinks he owns the earth." In the final sentences the narrator, taking to his pontificating pulpit, asserts that no one in New Mexico was "so vile a specimen as this bloodthirsty boy, whose chief delight was murder."

Regrettable, the East Coast author understood little about Billy and New Mexico. Doughty was the author of more than a thousand fictional works, including a series on Old King Brady, but his distorted comments undermined the authenticity of his fiction. Billy neither resided or hid out in Ojo Caliente in northern New Mexico nor lived in a cabin surrounded by a lake and rushing river. Once the Kid passed through the Silver City area in his flight to Lincoln County in 1877, he did not return to stay there; and he and old John Chisum were not hand-in-glove in mutually leading a murderous civil war in eastern New Mexico.

What Doughty's dime novel illustrated is that by the early 1890s a satanic Billy dominated portraits of him in fiction and biography. Nearly all the dime novels about the Kid—there were at least a dozen and perhaps as many as seventeen—portrayed a villainous Billy. When the dime novel depictions were combined with the dark views of Billy in contemporary national and New Mexican newspapers, a blackhearted Billy the Kid rode violently across fictional and biographical landscapes in the United States at the end of the nineteenth century and for the next quarter of century as well.

Three conclusions, among several others, about Billy the Kid dime novels are in order. First, these works rarely revealed much correct information about Billy; most were pure fiction rather than empirical history or biography. Second, nearly all the authors knew little about the Kid, his

bad-good character, his roles in the Lincoln County turmoil, or his strong contacts with Hispanics and romances
with several young women. But most importantly in their
excessively negative portrait of Billy the dime novelists, along
with newspaper stories coming to similar conclusions, sent
the Kid along the trail of legend as a murderous desperado.
These dime novels were the main ingredient of the satanic
Billy who rode through history as a bloodthirsty villain of
the worst order until the mid-1920s.

In spring 1882 the *Santa Fe New Mexican,* under the
name of New Mexican Printing & Pub., issued a pathbreaking book, *The Authentic Life of Billy, the Kid, the Noted
Desperado of the Southwest, Whose Deeds of Daring and
Blood Made His Name a Terror in New Mexico, Arizona
and Northern Mexico.* The listed author, "Pat. F. Garrett,"
is identified as "Sheriff of Lincoln C[ounty]., N. Mex., by
Whom He [Billy the Kid] Was Finally Hunted Down and
Captured by Killing Him." The author and publisher promised that the book would be a "Faithful and Interesting Narrative." The volume was a brief book, about 150 pages of
text with a half-dozen illustrations, and sold for fifty cents.
Some negative critics thought the title page carried as many
words as the book. Although Garrett's book became one
of the half-dozen most-important accounts in shaping later
stories about Billy the Kid, it flopped. The publisher, the
Santa Fe Daily New Mexican, was a leading daily newspaper in the territory. The newspaper company itself was
not a book publisher. The firm's naiveté and disorganization helped sink sales of the book, which sold but a few
hundred copies, was remaindered, and soon went out of
print. Ironically, however, *The Authentic Life* became the
chief source of information for other writers during the
next forty years and for other writers and movie-makers
well beyond the 1920s.

The back story of the book's production and publication, though little known and hazy, led to some of the dif-

ficulties in issuing Garrett's account and to its jumbled and unsatisfactory contents. Much more handy with a pistol than a pen, Garret was no wordsmith. Soon after the killing of Billy, Garrett became convinced that he had to shield himself from criticism and to compete with the sensational "yellowback fiction" (dime novels) then appearing and telling distorted stories about him and the Kid. Garrett had to tell his side of the Lincoln County conflict and the killing of the Kid, but he realized that he could not write that story and would need help—lots of it—with spinning the narrative. For that assistance he turned to his friend Marshall Ashmun "Ash" Upson, an experienced journalist and writer, who had lived for a time with the Garrett family. It is said that Garrett was offered $1,000 by the Santa Fe company, which he would divide with Upson.

Although Upson had urged Garrett to seek a nationally known publisher, the sheriff, with Ash in tow, began the book in fall 1881. Some are convinced that Upson, the ghostwriter, completed the book in less than three months before the end of the year. The publisher had promised publication in a month after receipt of the manuscript but, fumbling that end of the agreement, took up to five months to produce the book for sale. More specific conclusions about the writing and publishing of the *Authentic Life* are impossible to draw because no manuscript or correspondence are extant in an archive.

It is a near-fatal mistake, however, to focus only on the multiple miscues in the Garrett-Upson book. Although the volume is error-ridden, it was not seen as such by contemporaries. Early readers indeed viewed it as the first book-length biography of Billy, an authentic and factual account with more extensive coverage of his life than any previous work, and as the product of a writer who was an eyewitness to some of the happenings.

To understand the impact of the book on readers in the 1880s, however, one should emphasize how the Garrett-

Upson depiction of Billy clearly stood apart from the vitriolic portraits of him in most contemporary newspaper and dime novel accounts. In their first references and throughout most of their volume Garrett and Upson parted company with the journalists and dime novelists who delineated Billy as a heartless killer. In this departure, the Garrett-Upson account, the most important biographical account written about the Kid before the 1920s, pictured him as a bifurcated Billy. On the one hand he often resembled a trigger-happy shootist willing, as in the cases of Windy Cahill and J. W. Bell and Bob Olinger, to shoot others to protect his freedom or benefit his own future. On the other hand, the Kid was described as friendly, cheerful, congenial, courteous, and courageous, as many of his friends and acquaintances from his childhood in Silver City until his death in Fort Sumner remembered him during his short life.

Garrett and Upson paint Billy the Kid in these ambivalent hues. From the first references onward, Billy is a divided boy. Early on he "exhibited a spirit of reckless daring" but also "generous and tender feeling" that "rendered him the darling of young companions in his gentler moods, and their terror when the angry fit was on him." When just shy of ten he could be "bold, daring, and reckless" yet "open-handed, generous-hearted, frank and manly." Billy loved his mother, was helpful to the poor, and kind; on other occasions, when directly challenged "he sought such arms as he could buy, borrow, beg, or steal, and used them, upon more than one occasion, with murderous intent."

But when Garrett and Upson describe Billy's involvements in the bloody Lincoln Country War, they are more reproachful than sympathetic. For example, the Garrett-Upson duo write that the killing of Sheriff Brady, in which Billy participated, "would disgrace the record of an Apache." That murder, the authors add, "was a most dastardly crime on the part of The Kid, and lost him many friends who had, theretofore, excused and screened him." The writers also castigate Billy for his relentless rustling and unceasing violence.

Yet, in the final pages, in the midst of describing Billy's final days, Garrett and Upson salute the positive side of the Kid's character. Probably in Garrett's words more than Upson's the writers state that Billy "expressed no enmity towards me [Garrett] for having been the instrument through which he was brought to justice." In fact the Kid had shown "respect and confidence" in the sheriff, agreeing that he "had only done [his] duty, without malice."

Read as a whole, the Garrett-Upson volume notably departs from most of what was being written about Billy the Kid in the 1880s. Had other authors from the 1880s to the mid-1920s followed more closely the two-sided Kid portrayed in the *Authentic Life,* he might not have continued as the satanic Billy launched and elaborated on in pioneering journalistic and dime novel accounts.

The number of writings about the Billy the Kid never spiraled upward after 1890. And they would not pick up until after the appearance of Walter Noble Burns's *The Saga of Billy the Kid* (1926). Even though Frederick Jackson Turner came on line in the 1890s with his pathbreaking frontier thesis, Owen Wister's novel, *The Virginian,* (1902) became a bestseller, and the pioneering Western film, *The Great Train Robbery* (1903) stirred interest in a Wild West, that interest did not spark a plethora of biographies and novels about the Kid, and no extant films featuring a Kid character would be released until 1930. Perhaps readers were not interested in hearing more about a violent desperado, or perhaps even more importantly none of the leading Wild West demigods—for instance, George Custer, Wild Bill Hickok, Wyatt Earp, Calamity Jane, and the best-known Indian chiefs—were receiving much biographical attention. They would become notable attractions, however, for writers, readers, and moviegoers in the 1920s.

In the years from the mid-1880s to the early 1920s two writers provided nearly half the books and essays about Billy the Kid that gained notoriety among American readers. Cowboy writer Charles Siringo and journalist Emerson Hough wrote several books and essays about Billy in these years, and their differing conclusions about him belie the easy conclusion that from the dime novelists to the mid-1920s all writers portrayed the Kid as a notorious, murdering desperado.

In 1885 Siringo published his first book, *A Texas Cowboy: or, Fifteen Years on the Hurricane Deck of a Spanish Pony.* This rambling account of the newly popular cowboy—"the hired man on horseback"—and trail drives and open-range cowboying grabbed readers by the tens of thousands. The rapidly paced story remained steadily in print for nearly a half century and has been repeatedly reprinted since. Although Siringo probably rode hard into the land of exaggeration when he bragged his book sold a million copies, it did very well in the book market, giving American readers an engaging account of cowboying and ranching. If Siringo lived life at a gallop, his writings captured some of this high-speed, breathless action.

In chapters 18–30, the final third of *A Texas Cowboy,* Siringo moves in and out of the life of Billy the Kid. He had met the Kid for a few days in Texas during fall 1878, when Billy and his riders brought over a "herd of ponies" they had stolen in New Mexico and were trying to sell in the panhandle. In the three or four weeks that Billy remained near the sprawling LX Ranch, he and Charlie became well acquainted, chatting on several occasions and possibly exchanging gifts.

Perhaps Charlie identified with Billy's life. Early on nearly orphaned, both boys became teenage nomads, drifting from place to place without secure homes or jobs. Both had lived inside and outside the law, Billy mostly outside, Charlie mostly inside. From the first Charlie liked Billy and his riders; they were a "jovial crowd." After those weeks near Tascosa, Texas, Charlie never met Billy again, although two years later he rode with a Texas contingent hoping to track down and capture the Kid, after they recovered the Texas cattle Billy and his gang had stolen and taken to New Mexico. During those weeks in late 1880, Siringo got updates on Billy's doings, including his capture and jailing. He heard too about the jail break in spring 1881 and Billy's death at the hands of Pat Garrett.

After alluding to these unfolding events, Charlie provides in chapter 27 an eight-page essay entitled "A true sketch of 'Billy the Kid's' life." Siringo claimed he received or collected his information for this biographical sketch and other comments about the Kid from Billy himself, Ash Upson, and others who knew Billy firsthand. Much of Charlie's pen portrait is obviously taken whole cloth, errors and misinformation included, from the Garrett-Upson account published three years earlier. The cowboy writer claimed to be following first-person stories dealing with the Kid, but the abbreviated chapter follows much too closely the fabricated and error-riddled path of the Garrett-Upson volume. Charlie messed up on chronology, misspelled names, and stuck to the false information about Billy sojourning in Mexico. He also included such dramatic nonsense as Billy playing the piano in the McSween's burning house in Lincoln in July 1878.

More important, however, are Siringo's interpretations of Billy's character and the ways in which the cowboy writer directed and added to the legends beginning to surround the Kid. Siringo's Billy was "cool in time of danger," he "was not the cruel hearted wretch that he was pictured out to be in the scores of yellow-back novels [dime novels]," and was "noted as being kind to the weak and helpless." Overall, William H. Bonney became and remained "one of the coolest-headed, and most daring young outlaws that ever lived."

Still, Stiringo did not picture the Kid as a flawless saint. He was driven to kill men, especially those involved in the Tunstall murder. Even worse, "he would kill a man now and then, for what he supposed to be a just cause." And when seen whole, "maybe [he was] a very wicked youth." Accepting these damning aspects of the Kid's character, Siringo also wanted readers to remember that Billy "had some good qualities [too] which, now that he is no more, he should be credited with."

Hoping to cash in on Billy stories, Siringo brought the Kid into several later volumes but never with the success of his first Billy tales. In *A Lone Star Cowboy* (1919), Billy is not a major figure, and much of the brief description of the Kid repeats what Siringo said in *A Texas Cow Boy*. The cowboy author mentions Billy's violent crimes, but he is not pictured as a murderous desperado bent on killing at will. Charlie says that he and Billy "became quite chummy" in Tascosa in their only meeting in fall 1878. He claims too that he had gained further information about Billy from Charlie Wall, a fellow prisoner with the Kid in Lincoln in spring 1881. Charlie's descriptions of Billy's breakout in Lincoln and his death at the hands of Pat Garrett are straightforwardly told with concise, rather neutral, comment about Billy's character.

By time Siringo wrote his short biography, *History of "Billy the Kid,"* in 1920 he was coming to less forgiving conclusions about Billy. Written thirty-five years after his first work on Billy, this brief life story still followed closely the content of the Upson-Garrett biography, including many of the still-uncorrected errors. Although abbreviated, the book was Siringo's most extensive work on Billy. From its opening pages Siringo's biography speaks well of Billy. He was "a bright scholar" as a boy. He loved his "dear" mother and tried to protect her from evil men. He was "a good natured young man," loyal to his friends and "always cheerful and smiling." And he avoided drinking and helped people in need.

But Siringo's Kid is no paragon of virtue. Early on Billy was "associating with tough men and boys." Although usually of a "sunny disposition," Billy "had an ungovernable temper" when inflamed. For instance, after Tunstall's assassination, Billy was driven by "vengeance and hatred." Throughout his book, Siringo's tributes to Billy's good qualities are tempered by his denunciations of the Kid's serious faults. Near the end of his volume, Siringo speaks of Billy as "once the bravest, and coolest young outlaw who ever trod the face of the earth."

To his detriment Siringo was more a gatherer of tales than an energetic researcher, and he was careless with details. His chronology is jumbled, he misspells names, and gets several key events wrong. Even after thirty-five years of telling Kid stories, Siringo was still following the deeply flawed Upson-Garrett account, making little or no effort to search for verifiable, much less new, facts. Although Charlie promised to follow exactly what he learned from the Kid himself, Pat Garrett, Manuela Bowdre, and several other eyewitnesses, he plainly falls too often into the tangled thickets of error.

Surprisingly, this book was privately printed in 1920, as was *A Lone Star Cowboy* the previous year. Siringo's *Texas Cowboy*, his first book, had been wildly popular but not these two books published in 1919–1920. Had Billy—and Siringo too—fallen that far in notoriety? Second, Siringo moves little beyond the research contained in his earlier writings. Third, he fails to deal with several important persons in the Lincoln County story, including Alex and Susan McSween, Jimmy Dolan, and Lew Wallace.

Most of all, however, Siringo should be remembered as a clear exception to the negative portraits of Billy the Kid that dominated newspaper stories, dime novels, and other books and essays published from 1880 to 1925. If Siringo's Billy was no saint, neither was he a devilish desperado.

Emerson Hough's background and experiences differed markedly from those of Charlie Siringo. The author of *A Texas Cow Boy* learned his western yarns in the saddle on a cowpony and around a cattle-drive trail, but Hough gained his education through a philosophy degree at the University of Iowa and a subsequent law degree, and in his work as a writer and journalist. After failing at several jobs, Hough moved to White Oaks to practice law and write for newspapers and magazines. After nearly two years in New Mexico, Hough returned to the Midwest and eventually became a very successful author of numerous books, including several on the American West. But like Siringo, Hough would never have won a gold star for accuracy.

From his earliest writings dealing with New Mexico Hough clearly exhibited his dislike of Billy the Kid. *The Story of the Cowboy*, and an essay, "Billy the Kid: The True Story of a Western 'Bad Man,'" published in *Everybody's Magazine* (1901) illustrated Hough's hostility toward the Kid. Even though the Southwest was a place "full of horse thieves and outlaws," the "worst of those" obviously was "the notorious cutthroat . . . Billy." Backed by his violent followers, Billy "inaugurated a reign of terror, which made his name a dread from one end of the country to the other." Even worse, Billy on one occasion captained a murderous ride that led to the killing of seven Mexicans, which, Hough asserted, Billy had done "just to see them kick." Although the Kid had many friends, it was dangerous to oppose him in any way. If so, "he simply shot the man, laughed about it, and rode on."

Hough's motivation to depict a dark and malevolent Billy continued in his essay, "Billy the Kid." For Hough, Billy was the "most thoroughly bad of all the bad men in the really bad times of the West." Moreover, he was a "little wild beast," "an animal . . . born with a cat soul, blood-thirsty, loving to kill."

246

In many of these negative comments about Billy, Hough was far off the mark. In *Story of the Cowboy,* Hough contends Billy had killed twenty-three men, one for each of his twenty-three years. Four years later in "Billy the Kid," he states that the count was twenty-one deaths in twenty-one years, not counting those Mexicans he murdered "just to see them kick." Hough's errors add up. He has Billy at age fourteen—in Arizona—killing a man who insulted his mother. The details of Billy's escape from the Lincoln jail and his death at the hands of Pat Garrett are mostly wrong. He also greatly exaggerates the violence of the Lincoln Country War, declaring that four hundred people were killed in the clashes.

For Hough, the West was a wild place, with thousands of unruly and uncivilized men mostly mixed-bloods including "Greasers" [Mexicans]. There were "few [women] entitled to the name of womanhood," and he concluded, "Of civilization . . . there was nothing." Billy grew up in these wild surroundings, both influenced by the lawless setting and adding to the widespread violence.

In *Story of the Outlaw* (1907), Hough repudiated Billy less than in previous works. In a chapter entitled "Biographies of Bad Men," Hough provides a compact personal portrait of the Kid and treats him in other chapters as well. Perhaps the more favorable portrait of Billy and the correction of several egregious factual errors resulted from Hough's additional research into Billy's life and his conversations with Pat Garrett. Hough, after boasting about his research, states that this book told "the story of the Lincoln County War of the Southwest . . . truthfully for the first time, and after full acquaintance with sources of information now inaccessible or passing away."

An ambivalent tone emerges from Hough's descriptions in *Story of the Outlaw.* The author trots out the familiar boast that Billy killed one man for each of his years, but he later admits that this is "a matter of disagreement," with

Garrett reducing the total to eleven or less. Then Hough goes off track to say Billy killed several Apaches, several gamblers, then more Apaches, Mexicans, Frank Baker and Billy Morton, Bob Beckwith, Sheriff Brady, Morris Bernstein, Joe Grant, Jimmy Carlyle, and finally J. W. Bell and Bob Olinger. When Billy and his gang were involved in a group killing, Hough usually singles out Billy as the killer.

Yet, after listing all these horrendous acts of violence, Hough can admit that the Kid had another side to him, something the writer was reluctant to do in his previous writings about Billy. He "had very many actual friends, whom he won by his pleasant and cheerful manner," and he "was very popular among the Mexicans." Most of all Billy was gregarious, "hopeful and buoyant, never glum or grim, and he nearly always smiled when talking."

Lest one misread Hough's point of view, he ended with a negative but satisfying image. The conclusion of his pen portrait of the Kid states that "his deeds brought him his deserts at last." He must be remembered "as one of the most desperate desperadoes ever known in the West."

Four years after Hough's earlier excoriation of Billy in *Everybody's Magazine,* journalist Arthur Chapman turned out a similarly dark vignette of the Kid. Published in *Outing Magazine,* Chapman's "Billy the Kid: A Man All 'Bad,'" repeats Hough's assertion that Billy killed Mexicans "just to see them kick." He also charges the Kid with killing Chisum cowboys. Billy is, according to Chapman, "the only white man who slew out of pure wantonness." Chapman's Billy is an "effeminate individual," "the worst desperado in the history of the frontier." He killed a man for every one of his twenty-one years. Chapman was also the person who traveled the story that when Judge Warren Bristol sentenced Billy to hang "by the neck until you are dead, dead, dead," Billy fired back "And you can go to hell, hell, hell!" No facts substantiate either of these distortions.

Chapman depicts the Lincoln County War as a bloody, destructive conflict between legitimate cattle ranchers and lawless livestock thieves. Billy, for Chapman, captains the thieves. There is no mention here of the Murphy-Dolan gang or The House. Nor does he bring in Thomas Catron, the Santa Fe Ring, and the anti-Billy forces in the courts. Chapman describes Pat Garrett as a sturdy, heroic lawman.

Chapman's brief essay fits comfortably into the dark pictures of Billy the Kid that appeared from the 1890s to mid-1920s. In addition, it suffers from many of the same mistakes that undermined most of these writings.

Not many writers of fiction or drama chose Billy the Kid as subjects for their novels or plays, but a few did. These writers were on both sides of the Kid, some viewing him as a blackguard of the worst sort and others as a young man shaped by the unfortunate circumstances of his life.

Not surprisingly, Emerson Hough condemned Billy in his early novel, *Heart's Desire* (1905). The Kid plays a distant, minor role in this romantic, sentimental novel set in edenic Heart's Desire, Hough's fictional version of White Oaks, New Mexico. Billy never appears on scene, although Hough includes a short and largely imagined chapter on Billy's capture at Stinking Spring. Sheriff Ben Stillson (Pat Garrett) and a small posse capture Billy and some of his gang and haul them off to Las Vegas, after, Hough mistakenly says, they had broken out of jail. Hough was as careless with his history in his fiction as in his histories.

Rather, Hough portrays a woman-starved passel of men in Heart's Desire who see their place as a Valhalla, until a married woman with daughters, another woman, and two young twin girls invade their domicile. The women represent civilization (the East, the "States") and disrupt the outlook of a gaggle of cowboys, errant former husbands, miners, and men at odds with the demands of family, occupation, and responsibility. Hough evidently had tongue in cheek in most of his comments on women as barriers to masculine independence. When given the opportunity, the freedom-loving men welcome the females who come on scene. The author seems uninterested in linking the disruptions of Billy the Kid to areas surrounding Heart's Desire and to the contest of genders inside the small town.

O. Henry (William Sydney Porter) obviously drew on the Billy the Kid story in his short fictional work, "The Caballero's Way," which appeared in 1905 in his short story collection, *Heart of the West*. Most of the historical details are radically changed in O. Henry's tale. The young, "quick-tempered" hero, named the Cisco Kid—but "Kid" for short—has killed a large number of men, "mostly Mexicans." When O. Henry writes that the Kid killed Mexicans just "to see them kick," he was obviously referencing Hough's wrong-headed history and racist conclusions in his earlier writings. O. Henry's Cisco Kid can shoot faster "than any sheriff or ranger," and the señorita, Tonia Perez, loves him.

Things change overnight for Tonia and the Kid when Lieutenant Sandridge, a blond sun god, is sent to capture the desperado Kid. The half-Mexican Tonia, of Spanish Basque heritage, and the soldier immediately fall for one another, imperiling the Kid's love. He learns of Tonia's infidelity, overhearing her comments about him as El Chivato but also her new-found love for the blond giant. Later after the lieutenant leaves the Kid rides to hug Tonia and acts as if nothing is amiss.

In a quick O. Henry ending, the Kid writes the lieutenant a letter. Disguised as having been writing by Tonia, it says the Kid will be dressed as the Mexican girl and urges the officer to kill the disguised girl immediately. Thinking he has been told the truth, Sandridge smiles and shoots several times, only to find that the Cisco Kid has gotten his revenge by inducing the lieutenant to murder his novia rather than the outlaw.

The popularity of the Cisco Kid in subsequent writings and movies indicated that Kid-like figures in disguise could attract large crowds of readers and viewers. As time went on, however, the depictions of the Cisco Kid were less racially derogatory and increasingly modeled on Billy the Kid.

Four years after Hough's *Heart's Desire* appeared as the first novel dealing with the Kid after the sensational dime novels, Irish American writer P. S. McGeeney published *Down at Stein's Pass* (1909). McGeeney's novel was similar to Hough's in several ways. Both avoided the sensationalism of the dime novel Billy, but both depicted the Kid as a despicable villain nonetheless. The two novels portrayed Billy (or "Billie" in McGeeney's book) as a minor character who is absent for most of the plot.

In other areas, however, McGeeney moves in new directions. He sets his work in western New Mexico in the town of Stein's Pass and nearby ranch areas. Alden Raymond is working as a government engineer in the area before the arrival of Billie who heads up a group of gunslingers. Billie's gang captures and ties up Patrick Livingston, who then befriends Raymond after the engineer frees him. The growing friendship of these two and Raymond's conflicts with Livingston's stepbrother, Frances Livingston, who has hired Billie and his gang for support, are the cruxes of the novel.

Down at Stein's Pass is largely ahistorical, capturing little of the real life of Billy the Kid. True, Pat Garrett is on scene as sheriff of Grant County and something of a hero. But his actions and those of Billie, save for the sheriff's killing of Billie at Maxwell's "ranch," are far removed from their actual lives in Lincoln County. Indeed, McGeeney so manipulates his plot with manufactured surprises, mistaken or mysterious identities, and convenient memory losses that his novel fails as historical fiction.

On the other hand, McGeeney's novel fits comfortably into some interpretive modes of Billy trending in the early twentieth century. The Kid is not the sensationally murderous young man of the dime novels, and his death in *Down at Stein's Pass,* as it will be in Burns's forthcoming biography, is a significant harbinger of the future constructions of Billy. As the narrator puts it, Billy's demise brought the end of "outlawry in New Mexico" and paved the way "to times of peace and security."

In another area of interpretation, the first drama to circulate widely, Walter Wood's *Billy the Kid* (1903, 1906), avoided the disparaging views in the Hough and McGeeney novels and the O. Henry short story, instead dramatizing the Kid as the product of a fractured family, a legacy that he is able to overcome. Registered first in 1903, then revised, copyrighted, and produced on stage in 1906, the play was immensely popular, drawing, one source says, six million viewers in the first six years of its performance from 1906 to 1912. Wood's play portrayed a Kid much at odds with the Billy of most literary depictions from the early twentieth century. Billy has been driven off course by the lying, cheating, and betrayal of his father, who kills the Kid's mother and stepfather. These vicious acts send Billy reeling into a life of outlawry. But as the drama makes clear, Billy has a good, virtuous heart even if he has broken the law on several occasions—all off scene. Given an opportunity for redemption, he finally chooses that path in the closing scene.

Despite all the usual conventions of melodrama—several mistaken identities, fortuitous chance and circumstances, Billy dressed as a maid, and some attempts at Irish humor— the drama raises intriguing questions. Had Billy gone bad because he was forced or driven in that dark direction, or was he a bad man at heart? The playwright clearly thinks the former, showing that Billy prays, has a sense of God's "divine will," and realizes he can change direction, which he does in the closing lines, embracing his beloved Nellie and heading east "where there is no trouble, sin or sorrow."

In 1925, New Mexico writer Harvey Fergusson raised another important question for those interested in Billy the

Kid—then and now. "Who remembers Billy the Kid?" Fergusson wrote. "He is no more than the echo of a name today. . . ." The author went on to claim that Billy epitomized the "primitive pastoral epic" of the West's history that emerged after the Civil War and flourished into the 1880s.

Although Fergusson had already gained a reputation as a compelling historical novelist, his account of Billy, published in the American Mercury in 1925, was rife with errors. He has Billy hating stepfather William Antrim, stabbing a man to death in Silver City, and befriending outlaw Jessie Evans there. Arizona is overlooked in Fergusson's brief piece, and then the author sends him to Mexico, killing often when he thinks the violence is warranted. He also mistakenly depicts Billy as Alex McSween's leader early on in the Lincoln County fight. But he gets right the conflict between The House (Murphy-Dolan) and the Chisum-Tunstall-McSween combine, much more specifically and correctly than most others writing in the early twentieth century.

One of Fergusson's quickly made and undeveloped conclusions embodies an important insight for understanding interpretations of Billy the Kid by the mid-1920s. Fergusson views the Kid as the last gasp of the Wild West in New Mexico that, with Billy and others like him gone, could transition into a more civilized, forward-looking place. That view, of a closing frontier and an approaching postfrontier society, fits well with ideas about the West during the Progressive Era of the late nineteenth and early twentieth centuries. The historical writings of Theodore Roosevelt, Frederick Jackson Turner, and Frederic Logan Paxson, the novels of Owen Wister, B. M. Bower, and Zane Grey, and the movies starring Broncho Billy Anderson, William S. Hart, and Tom Mix subscribed to the closing-frontier thesis. For the most part these writers and actors reacted more ambivalently to the vanishing frontier than did Fergusson in his essay, and these writers and actors might not have seen Billy the Kid epitomizing the dying frontier and Pat Garrett ushering in a new law-and-order West. But all saw a West in transition, moving from a violent open frontier to what . . . they were not quite sure.

There was a second stage to the closing-frontier story. One might, like Hough—and Upson-Garrett earlier—view Garrett as helping end a lawless Wild West, but these writers, especially historians and novelists, were reluctant to move on to writing about a postfrontier, maybe a new West with its own regional identity. For well more than a half century, in some cases up to the 1970s, writers, filmmakers, and aficionados of popular culture remained fascinated with the Old West. They were fixated on a frontier alive with larger-than-life characters such as Billy the Kid or depicting a closing frontier with agents of civilization such as Sheriff Garrett ending the Kid's wild ways and opening the West to families, farms, and towns. The popularity of Buffalo Bill's traveling arena show, Wild West, from the 1880s to World War I, the huge sales of Owen Wister's bestseller, *The Virginian* (1903), and the names of Broncho Billy, William S. Hart, and Tom Mix on movie marquees were revealing illustrations of the celebration of the Kid's Wild West and the coming of law and order to end an Old West that had outlived its time. And that love affair with the Wild West, as we shall see, continued well past the mid-1920s.

14

Billys of Another Kind, 1926–1960

The Old West was reborn in the 1920s. Like the closing decades of the nineteenth century and the later 1950s, the decade and a half following World War I seemed aflame with interest in a Wild West. This fascination burned across nearly every facet of American cultural life. In the 1920s Zane Grey's yearly fictional Westerns topped bestseller lists, and cinematic Westerns, by far, were the most-popular movie genre. Likewise in the twenties frontier histories by Frederick Jackson Turner and Frederic Logan Paxson won major acclaim, and hundreds of thousands of Americans flocked west to rough it easy on dude ranches sprouting up all over the West. For the next two generations until about 1960, biographers and historians, novelists, and filmmakers produced numerous treatments of Billy the Kid. Some moved in new directions to depict a more heroic young man, others continued to portray him as a violent desperado, and still others were already giving hints of the bifurcated Billy— both rascal and hero—that would dominate depictions of him after 1960.

Journalists and historians were the most prolific of those treating Old West figures, churning out in the 1920s and early 1930s more than two dozen book-length biographies of lively western heroes and heroines. These appealingly written biographies were part and parcel of the Old West story that gradually solidified in the first decades of the twentieth century. Buffalo Bill Cody, Wyatt Earp, Wild Bill Hickok, Calamity Jane, and Billy the Kid—all these demigods were the subject of at least one biography in the decade stretching from the mid-twenties to the mid-thirties. Nearly all the biographies came from journalists; nearly all these writers wrote positive or at least sympathetic portraits of their subjects and of the closing frontier they depicted.

Walter Noble Burns's romantic biography *The Saga of Billy the Kid*, published in 1926, illustrated and enlarged on these appealing pictures of the Old West. This life story by a Chicago journalist about one of the Old West's most written-about characters won immediate attention, laurels, and mounting sales. Reviewers in the *New York Times Book Review*, *Harper's Monthly*, and several newspapers, including some in New Mexico, praised Burns's *Saga* as a dramatically written, interesting, and authentic account of Billy the Kid and the Lincoln County War. And Bernard DeVoto, who in subsequent decades would be lionized as a western historian of distinctive narrative power, praised Burns's story of the Kid as "a serious biography done with considerable literary charm." No previous biographers, DeVoto added, could match Burns's "detached and scholarly approach to the facts and, notably, his literary skill." It was a book "not only fascinating in its subject but equally fascinating in its content and final in its decisions."

The praise for Burns was not universal, however. Maurice Garland Fulton, a professor at the New Mexico Military Institute then beginning his thorough, decades-long research on the Lincoln County War, worried about what he considered "inaccuracies" in Burns's research. He also thought the author had sensationalized Billy's story. One year after the publication of *Saga*, writer Eugene Manlove Rhodes, already a New Mexican author with a national reputation, published in *Sunset Magazine* an essay entitled "In Defense of Pat Garrett." Although Rhodes praised the

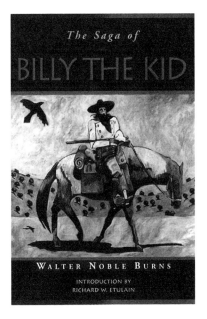

Walter Noble Burns, *The Saga of Billy the Kid.* First published in 1926, Burns's biography presented, for the most part, a positive portrait of Billy the Kid. Burns romanticized the Kid's life story and encouraged more-sympathetic pictures of Billy in following years. This reprint of the *Saga,* published in 1999, includes an introduction by historian Richard W. Etulain. Reproduction of book cover courtesy of the University of New Mexico Press, Albuquerque.

"color, fire and charm" of Burns's book, he thought the Chicago journalist had made Billy into a "hero" and Pat Garrett "the heavy" and thus had produced a "misleading" history. Burns himself might not have castigated Garrett, but he had allowed, Rhodes added, for a full airing of the criticisms of Garrett and his actions in killing Billy. Rhodes's comments are all the more surprising since Burns ended his book with praise for Garrett, concluding that in shooting Billy, Garrett had ended a lawless era of frontier history and helped bring to New Mexico badly needed law and order.

Rhodes was also mistaken in suggesting that Burns had produced a one-sided story favoring Billy the Kid. This biography instead featured a more complex, nuanced account of the Kid. True enough, Burns was much less dismissive of Billy than were the earlier newspapers, dime novels, and writings of Emerson Hough. Burns opens his book by noting how much Billy was embraced in New Mexico. Many residents adored Billy, with men often speaking "of him with admiration" and women touting "his gallantry and lament[ing] his fate." So loved was Billy, Burns states, that his "crimes are forgotten or condoned, while his loyalty, his gay courage, his superman adventures are treasured in affectionate memory."

After detailing New Mexico's admiration of the Kid, Burns reveals his own attitudes toward Billy. He was not, by any means, "an inhuman monster reveling in blood." Rather he was "bright," had an "alert mind," and was "generous, not unkindly," a young man of "quick sympathies." Moreover, he "was cheerful, hopeful, talkative, given to laughter." And he was honest, courteous, especially to women, and loyal beyond expectation. Burns finds much about Billy's character to praise.

Conversely, Burns also speaks about the Kid's darker side. Billy was a killer, and Burns cannot accept the Kid's part, for example, in the murder of Sheriff Brady on Lincoln's main street. These were deeds of "desperate and lawless men." Where Billy might be saluted for his "knightly devotion" to his friends and women, he was also driven by "a spirit of primitive savagery." In fact Billy had a split personality, his noble characteristics continually vying with his "desperado complex" for control of his life.

Well before a Jekyll-and-Hyde Billy came on the scene in the 1960s and 1970s and dominated interpretations of him for nearly a half century, Burns had introduced this conflicted character in the mid-1920s. Burns might be guilty of romanticizing the Kid, of embellishing the facts of the Lincoln County story, and in introducing inaccuracies, but in the long run his characterization of Billy as a bifurcated young man with both positive and negative personal attributes, foreshadowed a later, more thoughtful, widely accepted view of a complex Billy the Kid.

The Saga of Billy the Kid so dominated the scene from the mid-1920s to the 1950s that other writers were hesitant to undertake a full-scale biography of Billy. Some writers, including Miguel Antonio Otero Jr., William A. Keleher, Maurice Garland Fulton, and Philip Rasch, were able to escape the overshadowing influences of Walter Noble Burns, but most of the other writings in these three decades were reminiscent or hearsay accounts.

Otero, former New Mexico territorial governor (1897–1906), published his brief book, *The Real Billy the Kid* in 1936. Part biography, part memoirs of the Lincoln County War participants, and part imagined conversations, Otero's life story of the Kid had limited sales and elicited little national attention. Clear contributions of Otero's work conflicted with equally evident limitations.

In New Mexico, Otero obviously traveled with those who much admired the Kid—indeed unabashedly loved him. On one occasion Otero evinces his support for the outlaw by stating baldly that he wishes the Kid could have escaped when he was in jail in Santa Fe. In 1926, accompanied by photographer and note-taker Marshall Bond, Otero traveled to southeastern New Mexico in the summer following the publication of Burns's *Saga of Billy the Kid*. The former governor interviewed several persons who knew Billy, some of whom had even taken part in the fighting in Lincoln County. He spoke to, among others, Susan McSween Barber, Paulita Maxwell Jaramillo, George Coe, Frank Coe, and "Don Martin Chavez." He also read some of what Ash Upson and Pat Garrett had written or told others. Otero paid special attention to Hispanics and their remembrances of Billy and the Lincoln County War. Although in the book Otero claims his aim was "to write a story, without embellishment, based entirely on fact," he often creates conversations and frequently inserts quotations of Billy, for which there are no clear sources.

In all ways Otero's Billy was a young man to ride the river with. Courageous, energetic, and willing to move on, Billy drew people to him, especially women and Hispanics. For

Otero, Billy "was good and had fine qualities," and returning a stolen horse after his Lincoln jail escape proved him a "perfect gentleman." Yes, when "hounded like a mad dog," as he often was, and "when finally aroused," his "ungovernable temper" took hold, and in "angry moods" he could embark on violent journeys. But these were the exceptions in his life.

In several ways the accuracy and value of Otero's abbreviated biography is foreshortened through his errors. The reminiscences of Otero's interviewees, such as the Coe cousins, and the accounts of writers such as Upson and Garrett were followed too closely without the author's raising questions about many of their shaky conclusions. If Otero had made more use of earlier newspaper stories, government reports, and county records, his book could have been more authentic and reliable. In general he believed too forcefully the accounts of others without clearing up discrepancies, correcting mistakes, and keeping his voice at the forefront of the narrative. Otero's inadequate research, a failing in most accounts of Billy written before the 1950s, also limited the value of his book.

In roughly the thirty years after the appearance of Walter Noble Burns's *Saga of Billy the Kid,* three other writers came to the fore as thorough, solid, and indefatigable researchers on Lincoln County stories. Maurice Garland Fulton, a longtime professor of literature at the New Mexico Military Institute in Roswell, began his work on southeastern New Mexico in the early 1920s although his major work, *History of the Lincoln County War* (1968), was not published until well after his death in 1955. Albuquerque lawyer and historian William A. Keleher launched his research on New Mexico history in the 1920s and published in the 1940s and 1950s several solid books on New Mexico. The third member of the triumvirate was Philip J. Rasch, a Ph.D. in physical education, who began publishing his numerous essays on Billy the Kid and contextual stories in the late

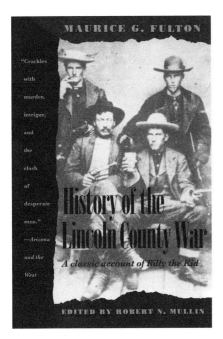

Maurice Garland Fulton, *History of the Lincoln County War,* 1968. Based on the thorough research of Professor Fulton and edited by his friend, Robert N. Mullin, this well-written history provides a thorough and still-valuable overview of the Lincoln County War and its major conflicts. Reproduction of book cover courtesy of the University of Arizona Press, Tucson.

1940s and continued producing his valuable, brief writings for the next four decades. Fulton, Keleher, and Rasch were trustworthy researchers, fact-finders, and no-nonsense historians. Breaking from the romantic approach Burns introduced in the 1920s, Fulton and Keleher provided the first extensive works on the Lincoln County War, and Rasch produced the first well-researched essays on Billy and his family. Although Fulton and Keleher saw Billy as a latecomer and rather minor figure in the conflict until after July 1878, Rasch focused much of his path-breaking research on the Kid and his family. All three authors won more laurels for their detailed, balanced research than for the literary qualities of their books and essays.

Fulton, the son of a professor and university chancellor and himself the holder of a master's degree with college-teaching experience, was the first academic scholar to write a book about the Lincoln County War and Billy the Kid. Although often promised and repeatedly delayed, his *History of the Lincoln County War,* edited by Robert Mullin, proved to be a turning point in the examination of the life and legends of Billy the Kid. Even left unfinished at his death, the content and point of view of this significant book had been partially introduced in the decades from the 1920s to the 1950s. Fulton's volume introductions and comments, his essays, and chiefly his voluminous personal correspondence foreshadowed what would appear later in his book.

Within a half-dozen years after his arrival in New Mexico in 1922, Fulton was recognized as a dependable source on the history of Lincoln County and writings about Billy the Kid. In fact, five years after landing in Roswell, Fulton displayed his assertiveness and his knowledge of his new home region by taking on Walter Noble Burns. Reading a Burns essay, based on his forthcoming *Saga,* in *Frontier* magazine in 1925, Fulton wrote the author to point out what he considered mistakes in the essay and to suggest the book itself might also contain misleading information. Not surprisingly, Burns replied that he had carefully researched the book, and it would not contain errors.

Two years later, in a sign of Fulton's rising eminence as an authority on Lincoln County and Billy the Kid, the well-known publisher Macmillan asked him to serve as editor of a reprint of Pat Garrett's *Authentic Life of Billy, the Kid.* Fulton's introduction and brief editorial notes illustrated how much regional history he had learned by 1927, after only five years in New Mexico. As editor and annotator, Fulton aimed at a "refurbished" Garrett biography of the Kid. These changes entailed cleaning up writing errors, stylistic miscues, and obscure language. Fulton also corrected chronological slipups such as placing the shooting of Buckshot Roberts before rather than after the murder of Sheriff Brady and reducing Billy's possible killings from the widely and falsely reported twenty-one and the estimated eleven of Pat Garrett. Alongside the corrections, Futon added information from newspapers, interviews with eyewitnesses such as John P. Meadows, and Kid quotations to expand Billy's story.

Like his later writings, Fulton's comments and annotations in this new edition were balanced and reasoned. As a scholar, Fulton did not angle to boost one side or the other in evaluating Garrett's book. Even while noting the excesses of Ash Upson in the opening pages of the new edition, he praised the volume as factual and its "faithfulness" to "true facts." The biography, Fulton insisted, was a "fair and sympathetic portrayal of the Kid."

This evenhanded approach carried over to Fulton's contentions throughout his contributions to the reprint of *The Authentic Life*. He agreed with Garrett's refusal to depict the Kid as a "murderous, super outlaw" and concluded that Billy was the product of a violent, uncivilized West. The Kid's "zeal for vengeance" after Tunstall's assassination and his "native capacity for leadership" undoubtedly powered Billy's behavior and choices from 1878 forward.

An even more sympathetic portrait of Pat Garrett emerges. The sheriff did his job, even if that meant doggedly pursing an acquaintance, although not a close friend. Most of all, through his courageous actions Garrett brought much-needed law and order to southeastern New Mexico, thereby helping to rein in an often unstable and dangerous Wild West.

Fulton was guilty of a few mistakes and left out other key facts. He wrongly listed Billy's first killing as that of a man in Silver City who had insulted his mother, incorrectly cited Fort Bowie as the site of Billy's shooting of Windy Cahill, and seemed willing to admit that Billy probably killed a few unnamed Mexicans and Indians. Nor did Fulton clarify anything about Billy's role in the possible killing of Jimmy

Carlyle at the Greathouse Ranch shootout or the likely romantic relationships between the Kid and Paulita Maxwell or any other young women in the Fort Sumner area.

Several other writers responded to Fulton's edited edition of the Garrett volume. Noted New Mexico novelist Eugene Manlove Rhodes wrote to Fulton in May 1927, praising the reprint of Garrett's book and noting that he thought an all-out war explained and maybe even permitted such actions as the murder of Sheriff Brady. The Chisum-Murphy conflicts were similar to the violent, senseless, and bloody battles of World War I and the frenzied combat between the "damyankees and johnnyrebs" in the Civil War. But Rhodes wanted Fulton to know that he considered Burns's *Saga of Billy the Kid* "one-sided," with the journalist allowing "his enthusiasms to runaway with him."

On 12 December 1927 Burns wrote to congratulate Fulton for his editorial work on Garrett's book. Fulton thanked the Chicago journalist for his "kind letter" and then explained that he hoped his annotations helped bring to light the "conflicting accounts" of the Kid and thus "promote discussion." Fulton also provided an early inkling of what would prove to be his long-delayed work on Lincoln County. He told Burns he was now writing a history of the Lincoln County War, on which he had "gathered a good many forgotten and overlooked details." He hoped "that this book . . . [would] be completed by spring [of 1928]." Fulton was even thinking of organizing "a Societry [*sic*] of Writers on Billy the Kid" and thought Burns "should be a charter member." But thirty years later the promised book was still not finished. Fulton often dreamed well beyond his ability to complete major projects.

Fulton was on the fast track to gather information, however. No facts were more valuable than the information and opinions he gathered from Susan McSween Barber. Soon after arriving in Roswell, Fulton made contact with McSween Barber, who, after a successful career as a cattle rancher, had retired on diminishing returns to a very modest home in the semi–ghost town of White Oaks. Lying only about a hundred miles northwest of Roswell, White Oaks nonetheless seemed something of an unbridgeable distance because Fulton did not drive, and his teaching duties at the New Mexico Military Institute kept him busy six days a week. He frequently missed opportunities to visit with Susan or failed to keep his promises of scheduled trips. In nearly every letter between the two from 1925 to Susan's death in 1931 Fulton, counter to Susan's desired partisan account of the county war, tried to explain he was attempting to write a nonpartisan story of the battles. He assured her, in a lengthy letter dated 21 July 1928, that he was convinced "the McSween party were more in the right than the Dolan party." But when Susan heard that Fulton would edit a reprint of Garrett's biography, that he talked to Murphy-Dolan partisans, and that he contacted Lily Casey Klasner, whom Susan detested, these research efforts, McSween Barber confessed, "sent a dagger to my heart." Susan wished for a strong, full book on the Lincoln County story, but not surprisingly she wanted it to advocate and confirm her point of view.

Over time Fulton proved to be an indecisive scholar and a long-term procrastinator. Nothing major came from his pen in the next few years. He did locate a dime novel–like biography on the Kid published in the *Santa Fe New Mexican* in late 1882. Fulton published excerpts from that newspaper series in folklorist B. A. Botkin's regional magazine, *Folk-Say* (1930). He also contributed in 1949–1950 a brief piece entitled "Billy the Kid in Life and Books" to the *New Mexico Folklore Record*.

Fulton was also called on to prepare an introduction to a reprint of John W. Poe's *The Death of Billy the Kid* (1933). Fulton's comments in this account by Pat Garrett's deputy clearly indicate his increasing distaste for the Kid. Billy was a "young hotblood," and "if not literally the scourge of the

Southwest," he obviously was "a general nuisance, not to say an appreciable menace." Fulton also revealed his conclusions on several controversies roiling about Billy: he had killed Jimmy Carlyle at the Greathouse Ranch; he had not gone to Fort Sumner to see Paulita Maxwell; and he had not carried a pistol into Pete Maxwell's darkened bedroom late on 14 July 1881. On the Paulita rumor Fulton was explicit. Even though stories of a Billy romance with "one of the Maxwell daughters [Paulita]" abounded in New Mexico and beyond, Fulton dissented: "The present writer himself discounts heavily the echoes of the old gossip [about the romance] that may still be heard or found in print."

In the next two decades Fulton pursued the long-delayed book on Lincoln County. His papers now on file at the University of Arizona Library overflow with information from his tireless tracking of Lincoln County and Billy the Kid stories. He often corresponded with other Kid aficionados, including a wide array of lay and professional historians and biographers also researching Billy the Kid. Sometimes Fulton revealed his findings to these correspondents; on other occasions, he abruptly refused to divulge his hard-wrought discoveries, telling others of his lack of funding, his heavy teaching schedule, and the necessity of keeping his research private. The Fulton manuscript collection is packed with his lengthy, fact-filled correspondence, suggesting that writing letters came easier to him than drafting his long-promised book. On occasion Fulton would write several pages to novelists such as Edwin Corle and Charles Neider, urging them not to mistreat historical fact as they pursued their fictional purposes. A professor of English with a sensitivity to literary goals and achievements, Fulton was much more friendly and helpful to novelists than to most biographers and historians dealing with Billy the Kid and the Lincoln County story.

Among correspondents with Fulton was Robert N. Mullin, a Billy the Kid collector and an occasional writer. After Fulton's death in 1955, Mullin became his literary executor.

For nearly a dozen years, Mullin pieced together a lengthy volume from Fulton's scattered publications, notes, and outlines. With no complete manuscript or its evolving parts extant, one must accept Mullin's explanation that the extensive book, *The History of the Lincoln County War* published in 1968 under Fulton's name with Mullin listed as the editor, was indeed nearly all Fulton's work except for the final chapter, which Mullin claimed he had prepared.

A full-scale history of the Lincoln County War based on wide and thorough research, Fulton's volume proved invaluable for the next generation of historians. Fulton's book, both similar to and different from William Keleher's *Violence in Lincoln County, 1869–1881* (1957), provided extensive background to the violent acts of 1878 and devoted the heart of his book to events during the months stretching from February through July 1878, with bits and pieces after 1878 covered in later chapters. Four of his chapters (46–49) are focused largely on Billy the Kid.

Fulton was clear on his major themes. The competition for money, for economic dominance, was the major cause of the escalating violence in Lincoln County, particularly in the mid- to late-1870s. On one side, the Murphy-Dolan-Riley contingent, whom Fulton viewed as unscrupulous, thieving rascals, attempted to drive out of Lincoln County the other side of John Tunstall, Alex McSween and, to a lesser extent, John Chisum, whom Fulton does not salute but considers upright and fair in most of their dealings. According to Fulton, other major contributing factors to the violent upheavals included weak county leadership in politics and law enforcement. The Santa Fe Ring, headed by dictatorial Thomas Catron, sided with the Murphy-Dolan faction; so did the exceptionally partisan—if not crooked—regional court officials, District Attorney William Rynerson and Judge Warren Bristol, whom Fulton frequently castigated. The author also makes clear that the operations of Fort Stanton's commanding officer, Lieutenant Colonel

Nathan A. M. Dudley, did more to muddy than clear up the confusion and clashes that vexed Lincoln County.

Fulton lards his narrative with several inviting pen portraits. All the major characters—Murphy, Dolan, Tunstall, the McSweens, Chisum, Wallace, Dudley, and the Kid—appear in smoothly worded vignettes that attract and hold readers. Similarly, Fulton's use of numerous brief and direct chapters adds to the appealing literary quality of his narrative.

Fulton's Billy is a contradictory character, one with competing positive and negative characteristics. The Kid of these pages steps away from the despicable desperado of the dime novels but does not quite measure up to the romantic depiction of him in Burns's *Saga*. In fact Fulton treats Billy somewhat like he does a majority of the Tunstall-McSween partisans: most of the time they moved in the right direction but on occasion faltered. Billy could stand loyally for Tunstall and McSween, but his overpowering thirst for vengeance drove him into the mob-like killing of Morton and Baker and of Sheriff Brady.

Fulton's *History of the Lincoln County War* illustrates one of the clear directions that interpretations of Lincoln County and Billy the Kid were taking in the period from the mid-1920s to 1960. The author's research had turned up dozens of new sources of information in contemporary newspapers, manuscript letters, and government documents; he also was not writing primarily about Billy the Kid but about the contexts that surrounded him in territorial New Mexico. And he put before later readers the important cross-continental forces (particularly Washington's influences on New Mexico) rather than just those arising out of the Southwest that shaped the life and times of Billy the Kid. These were notable contributions, as many later readers and scholars would realize.

Another writer, William A. Keleher, spent most of his life in New Mexico and early on developed a deep, abiding interest in the state's nineteenth-century history. Trained as a lawyer, Will (as he was known) Keleher began his wide reading and research in the 1920s and 1930s, which led to publication of his first book, *Maxwell Land Grant* (1942). In the next fifteen years, three other books—*Fabulous Frontier* (1945), *Turmoil in New Mexico* (1952), and *Violence in Lincoln County, 1869–1881* (1957)—testified to Keleher's achievements as a skilled, committed historian as well as a well-known and respected lawyer. Throughout his writing career, Keleher won repeated accolades from reviewers and other historians for his broad and deep research and adept handling of documentary evidence.

The Fabulous Frontier: Twelve New Mexico Items illustrates Keleher's approach to New Mexico, Lincoln County, and Billy the Kid histories. In this study of people and events that shaped southeastern New Mexico shortly before, during, and after the 1870s, Keleher wants to capture the "atmosphere" of the territory in transition. He infrequently evaluates the personalities or actions of his major characters but frequently cites and quotes extensively journalists, government officials, and eyewitnesses with decidedly strong opinions. In this volume or later ones, Keleher rarely comments, one way or another, on the views of the onlookers and participants. Instead, he employs the long quotations from newspapers, personal correspondence, and legal documents for their historical information without providing evaluations of the viewpoints expressed.

An article that appeared in the 15 September 1883 issue of the *Lincoln County Leader* illustrates this noncommittal approach. The reporter praises Pat Garrett for "exterminating" Billy the Kid and characterizes John W. Poe, Garrett's successor as Lincoln County sheriff, as a "terror to evildoers," but Keleher provides no reactions about these explicit interpretations of the two sheriffs, merely suggesting they were agents of change in a shifting Lincoln County. In another case, Alexander Grzelachowski, a merchant in Puerto de Luna often dubbed "Padre Polaco," told his workers, "Always give the Kid anything he wants; never argue." This unusual and revealing comment about the merchant and Billy elicits no comment from Keleher. Such silence on intriguing, conversational statements pervades nearly all of Keleher's writings.

If *The Fabulous Frontier* dealt with all of territorial New Mexico, *Violence in Lincoln County* focuses almost entirely on the county and its violent history from the end of the 1860s to the opening of the 1880s. Keleher seemed convinced that during these years New Mexico had broken from its Spanish and Mexican heritage, most of its contacts with Indians, and its military conflicts and become, gradually, a region descended into something of a civil war.

Like nearly all writers dealing with the Lincoln County War, Keleher defines the deadly conflict as primarily a violent contest for economic control. But unlike most commentators, Keleher does not take sides. His is a story without heroes, largely a tortuous tale of many men demonstrating their less-than-upright actions. Whether Keleher is dealing with the Murphy-Dolan-Riley partisans or the Tunstall–McSween backers, he utilizes lengthy extracts from numerous documents pointing to villainous actions on both sides. Generally the flaws, failures and prejudices of participants rather than their strengths or contributions appear primarily in the numerous, extensively quoted sources.

Keleher's hefty volume was to date in 1957 the most thorough account of the Lincoln County War and remains one of a handful of the most important books devoted to that subject. The author followed the format of his previous books, quoting extensively from newspapers, manuscript correspondence, and court cases. These documents did much more than focus on local details, however. By quoting extensively from newspapers outside New Mexico and particularly by thoroughly utilizing letters exchanged between New Mexico leaders (especially the letters of Governor Lew

Wallace) and national officials in Washington, D.C., Keleher provided a cross-continental perspective missing from most previous—and many recent—books on New Mexico's Lincoln County.

After paying scant attention to Billy the Kid in his earlier chapters Keleher turns to a much more thorough treatment of the Kid about three-quarters of the way through his heavily detailed book. Chapters 13–15 emphasize Billy, with notable coverage of events in late 1880 and the first half of 1881. A few bits and pieces of Billy's life before 1880 also appear in these chapters.

Several scholars tracing the shifting interpretations of the Kid over time assert that in the decades following the publication of Burns's *Saga* in 1926 profiles of Billy pictured him as a good, if not heroic, young man. Keleher did not follow that path. His document-rich and fact-filled volume did not advance an explicit view of Billy the Kid. In the first place, Keleher was much more interested in the Lincoln County War than in the Kid, and the chapters on Billy pinpoint his participation in the events of 1880–1881 rather than on the earlier years up to 1880.

Consider, for example, one of Keleher's most extensive quotes concerning Billy. In this instance, Keleher is speaking of the differences between Governor Wallace and the Kid as they maneuvered cautiously toward their meeting and agreement in Lincoln in March 1879. Wallace was, according to Keleher, "a mature man of great prestige," the territorial governor, "a man of acknowledged pre-eminence in letters and literature," and much more. Billy, on the other hand, was "scarcely of legal voting age; almost illiterate; . . . a desperado, gunman and outlaw; a man who had not hesitated to take human life on more than one occasion, whether just or unjustly was yet to be determined."

That capsule description of Billy contained more disparaging words than any other Keleher comment about the Kid in his entire book. But other, more supportive comments came as easily as the critical ones. One of Billy's responses to Governor Wallace, Keleher asserted, proved the Kid "was entirely willing and unafraid to risk a fight in the open; that he had a native, inherent shrewdness, and a capacity for intelligent leadership." In fact these negative and positive comments are entirely out of character in Keleher's writings; most often he speaks about Billy's involvements in events, such as the shooting of Sheriff Brady, the frenzy of McSween's house burning on 19 July 1878, and the killings of Buckshot Roberts and Jimmy Carlyle, without making value judgments about the Kid's actions in these events. For later writers who used these events to limn an interpretive portrait of Billy the Kid, Keleher seems a curiously detached writer.

These later authors were right in part but in a way different from what they intended. Keleher's refusal to take sides, to push to strong conclusions, may have led to a balanced approach, but the nonpartisan distance also greatly reduced the narrative power of a story with such inherent peaks and valleys. The drama of Lincoln County history, particularly the controversial personalities on the two warring sides, is reduced in Keleher's book to a clear, straightforward narrative without the spice of a narrator's opinions or conclusions. In drafting the history, Keleher had not realized the importance of capturing readers' interest, as would a few historical novelists and moviemakers or as would historians Frederick Nolan and Robert Utley later in their lively books and essays.

The largest problem for Keleher was his inability to rein in his desire to lard his narrative with excessively long quotations from historical documents. For instance, in one of the most glaring examples of this overkill and of relinquishing his authorial voice to his documents, Keleher includes extraordinaryly lengthy quotes from a Robert A. Windenmann statement and an Alex McSween testimony to U.S. Special Investigator Frank Warren Angel. Those two extracts take up pages 260–80 of his text, in other words nineteen pages of quotation in 20 pages of text. Completely lost in between the gargantuan and dulling quotes is the book's author.

Yet, in the end Keleher's book proved to be an extraordinary contribution to the study of the legendary Billy the Kid because of his exhaustive research. He uncovered large amounts of new information on Lincoln County and the Kid. In the post–Walter Noble Burns years, Maurice Garland Fulton and Will Keleher proved just how much new information could be discovered and demonstrated that it need not be cast into an excessively romantic saga of the Old West.

Of the three energetic fact-finders researching the Lincoln County War, Billy the Kid, or both, Philip J. Rasch was the most relentless in his pursuit of Señor Billy. He was also the most prolific, turning out nearly 170 essays on the Kid and Lincoln County. Regrettably he was likewise the most difficult of the three to work with, often alienating others with his blunt, opinionated ways.

Philip Rasch never gave up his hunt. Whether with his education, including graduate studies in several fields, his work with the military, or his writings on a welter of subjects, he kept going. He lacked training in history and biography and was not a skilled narrative author, but none of those deficiencies kept him from endless, dutiful research.

Rasch began his investigations and writings on Billy and Lincoln County in the late 1940s and early 1950s. At first he seemed intent on publishing several of his "papers" (as he called his essays) or a book on the Lincoln County country or even a biography of the Kid. The dream of a full-length book faded when publishers rejected a projected volume based on his already-published essays, but that disappointment did not blunt his drive to publish more articles. In a forty-five-year career, Rasch published an average of four essays a year, while usually working full time, and was even more prolific in the 1950s and 1960s. Meanwhile, he produced several books and essays in the fields of physical education and exercise, the field in which he had earned a doctorate. The work on Billy, his avocation, became nearly an obsession.

Rasch seems to have launched his quest for Billy as a college undergraduate preparing a term paper for a literature course. Dissatisfied with sources available to him on the Kid, in 1946–1947 he began corresponding with anyone who could add to his thin information, an exercise that foreshadowed his lifetime of digging out new facts on Billy and Lincoln County. He likewise illustrated some of his limitations as a researcher, roundly criticizing previous authors, displaying his lack of tact in dealing with opinions different from his impressions, and expressing supreme confidence in his own conclusions.

While searching for a more factual Billy the Kid, Rasch encountered Robert H. Mullin, also an aficionado of New Mexico territorial history. A businessman with a lifelong interest in Billy the Kid and Lincoln—and who, as a boy, had met Pat Garrett—Mullin had already corresponded and bonded with Maurice Garland Fulton. Now he had a new trail mate in Rasch. In tandem, they dug deeper in new fields and sources about Billy. Their strong results changed much that was known about the younger Kid.

Rasch as a writer followed no discernable theory, system of organization, or consistent point of view. His eccentric approach, never stated directly, was to turn up "all the facts" about Billy the Kid and the Lincoln County War and in doing so smash into oblivion the legend-driven and wrongheaded views in the Garrett-Upson and Burns books. Year by year, he piled up an amazing mountain of new information and was increasingly pleased with himself in what he had accomplished.

In his first years of diligent work during the late 1940s and early 1950s Rasch focused primarily on Billy, the McCarty-

Antrim family, and those who traveled with or competed with the Kid. Rasch's research methods were similar to those of Maurice Garland Fulton and Will Keleher. All three ransacked contemporary newspapers, spoke or wrote to eyewitnesses or their descendants, examined published books and essays on the Kid's story, and hunted for available, unpublished manuscripts. More than the other two authors, Rasch's relentless pursuit of and success in gathering information through personal correspondence loaded his essays with new facts. He flooded the mails to gather even the smallest tidbits of new information. In some of these early papers he worked with Mullin, who had already been a Kid hunter of sorts since boyhood. At first it was a fortunate partnership; later, it became an acrimonious verbal battle.

Some of the earliest Rasch essays contained the most valuable findings. With Mullin he wrote "New Light on the Legend of Billy the Kid" (1952–1953) and "Dim Trails— The Pursuit of the McCarty Family" (1953–1954). On his own he authored "The Twenty-One Men He Put Bullets Through" (1954–1955), "Five Days of Battle" (1955), and "The Rise of the House of Murphy" (1956). These pioneering essays dealt with Henry Antrim/Billy Bonney/ Billy the Kid, his brother Joe McCarty Antrim, and step-father William H. Antrim. With Robert Mullin, then more comfortably by himself, Rasch added new information year by year on these three men. Gradually realizing fresh facts on the pre-1873 period were unavailable, Rasch zeroed in on the Silver City years and Lincoln County, and some on Arizona. Rasch and Mullin published their pioneering work about the discovery of the marriage of William Antrim and Catherine McCarty in the Santa Fe Presbyterian Church on 1 March 1873, and Rasch bragged of being the first to uncover the story of Kid Antrim's initial killing, the shooting of Windy Cahill on 17 August 1877 in a saloon near Camp Grant, Arizona. Rasch also provided early on the fullest and best-researched account of the horrendous Five-Day Battle in Lincoln in July 1878.

Soon, Rasch expanded his research to deal with other figures and events. As he rethought his topical coverage, he wrote essays on Lawrence G. Murphy, Jessie Evans, the Horrell and Pecos Wars, John Tunstall, Juan Patrón, and several other people and topics. He even dealt with federal investigations of violence and corruption in southeastern New Mexico. On the other hand, he did not produce essays on Alex and Sue McSween, the Santa Fe Ring, or William Rynerson and Warren Bristol, although those persons and topics appear in several Rasch essays.

By the mid-1950s Rasch had decided to write a book about Lincoln County, covering the period from 1873 to 1883. While preparing for his comprehensive examinations in his doctoral program in physical education, he turned out chapters on the "wars" of Lincoln County. But when he tried out his book plan with a least one or more publishers, they rejected his proposal, telling him his book was too much a mere reprinting of his previously published essays. Forty years later, Rasch's friends accomplished what he dreamed of, reprinting nearly seventy of his essays in three important collections: *Trailing Billy the Kid* (1995); *Gunsmoke in Lincoln County* (1997); and *Warriors of Lincoln County* (1998). Still other collections of Rasch's essays were planned but never completed.

Rasch's "papers" make abundantly clear what he thought of other authors writing about Lincoln County and Billy the Kid. The Garrett-Upson biography became and remained Rasch's favorite target for barbed criticism. He agreed with another writer that the book published in 1882 was "a storehouse of misinformation" that led readers and other writers astray for more than a half-century. Ash Upson, whom Rasch credited with writing the biography (especially the opening chapters), particularly earned Rasch's wrath through his imagined stories "of pure fabrication."

More than thirty years later, Walter Noble Burns, according to Rasch, loaded up his *Saga of Billy the Kid* with "folklore," Rasch's favorite word for false or misleading stories that helped to create destructive legends. Burns misspelled names, placed Henry/Billy in places not yet established, and created episodes in which the Kid never participated. Early on in his career Rasch dismissed Burns's book as "woefully inaccurate."

Rasch also fell out with other writers. One of these was Maurice Garland Fulton. When Rasch asked the Roswell scholar for help with a source, he thought Fulton responded with "a churlish letter"; Rasch replied in kind. Even more importantly, he thought Fulton's book, *History of the Lincoln County War*, edited by Robert Mullin and published in 1968, was "simply ten years out of date the day it was published." Left unsaid, of course, was that Rasch's publications in those ten to fifteen years had added much new information not included in Fulton's book. By the mid-1950s Rasch credited Miguel Antonio Otero Jr.'s book, *The Real Billy the Kid* (1936), the most recent book on the Kid as the best on that subject. Still, it fell far short of what Rasch thought could be done with Billy, and Rasch frequently hinted he was at work on such a book.

Within a half-dozen years of his first publications on the Kid, Rasch had made explicit his conclusions about that controversial figure. Quite simply, Billy was "a psychopathic young man." Or at nearly the same time he contacted another Billy-hunter and stated, "I am prepared to say that Billy the Kid was a psychopathic personality with an I.Q. of around 100 to 110." Later, in the 1970s when still another correspondent challenged his labeling Billy "psychopathic," Rasch referred him to the fourth edition of *The Abnormal Personality* published by Robert W. White and Norman F. Watt (1973). The authors defined the "psychopathic personality" as those who "failed to respond adequately to the process of socialization." They made "an unusually pleasing impression in interviews," but they "are very unreliable, inclined to lie and deceive." Nor did they "accept blame for . . . [their] misconduct nor felt shame about it, but readily give . . . a plausible excuse for everything that has occurred." Rasch concluded that "you will never read a better description of the Kid's personality."

Although Rasch was clearly no fan of the Kid, he was certain that previous writers had badly misconstrued Billy by delivering up false factual information or creating a legendary figure far from the real one. In his essay "The Twenty-One Men He Put Bullets Through," Rasch abruptly dismissed most of the "folklore" stories of earlier authors as lacking credibility. Instead Billy was alone guilty of four shootings: Windy Cahill; Joe Grant; J. W. Bell; and Bob Olinger. And he was involved in five other "gang killings" at most: William Brady and George Hindman; William Morton and Frank Baker; and James Carlyle. If the numbers of murders had been vastly overestimated, so had Billy's character. Rasch saw no reason to characterize the Kid as courageous, brave, or valiant in any way. Obviously Billy had been overrated.

Rasch's opinions of other Lincoln County characters were equally self-assured. As author Frederick Nolan notes, Rasch "had very set ideas on certain things." For instance, in his early piece on Lieutenant Colonel Nathan A. M. Dudley Rasch provides a helpful overview of the officer's controversial roles in the Lincoln County contretemps but admits his "chronological account . . . affords little opportunity to assess a man's character." Later, in 1965 Rasch castigated writers who criticized Dudley and who, Rasch opined, had not read carefully the testimony supporting Dudley and were too "determined to cast him as one of the villains" in the Lincoln County story.

In the case of John Tunstall, Rasch was similarly adamant but in a different direction. In Rasch's view, even though other writers portrayed the newcomer to New Mexico "as a

saintly English lamb fallen among Lincoln County wolves
. . . he was simply a fortune hunter, determined to get everything on which he could lay his hands." Rasch added that
Tunstall was in part the reason for his own violent demise
when he "relentlessly closed in to eliminate his opponents."
Rasch matter-of-factly recounts Tunstall's murder but provides no discussion as to the possible merits of the man's
character.

Rasch is particularly hostile toward Alex and Sue
McSween. He summarizes his animosity toward the lawyer
by describing him "as crooked as a dog's hind leg." Alex
was an embezzler, a manipulator, and a liar who misspent
the Fritz insurance payment to build his house and stock
the Tunstall store in Lincoln. When a correspondent with
Rasch cast doubt on the ugly rumors submitted to court by
those who wished to denigrate Sue McSween's moral standards and character, Rasch told him she was not worthy
of his support. In Rasch's mind, she was indeed a woman
of questionable morals. In his letters to other researchers,
Rasch was even more bluntly critical of the McSweens than
in his published essays.

Toward the Murphy-Dolan side, Rasch was ambivalent. In his early, long piece, "The Rise of the House of
Murphy" (1956), he lists fully Murphy's numerous sins as
a business conniver, prevaricator, provocateur, and drunk
but nevertheless shies away from providing an interpretative
portrait or sketch of the dominating businessman. Rather
he provides more information on Lincoln County affairs
than on Murphy's House actions. The essay ends not with
a summing up of Murphy's life or actions but with two
sentences on "a psychopathic young rustler named Henry
McCarty, alias William Antrim, alias Billy Bonney, alias Billy
Kidd [sic], alias Billy the Kid," who had arrived in Lincoln
County where he was "destined to play a leading role in the
explosion which was about the [sic] engulf the House of
Murphy and bring it crashing down upon its proprietors."

Interestingly, elsewhere in the piece Rash assigns Billy no leading role in the events of 1877–1878 as he does in this one sentence.

On Jimmy Dolan, who may have come closest to playing the antihero's part in Lincoln County in 1877–1879, Rasch has much less to say. He hardly mentions Dolan in regard to House affairs or events in late 1877 or the shootouts in 1878, even though Dolan played a large role in those happenings. Nor does Rasch think Dolan shot Huston Chapman on the street in Lincoln in early 1879. Some writers, looking closely at Rasch's sources, think his connections with Dolan's family as sources of information kept him from saying anything that raised questions about or cast a shadow over Dolan himself.

Perhaps Rasch's hesitancy to provide strong, useful generalizations about Billy and the Lincoln County War had more general origins. It is clear that he relished historical facts and details, especially when they demolished earlier interpretations of southeastern New Mexico he considered wrong or misleading. In an essay published in 1959 Rasch made distinctions between "chronicle-like records of what happened" and "historical narratives in which the happenings are interpreted and/or explained." Rasch manifestly belonged to the "chronicle-like" writers rather than to the "historical narrators." Even toward the end of his long career in the 1980s and 1990s, he was reluctant to furnish overarching conclusions about the origins or reasons for the Lincoln County War or an extended essay on Billy the Kid's character or personality.

In 1955 Rasch provided another hint about his approach to history. He informed a friend that he agreed "that we need to capture the psychology of our subjects," but in his essays or in his letters Rasch rarely moved beyond a few hints of interpretation. He adored and coveted bits and pieces of history and perhaps abhorred and shunted large, general frameworks of historical analysis, evaluation, and conclusion.

On the other hand, one must credit the significant role that Rasch played in the trajectory of Billy's legendary path. In his view everyone who had written extensively about the Kid—historians and biographers such as Garrett and Upson, Burns, Fulton, and Otero and memoirists such as the Coe cousins—was mistaken or misleading. So he set out to correct their erroneous accounts and thereby topple the ever-rising legends about the Kid. Billy had not killed twenty-one men in twenty-one years, he was not a leader in the Lincoln County War in the first half of 1878, he and his family had not gone to Kansas in the 1860s, and he had not killed a man for insulting his mother in Silver City. By eliminating these false stories and replacing them with new research-based information, Rasch reined in the legend-making about the Kid that began with the Garrett-Upson book in 1882 and expanded for the next seventy years.

In the mid-1950s Rasch and other historians and biographers had to address a new kind of legend about the Kid, one that bedeviled Billy pursuers well into the twenty-first century. In their short book *Alias Billy the Kid* (1955), English professor C. L. Sonnichsen and paralegal researcher William V. Morrison provided the first installment of the new legend. This story line pronounced that Pat Garrett had not killed the Kid in Pete Maxwell's bedroom but instead shot an unknown young man named Billy Barlow. The unusual narrative then stated the Kid had survived, lived a nomadic life in Mexico and throughout the West, and went into semiretirement in Texas, where he was known as O. L. "Brushy Bill" Roberts. In the late 1940s, Brushy Bill told Morrison he was the real Billy the Kid and, now at ninety, wanted an official pardon for his misdeeds.

Sonnichsen and Morrison, with at least a dozen other writers later on, accepted Brushy Bill's unique story largely because, they argued, he knew so much about the Lincoln County story. His knowledge of obscure detail astounded some, especially those already drawn to conspiracy theories. Robust researchers such as Rasch, however, dismissed the team-written book as folklore, trash, or unbelievable speculation. Although Brushy Bill failed to gain his pardon and died a few months after interviewing the New Mexico governor to obtain the pardon, with most scholars dismissing his questionable story, the legend of a resurrected or "beyond the grave" Billy circulated for more than another sixty years. Although the Billy-didn't-die-in-Fort-Sumner legend never became a widely accepted view among serious biographers and scholars, the fantastic idea would not disappear from debates over the Kid, remaining on the margins for decades.

After the flurry of a dozen or so of dime novels about the Kid in the 1880s and 1890s, fiction writers in the next thirty years seemed hesitant to tackle Billy the Kid. The same hesitation continued from 1930 to 1960, with only a handful or two of Billy novels appearing in these long years. None of the scattered novels, until Edwin Corle's *Billy the Kid: A Novel* (1953) and Charles Neider's *The Authentic Death of Hendry Jones* (1956), should be considered as significant or influential as the dime novels in the late nineteenth century or several other novels published from the 1960s onward.

Ambitious writers wishing to embed Billy in a historical novel faced three large barriers in the first half of the twentieth century. First, negative images of the Kid in fiction still predominated, reflecting the dark pictures of Billy in dime novels. Second, popular western fiction writers, following the model in the widely popular hero in Owen Wister's bestselling novel, *The Virginian* (1902), peopled their novels with heroic and romantic protagonists. Wister, Zane Grey, Max Brand, and B. M. Bower (the only woman writing well-known Westerns at the time) repeatedly depicted their leading men as agents of law and order, defenders of community standards, and models of virtue and morality for a wide spectrum of American readers. Billy the Kid did not fit that pattern. Third, the popular Westerns of Grey, Brand, and others followed a triplex of character types in their plots: hero, villain, and heroine. If Billy failed as a hero, Pat Garrett was certainly not a villain (although Lawrence G. Murphy or Jimmy Dolan might have been), and no obvious heroine came on scene, unless one was created and treated as a historical figure. Any writer trying to create an appealing fictional portrait of Billy in the period from 1900 to 1950 would have to hurdle these daunting formidable barriers to achieve their dreams. No one did.

Before the mid-1920s novelists lacked a strong, credible biography of Billy the Kid on which to base their historical fiction, even though some thought the Garrett-Upson work, *The Authentic Life of Billy, the Kid* (1882), was a dependable source. A dramatic change in direction occurred after the publication of Walter Noble Burns's romantic, somewhat-sensational life story of Billy in *The Saga of Billy the Kid*. Now writers had a biography that depicted the Kid, at least in part, as a hero and told a new kind of life story on which to base novels. Commentators on the historiography surrounding Billy the Kid have made much of the large impact of Burns's book on subsequent Kid biographies, but they have failed to notice how that book also influenced novelists.

Historical novelists faced two other conflicting trends in western American literature in the 1920s, 1930s, and beyond. The first trend, which had little impact on novels dealing with Billy the Kid, was the rapid rise of western regionalism in the interwar years. As it did in the American South, the regional movement took the West by storm in the twenties and thirties. Rooted in the Local Color movement of the late nineteenth century and in the works of early twentieth-century writers such as Mary Austin and Willa Cather, then encouraged by the plethora of little magazines that sprang up in the 1920s, writers about the West were motivated to show how western history and physical settings shaped diverse western characters. However understandable, this regionalist approach did not entice novelists writing about Billy the Kid.

But historical novelists did find a place for Billy in the stylized, formula Western novel that arose after Wister's *Virginian* was solidified, especially in the writings of Zane Grey and Max Brand and, before and after World War II, in the Westerns of Ernest Haycox and Luke Short (Frederick Glidden). Before Burns's *Saga,* western writers lacked an appealing Billy-as-hero figure; now they had a model for that attractive protagonist and a rascally villain in Lawrence G. Murphy, the "Lord of the Valley" figure in Burns's *Saga.* With imagined heroines, historical novelists now had the triumvirate of characters they needed for formula Westerns.

Hollywood overnight also capitalized on the new Billy hero in Burns's biography with its *Billy the Kid* (1930), directed by King Vidor, and starring former football legend Johnny Mack Brown. But immediately after the appearance of Burns's *Saga,* novelists were still reluctant to place heroic Billy characters in their western historical fiction. Most of the novels appearing in the late 1920s remained locked into the earlier demonic pictures of Billy or dealt with him as a largely off-scene character.

Four novels with Billy the Kid in either major or minor roles were published between 1926 and 1929. This quartet of novels revealed that the reach of Burns's *Saga* was longer and clearer in nonfiction than fictional works. The closest to history, although quite different in their portrayals of the Kid, were Dane Coolidge's *War Paint* and William MacLeod Raine's *The Fighting Tenderfoot,* both appearing in 1929. Coolidge follows the now-familiar hero, villain, and heroine format of the formula Western, but he turns Billy into a devilish villain. Even though the Kid is a distant figure in much of the plot, his reputation as a killer with nearly twenty vic-

Billy the Kid, 1930. This early sound movie starring the former football star Johnny Mack Brown and directed by King Vidor, portrayed Billy the Kid in a heroic light, an interpretive precedent and shift championed by Billy biographer Walter Noble Burns. A contrived, upbeat ending to the movie allows the Kid to escape from his killing of Pat Garrett's deputies and ride off with the heroine. Courtesy Paul Andrew Hutton.

tims to his name hovers over and threatens to bedevil the good guys and their attempts at communal acts. Named Tuffy Malone here, the Billy-like character is described as "bad medicine," "the best pistol shot in the country." Or one character admonishes, "You'll hear from him [Tuffy-Billy]," for "there is one of the worst characters on the whole frontier, a city tough, gone wild in the West." True events in Billy's life appear in the story, but the stereotypes of popular Western fiction abound: a speedy plot loaded with action; a stalwart hero (not Billy); deplorable villains; and a vivacious heroine. In addition Coolidge, like Zane Grey, is unconvincing in handling human emotion, overblowing his characters' passions, fears, and stubbornness.

Raine, the British-born author of more than eighty Westerns, flooded the markets of popular fiction from 1908 to 1958. In *The Fighting Tenderfoot*, Raine's plot, characterizations, and bits of setting reveal his indebtedness to the dark

Kid story. His Billy character, named Bob Quantrell, is the fastest gun, haughtiest killer, and most-arrogant rider in the territory of Jefferson County. He is caught in a violent civil war between cattle baron Wesley Steelman (John Chisum), and smaller cattlemen and merchants, the latter reminiscent of Murphy and Dolan. But other ingredients of the plot are Raine-imagined, not history-inspired. Hispanics, although supporters of Quantrell, are referred to as "greasers" and, on one occasion, "not civilized." A romance between hero Garrett O'Hara, the lawyer "tenderfoot" of the title, and widow Barbara Steelman, allows love to win over war. But closely following Wister's format in *The Virginian*, O'Hara has to go after the villainous Kid Quantrell before he can win the heroine. Conventional stereotypes inherited from the formula Western keep this work from being a strong historical novel about the Kid.

Even Zane Grey, like Dane Coolidge, dealt tangentially with Billy in *Nevada* (1928). The Kid is a friend of the hero, Nevada, and is referred to nearly ten times in the novel. Early on, Billy is depicted as a gunman-desperado in the vicious Lincoln County War. But in the final pages Grey dramatically changes the direction of the fictional Kid. In *Nevada,* a central, well-respected figure argues that characters such as Billy, Wild Bill Hickok, and Wess Hardin (John Wesley Hardin) are not "bloody murderers." Instead they are necessary for settling and civilizing the West. He declares, "There are bad men and bad men. The West could never have been populated without them." This comment is an almost–O. Henry–like ending to a Zane Grey novel.

The most innovative and sympathetic portrait of Billy appeared in Eugene Manlove Rhodes's classic novella, *Pasó por Aquí* (1927). Rhodes speaks only once of Billy, referring to Pat Garrett as "the man who killed Billy the Kid," but he clones a young Billy in Ross McEwen to tell a favorable, even compassionate story about the Kid. McEwen has robbed a bank and is galloping south to escape when he encounters a Mexican family near death from diphtheria in their adobe. Rather than abandoning and fleeing the very sick family, the hero announces, "I'm here to help you." He nurses the family. A few days later Pat Garrett, pursuing McEwen, arrives at the adobe, sees the good the young robber is doing, and looks the other way in allowing the thief to escape. Rhodes provides a good-Billy story, a type that would appear with more frequency later in the century. At the same time, the author is a Garrett defender, painting an exceedingly positive portrait of the diligent but sympathetic sheriff.

Although these novels were published soon after Burns's biography, less than a handful appeared in the next quarter century. The early thirties were a high point of interest in the American West, but novelists did not turn to the story of Billy the Kid for their historical fiction.

Unfortunately, E. B. Mann's *Gamblin' Man* (1934) was particularly disappointing as historical fiction because the author's perversion of the facts badly distorted what was then known about Billy. Even though the author warned readers at the onset that his book was a novel, not a work of history, he essentially abandoned the main contours of Billy's life. Mann grafts a romance story—Billy's love for pretty, vivacious Kathie Haskel—onto his action plot. Revealingly, no Paulita Maxwell or Hispanic señoritas walk through these pages. Instead we get the author's imagined and not very believable heroines.

Other changes by Mann misinterpret Billy's life. The author removes Billy from the Buckshot Roberts incident and from the killing of Morris Bernstein at the Mescalero Agency, and he makes Billy the very-close friend of Pat Garrett and, for the most part, the close partner of John Chisum. He overemphasizes John Tunstall's support for Billy, makes Susan McSween a dear friend, and changes the details of the Five-Day Battle in Lincoln. Meanwhile Alex McSween is a stick figure reduced to a Bible-caressing caricature. Most importantly Mann has Garrett killing a Billy look-alike in Pete Maxwell's bedroom, the mistake allowing Billy and sweetheart Kathie to ride off to Mexico or elsewhere and begin a new life. Appearing in Mann's fiction was an early version of the later legend of a resurrected Billy.

If the historical novelist should be true to known history as many specialists dealing with historical fiction contend, Mann fails miserably with his changes to and mistakes of historical fact. Those missteps lead to distortions in the Kid's biography. Mann's alterations and miscues large and small shift the Billy the Kid story away from history and allow the author's transformed and imagined Billy, rather than the historical Billy, to ride through these troubling pages.

Published a few years later, Nelson Nye's *Pistols for Hire* (1941) proved to be an anomaly, the most-damning novel about Billy in the mid-twentieth century. Nye's hero and narrator Flick Farsom, a twenty-something cowboy who begins riding with Chisum but transfers his loyalties to the Murphy-Dolan side, views Billy as "a murderer and thief. He would drive a bullet through a fellow's heart as lustful as he'd rape a woman; and times beyond count he did both. He was a man without remorse—without regret or pity." And if someone tried to write something about a "good" Billy, he was lying through his whiskers. Nye's novel proved a piece of partisan fiction with faulty uses of history and a distorted viewpoint.

Zane Grey even tried a second time to treat Billy in *Shadow on the Trail* (1946), with results similar to his first effort. In this story, the Kid is still off scene, and the descriptions are equally dark and unforgiving. One character describes Billy as "the chain lightnin' an' poison of the frontier," and another, as "all that's bad on the frontier rolled into one boy of eighteen years." Major errors also abound. Among them are naming a character, "Henderson," as an actual member of the Kid's gang, stating that Billy played a central role in igniting the Lincoln County War, and reporting that

Pat Garrit (Garrett) shot down Billy in the town of Lincoln. In the familiar format of the popular Western, Billy plays a villain, not a hero, in Grey's *Shadow*.

At the end of the 1950s, two novels gained and would retain notoriety as pioneering, robust fictional works about Billy the Kid. During the 1950s, in the diligent and path-breaking published research of Philip Rasch and, to a lesser extent, of William A. Keleher, Robert Mullin, and Maurice Garland Fulton, novelists had at their fingertips larger amounts of historical information about the Kid. Edwin Corle's *Billy the Kid: A Novel* (1953) illustrates and exploits this new fund of historical information now available to writers. Some sections of his work read more like history and biography than fiction. The major characters seem historical and quite true to historical form.

Despite this trove of historical work on Lincoln County and the Kid, Corle utilizes mistaken facts that historians had not yet corrected. Once in Silver City, Corle's Billy pals around with badman Jessie Evans, and he stabs a Chinese laundryman during a robbery spree with Jessie. Billy also kills a "nigger" when he is next in Arizona and two Mexicans while in Mexico, before riding into Lincoln County. All wrong.

Corle pictures Billy as an irrational killer. He murders on several occasions because he is angry or uncomfortable, not because he is threatened or violently confronted. These frequent killings place Billy among the earlier devilish Billys. Even though Corle's novel was published in the 1950s, it had been drafted in the 1930s, closer in time to the images of a murderous Billy. The novel certainly did not follow the more likeable Kid in the Burns biography.

Besides his killer instinct, Billy is also a lover in the Corle novel. His novia is Abrana García, said to be one of the señoritas he coupled with in Fort Sumner. The Kid bullies his way into her heart and then her bed, even though she is already married to an older man. Nothing is suggested in the novel that Paulita Maxwell is the woman to whom Billy returns after escaping from the Lincoln jail.

Most intriguing about Corle's novel and about historical fiction in general is the license historical novelists are convinced they have to fill in the spaces between known history. For example, what did Billy *feel* when his mother died, when he killed Windy Cahill or Joe Grant, and when he slept with Paulita, Abrana, or Celsa? What did he *say* to his stepfather, to John Tunstall or Alex McSween in Lincoln, or to Governor Wallace? By combining history and imagination, Corle tries to fill the silences in so many of Billy's emotions and thoughts.

Charles Neider also served up large slices of history in his novel, *The Authentic Death of Hendry Jones* (1956), but he made so many changes that the history in this work of fiction is deeply flawed. He shifts the setting of his story from Lincoln County to the coastal area of Monterey, California. In making this major transfer of location Neider abandons the cattle-country culture and isolation of remote territorial New Mexico and places the action in the more-settled seacoast of California. In the new scene mists, gloom, abalone fishing, and a trip to Old Mexico replace sun, heat, open-range ranching, hunting, and Texas connections. The shift in setting undercuts what could have been a regionalist's strong desire to show the shaping power of place on unfolding events and character formation.

Another major change is in the cast of characters, especially in the narrator role of Doc Baker. Doc says little about the background of Hendry Jones (the Kid); but he speaks extensively about the Kid's character in the months immediately before his violent death. Doc's Kid is courageous, often cheerful, and gregarious; he is also a callous, casual killer. He is secular, even antireligious, and sexual, and disposes of a close acquaintance with no apparent reason. Despite Doc's prudent advice, the Kid follows his own murderous ways. Several literary scholars and other writers have praised Neider's novel as a breakthrough in fiction about Billy the Kid. They and film historians also make much of the movie, *One-Eyed Jacks* (1961), based on Neider's work, and directed by and starring Marlon Brando. Neider's novel is an innovative, appealingly written work of fiction, but it fails as a believable historical account of Billy the Kid, particularly without the Lincoln County setting. The author's new settings—physically, occupationally, and socioculturally—do not work as truthful, accurate accounts of the historical Billy the Kid and the weeks leading up to his death. If Neider avoided the violent-desperado legends about Billy in dime novels and early journalistic accounts, he furthered counternarratives with few strong ties to the actual Billy.

The Corle and Neider novels provided a bridge from the earlier, very flawed dime novels and other book-length works of fiction to the stronger, more satisfying novels that followed. They were limited by the inadequate biographical information, however, then available on Billy the Kid.

In the 1960s, especially toward the end of the decade, two trends began to impact writings and films about Billy the Kid. As we have seen, several diligent scholars turned up new information about Señor Billy, particularly details on his earliest years and family life. At the same time, American society and culture were undergoing dramatic transitions. Spurred on by negative reactions to the Vietnam War and the activism of many Americans, especially on college campuses, Americans became less inclined to embrace historical figures as heroes and heroines. In fact the trends were in the opposite direction, finding warts and blemishes in politicians, cultural figures, military leaders, and many others. This growing disposition toward dissent, sometimes accompanied by an expanding cynicism, threw a large, wet blanket of doubt over the roles of the demigods of the Old West.

These trends helped shape novels being written about Billy the Kid. Rather than the evil desperado of the early dime novels or the more heroic character of Burns's biography dominating the pre-1960s period, the Kid instead became an ambiguous Billy, a young man combining *both* negative and positive characteristics. In short, neither a black nor a white hat, the outlaw and the cheerful comrade sides were united and blended into a New Grey Billy.

From the late 1960s onward, novelists, following this emerging two-sided figure, depicted Billy the Kid as a Janus-faced character. He might veer toward violence and cruelty, but he also warmly embraced Hispanics and women as well as several male colleagues. This dualistic Billy has dominated historical fiction about him in the past half century.

Moviemakers from 1930 to 1960 paid little attention to the known facts of Lincoln County history or the life of Billy the Kid. Rather they displayed, as they often did—and still do—in films about the Old West, what might be dubbed Hollywood history. When weighed in the balance sheet of a Hollywood studio or production company, action, lively imagined characters, dramatic events, and sensational story lines counted much more than verifiable, less dramatic historical details. In these decades, movie production proved how difficult it might be to follow a path of factual accuracy in cinematic portraits of Billy the Kid.

Critics of early Billy the Kid movies often dismiss most of these films as hopelessly second or third rate, if not entirely banal. They point to stereotyped characters, incessant frenetic action, and hackneyed plots as the culprits in the inferior quality of these films in the 1930s and especially in the early 1940s. These detractors are in large part correct and fair, if their assessments derive solely from aesthetic considerations. Most of the first Kid movies were innocent of polish, substance, believable action, and sound characterizations.

But more than a few students of legend-making move in other interpretive directions. Just as examinations of the rise and persistence of legends pay close attention to Zane Grey and Max Brand fictional Westerns, so these evaluations scrutinize B-Westerns for plot patterns, character types, and stylized action. For specialists in American popular culture these patterns, stereotypes, and other repetitions are important ingredients worthy of close attention. So it is with many of the earliest Billy the Kid movies; the patterns evident in these films suggest how extraordinarily popular the Kid became in the period from 1930 to 1960.

The initial Billy the Kid movies made in the silent era, are gone with the wind, leaving only reviews and cursory comments in movie magazines for the historian and critic to follow. Two were made; both are lost. *Billy the Kid* (1911) features a character who is thought to be a boy until age sixteen and then is revealed as a girl, who marries a range rider. So this Vitagraph movie, starring Edith Story as Billy, is not at all about the real Kid. A similar disconnect occurs with the second silent film, *Billy the Bandit* (1916). As noted in the previous chapter, Thomas F. Daggett's dime novel, *Billy LeRoy, the Colorado Bandit; or, the King of the American Highwaymen* (1881), dealt primarily with the actual Colorado outlaw, Billy LeRoy, with a few disjointed pages about New Mexico's Billy. If this movie followed Daggett's dime novel—no extensive plot summary of the film exists—it too ventured far from the historical Billy, and it did not please commentators. One referred to the film as featuring Billy selling "a sand lot to an unsuspecting woman purchaser, and then abducts his girl in cave man fashion." Another source on the film, which starred Billy Mason, dismissed the movie because of its "jerky" action, which "interferes with the plot development." Obviously these first two cinematic efforts did not promise much in films about Billy the Kid.

But that would all change beginning in 1930 and stretching into the next fifteen years. More than twenty movies, nearly all of which were filmed by the Producers Releasing Corporation (PRC), featured Billy the Kid as a major cinematic character. As much as historians and critics wish to locate and identify general trends in a succession of biographies, histories, novels, or films, such clear patterns are not available or demonstrated in the Kid movies from 1930 to 1945, but the one credible generalization is that in most of these films Billy was not the violent outlaw he had been in newspaper accounts, dime novels, and some early biographies. The first cinematic Billys owed more to Walter Noble Burns's favorable, sympathetic image advanced in *The Saga of Billy the Kid* than to the dark, malevolent desperado featured in dime novels and some earlier histories.

Two impulses helped to launch Director King Vidor's 1930 *Billy the Kid*. First, Hollywood was awash in Westerns, and the game-changing entrance of sound technology in the late 1920s sent producers and directors scrambling in new directions. Hollywood dashed forward to adapt to the "talkie" breakthrough in its new Western movies, the most popular film genre of the 1920s. Three Westerns released in 1929 gained considerable public attention and enjoyed attendance by tens of thousands of filmgoers: *In Old Arizona,* which earned an Oscar for actor Warner Baxter; *The Big Trail* starring John Wayne in his first major role; and *The Virginian* featuring Gary Cooper as the hero. Their warm reception by critics and at the box office convinced Vidor that he could duplicate those successes with a new movie about Billy the Kid.

Equally important, Vidor was enamored with Burns's *Saga* and wanted to base his new Billy film on that dramatic book. The more positive legends surrounding Billy had come to the fore during the mid-1920s, with the powerful influence of Burns's book clearly evident in Vidor's pioneering Kid film. It is true that Vidor's cinematic Billy, like the historical Billy, vows revenge after John Tunston (Tunstall) is killed and follows up on his promise to wipe out his enemies. Billy declares in the film, "Killing rats comes naturally to me," and one of his competitors calls him the "most dangerous man in Lincoln County." But the film depicts the Lincoln County contest as a war, and Billy courageously and defiantly fights his opponents, beginning with Donovan (Lawrence G. Murphy) and later including his chief henchman, Ballinger (Olinger). Billy not only fights the black-hatted "bad guys" but moves toward the white-hatted "good guys." Pat Garrett is attracted to Billy, even though the Kid's escapades challenge the lawman's leadership.

Important too in the formulation of the sympathetic Billy are his connections with Hispanics and women. Billy reciprocates the warmth of the Mexican people, who welcome him, love his support of them, and encourage his enthusiastic dancing. Even more revealing, Billy's magnetism pulls women to him. After Tunstan is murdered, his newly arrived fiancée, Claire, discovers Billy, admires his gentlemanliness and gentleness toward her, even though she knows about his violent deeds. A romance blossoms. Part Hollywood, and part the emerging refurbished legend of a heroic young man, the mutual romance leads Pat Garrett to allow the couple to ride off, out of town, in the final scene rather than bringing about Billy's death.

Vidor's close adherence to Burns's book led to a few inaccuracies. Two incidents in *Saga* and *Billy the Kid* were particularly galling to Sue McSween Barber. Vidor, following Burns, has Sue playing *The Star-Spangled Banner* on her piano while her Lincoln house burns to the ground, and her husband, Alex, holds his Bible in the flaming house, then outside in the street when he is shot down. (Sue had upbraided Burns for these inaccuracies, which he admitted to, but he defended himself by stating those stories were so widespread among persons he interviewed in Lincoln that he had to use them.) When these cinematic stretchers reappeared in *Billy the Kid*, Sue stormed out of the theatre, branding the film as "all lies." Sophie Poe, who had married one of Pat Garrett's deputies after Billy was shot, also thoroughly castigated Vidor's movie. Billy the Kid, she burst out, was nothing like the young hero portrayed by Johnny Mack Brown, the former University of Alabama football star. The Kid, Sophie asserted, was a "little buck-toothed killer." In the end, Director Vidor's response helps clarify the powerful influence of public opinion on legend-making. "I understand your feelings," he told Sophie, "but this is what the people want." The movie also received the blessing of noted Western film star William S. Hart, who served as a consultant for the film.

Throughout the 1930s filmmakers experimented with sound and how best to employ it in new films. Directors of "talkie" Westerns encountered special challenges because so many scenes of action were out of doors and distant from needed sound technology. To overcome this problem of distance and the complications of utilizing sound, several film companies turned to singing Westerns. In these hour-long movies, three or four songs were sung around a campfire, in a saloon, or at a dance, usually performed by the hero or another leading male character. By the mid-1930s Gene Autry had ridden to center stage as a rising star in singing Westerns. When he and his studio fell out over contractual matters, the studio turned to Roy Rogers, a newcomer, to ride at the head of their singing Westerns. Three years into his Hollywood career, Rogers starred in *Billy the Kid Returns* (1938), the first singing Western about the Kid.

The Rogers film, casting Smiley Burnette as the humorous sidekick, Frog Millhouse, and Wade Boteler as Pat Garrett, depicted Rogers's Billy the Kid in a uniquely structured plot. In the opening minutes of the movie, the McSween house burns, McSween is killed, and shortly thereafter Garrett rouses Billy from sleep and outdraws and shoots the Kid. In a second section of film, which is longer, Rogers appears on the scene in Lincoln. He so resembles Billy physically that Lincoln residents are certain he is actually Billy. Legal officials, including Garrett, reluctantly accept the ruse that Roy will become Billy and help the nearly defeated nesters to try again to put down roots despite the brutal opposition of characters resembling Murphy and Dolan.

Rogers's Billy, like so many popular figures in the post-Burns era, is treated as a champion of the people. In a series of fast rides, musical solos, shootouts, and humorous incidents (with Burnette involved), Rogers stands up for the underdogs and defeats the evildoers. The mediocre action, the depiction of Rogers on one occasion singlehandedly standing off four villains, and the hero's ludicrous romantic attention to a pretty young woman, while undermining a viewer's credulity, nonetheless maintain the legend of a heroic Billy doing good deeds for needy others, the helpless nesters in this case.

A critic or two has asserted that *Billy the Kid* (1941), starring Robert Taylor, was a remake of the 1930 *Billy the Kid*. Not so. The differences between the two films outweigh the similarities. In fact the Taylor-led movie diverged from most, but not all, of the Billy the Kid movies released up to the early 1950s.

The distinctions emerge in critical comparisons of the 1930 and 1941 films. Although both films deal with more Lincoln County and Billy the Kid history than the nineteen segments of the Producers Releasing Corporation (1940–1943) soon to come, the 1930 film sticks much closer to the Burns account than does Taylor's film. In the 1941 production, nearly all the leading characters of the Lincoln County War are elided, including John Tunstall (for the most part), Alex and Susan McSween, the Santa Fe Ring, and conniving New Mexico territorial officials. A more explicit Pat Garrett figure appears in the 1930 film as well as a more evident romance for Billy. In the Johnny Mack Brown film, Billy is allowed to escape, whereas eleven years later, the left-handed cinematic Kid character seems to invite his own demise by switching to his right hand and is shot down by Garrett, a long-time friend, then competitor.

The two films most diverge in the depiction of Billy's character. Brown's Billy is primarily a heroic character with bits of backsliding into violence. Taylor's Billy is hardly a tragic figure, although some participants in the making of the film labeled his life a tragedy,. He cannot control his volcanic temper, violently kills, and becomes a murderous villain more than does Brown's Billy, who keeps primarily on the positive side of the law. Controlled by deadly revenge, Taylor's Billy frequently gallops up the trail of killings. On two or three occasions the Kid in the 1941 film ponders his redemption, then suddenly reverts to his vicious, murderous ways.

Strangely, even though Taylor's Kid movie suffered from serious inadequacies in character development and from distorted history, it was a box-office bonanza for MGM, whereas the 1930 Vidor film was a bust, also for MGM. Perhaps the brilliant Technicolor format, the authentic southwestern scenes, and the popularity of movies about western outlaws, such as Jesse and Frank James and the Dalton brothers in 1939–1940 were spurs to the popularity of the 1941 film. At any rate, Taylor's Billy was the most negative, dark Kid protagonist in movies from 1930 until well into the 1940s.

By the early 1940s, large numbers of Westerns in Hollywood had begun to follow familiar patterns. Some were the singing Westerns of Autry and Rogers. Others, identified as B Westerns, were low-budget films featuring little-known actors and packed with nonstop action. Nearly all these Westerns also contained a minor strain of romance, with the hero attracting a beautiful, virtuous young woman with his courageous and upstanding actions.

Nineteen films about Billy released by the small Producers Releasing Corporation (PRC) between 1940 and 1943 established Billy the Kid as a widely filmed protagonist. Indeed, the PRC films consist of about one-fourth of all the Kid films in this period, helping to make him the most widely portrayed Western movie character. None of these films closely followed Billy's actual history, and over time they became increasingly hackneyed and trite. But as noted western historian Paul Andrew Hutton perceptively states, despite their historical and aesthetic shortcomings, "the films created a Billy the Kid brand name that elevated the outlaw into a position alongside fictional westerners such as Red Ryder, Hopalong Cassidy, and the Lone Ranger."

The PRC series opened with *Billy the Kid Outlawed* (1940) and closed with *Blazing Frontier* (1943). These briskly made films soon fell into increasingly recognizable patterns and stayed with the formula throughout the series' existence. The lead figures—Bob Steele in the first six films from 1940–1941 and Buster Crabbe in the next thirteen films from 1941–1943—were featured in fifty- to sixty-minute plots of hard riding, furious shooting, and several fistfights. Throughout the series, Al St. John rode along as Fuzzy Jones, a fumbling, bumbling sidekick, comic relief to the serious roles of Steele and Crabbe as Billy the Kid. In the first films in the series, another sidekick, Jeff, journeyed with the leading duo, but diminished budgets evidently caused his eventual disappearance. All of the series epitomized what had happened in the 1930s and 1940s in Poverty Row in Hollywood, pumping out dozens—even hundreds—of low-budget Westerns for Saturday afternoon audiences, particularly youthful watchers and other Americans addicted to a cinematic Wild West overflowing with action and adventure.

The PRC series invoked little of Lincoln County in its nineteen installments, although most were set in fictional New Mexico settings. Almost nothing dealing with the main Lincoln County figures appears in these films: John Tunstall, Alex and Sue McSween, John Chisum, Lawrence

G. Murphy, and Jimmy Dolan. There are no complex grey-hatted characters, but the PRC films were built around some of the economic and legal civil wars between good and bad guys. In the initial Bob Steele film, *Billy the Kid Outlawed* (1940), in *Billy the Kid's Gun Justice* (1940), and in the final installments, *Cattle Stampede* (1943) and *Blazing Frontier* (1943), a brutally contested war, much like one in the historically divided Lincoln County, is featured. Usually, as in *Billy the Kid Wanted* (1941) and *Billy the Kid's Fighting Pals* (1941), the villainous characters resemble the Murphy-Dolan contingent, co-opting and controlling the small farmers and other virtuous county citizens. Toward the end of the series, in such films as *The Kid Rides Again* (1943) and *Fugitive of the Plains* (1943), a minor female character appears, but no woman plays a major role or enters into a warm romance with Billy.

The Billy the Kid actors appearing in the PRC series generally resembled the benign or nonthreatening Kid character constructed in writings about him from the 1930s to the 1950s. But Billy has to show himself as an upright young man because nearly all the series films open with his public reputation as an outlaw or, even worse, a murderer. These plots feature the Kid as a visitor to a new locale, where residents think of him as a criminal and are convinced he should be shunned or even kept from entering the area. In *Billy the Kid in Texas* (1940), the Kid has to prove he can be a bringer of peace. The same is true in *Billy the Kid Wanted* (1941) and in *Billy the Kid Trapped* (1942), where a trio of rascals masquerading as Billy and his two chums, have to be defeated and exposed before the Kid is accepted.

Sometimes the challenges of proving his sterling qualities are doubly difficult for Billy. *Fugitive of the Plains* (1943) includes a sheriff who dislikes the Kid and thinks of him as a common criminal. Billy has to convince the sheriff, as well as the county's residents, that he will stand up for them. Until the final film in the series, this defeat of bad rumors and the proof of honest, courageous acts are necessary to prove Billy is one of the good guys. *Billy the Kid's Range War* (1941) illustrates what the Kid is up against in scotching these damning, false rumors when he laments, "I'm wanted from Maine to California, and I've never been out of the Southwest."

Gradually, the sameness, the numbing repetition of ideas, actions, and plots in the PRC series doomed it to extinction. Buster Crabbe, as Bob Steele had before him, tired of the banal qualities of the Billy films. Forced into lower budgets with diminishing audiences, the series ended in 1943. Interestingly, some thought the growing unpopularity of outlaw and gangster movies also undermined the faltering PRC series. Yet the series ideas were still sufficiently popular to spawn a new spate of twenty-three Billy Carson movies that cast Buster Crabbe as the hero and appeared from 1943 to 1946. Even with the declining popularity and eventual end of the PRC Billy series, the Kid had arrived as a well-known, attractive character, even a hero. More Billy films had been made about him than about any other western demigod by the mid-1940s.

The Outlaw (1943), with Jack Beutel, Thomas Mitchell, and Jane Russell respectively as Billy the Kid, Pat Garrett, and Rio McDonald, was clearly the most unusual Kid film released before 1960. It was also the most popular, playing to burgeoning audiences in subsequent, revised releases. At the same time the film markedly diverged from historical accuracy.

Sex, more than Billy the Kid, drew viewers to *The Outlaw*. The physical features of the buxom Russell, augmented by a new "heaving bra" Director Howard Hughes had designed for her, attracted voyeurs and critics. At first derailed by censors the film featured Rio (Russell) as the Kid's bed partner in their first meeting and also later. The blatant sexual content startled fans of the Kid; no previous film or novel about Billy had played up such erotic themes. By the early 1940s, some Billy biographers had gathered information, mainly in the form of later rumors, about the Kid's romantic links to señoritas, señoras, and other young women such as Paulita Maxwell, but most of those scholars chose not to publicize the sexual tales that indicated Billy might have fathered children in the Fort Sumner area. That meant the sexual emphases in *The Outlaw* highlighted a new, controversial, and scintillating part of the Kid's character. Sex was a new, unexplored frontier in Billy the Kid studies.

In addition to depicting Billy as a sexual animal, the Hughes film greatly rearranged or abandoned history. Conflicts between Billy and Pat Garrett (the sheriff was marvelously played by the Oscar-winning Thomas Mitchell, just coming off his Oscar for starring as the drunken doctor in the blockbuster Western *Stagecoach* in 1939) are addressed but in revised form. Even though Russell's Rio is a central figure—or her figure is central—she suffers from the blatant misogyny of both Billy and Pat. They vie for a strawberry roan horse, Red, as much as for Rio; in fact the horse beats out Rio in the masculine contests. Billy also abandons Rio more than once and even ties her to a fence in another scene.

The largest historical inaccuracy, however, is the insertion of Doc Holliday (John Henry Holliday) into the story, casting him as a good and close friend of Pat and Billy. No historical evidence indicates that either the sheriff or outlaw knew the gambler, even marginally. Yet Director Hughes uses Doc to illuminate what might be important facets of Billy's character. On one occasion Billy salutes Doc as "never having cold feet in his life," and in the next episode Billy says to Doc, "You're the only partner I've ever had." Maybe Doc serves as the big brother or father figure that Billy had enjoyed briefly in Tunstall and McSween—and quickly lost to blazing gunfire.

Even though *The Outlaw* introduced new themes and subject matter into the Kid's story, the mediocre acting of Beutel and Russell weakened the film. The two young actors, just beginning in Hollywood, were in over their heads in these demanding roles. The disregard of history also weakened the movie. In a final break with facts, the film has Garrett shooting Doc in mid-July 1881. In fact Doc was alive three months later to fire away in the famous Gun-fight at the OK Corral shootout in Tombstone, Arizona. He died from tuberculosis in Colorado in 1887.

Between 1942 and 1960, especially during the 1950s, about fifteen other films featured Billy the Kid characters in major or supporting roles. Few gained much attention, won over critics, or exhibited a notable impact on evolving Kid legends. Intriguingly, four films depicted a Billy who had escaped Garrett's guns in 1881: *West of Tombstone* (1942); *Son of Billy the Kid* (1949); *Last of the Desperados* (1955); and *The Parson and the Outlaw* (1957). Another picture, *Badman's Country* (1958), treats Garrett after Billy's death. On the other hand, three Billy films did capture audiences and engendered considerable comment: *Four Faces West* (1948); *The Kid from Texas* (1950); and *The Left Handed Gun* (1958).

Four Faces West drew heavily on New Mexico writer Eugene Manlove Rhodes's novella, *Pasó por Aquí* (1927). Although Billy the Kid is already dead, the central character in the movie, Ross McEwen, many are convinced, is based on Billy. McEwen robs a bank of $2,000 to aid his needy father, gallops out of town, and even rides a steer to befuddle the pursuing Marshal Garrett. The young robber then runs into a desperate Hispanic family in near-death condition, rumored to be from diphtheria. Deciding to restore the ailing family to health, McEwen abandons his getaway and surrenders to Garrett. Realizing McEwen's humanitarian efforts (he has also begun to repay his stolen money), the marshal promises to plead leniency for the young man.

Western novelist and Kid-movie authority Johnny D. Boggs writes that "many film historians have suggested that the character of Ross McEwen is loosely based on Billy." Indeed, McEwen's generosity, gentlemanliness, his connections with Hispanics, his romantic inclinations—all resemble those of the "good" Billy surfacing in the 1930s and 1940s.

Four Faces West, featuring the quartet of McEwen, Garrett, Frances Dee as Fay Hollister, and Joseph Calleia as Monte Marquez, was a popular movie with reviewers and critics but failed at the box office. The nonviolent film—not a single shot was fired—disappointed aficionados of violent, action-filled Westerns. Youthful audiences evidently disliked the romance and talking scenes. But Joel McCrea as McEwen and Dee as Hollister were strong actors, and so was Charles Bickford as Garrett. If one accepts the conviction that McEwen is actually modeled after Billy the Kid, then Johnny Boggs may be correct in concluding that "*Four Faces West* is easily the best movie about Billy the Kid."

The Kid from Texas (1950) illustrated how much the person starring as the cinematic Kid could shape not only the content of the movie but also its reception. By time the film was released in 1950, its lead actor, Audie Murphy, was a highly touted and widely recognized war hero. The real "Kid from Texas"—Murphy, not Billy—had risen up from poverty and an orphanage. He won numerous laurels for his valor in Europe, killing more than two hundred enemy soldiers in combat. Soon he became "the most widely decorated American soldier in history." Meanwhile his autobiography, *To Hell and Back* (1949), had raced to the top of the bestsellers. Few actors came to a movie with such a dramatic personal story and so little acting experience as did Audie Murphy.

One scholar, in examining Murphy's role as the Kid, said his portrayal of Billy oddly "mirrors Murphy's [own] life." There was indeed a close fit between Murphy and his filmic alter ego. Both were underlings trying to push their way upward and outward toward respect and prosperity. The movie Kid finds work with English rancher Jameson (Tunstall) and connects some with lawyer-merchant Alexander Kain, although Kain differs greatly from Alex McSween. Most names in the movie are changed, but Billy's revenge oath sworn against the killers of Jameson follows history. The Kid shoots down several opponents, who resemble the minions of Murphy and Dolan. Finally, Billy shows up in Fort Sumner and falls before Garrett's gun.

At the beginning of the film, the narrator promises that, despite name changes and "altered chronology," "the facts" in the movie "were as you see them." Why the necessity of name changes and the disrupted chronology is unclear. But the largest mystery is in the transformation of Alex and Irene Kain (Alex and Sue McSween). Kain is a hard head who dismisses Billy and even threatens to kill him while the beautiful Irene, played appealingly by Gale Storm, catches Billy's eye romantically, and maybe she him. In the final scene, Billy goes to Fort Sumner not to see Paulita Maxwell but to seek Irene Kain who is there.

The Kid from Texas was a box office hit, setting attendance records. Murphy quickly became something of a film hero, even though his depiction of Billy in the movie was less than captivating and convincing. One has to conclude that the notoriety of Audie Murphy as a national hero probably drew more attendees than any other facet of the film. In retrospect, the parallels between Murphy's life and that of Billy the Kid are perhaps the most memorable parts of the film.

The Left Handed Gun (1958), both a segment of the long Billy the Kid movie tradition and something of a window into the temper of the late 1950s, symbolized a sharp break from most of the previous Billy movies. The marriage between Kid history and sociocultural currents of the Eisenhower era pushed this cinematic Kid in new directions.

Paul Newman's adept handling of the central Billy character in this film dramatizes, for the most part, the "dark side" of the Kid. The revenge motive that fueled the historical Kid after Tunstall's murder also drives Newman's Kid, who becomes a vicious gunman, even though hints of his sympathetic qualities remain. Selfishness reins when he leads a band in the killings of Morton and Baker and seduces Celsa Gutiérrez in her own home. Even though close to his fellow riders Charlie Bowdre and Tom Folliard, Billy thinks first of himself and saving his own skin.

Arthur Penn deserved accolades for his superb direction of the movie, but he and his advisors played havoc with history. Those changes shape—possibly misshape—some of the Kid's story. For one, the film's pace, almost a canter, leaves little time for any reflection or indecision for Billy. Immediately after the Kid and his riders shoot down Sheriff Brady in Lincoln (April 1878), the Five-Day war also in Lincoln (July 1878) takes place. Then quickly comes the Kid's escape from the Lincoln jail (April 1881) and his death before the gun of Pat Garrett (July 1881). The rapid sequence of these events, much brisker than they actually were in historical Lincoln County, not only keeps the film dashing forward but reduces Billy to little more than a psychotic serial killer.

Conversely, other scenes suggest another kind of Billy. He admires and perhaps loves John Tunstall, who symbolically adopts the Kid. Tunstall also preaches peace and nonviolence to Billy. He gives the Kid a Bible and suggests that what now seems like "seeing through a glass darkly" would eventually become clear to the young wanderer. The Kid also feels at home with Bowdre and Folliard, relishing the rides with them.

Some have opined that *The Left Handed Gun* owes much to its cinematic times, citing James Dean's role in *Rebel Without a Cause* (1955) and the depiction of other youths in *Blackboard Jungle* (1955) as influences and models for Billy in this Arthur Penn film. Those comparisons are perhaps partially true. But Newman's Kid is more nuanced and complex than the juvenile delinquents of the fifties films. He is equally—or maybe more—a masculine type of the late Gilded Age and frontier America trying to sort out the present and looming future—but now only seeing through that glass darkly.

By the end of the 1950s, a different kind of Billy the Kid had emerged from the one depicted in dime novels, newspapers, and other negative accounts before the mid-1920s. Walter Noble Burns in *Saga of Billy the Kid* prepared the way for the new, less dark and more hopeful Kid. If not entirely heroic, his Billy was at least not the senseless murderer of the earlier interpretations. The historical writings of William Keleher, Maurice Garland Fulton, and Philip Rasch, the novella of Eugene Manlove Rhodes, and such films as *Billy the Kid* (1930), the PRC series, and *Billy the Kid Returns* featured a Billy with good sides as well as dark moments. That meant the earlier negative legends about the Kid had receded in large part and were replaced with another legend that could sometimes depict Billy as something of a Robin Hood, a person standing up for the downtrodden against their oppressors. Then in the 1960s and beyond, a third legendary Billy came on the scene. If the two earlier Billys followed an *either-or* pendulum swing, the third took on a *both-and* complexity. The third legendary Billy could be, at the same time, a young man of both bad and good inclinations. A New Grey Billy was born and would remain on the scene for most of the next half century.

15

The Rise of a Bifurcated
Billy, 1960–1995

The writings of Frederick W. Nolan and Robert M. Utley, like the books by Pat Garrett and Ash Upson and by Walter Noble Burns in earlier years, proved to be flash points in the interpretive history of Billy the Kid in the years stretching from 1960 to 1995. Rather than seeing Billy the Kid as villain or hero, Nolan and Utley brought into view a bifurcated Billy, a historical figure embodying both negative and positive characteristics. And deservedly so. Their pathbreaking books, articles, and essays from the 1960s to the 1990s still dominate writings about Billy the Kid decades later.

But even before Nolan and Utley came to the fore with their most valuable books, several other historians and biographers were turning up valuable new information on Billy the Kid. Philip Rasch continued publishing his diligent, hard-nosed "papers," and such grassroots historians as Waldo Koop and Robert Mullin were discovering extraordinarily valuable missing pieces in the Kid's early life.

The indefatigable Rasch persisted in churning out dozens of essays from 1960 until his death in October 1995. But rather than focus on Billy and the Antrim family as he had in the early 1950s, Rasch now turned to filling in many more details on those who rode with Billy, who took part in the Lincoln County War, and who played other parts in the history of southeastern New Mexico in the 1870s and 1880s.

Over time Rasch's views rarely changed in noticeable ways. Instead he generally buttressed earlier conclusions with new information. He still remained less critical of contributions of Murphy, Dolan, and Dudley than those of Tunstall and the McSweens. And intriguingly he did not write extensively about John Chisum. He viewed Tunstall, the Englishman, as a naïve conniver and Alex McSween as an embezzler, who used the Fritz insurance money to fund the Tunstall store and his house.

Rasch also maintained his dark view of Billy the Kid, summing up the Kid in his essay, "The Bonney Brothers" (1964–1965), as a "juvenile delinquent, horse thief, cattle rustler, and murderer." In another essay, "A Second Look at the Blazer's Mill Affair" from 1963–1964, Rasch curtly dismissed Billy's views on the shooting of Buckshot Roberts, stating that "there is little reason to give credence to the vainglorious claims of New Mexico's most famous psychopathic personality." Billy might not be an "adenoidal little moron," but he was "an expert at looking out for his own hide." For Rasch, the problem to overcome was the "fog of folklore" that Ash Upson and Walter Noble Burns had turned out in their biographies, both of them "either patently false, of questionable accuracy, or distortions of facts." Rasch found no sunny qualities in Billy's personality to praise.

Note by research note, Rasch's opinions on Billy-related facts became more set and uncompromising. Throwing out all stories about Billy's New York City origins, Rasch was more inclined to accept the 1880 census report that his parents resided in Missouri and that Billy was born there in 1855. The author also believed that Catherine McCarty took her family to New Orleans after living in Kansas and before she moved farther west. Although Rasch claimed to be the researcher who turned up Billy's killing of Windy Cahill in August 1877, his details on Billy's sojourn in Arizona from 1875–1877 are often vague.

Rasch's blunt personality shaped his writings about the Kid and other persons. Unable to be self-evaluative, Rasch frequently bludgeoned other writers such as Robert Mullin, his former collaborator, and Maurice Garland Fulton. In fact Rasch seemed unable to compliment the writings of others. For instance, he built on the pathbreaking research of Mullin and Waldo Koop without giving them well-deserved credit for their valuable findings. On the other hand, Rasch repeatedly pointed to his own important work; one of his essays contains thirty-nine footnotes, with eighteen references to Rasch essays. He found few, if any, characters in the stories of Lincoln County and surrounding areas who deserved his sympathies. And as Robert Utley has noted, Rasch's increasing tendency to publish in obscure outlets, particularly the *Brand Books* of grassroots Westerners organizations, meant that many of his essays never gained the attention he so craved.

Reservations about Rasch's difficult personality should not lessen his extraordinary value as a researcher on Billy the Kid, however. Along with later writers such as Nolan and Utley, Rasch did much to correct the misleading Kid legends created or perpetuated in the Garrett-Upson and Burns biographies and in numerous stories published in popular magazines and newspapers. He replaced these less-than-adequate accounts with new, solidly factual information about the Kid, his acquaintances, and his opponents that informs work a half-century later. Even if Rasch cannot be credited with smoothly written narrative histories with illuminating conclusions about the Kid, he must be remembered for his diligent research that cast fresh light on complex subjects related to the Lincoln County War and its warriors.

In 1965 another grassroots historian, Waldo Koop, published one brief monograph that cleared up several mistaken notions about Billy the Kid's early life. In his *Billy the Kid: The Trail of a Kansas Legend,* the Kansas writer adds much about the Kid's life from the mid-1860s to 1871. Koop does not focus on the possible life of Billy in New York City but on his years in Indiana and Kansas with his mother, his brother, and William Antrim, his eventual step-father.

Koop fills in missing gaps in previous accounts of Billy's life. In the opening paragraphs of his essay, relying on official documents recently discovered, Koop reveals that Catherine McCarty and William Antrim had known one another for about six years before coming to Wichita, Kansas, in about 1870. In 1868 the city directory of Indianapolis also indicated that Catherine was a widow of Michael McCarty and that she lived in that city near the residence of the Antrim family.

Arriving about June 1870, Catherine and her two boys quickly took up a vacant lot in newly established Wichita. Soon thereafter she opened a laundry, which was lauded in the local newspaper as an ideal place for cleaning clothes. In early 1871 Catherine was living on her small farm on the outskirts of Wichita, residing in a tiny home Antrim had built for her and raising crops and flowers. She also bought other small properties in town. Then suddenly Catherine sold her properties and left Wichita. Why the quick in and out movements? Koop suggests and others agree that Catherine's tuberculosis probably had been diagnosed and that she realized she had to go west to higher, drier country. By August 1871 the McCarty family, probably with Antrim, left Wichita and maybe headed for Colorado.

These valuable findings necessitate corrections and additions about the McCarty family. Catherine and Antrim had known one another since 1868 and perhaps as early as 1865 in Indiana. He was not a selfish, uncaring man but, in the months in Wichita, proved himself to be a warm-hearted, supportive friend for a single woman and her two growing boys. And the McCartys were not a dirt-poor family, for the mother and sons had sufficient funds to buy lots, take on a farm, and later to sell those properties and gain some income when they left Kansas for points farther west.

Like Koop's brief piece, Mullin's longer essay on Billy's early years, *The Boyhood of Billy the Kid* (1967), did not so much run counter to the conflicting legends of the Kid as outlaw or hero but was a revealing, factual overview of Billy's early years. Mullin achieved more broadly and deeply for Billy childhood what Koop had done with the Indiana-Kansas connections of the McCarty family. After attempting to explain the unsolved mysteries of Billy's origins and first years, Mullin draws on Koop and other sources to trace the McCarty history up to their arrival in Silver City in 1873. Then utilizing newspaper stories, interviews, and personal correspondence, Mullin provides the most dependable coverage of Billy's two years in Silver City, 1873–1875, at least until Jerry (Richard) Weddle published his 1993 monograph, *Antrim is My Stepfather's Name: The Boyhood of Billy the Kid*.

Not only does Mullin pull together reliable information on the first fifteen years or so of the Kid's life, he also discounts several of the legends that had surfaced about Billy's boyhood. Billy did not kill a man in Silver City for insulting his mother, and he was not already a hardened outlaw, or even labeled a juvenile delinquent by time he "skinned out" for Arizona. Unfortunately, Mullin points out, the highly charged Garrett-Upson biography had sent readers up the wrong trails in 1882, with those inaccurate directions still influencing writers three-quarters of a century later.

Mullin is particularly perceptive in noting the contending legends of Billy that had evolved by the 1960s. Those competing notions had laid "the foundation for the contradictory views of his [Billy's] character." On one side were those writers and readers who believed the Kid was "the most thoroughly bad man of all the bad men ever known in the West . . . the only white man who slew out of pure wantonness." On the opposite side, supporters contended the Kid was "a modern Robin Hood . . . a friend of the poor, a protector of innocence and virtue, a knight in books and *chaparejos* [chaps] slaying dragons on the plains of New Mexico."

Mullin traveled on neither side of this divide of conflicting views, although he avoided the darkest views of Billy. And in evaluating Billy's boyhood he saw a young man neither villainous nor saintly; rather, the Kid was "no better and no worse than any other of that area and era."

If Koop and Mullin focused on Billy specifically, Frederick Nolan in his book *The Life and Death of John Henry Tunstall,* released in 1965, thoroughly wove the story of one of the half-dozen men most influential to the Kid during his years in Lincoln County. This valuable book also launched Nolan as one of two most-important recent writers on Billy and kicked off his career of writing numerous books and articles on the Kid, Lincoln County, and other western American subjects.

Nolan's path to the top of the Billy specialists is all the more remarkable because he is an Englishman and wrote his first book on Tunstall without having set foot in the United States. Although the book on John Tunstall was Nolan's first dealing with the Lincoln County troubles, he would eventually turn out more than seventy other works of fiction and nonfiction, with even more essays added, in the next half century. In addition to historical works on New Mexico and the America West, Nolan wrote the Angel series of western novels, served as a founding father of the English Westerners organization, and even penned books about American musical theater. Building on his earlier editing and publishing experiences, Nolan was so prolific that he needed the pennames of Frederick H. Christian,

Daniel Rockfern, and several others to market his extraordinary output of books. On one occasion in July 1973 Nolan resigned from a well-funded position to sign a contract to produce eight book-length novels in a year's time. Once smitten by the Lincoln County story, Nolan contacted and corresponded with other researchers such as Maurice Garland Fulton, Robert Mullin, and Philip Rasch to expand his knowledge of the U.S. West and New Mexico

Nolan's book on Tunstall foreshadowed much of his approach to later books and essays dealing with Lincoln County and Billy the Kid. His thorough research, especially in original and obscure sources, was instantly apparent. Equally clear were the hallmarks of a creative writer, an author of fiction utilizing his appealing style to entice readers into an engrossing story. No one could have missed Nolan's talents in using his narrative framework to incorporate extensive quotations from Tunstall's dozens of letters to his family in England. Finally, photographs played a central part in the attractiveness of the book's contents.

Even though writers dealing with Lincoln County and Billy the Kid stories had been notoriously partisan, at first depicting the Kid as a despicable outlaw and later as something of a hero, Nolan avoided these simple, narrow extremes. Given that Tunstall did not refer once to Billy in his numerous letters home, all the information here on Billy comes from Nolan's perspective—and it is remarkably nonjudgmental. In a brief profile in a lengthy footnote, Nolan first dismisses "the web of folklore spun around the name of the Kid" in the Garrett-Upson biography. Then he encapsulates his own view of Billy in one line: he was a "lost waif who died before he had really started to live" and became "the one to gain immortality." Admitting the difficulties in turning up the Kid's origins and tracing his early years, Nolan summarizes Billy's life up to his meeting Tunstall in late 1877—all in amazingly neutral terms.

The same middle-of-the-road approach characterizes Nolan's treatments of major figures in the Lincoln County drama. Murphy and Dolan are not castigated as they are so often in biographies sympathetic to Billy. Nolan briefly mentions Murphy's "stranglehold on the mercantile business of Lincoln County" and his "virtually unbreakable monopoly" on supplies for the Mescalero Reservation and Fort Stanton, but he avoids tarring Murphy as a drunken, murderous dictator as so many Kid aficionados do. Nolan brings the same judicious assessment to Dolan. As he had with Murphy, Nolan quotes unflattering, often bellicose descriptions of the two leaders of The House, without endorsing these criticisms or drawing his own conclusions about the attacks. The closest Nolan comes to aversion toward Dolan is his statement that opponents of Jimmy did not realize that firing up his enmity "could often have fatal consequences." On the other side, the same balance marks Nolan's depictions of Alex McSween. Admittedly the lawyer was not always organized and sometimes naïve, and perhaps "one of the shadowy proponents of Lincoln County troubles," but he was not villainous or evil in any way. Others have criticized McSween for his mysterious and maybe self-serving handling of the Fritz insurance settlement, but not Frederick Nolan. And he makes clear McSween was a supporter of Chisum and Tunstall.

Of course, the fullest picture is of John Henry Tunstall, the central figure in this volume. The balance evident in the handling of other protagonists in the Lincoln County story is especially clear in Nolan's treatment of Tunstall. Without saying so explicitly, Nolan suggests that Tunstall's boundless ambition sometimes carried him away into unwise decisions and that he was too idealistic and unworldly (at least in the Lincoln County setting), yet he was by and large a supportive friend, an exceptionally warm son, and more obedient to law and order than most of his opponents.

Nolan's Tunstall exhibited a "forceful . . . personality," but unfortunately that personality was "full of youthful impatience and intolerance that comes in the early twenties and late 'teens, [and] occasionally dogmatic but more frequently sympathetic and friendly."

Tunstall's overwrought ambition and unwise decisions, Nolan implies, led to his tragic death in February 1878. In Tunstall's drive to establish his own "ring" to compete with The House and powerful territorial officials and to capture business leadership in Lincoln County, he was repeatedly imprudent, stirring up a volatile and angry hornet's nest that led to his sudden, tragic demise. Nolan's Tunstall is not a bad man—in fact a good man. Still, the sometimes-foolish newcomer took on much more than he could handle.

During much of the next thirty years, Frederick Nolan kept after the Lincoln County and Billy the Kid stories. His relentless pursuit of the stories led to the publication of his huge book, *The Lincoln County War: A Documentary History* (1992; updated in 2009). This six-hundred-page, oversized history immediately gained attention as the most extensive study of the Lincoln County War, and the book retains that sterling reputation nearly thirty years later.

Nolan's "documentary history" was appropriately titled. He had investigated and brought to his book the lives and actions of the major actors in the Lincoln County drama. Turning up new information through his diligent research in major archives, newspapers of the day, and government repositories, and through contacts with other specialists on Lincoln County and Billy the Kid, Nolan surpassed all previous scholars in the breadth and nearly always in the depth of his coverage. For example, in addition to his lengthy narrative covering the leading protagonists and central events, Nolan added ninety-eight biographical vignettes of less-well-known participants and a twenty-six page chronology of happenings from the early nineteenth century, with especially thorough coverage in the late 1870s through Billy

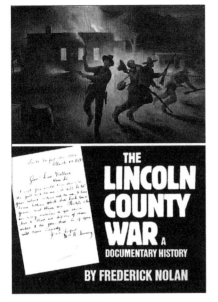

Frederick Nolan, *The Lincoln County War: A Documentary History*, 1992. Nolan's lengthy overview of the Lincoln County War remains the most thorough source on that large, controversial topic. The author's wide research, comprehensive point of view, and skillful employment of sources and photographs add much value to this magisterial volume. Reproduction of book jacket courtesy of the University of Oklahoma Press.

THE
LINCOLN
COUNTY
WAR A
DOCUMENTARY HISTORY
BY FREDERICK NOLAN

the Kid's death in July 1881. Nearly one hundred pages of photographs and maps add much to the comprehensiveness of Nolan's book.

Nolan holds back in the extensive evaluation of characters and their actions in much of his book, choosing instead to allow documents to contribute those often-conflicting conclusions, but he does not restrain his personal views in his closing three-page "Valedictum." It is the darkest picture Nolan had yet provided of the Lincoln County War. "Thirty years ago," Nolan wrote, "serious treatments of the causes of the Lincoln County War and the motives of its participants were very few." So at that earlier time he chose to see the events through the perspective of John Tunstall because he had become well acquainted with that young man's adult life. By the 1990s he needed to cast a much wider, more complex net. And he did so, with surprisingly bleak results.

It was now time, Nolan ventured, "to render sterner judgment on Tunstall and especially on Alexander McSween." And he did just that. Those two participants, so often treated as the "good guys" in the conflict, "were intent on a domination of Lincoln County as complete as that of Murphy and Dolan." Tunstall and McSween were "reckless," and Tunstall, a "fortune- hunting" young man, should have realized he was headed for a doom in his deadly competition with The House leaders. The "money-hungry McSweens" (perhaps Susan even more than Alex) were guilty of "pushing, needling, cajoling, intent on getting rich." In addition, Nolan asserts that lawyer McSween "manipulated the law to give the Regulators legal license to kill," which forfeit "all credibility, his own pious handwringing notwithstanding."

If the Tunstall-McSween partisans were often evildoers, The House dictators may have been worse. In fact, judging the Regulators harshly was "not in any way to attempt to justify or condone the autocratic arrogance of Murphy or the murderous deviousness of his chief adjutant [Dolan]." To put it succinctly—and in stiletto-like directness—The House scoundrels were "proven embezzlers of government funds, procurers and condoners of violence and murder, extortion and wholesale rustling—men without scruples of any kind."

Nolan dismissed nearly all the Lincoln County leaders as scoundrels of the worst sort. Dick Brewer, Juan Patrón, Lew Wallace, and Ira Leonard were less culpable, but they too carried large blemishes. Under pressure Brewer turned to violence, Patrón wobbled in his support at the Big Killing, Wallace failed to keep his promises, and Leonard seemed to disappear when the Kid needed him most. In short, Nolan concludes, "The Lincoln County War established nothing and proved nothing. . . . Nobody won, everybody lost."

It is revealing that Nolan makes no judgments about Billy the Kid in these gloomy conclusions other than to suggest that the town of Lincoln and perhaps the story of the Lin-

coln County War live primarily on the back of Billy's enduring, evolving legend. "The history ends where the legend
began," Nolan concludes, and "the legend never ends."

Nolan does provide information about Billy's life during these tumultuous years, however, and even advances
a few brief analytical comments about the Kid's actions.
He devotes about six of his thirty-eight chapters wholly or
partially to Kid-themed chapters. After two brief sections
tracing Billy's life to 1877 and his appearance in Lincoln
County, Nolan skims over Billy until after the Big Killing in
July 1878. Not surprisingly, the closing chapter treats Pat
Garrett's pursuit and killing of Billy.

Despite the brevity of Nolan's treatment of the Kid, he
spotlights important dimensions of Billy's character. He
notes that Billy, as early as his Arizona years and often later as
well, could not break way from the familiar places and paths
in his life and near at hand. He seemed unable to branch out
in new ways and become more far-sighted to avoid conflict
that would dramatically and tragically shorten his life. That
shortsightedness, Nolan insists, led to the Kid's eventual
demise. Whereas others fighters such as the Coe cousins and
Doc Scurlock could see the bleak and literal dead end in rustling, Billy could not break off his disastrous criminal journey,
remaining in place to steal for a living. Nor could he avoid
returning to a dangerous Fort Sumner where Pat Garrett
might be lurking. The Kid was roundly warned; he would
not—maybe could not—heed those warnings. Instead he
returned again to his friends and supporters and maybe to
his sweethearts in an act lacking courage and foresight.

Conversely, Nolan credits Billy with keeping his promises
to Lew Wallace, but the governor was unwilling to fulfill his
pledges. As Nolan puts it, Billy, "true to his word," helped
Wallace—in fact, he "put his life on the line for Lew Wallace." The Kid had "kept his word," but the governor, Nolan
continues, "never had any real intention of fulfilling any of
the promises he made." Nolan is convinced that Wallace's

failure to deliver on his pledges, as well as the earlier broken promises of Tunstall and McSween, was life changing for the Kid. Others had failed him, so "from now on, he would profit from the lesson: look out for Number One, and never buy anything you can steal."

On a few occasions Nolan overlooks, diminishes, or adds new wrinkles to the Kid's roles. The author is mute on much of Billy's reactions to Tunstall's murder, downplays his participation in the killing of Morton and Baker, and does not make much of the youth's emerging role in the Five-Day Battle. On the other hand, Nolan says more than most earlier writers about Billy's sweethearts and his possible paternity and asserts that Billy had just made love to Celsa Gutiérrez in a peach orchard in Fort Sumner before he walked to his death in Pete Maxwell's bedroom.

One should remember, however, that this book is a documentary history of the Lincoln County War, not a biography of Billy the Kid. That life story came six years later in Nolan's *The West of Billy the Kid* (1998). One should also keep in mind Nolan's astute and in all ways defensible observation that the escalating and enticing attractions paid to Billy the Kid have kept alive the ongoing attention to the Lincoln County War, not the reverse.

The authorial path of the other major interpreter of Billy the Kid, Robert M. Utley, followed a route as unusual as that of Frederick Nolan. As Utley noted, he had "devoted three decades to Indians and soldiers," and now he "was seeking a fresh field to plow." Viewing the film *Chisum* (1982) starring John Wayne, making a trip to the town of Lincoln, and perhaps hanging out with his neighbor, friend, and fellow western historian, Paul Andrew Hutton, drew Utley to the Lincoln County story with its "cast of vivid characters in a dramatic conflict and a case study of frontier violence."

With his usual energy and forthrightness, Utley was quickly on the Lincoln County and Billy the Kid trails. The initial product of this new-found interest was the first of a quartet of Utley books on these fresh subjects, *Four Fighters of Lincoln County* (1986). Soon to follow were *High Noon in Lincoln: Violence on the Western Frontier* (1987), *Billy the Kid: A Short and Violent Life* (1989), and most recently *Wanted: The Outlaw Lives of Billy the Kid and Ned Kelly* (2015).

Four Fighters of Lincoln County was the product of Utley's four lectures as the first presenter of the Calvin P. Horn Lectures in Western History and Culture at the University of New Mexico, an annual series that continues today. Utley's lectures and the book that followed were biographical in format. In his four talks and the four resulting essays, Utley dealt with Alexander McSween, Billy the Kid, Lieutenant Colonel Nathan A. M. Dudley, and Governor Lew Wallace. The lectures and essays were succinct, thoroughly researched, and clearly analytical. The conclusions of this brief volume would reappear in expanded treatments in Utley's two later books in the 1980s.

Hurtful flaws plagued Utley's major characters. Although an intellectual, religious, and nonviolent man, Alex McSween's excessive ambitions and naiveté, perhaps fueled further by his driven, stubborn wife, Susan, tried to push aside The House competitors through increasingly alienating means. He may even have urged his Regulator followers to kill Sheriff Brady. Even more flawed was Colonel Dudley, a man driven by a fiery, erratic temperament and a bombastic, crude demeanor. He clearly changed the balance of action on the day of the Big Killing. He should have stepped in and stopped the fighting, Utley contends. Even more disappointing were the procrastinating and delayed actions of Governor Wallace. Rather than diligently advocate for martial law, he waffled and seemed more interested in writing his novel *Ben-Hur* than in addressing the large, apparent needs of Lincoln County.

Utley's Billy the Kid is similarly marred. Early on he proved to be a "scrappy tough" and "drifter." He was not a leader in his early days in Lincoln County in 1877–1878 but was "always the diligent, active soldier," taking part in the Morton and Baker, Brady, and Roberts killings. After the violent shootout in July 1878 Billy, unwilling to change his ways, moved increasingly outside the law; he became an "outlaw chief." Utley portrays a young man who, on one side, could win over Hispanics, appeal to others on the owl hoot trail, and impress still others as optimistic and gregarious; but on the other side he could be willingly involved in violence and murder. Utley moves beyond earlier interpreters in suggesting a chronology of Billy's conflictive development: until the Lincoln County War, he seemed more the lively young man who loved to ride and shoot, but after the horrendous events of the first half of 1878, he moved toward the bad side, becoming more and more a thief and outlaw. The final pages of Utley's chapter on Billy the Kid contain a valuable, brief discussion of the shifting legends that arose around Billy and continued for many decades.

High Noon in Lincoln, building on central ideas in Utley's *Four Fighters,* greatly enlarged his coverage of the Lincoln County War from February to July 1878. Utley also made exceptionally clear one of his central themes in both books: the Lincoln County upheaval was a "war without heroes," an idea unanticipated when the author began his work on the two volumes. Although the actions of Sheriffs William Brady and George Kimball (Kimbrell) and Captain Henry Carroll might deserve limited praise, the deeds of Murphy, Dolan, Tunstall, Dudley, the McSweens, and Billy the Kid proved more villainous than heroic. In these critical conclusions, Utley was not so much attacking legends as countering and dismissing what he considered false information. The war, featuring a "collision of personalities," was fueled, as so many frontier "wars" were, by whiskey, guns, a "quest for money and power," and the Code of the West, which encouraged combatants not to retreat in face-to-face conflicts.

Utley spins his "high noon" story differently from what others historians say about the Lincoln County War. For one, he draws on his extensive knowledge of frontier military history to place Lieutenant Colonel Nathan Dudley's actions in larger, more complex contexts. He also criticizes Alex and especially Susan McSween more roundly than most other historians. In addition, Utley rightly notes that the war did not end with the killing of Alex McSween in the summer of 1878; it rolled on with familiar as well as new conflicts for another year.

Utley's Billy the Kid plays little or no role in the narrative through the Five-Day Battle. He is barely mentioned before the second half of 1878, making again clear that this book is primarily a history about the Lincoln County War, not a biography of Billy. But even Billy's post-1878 life is tightly condensed, with Utley covering the Kid's life from April 1879 to July 1881 in only a few pages.

Still, Utley reserves a special role for Billy in his Lincoln County narrative. The Kid, Utley writes, came out of this story as "a figure of towering significance," a result of "the standing he achieved in American folklore." Many of Billy's biographers, including Frederick Nolan, think that the Kid's expanding notoriety kept the Lincoln County story in the histories of the American West and of U.S. outlaws. Not so, Utley counters, for "the Lincoln County War did more for the Kid than he for it. For the Kid of legend, the war provided a setting for feats of prowess and adventure and acts expressive of character that would be endlessly chronicled with creative hyperbole." Although the Kid of history is treated as something of a minor supporting player in this drama, two years later he moved to center stage in Utley's very successful biography of Billy the Kid.

If the sales and reviewer attention of *Four Fighters* and *High Noon in Lincoln* disappointed their creator, the mounting sales and commentary on *Billy the Kid: A Short and Violent Life*, published in 1989, were much more than

Robert M. Utley, *Billy the Kid: A Short and Violent Life*, 1989. Utley's smoothly written, richly researched biography remains the premier life story of Billy the Kid. It is balanced, insightful, and appealing. Reproduction of book cover courtesy of the University of Nebraska Press.

satisfying. Utley's biography exploded on the scene, selling much better than his previous two books about the Kid and Lincoln County. His royalties quickly zoomed up to $50,000—and beyond. Reviewers showered the book with praise, calling it the best biography yet written about Billy the Kid and a model for stories dealing with other western demigods.

The accolades were richly deserved. Through its subject matter, organization, and even-handedness, Utley's book adds up to the best life story of Billy the Kid to this day. In his opening pages, Utley succinctly summarizes the purpose of his book: "stripping off the veneers of legendry accumulated over a century exposes neither hero nor villain, but a complex personality. Of the Kid as person and the Kid as outlaw, the reality both sustains and contradicts the legend." Here are Utley's explicit depiction of the bifurcated

Billy and the author's intentions to clarify when legends and reality overlapped and when they diverged. In this balanced, complex approach, Utley clearly moves away from the one-sided portraits of the earlier biographies by Pat Garrett and Walter Noble Burns.

If Utley portrays a two-sided Billy, he also describes a Billy moving through clear stages in his short life. The Kid is introduced as a lively, rather aimless juvenile in Silver City and something of an apprentice thief in Arizona and his first weeks back in New Mexico in Lincoln County. Until midsummer of 1878, he was a follower rather than a leader. After the shootout in Lincoln in July 1878, Billy gradually became a wandering rustler chieftain in southeastern New Mexico and the Texas panhandle. Utley's Kid was never the leader of an ongoing, well-organized gang of thieves, but he nonetheless moved through three transitions from innocent youth to beginning thief and on to veteran rustler.

Utley's skills as a historian and writer also lift his work above other biographies preceding his work. He avoids reproducing or replicating the rather formless works of Keleher and Fulton and also eschews their approach of excerpting in their narratives numerous long and sometimes undigested quotations of first-person accounts. Instead his compact chapters move along briskly, often organized around an interest-whetting event or two. In addition Utley's thoroughness as a researcher moves well beyond the notes of Fulton, who included almost no specific documentation in his text or skimpy notes. While prioritizing his fast-moving narrative and minimizing the quotation of historical sources, Utley still provides numerous comments on varying viewpoints and conflicting conclusions in his extensive footnotes.

Especially helpful are Utley's interpretive comments concluding many of his chapters. Several of these final comments deal with Billy's transitions in maturing, the conflicts between his lawful and unlawful actions, and his ties to

Tunstall, McSween, and the Regulators and their wars against The House partisans. Other summary observations disclose how much Billy's life illustrated the escalating violence and political and moral corruption of New Mexico and the country as a whole during the Gilded Age. These analytical paragraphs in chapter conclusions mesh well with the overarching narrative power of Utley's biography.

In his final chapter Utley furnishes a succinct overview of interpretations of Billy from the Kid's final months to the late twentieth century. Utley deals extensively with the shortcomings of the Garrett-Upson and Burns biographies and briefly mentions the Kid's treatment in literary works and movies. The ending pages, reflecting Utley's rather unique viewpoint, place Billy in the context of western violence. He also returns to the two-sided Kid he has introduced in his preface. If Ash Upson's earlier depiction of Billy as a "happy, likeable youth who was also a merciless killer laid a solid foundation for the rise of two towering and contradictory figures"—Billy as hero and as antihero— the latter image ruled for two generations into the 1920s. Then Billy as "engaging boy" followed Burns's romantic path. "Ultimately," Utley adds, "the struggle between the two [villain and hero] reached an uneasy equilibrium." It is this Janus-like figure who gallops through Utley's masterful biography of Billy the Kid.

Once a historical person, event, or idea comes on scene, takes root, and flowers with extraordinary growth, the role of ambitious historians resembles that of a skillful, perceptive gardener. Just as the gardener surveys those plants that grow best and worst in his or her garden and plans the future accordingly, so the insightful historian examines what has been written about a subject, evaluates the achievements and shortcomings of those writings, and suggests future approaches and topics to others. Historians call the survey and evaluation of a body of historical writing "historiography." For example, we have a historiography of the American Revolution, Civil War, Abraham Lincoln, the American West, and dozens of other topics. And there is a historiography of Billy the Kid that merits brief examination.

As biographies of Billy the Kid and his role in the Lincoln County War proliferated, historiographers turned to reviewing and evaluating the trends, the high and low points, and the future possibilities of essays and books focused on the two intertwined topics. Brief essays by Maurice Garland Fulton and William Keleher paved the way early on in the 1930s, and N. Howard Thorp and Neil McCullough Clark were some of the first scholars to evaluate the legends growing up around Billy in a chapter of their book, *Pardner of the Wind* (1945).

The most important breakthrough in the historiography of the Kid, however, came in J. C. Dykes's *Billy the Kid: The Bibliography of a Legend* (1952), an invaluable compendium. After well more than a half century, it remains the most extensive annotated bibliography of writings about the Kid. More bibliography than sustained narrative, Dykes's book contains comments on 437 items including biographies and histories, novels and other literary works, movies, newspaper stories, and ephemera. The annotations are extremely helpful, pointing to major contributions of books and essays and to glaring errors. Dykes knew his Billy biography and history and took a middle-of-the-road approach to the Kid, as his insights repeatedly attest.

In the early 1960s, two book-length studies pioneered with competing approaches to the Kid, approaches that continue to compete into the present. The introductions in the two books make entirely clear their exact but divergent purposes. One of the books, *A Fitting Death for Billy the Kid* (1960) by Ramon Adams, a candymaker by trade but also an energetic student of western history, was but one of his several books and essays about western demigods. The first of these was the helpful annotated bibliography *Six-Guns and Saddle Leather: A Bibliography of Books and Pamphlets on Western Gunmen and Outlaws* (1954, rev ed., 1969). In the prologue to *A Fitting Death* Adams tells readers he proposes "to correct . . . false history," to "point out and correct the various legends which have been repeated for more than seventy-five years. Surely it is time we learned the truth." On the other hand Kent Steckmesser was a historian with a deep background in literature and folklore. In *The Western Hero in History and Legend* (1965), Steckmesser wants to trace four western heroes—Kit Carson, Billy the Kid, Wild Bill Hickok, and George Armstrong Custer—in legend as well as history. "To ignore legends simply because they are by definition historically unfounded," Steckmesser provocatively states, "is an error which too many professional historians have made. Legends are of great importance in any interpretation of our national past."

Both writers achieved their opposing goals. In his research Adams tracked down and labeled hundreds of errors in books, essays, and newspaper stories beginning with accounts emerging in the 1880s. And not surprisingly, he devotes several pages to cataloguing errors in the Garrett-Upson and Burns biographies but also the numerous mistakes in the writings of Charlie Siringo, Emerson Hough, and the memoirs or histories of Miguel A. Otero, George Coe, and several other old-timers. For the work of Philip Rasch, William A. Keleher, and Frazier Hunt (whose book *The Tragic Days of Billy the Kid* [1956] draws on the extensive research of Maurice Garland Fulton), he has a much higher regard because of their factual accuracy. Hunt's work, Adams concludes, was at last a biography of the Kid he found "both reasonable and believable."

In *The Western Hero in History and Legend*, Steckmesser provides four succinct chapters in his discussion of Billy. After a brief biographical essay, he devotes the next two chapters to the two early legends about the Kid: "The

Satanic Billy" and "The Saintly Billy." The fourth chapter, "The American Robin Hood," traces legends spun about the Kid since the 1940s, with major emphases on Hunt's biography and western movies. Steckmesser is convinced that the essentially heroic stories of the Kid have dominated since 1940 because they play appealingly on the theme of betrayal by Governor Wallace and Sheriff Pat Garrett, as well as on the upbeat, winsome personality of Billy, his skills as a shooter, and his clear sympathies for Hispanics. "As long as this nation needs a Robin Hood figure," Steckmesser concludes, the legendary but not the historical Billy "will continue to gallop through the biographies and ballets, [and] fiction and film."

The competing approaches of Adams and Steckmesser captured and retained students of Billy the Kid legends in the next half century. They were as prologue for what followed. None of these next studies was more important than the two books by Stephen Tatum and Jon Tuska appearing in the 1980s and 1990s.

Tatum's *Inventing Billy the Kid: Views of the Outlaw in America, 1881–1981* (1982) veered away from Adams's fixation on specific historical facts and more closely followed Steckmesser's history-and-legend approach to the study of the American West. Tatum was trained in literary studies at the University of Utah and hewed closely to the American Studies tradition of his mentor, Don D. Walker, who in turn was a student of Henry Nash Smith, the founder of the myth-and-symbol approach to the American West. Tatum's pathbreaking study of the Kid and his interpreters, based on his doctoral dissertation and aimed at placing evolving interpretations of Billy the Kid in shifting sociocultural contexts, frequently invokes the theories of cultural-intellectual scholars such as Hayden White, John Cawelti, and Gene Wise. Tatum proposes to show how the Gilded Age, Great Depression, and Cold War years, for example, encouraged shifting views of the Kid. He also utilizes the literary modes of romance, tragedy, and irony to elaborate on the changing "inventions" of Billy.

Tatum moves well away from the narrow, uncompromising factual approach of Ramon Adams and other nitpickers by greatly enlarging on the changing meanings of the Kid's legend over a century's span. He urges readers to see how American society in the Progressive Era, the late 1920s, and the 1960s, for instance, encouraged writers and filmmakers to view the Kid differently because they were seeing their lives and their worlds diverging from and at odds with the political and social values of previous generations. Invoking the interdisciplinary methods of the American Studies field, Tatum draws on the insights of literary critics, sociologists, psychologists, and cultural anthropologists among others, to frame close readings of and produce fresh and deeper meanings for the transitioning images of Billy.

At the same time Tatum pushes his views so strongly that he overlooks a few points. He fails to see that historiography—the varying viewpoints of historical periods in this case—is not set in stone. What one generation of historians sees as central to an understanding of a decade or two in American history is not static and may indeed change dramatically over time. Historical interpretations of the 1890s, 1920s, and 1950s, for example, have altered markedly in the half century following the 1950s. In his criticism of Ramon Adams and other devoted fact-finders Tatum downplays too much the value of newly discovered facts and corrections to the narrative and overlooks their continuing impact on what later historians and novelists write about the Kid. Historians who read Tatum's study probably realize too the distance between their work and his conclusions when he asserts that Michael Ondaatje's innovative and in some ways absurdist volume of poetry, *The Collected Works of Billy the Kid* (1975), "is to my mind the most significant publication in the Kid's bibliography." Finally, Tatum's point that not much had been said about the Kid in the few years between the movie *Pat Garrett and Billy the Kid* (1973) and the publication of his book and his predictions about what might happen was overwhelmed by the explosion of histories by Nolan and Utley books, novels by N. Scott Momaday and Larry McMurtry, and the two *Young Guns* movies—all by 1990. Still, despite these and other small shortcomings, Tatum's book about the shifting cultural interpretations of Billy the Kid and their historical contexts remains the best book of its kind in the Kid bibliography.

Taking a position nearly opposite to that of Stephen Tatum is Jon Tuska in his *Billy the Kid: The Life and Legend* (1994, 1997). Tuska, who worked as a writer, an editor, and an agent, warns readers away from trying to link Kid historians, novelists, or filmmakers to their historical times and places and to the possible shaping influences in those cultural contexts. Instead adopting the techniques of Ramon Adams, Tuska pushes contentiously for the organization he uses in his widely circulated volume. For Tuska the facts about Billy the Kid can be gathered and structured in a dependable historical narrative as he does in the opening short biography in his book and the appended Kid chronology. Once those carefully researched facts have been obtained and rationally organized, in Tuska's view the historian or reader can move on to see how biographers, novelists, and filmmakers have dealt with the facts of Billy the Kid's life and legend. This method, labeled a "historical construction," must be adopted, Tuska was convinced, rather than Tatum's approach of viewing publications and films in the shaping contexts of their times.

Even though Tuska couched some of his discussions in theoretical terms, most of his pages are filled with extensive plot summaries of historical works, novels, and movies. More handbook than sustained analysis and evaluation, Tuska's book is informative and fact filled. In gathering all these facts, Tuska achieves his major purpose of putting together something close to his "historical construction" of Billy's life.

Major flaws limit the book's contributions, however. To his detriment Tuska is driven to attack other writers rather than merely to correct their mistakes or challenge their interpretations. He seems convinced that pointing out the weaknesses in other books will strengthen his own study. This is largely untrue. Noting the factual mistakes and incorrect conclusions in biographies by Garrett and Upson, and Burns is useful service, but Tuska calls the errors "fantasies" and unnecessarily assails the scholarship of Henry Nash Smith, Kent Steckmesser, John Cawelti, Stephen Tatum, and Robert Utley. In fact, his attacks are usually unwarranted. Tuska is especially wrathful toward Utley's first three books on Lincoln County and Billy, but most of the criticisms of these "fantasies" revolve around differences of opinion rather than factual mistakes, calling into question Tuska's understanding of the difference between historical fact and interpretation.

In general Tuska misunderstands or underappreciates the artistry of biographers, historians, novelists, and filmmakers. Too often following the facts-only approach of Ramon Adams, Tuska harshly criticizes major works of scholarship if they contain any factual errors, no matter how minor. Tuska seems to have had a blind eye and tin ear for all dramatic narrative. His own work lacks it.

In short the Tatum and Tuska volumes, the most recent book-length historical studies of writings and films (or the historiography) about Billy the Kid, provide two divergent approaches to understanding the legends surrounding the much-written-about western outlaw. Tatum, identifying with, incorporating, and elaborating on the methods of American Studies scholars such as Henry Nash Smith and Kent Steckmesser, urges researchers to see how shifting interpretations of the Kid have been profoundly shaped by the changing social, cultural, and intellectual milieus in which they were written and published. Tuska, on the other hand, stiff-arming Tatum's methodology and embracing the approach of Ramon Adams, calls for history first, special attention paid to plot details, and avoidance of partisanship he claims to see in the writings of Robert Utley. No one since Tatum and Tuska has provided overviews of the changing interpretations of Billy the Kid in the past twenty to thirty years. The next chapter in this work attempts to do just that.

Many fewer novels than biographies about the Kid appeared in the years between 1960 and 1995. Beginning in the 1960s, a cultural trend toward doubt, cynicism, protest, and even satire helped shape novels written about Billy the Kid. Rather than an evil desperado of the early dime novels or the more heroic character of Burns's biography, the two contrasting views of Billy in the pre-1960s period, the Kid became instead a Janus-like Billy, a young man combining *both* negative and positive characteristics. In short neither a black nor a white hat, the malevolent outlaw and cheerful comrade were united and blended into a New Grey Billy.

From the late 1960s onward novelists, following this emerging ambivalent figure, depicted Billy the Kid as a two-faced character. He might veer toward violence and cruelty, but he also warmly accepted Hispanics and women as well as several male colleagues. This two-sided Billy has dominated historical fiction about him in the past half century. Yet, as had been true prior to 1960, not all fiction writers featured this ambivalent Billy the Kid in their novels and short stories.

In 1967 historical novelist Amelia Bean published *Time for Outrage,* which, at 450 pages, was to date the most extensive work of historical fiction about the Lincoln County War. Bean focused on the events of 1877–1878, provided pen portraits of the major participants in the war, and dealt with the two competing factions in Lincoln, the Chisum-Tunstall-McSween and the Murphy-Dolan-Riley combines. Nor did she overlook the Santa Fe Ring members, territorial officials, and army officers who involved themselves in the horrendous violence.

Two imagined figures, Luke Pender and Magdalena Perez, dominate the plot in a torrid romance. And revealingly, Bean does not deal extensively with Billy the Kid. Following the histories by William A. Keleher, Taylor Ealy, and Frederick W. Nolan, the author concludes that Billy was "never . . . during the war a leader of any group or contingent." Or again she declares, "Bonney could not have been a leader of men fighting for McSween." Prone to strong opinions and quick violence, as illustrated in the Brady killing, Bean's Billy is pushed aside by Luke Pender, the main male presence in the novel.

In two ways Bean enlarges the fictional recounting of the Lincoln County War. She deals extensively with the ethnic or racial mix in the region, showing how Mexican-descent and African American people were intimately involved in the events of 1877–1878. Bean also integrates women more thoroughly into the Lincoln County story. Sue McSween is a lively, assertive, and sometimes-foolish participant in several events, and Mrs. Brady, the Mexican wife of Sheriff Brady, is known in Lincoln for her opinionated, outspoken ways. More intriguing is Tia Lupe, another local Hispana, a *médica* or curandera, who plies her skills as a healer and source of folk wisdom in the village of Lincoln.

Another novel, *The Outlaws* (1984), illustrates a trend increasingly popular in American fiction from the 1960s onward. More than a few publishers, recognizing the large, persistent interest in things western and capitalizing on the growing fascination with violent and explicitly sexual stories, catered to reader demands in the Adult Western genre. Featuring steamy sexual encounters and several scenes of violence, Adult Westerns were extraordinarily popular in the closing decades of the twentieth century.

Like many other Adult Westerns, *The Outlaws* was written under a pseudonym, in this case by Jane Toombs as Lee Davis Willoughby. It appeared as the forty-ninth entry in the multivolume Making of America Series. The author of dozens of books in several fictional genres, Toombs adopts the commonly used technique of many historical novelists: the creation of invented characters to ride along with historical figures.

One of the first authors to employ explicit sexual encounters in a novel about Billy the Kid, Toombs nonetheless keeps Billy's sexual activities off the page. But hero Mark Halloran (actually Mark Dempsey) and heroine Tessa Nesbit engage in electric lovemaking. Sex plays a more prominent role than violence does in this novel.

Toombs's Billy illustrates the ambivalent Kid figure who began appearing in fictional and historical accounts from the 1960s forward. He is cheerful and warm toward Tessa's younger brother, Ezra, and helps other needy persons. But he is also a selfish, self-absorbed, vicious, and predatory young man. For instance he takes advantage of a young señorita hopelessly enamored with him. Toombs features more the ugly side than the virtuous actions of Billy.

For the most part, Toombs closely follows the major events of Billy's life in Lincoln County. The killings of Tunstall, Brady, and McSween are mostly accurate, as are the depictions of the important happenings at the Greathouse Ranch, Stinking Spring, and Fort Sumner. In *The Outlaws*, the New Grey Billy and the Adult Novel are juxtaposed. The result is not a first-rate novel but one about Billy that is provocative, readable, and reasonably accurate.

Two major—and unusual—novels about the Kid appeared in the late 1980s, one diverging markedly from the bifurcated Billy figure and the other following it. Larry

McMurtry's *Anything for Billy* (1988) includes a portrait of an atypical Billy, here named Billy Bone. Uncertain, irrational, and weepy, Billy exhibits few, if any, of the characteristics of the historical Billy. Shrouding his youthful, diminutive protagonist in a less-than-courageous demeanor allows McMurtry to depict a lead man far different from those characters featured in most of the recent Kid novels or biographies.

McMurtry's Billy must have his way. Ben Sippy, the imagined narrator, and Joe Lovelady, Billy's cowboy buddy, try to bend to Billy's will and ways. He tolerates no disagreements with his opinions and actions, bullies his acquaintances into following his erratic ideas and deeds, and falls into depression when he dreams about the mysterious Death Dog and his own demise.

Storyteller Sippy, a western dime novelist, flees Pennsylvania and his termagant wife. He is all wide-eyed about his dreamed-up Wild West. He tries and usually flubs his attempts to understand a West and Billy sharply varying from his premonitions and his love for a frenetic frontier. His gradual perception of what the West is really like is a major ingredient of the novel.

Anything for Billy evolves into something of a spoof, although McMurtry's intentions were undoubtedly more serious. This novel is reminiscent of McMurtry's *Buffalo Girls* (1990), a novel about Calamity Jane issued in 1990. Both works satirize western demigods, Billy and Calamity, but move little beyond satire and black humor. When compared with the abundant strengths and major achievements of McMurtry's Pulitzer Prize–winning *Lonesome Dove* (1985), these two novels badly falter. They are laced with such large helpings of satire that Billy and Calamity become little more than western caricatures.

Ben Sippy tells readers that Billy "was violent all right . . . [but] in his case the reputation [as a gunslinger] just arrived before the violence." Billy moved without thinking;

he "was just a puppet to his instincts, jerked this way and that by strings whose pull he couldn't predict." How much of what Ben relates in first person represents McMurtry's thoughts about Billy the Kid is not clear. One might speculate, judging from McMurtry's general comments concerning a mythic West, that he attempts here to question the huge, dominating legends about the region, particularly in the person of Billy the Kid. And that is perhaps as far as the speculation ought to go.

Another unorthodox novel about Billy the Kid is N. Scott Momaday's *The Ancient Child* (1989). This experimental work combines several ingredients—Native American myth and lore, Old West legends, and modern Indian life—to help portray Billy as a supporting character. It was the first novel by Native American writer Momaday after his Pulitzer Prize–winning *House Made of Dawn* (1968).

Two characters stand at the center of the story. Set, an adopted Indian artist, is on a traumatic identity search, trying to find his real father and true self. His journey turns him toward Grey, a young Kiowa-Navajo medicine woman. Through Grey's dreams or visions the reader moves backward in time to view Billy the Kid and his milieu. Grey not only dreams of Billy, she time travels to his era, becomes his lover, and accompanies him on several of the most-written-about events of his life. It is she who delivers the note about a hidden pistol in the privy, which he uses to shoot down one of the deputies in his escape from the Lincoln jail. She also observes him in the killing of Sheriff Brady and watches his capture at Stinking Spring.

The images of the Kid in Grey's memories and dreams, and in the novel generally, are those of an ambiguous Billy. He readily kills (although he is never labeled a murderer), but is also a jolly, clever, and loving companion.

Momaday's novel is difficult to follow because it lacks a plot. Dreams and memories, descriptive passages, bits of poetry, strands of legends, and other experimental literary forms are piled together often without clear connections. But in focusing on Native perspectives and utilizing numerous dream sequences, Momaday added fresh ingredients to Billy the Kid fiction when the book appeared in 1989.

In the early 1990s a handful of other novelists attempted traditional as well as new approaches in historical fiction about Billy. Preston Lewis's *The Demise of Billy the Kid* (1994) adopts the most universally utilized trick in historical fiction: he creates an imagined character, H. H. Lomax, to journey alongside Billy in the Lincoln County War and until his death. Lomax speaks of the befriended Billy as a grinning, warm buddy who becomes increasingly negative, even a heartless killer in seething rage after Tunstall's murder. All of Lewis's major characters—the Murphy-Dolan-Riley gang on one side, the Chisum-McSween faction, including Susan, on the other—are flawed figures. Only Sheriff Pat Garrett seems upright and honest. A more-than-adequate historical novel, Lewis's work itself is artistically flawed, however, with excessive use of metaphors and similes and an ill-conceived romance between Billy and Señorita Rosalita, who plays musical beds with Lomax and the Kid.

Much more atypical is the novel of Rebecca Ore, the penname for Rebecca B. Brown. Her work of science fiction, *The Illegal Rebirth of Billy the Kid* (1991), which features the "rebirthing" of a "chimera" or rebooted clone of Billy the Kid in 2067. The author's Billy is lost in the present and future, understanding almost nothing after 1881. The meandering plot dramatizes the Kid's attempts to negotiate the chaos between the twenty-first century and the 1870s and 1880s. Clearly, Brown is a strong writer and knows a good deal about Billy's life and times, but her paranormal fiction likely attracts aficionados of science fiction much more than Old West readers.

Two other novels reveal how much novelists in the 1980s and 1990s could diverge from the good badman becoming highly popular in those decades. One is a throwback to the earlier desperado Billy, and the other is ahistorical in its treatment of the Kid.

Veteran novelist Matt Braun combines history and sheer imagination in his formula-driven Western *Jury of Six* (1980) and reverts to the one-sided, negative view of Billy popular earlier in the twentieth century. The author is well acquainted with the familiar events of Billy's life, employing them to create a dark portrait of the Kid.

Braun grafts the life story of Texas stock detective Luke Starbuck onto the journey of Pat Garrett, generating confusion, irregularities, and unbelievable events as a result. All historical novelists face the dilemma of how much history and how much invention will characterize their works. This author errs on the side of an overactive imagination.

For Braun, Billy the Kid is "nothing more than a common murderer." He had killed eight men (not true) and "had given none of his victims an even break." Even worse is that the Kid was like a "mad dog terrorizing the countryside," with his violence and murder having a "passing similarity to a rabid animal." On the other hand the author's fictional character, Starbuck, is a courageous, driven, and dependable man. Braun is clearly embracing the earlier legend of Billy as a violent desperado with little sympathy for anyone but himself.

Although B. Duane Whitlow avoids the negative image of the heartless, callous Kid in Braun's novel, he does break the golden rules of top-drawer historical novelists in his *Lincoln County Diary* (1991). He not only frequently reimagines the crucial events of Lincoln County conflicts, he also rearranges the known chronology of happenings and mistakenly dates other occurrences.

Whitlow's reshapings include the main characters. They are government officials from Washington, D.C., and soldiers from Fort Stanton, not the best-known figures from Lincoln County. The exception is Jimmy Dolan, the familiar character at the center of the story, although Governor Lew Wallace and others play minor parts.

Billy the Kid is primarily an off-scene, bit player. Whitlow deals with Billy the killer and also Billy the genial comrade, but the events of his life are so changed—even distorted—that he is not the Kid of history. For instance Billy is captured by Pat Garrett in Stinking Spring in December 1880, but afterwards he is taken to Lincoln, not to Las Vegas and Santa Fe. And there is no trial in Mesilla. Billy escapes from the Lincoln jail a few days after his capture, and Garrett guns him down shortly after his escape. In these instances alone, about six months of Billy's life are elided and events surrounding his last days rewritten.

Whitlow also turns the Lincoln County conflict into a story of government agents pursuing counterfeiters in southeastern New Mexico. In the plot focused on phony dollars in New Mexico and Mexico, John Chisum, Alex and Sue McSween, and the Regulators are absent for the most part. The author also has Billy working for Jimmy Dolan, with Jessie Evans operating one helm of the counterfeiting and a prominent member of the Santa Fe Ring pulling the levers of the counterfeiters in the territorial capital.

This novel illustrates how fast and loose authors of fiction can play with historical facts. Whitlow sidelines Billy the Kid and undermines the authenticity of his story and surrounding events, seemingly without any difficulty or reservations. While avoiding the three major legends surrounding Billy—villain, hero, or a combination of villainy and heroism—Whitlow creates a new story line greatly at odds with recorded history.

The opposite example is Elizabeth Fackler's *Billy the Kid: The Legend of El Chivato* (1995). Her work, containing more than five hundred densely packed pages of historical material, remains one of the longest historical novels about the Kid. Fackler's novel provides almost as much biographical and historical material as any nonfiction work on Billy.

For the most part she follows known facts and along the way adds conversations and thoughts based on the most-thorough historical research.

Fackler's Billy is an appealingly complex figure. At times fun-loving, genial, and loyal, he can also be violent, vicious, uncaring, and murderous. The author achieves depth and breadth in her Billy character. In one scene, for instance, the Kid can win the hearts of señoritas and señoras but, in the next episode, gun down those who stand in his way or challenge his actions.

Other additions to Fackler's novel increase its value. Her treatment of Hispanics and women is expanded much beyond most fictional accounts of Billy. The depictions of Susan McSween, Billy's señoritas, and his relationship with Paulita Maxwell are especially thorough. In general Fackler adds a great deal on the roles of women in what is usually a man's story. Indeed sexual relationships play a large role in this story, with Billy sometimes frolicking in bed more than shooting his pistol.

Many recent books on Billy are sympathetic to him; a few others, conversely, see him as a desperado whose selfish actions bring about his own demise. To Fackler's credit, she portrays Billy positively as well as negatively, showing that his complex character embodied humanity, even love, but also harbored violence and evil. Not many historians, biographers, or novelists have been as successful as Fackler in portraying Billy the Kid as a complex historical character.

Few films about Billy were made in the years from 1960 to 1995, but of those released some remain among the best of the Kid movies. It is revealing that the Billy films during these years featured the two-sided figure—the happy, congenial young man and the malicious, indiscriminate killer—although the balance shifted toward the dark Billy rather than the more attractive Billy appearing in most historical and biographical accounts.

One-Eyed Jacks (1961) starred Marlon Brando as Rio, the Billy the Kid figure. The script drew on Charles Neider's fictional work, *The Authentic Death of Henry Jones* (1956), but also broke from that novel. Rio's hatred for Dad Longworth, the emotional tension at the center of the movie, derived from Longworth's abandoning Rio in Mexico and forcing him to spend nearly five desperate years in a Mexican prison hell-hole. Dad, formerly something of a father and partner, and Rio become deadly enemies, even though Rio begins to pursue Dad's step-daughter, Louisa.

Rio, a young man distorted and bent from his harsh, cruel background, frequently erupts in dark behaviors. On one occasion he gives a half truth to an inquiring woman when he tells her "home is anyplace where I throw my saddle down" and that a saloon was his boyhood setting. Even though Rio covets a stable life, he frequently erupts in anger especially when driven to rage from what he considers Dad's mistreatment. Reluctantly in a later moment of illumination, Rio is able to recognize but not rein in his powerful emotions.

Conversely Rio exhibits few traces of the good Billy who had emerged in the Burns biography and more than a few life stories thereafter. Rio is not a happy companion willing to brighten the lives of his chums. Instead anger—sometimes fury—dominates his life. That seething temperament finally explodes into the killing of Dad Longworth at the end of the film.

Like Neider's novel, *One-Eyed Jacks* abandons the New Mexico setting. The film offers nothing of Lincoln County. In fact Monterey, California, the Doc narrative figure, and the downtrodden Hispanics found in Neider's work are weakly depicted in the film. Rather, the movie focuses on the interior struggles that drive Rio to emotionally lash out at others. In most ways the film is something of psychological study of an anger-driven Kid.

Chisum (1970), starring John Wayne as rancher John Chisum, moves clearly away from much of *One-Eyed Jacks*. First, it is a John Wayne film, and by this stage in Wayne's career, any movie in which he was the leading figure was a Wayne-dominated project. All the more intriguing is the image of Chisum that Wayne portrays in light of the types of Westerns being filmed at the time.

In the decade following the mid-1960s a passel of film Westerns presented the West, its leading men, and their actions in, at best, grey hues. Clint Eastwood's trilogy of "dollars" films, *A Fistful of Dollars* (1964), *For a Few Dollars More* (1965), and *The Good, the Bad and the Ugly* (1966), directed by Sergio Leone and known as Spaghetti Westerns, depicted Eastwood as the "Man with No Name," a violent, laconic, heartless protagonist lacking any measure of law or morality. Three later three films, *The Wild Bunch* (1969), *Little Big Man* (1970), and *Soldier Blue* (1970), were equally dark, picturing western law men as violent crooks and sexually driven misanthropes. In these films there were murderous or half-crazy soldiers, as George Armstrong Custer was depicted in *Little Big Man*. At the same, Indians were becoming the new heroes confronting a racist, violent, rampaging American civilization.

These dark Westerns were all the rage from the early 1960s to the mid-1970s, but *Chisum* was an exception. It is true that Wayne would never have starred in an Italian Western reorienting the genre and bringing anti-Westerns on the scene as Leone and Eastwood did. Instead, Wayne's Chisum role reorients history by making the cattle baron the central figure in the Lincoln County War. Much more than being the Cattle King of the Pecos in historical terms, the Chisum in Wayne's film marches forward to lead the attacks on The House partisans and the corrupt legal officials.

The dominance of the Chisum character in the film forces Billy, played by Geoffrey Deuel, into a supporting role. He comes on the scene as a murderer from Silver City, not Arizona where his first killing occurred, and takes a job with Englishman John Tunstall. And when the Murphy-Dolan-Brady supporters kill Tunstall, Billy swears an oath to avenge the killing and follows a desperate path of bloody vengeance.

In *Chisum* Billy is turned into a violent gunman bent on retaliation. He becomes a black-hearted villain, shooting down Morton, Baker, and Sheriff Brady. Before long he has also killed Jessie Evans and others. By the film's end, the differences between Chisum and Billy become clear: the rancher desires justice; Billy craves vengeance. In its rewriting of actual history, *Chisum* elides the positive side of Billy—his camaraderie, his connections with Hispanics, and his warm ties with older and younger woman—and turns him into an unfeeling, indiscriminate murderer. Hollywood obviously had its own historical agenda in mind, abandoning the ambiguous Billy who had emerged since the publications of Burns's *Saga of Billy the Kid* in 1926.

In 1972 *Dirty Little Billy,* sandwiched between *Chisum* (1970) and *Pat Garrett and Billy the Kid* (1973), suggested that the film was made in a Hollywood entirely foreign to an actor or director such as John Wayne. As was so often the case in such projects, *Dirty Little Billy* also proved that the film's makers, long on intended revisionism of the Kid and his legend, were way short on their historical knowledge of the Kid's life and what had been written and published about him in the past half century. The screenwriters drew not on the new findings coming out in the 1950s to the early 1970s but on the ill-conceived conclusions published in the Garrett and Burns biographies.

In the film Billy is a young man living in a fractured family in Coffeyville, Kansas. His stepfather, Henry McCarty, hates him, and the feeling is mutual. Thrown out of his home, Billy finds new friends, a somewhat older gambler named Goldie and his girlfriend, Berle, a prostitute. Billy soon descends into a maelstrom of guns, violence, and sex. Goldie befriends Billy but instructs him in the "dirty" deeds that suddenly dominate his young life. In explosive scenes of shooting and murder, Berle is killed, and Goldie and Billy are forced to flee Coffeyville.

If director Stan Dragoti and actor Michael J. Pollard intended to counter the more sympathetic cinematic depictions of Billy and instead to give viewers the "real" Kid, they badly failed. Their revisionist Western was more Hollywood fantasy than western history. Nearly every event in this dark film was either wrong or badly imagined. In the end *Dirty Little Billy* was something of a throwback to the villainous Billys of the late nineteenth and early twentieth centuries. Viewers shunned the unrelenting darkness—the grime, depravity, greed, and violence—and the film was a box-office disaster.

Movie director Sam Peckinpah had been interested in the Billy the Kid story for nearly a dozen years. In the early 1960s he tried to direct *One-Eyed Jacks*. That did not work out, but Peckinpah kept at the Billy story. It came back around to him in *Pat Garrett and Billy the Kid* (1973), hailed by some as the best of the movies about Billy.

Peckinpah's film, unlike nearly all other Kid movies, gave Billy (Kris Kistofferson) and Pat Garrett (James Coburn) equal billing. Following those dual interests, the film shifts back and forth between the two characters, who are nearly always filmed in separate scenes. The 2005 version, a special edition, which recovers scenes cut in the version first release in 1973, opens with the murder of Garrett in 1908 (not as the film mistakenly says 1909) and fades away into a scene of Billy and his followers shooting off chicken heads at Fort Sumner.

Naturally Garrett and Billy are the central characters, with the sheriff portrayed as a no-nonsense man appealingly dressed. He shoots without hesitation and also enjoys bathing in the nude, on one occasion with four enthusiastic

Pat Garrett and Billy the Kid, 1973. Many consider this the best movie on Billy the Kid. Sterling performances by James Coburn as Pat Garrett and Kris Kristofferson as Billy the Kid greatly enhanced the quality of the film. Courtesy Paul Andrew Hutton.

prostitutes. In addition, he tells Billy that in five days when he becomes sheriff, he will ride the Kid down. Garrett is pictured as the wave of the future, telling Billy, "Times have changed." Maybe so, Billy retorts, but "not me."

Peckinpah's Billy combines the historical Kid and Hollywood fantasies. His dual character comes into focus: he is an enthusiastic comrade as wells as a vicious killer. He connects well with Hispanics and is as sexually driven as Pat Garrett. His actions can also include dramatic U-turns. On the way to Mexico, when his friend Paco is shot down and his wife (or daughter) raped, Billy immediately changes his mind to return to fight for what he considers right. On another occasion the Kid dashes on scene, like a super gunman, to wipe out a clutch of bounty hunters.

The first-rate acting of Kristofferson and Coburn power this film. Their characters are not men in white or black hats but, by turns, grey figures almost heroic yet clearly villainous. The apt handling of the scenery reinforces the greyness

Young Guns, 1988. The famed Brat Pack—Emilio Estevez as William H. Bonney (Billy the Kid), Kiefer Sutherland as Doc Scurlock, Lou Diamond Phillips as José Chávez y Chávez, and Charlie Sheen as Dick Brewer—especially captured the attention of youthful audiences in the late 1980s. Late-twentieth-century attitudes on racial, ethnic, and gender topics also shaped the content of the movie. Courtesy Paul Andrew Hutton

of the characters, with numerous depictions of unflattering landscapes and unattractive, run-down buildings. The film clearly plays on the Janus-like figure of Billy increasingly popular in these times.

Young Guns (1988) followed the format and content of most Billy films of note in the late twentieth century. It combines bits of history, some social and cultural issues of the film's time, and Hollywood flavoring. Moviegoers were attracted to the film because it fit the times, appealed especially to young audiences, and depicted an alluring Billy the Kid.

Billy comes on scene as a reputed murderer. The movie misshapes history, however, in these opening tableaus: the Kid is rescued by John Tunstall partisans from vicious L. G.

347

Murphy riders. Then the film moves back on track in illustrating the civil war between economic interests and power-hungry competitors in Lincoln County.

The same combination of fact and imagination continues in the treatment of Billy in subsequent scenes. On the dark side he is depicted as a "little rodent" scurrying around the desert without an upstanding cause or direction. When the villains kill Tunstall, Billy loses his nascent home, and his possible new course to stability and virtue is now knocked off track; he is driven wild with revenge. He quickly canters up the vengeance trail, killing men with little reason. One cannot describe the *Young Guns* Billy as a hero, but at times he is motivated by courage and altruism. In fact, in the second part of the film, Billy rides back into deadly Lincoln to help Alex McSween, the lawyer with whom he has disagreed but, Billy thinks, now needs help.

The Big Killing scene in Lincoln in July 1878 is the climax of the movie, the action most emphasized and most distorted. Here the bifurcated Billy is on display. He sometimes seems the badly needed strong, forceful captain; in other scenes he is obviously an irrational youth fueled by murderous rage. One of his followers comprehends this conflicting urge: Billy is "like a whirlwind out there," he tells others. In the most contrived part of the Lincoln shoot-out, Billy climbs into a trunk, is thrown down from above, and pops out of the trunk, both guns blazing and killing several rascals. The Hollywood writers and producers had obviously rewritten the scene to maximize the drama and center Billy in the traumatic episode.

The screenwriters also wove their reflections of contemporary sociocultural issues into the script. They play up the questionable Apache heritage of Billy's companion José Chávez y Chávez, insert a crazy peyote scene Billy engineers, and show him holding forth on the white attack of an Indian village that did not occur. Doc Scurlock is enamored with a young Chinese woman who was not a part of the historical Lincoln County story. Adding more ethnic elements, the film indicates Charlie Bowdre marries a Hispanic woman (true enough) but obviously not just after he meets her the first time at a dance. Even more intriguing, this Billy the Kid has no love interest in women.

Hollywood also played its youth card. A group of young actors known as the Brat Pack played most of the leading parts, including Emilo Estevez as Billy, Kiefer Sutherland as Doc Scurlock, Lou Diamond Phillips as José Chávez y Chávez, and Charlie Sheen as Dick Brewer. The camaraderie among these young men moved well beyond what was known about Billy and his followers, with that warm vibe obviously appealing to youthful viewers.

The feeling of community and its attraction for moviegoers was one of the major reasons for the sequel movie in 1990, *Young Guns II*. The same Brat Pack played the characters of Billy, Doc Scurlock, and Chávez y Chávez in the second film. Along with the familiar characters were other carryovers from *Young Guns:* scene after scene of violence: an enlarged emphasis on the Billy-Garrett standoff; and the combination of historical references and Hollywood distortions.

The most significant change came in the adoption of the beyond-the-grave legend of Brushy Bill Roberts as Billy the Kid. The Texan's claim in 1950 to be the Kid and his attempt to gain a pardon from the New Mexico governor becomes something of a framework for this film. The movie never clearly backs Brushy Bill's claim but hints at acceptance— perhaps to add the element of conspiracy about the Kid's death, a dimension never entirely erased for many people in the Billy the Kid story.

As he was in *Young Guns,* the Kid is obviously a young man of conflicting urges, but his dark side emerges more often than the cheerful, friendly Billy. The Kid sees his popularity rising and rides the public interest to selfish, egotistical ends. He frequently falls out with Dave Rudabaugh over gang leadership and relishes the several clashes between Kid and Chisum riders imagined by Hollywood. Billy, aware of the nature of these conflicts, views the Lincoln County shootouts as essentially a "merchant war," but the film is too busy with other kinds of violence to demonstrate the economic reasons for the county's civil war.

Distortions abound in the movie, sometimes to bring novel elements into the story line. For instance, looking for roles for women in this male-drenched story, the movie replaces conniver Whiskey Jim Greathouse with a madam, Jane Greathouse. When Pat Garrett burns down her bordello, she rides out of town like Lady Godiva, without clothes. The details of the historical story are further jumbled in Garrett's urging Ash Upson to accompany him into the Lincoln area, observe the conflicts, and write an inviting book about the violent outbreak and the notorious Billy the Kid.

Details in the film after the Kid's escape from the Lincoln jail are clearly ahistorical. And his death in Fort Sumner is removed from the plot. Billy talks Garrett out of killing him and rides out of Fort Summer, like Brushy Bill Roberts, to live a long life.

Both the *Young Guns* films were popular box-office successes. Some think the new Brat Pack in both movies attracted many young watchers, a claim that is undoubtedly true. The two Kid films also helped rekindle interest in the Western, which had floundered in the 1980s. But as solid history, the two movies were greatly wanting, allowing Dream Land fantasies to capture more of the story lines than solid facts about Billy the Kid and the Lincoln County War. They were also revealing examples of how much old legends, Brushy Bill Roberts for instance, could resurface alongside new emphases, such as the Brat Pack, to keep the Billy the Kid story alive into the next decades.

16

Billy from 1995 to the Present

A few scattered books and essays on Billy in the early 1990s foreshadowed what was to come in the next twenty to thirty years among new interpretations of the Kid. Most of these publications embraced a two-sided Billy, combining the negative and positive facets of his character, but the approaches and subject matter of the interpretations varied widely. It is revealing that novels and movies about Billy were much less numerous than the biographical and historical treatments of the Kid, suggesting that fiction-writers and moviemakers found it more daunting than nonfiction writers to navigate the cluttered path of Billy interpretations.

Other kinds of Kid treatments surfaced in the early years of the twenty-first century. Controversies surrounding possible new photographs of the Kid stirred headlines, and even more contentious were the attempts to dig up Billy's bones to determine once and for all that it really was the Kid buried in the Fort Sumner cemetery and that the Brushy Bill Roberts story in Texas was entirely a hoax. And Gale Cooper, a new name in the Billy the Kid field, exploded on the literary scene, producing more pages about the Kid than any previous writer.

All this activity reinforced what many had believed for several decades: Billy the Kid continued to entice readers and viewers to consume books, novels, and films about his life and legend. His popularity as dramatic figure of the Old West continued to lead the field.

Two publications among several others in the early 1990s illustrated the kinds of new information about the Kid industrious researchers could still turn up and the innovative approaches one might adopt in dealing with Billy. Jerry (Richard) Weddle proved in his brief but exhaustively researched short monograph, *Antrim is My Stepfather's Name: The Boyhood of Billy the Kid*, how much the combined reexamination of known and rethinking of previously unknown sources could reveal about Billy. Weddle uncovered more sources on Billy's Silver City (1873–1875) and Arizona (1875–1877) years than anyone before or since. He did this by examining *all* available sources: newspapers; interviews; information in the major Billy the Kid manuscript collections; military and legal records; and a variety of other manuscript and published materials. The thoroughness of his research and the conclusions drawn from that remarkable investigation proved that more than a century after the Kid's death, a "tenacious and level-headed researcher," as Robert Utley calls Weddle, could uncover much fresh, valuable information and, in the process, rewrite the Kid's story for these four critical years of his life. (The history of Kid's life before 1873 needs other historians and biographers with Weddle's energy and tenacity to provide equivalent research.) Weddle's short book, about fifty pages of text with nearly twenty pages of footnotes and an extensive bibliography, furnished a clear example of what kinds of projects were still open on the Kid in the early 1990s.

Joel Jacobsen offered another path forward for historians and biographers in his book, *Such Men as Billy the Kid: The Lincoln County War Reconsidered* (1994). Making strategic use of standard historical studies by William Keleher, Maurice Garland Fulton, Frederick Nolan, and Robert Utley, Jacobsen provides a thoroughly dependable and briskly paced history of the Lincoln County War. But it is his adept handling of the complex, ever-shifting legal issues of the conflict that makes the largest contribution to the historiography on the war. He demonstrates that the Lincoln County story contained several narrative or interpretive strains deserving close scrutiny. As a lawyer, Jacobsen drew on his legal background to point out the important legal ingredients of the New Mexico story. If ambitious writers carefully study Jacobsen's first-rate book, they can see an approach for new books treating other threads of the Lincoln County narrative: the influences of New Mexico and national politics; the roles of Hispanics; the contributions of women and families; and the much-needed life stories of such participants as the McSweens, Chisum, Murphy, Dolan, and several others.

In the next quarter century some writers followed the exemplary examples provided in the books of Weddle and Jacobsen. Others moved in new directions, although the numbers of biographies of Billy the Kid and histories of Lincoln County were less numerous than those appearing in the period from 1960 to 1995.

Veteran historian, biographer, and novelist Frederick Nolan did not move in novel directions in his biography, *The West of Billy the Kid* (1998). Instead the appealing hallmarks of his previous work on Billy and the Lincoln County War shaped and strengthened his new book. In fact, more than thirty years after Nolan began his journey with the mysterious and convoluted story of frontier New Mexico through the murder of Englishman John Tunstall and after producing the most comprehensive history of the Lincoln County War, Nolan arrived at a specific focus on the Billy the Kid story. He delivered the truthful, fact-driven account he promised and avoided "conceptual history in which the facts are messaged to fit and support a preconceived theory." As he wrote this biography, his chief aim was not to construct Billy as a part of a larger, contextual narrative but to tell the story of a young man trying to make his way in a difficult, unstructured Old West.

Nolan's grasp of a two-sided Billy becomes clear in his book's preface. In the process of clearing away misleading legends, misconceptions, and outright mistakes, Nolan discovers a bright, alert, intelligent boy possessing an impish sense of humor and thrown early and unprepared on his inner resources. He was also a brave boy forced to live on the sharp edge of frontier life, doing the best he could in a world that rarely extended a helping hand. There was no pretension in the kid. Although by no means a perfect human being—there was a dark and vengeful streak in his nature too—he was understandable, whole, and real.

The notable benchmarks of Nolan's contributions to the Lincoln County War and Billy the Kid stories are everywhere clear in this readable biography. He adapts his obvious literary talents, especially his descriptive powers, successful characterizations, and attention-whetting anecdotes, to provide an engrossing life of Billy. Extensive quotations from original sources, both manuscript and published, add much to the narrative. Over the years Nolan had done his homework in the archival and other sources on which to build this Billy biography. And he utilized up-to-date sources, his notes citing essays and books published right up to the eve of his own book. No reader can be unaware of the numerous photographs that grace Nolan's story. More than 250 photographs and their captions, some like minibiographies, provide an extra visual dimension to the deep scholarship so evident in Nolan's books.

Nolan's depictions of the Kid fulfill his promises in the preface. The author's purpose was not to aim at destroying legends but in correcting them by keeping only to provable points in his text. Drawing on the most recent historical findings, carefully examining manuscript and published accounts, and questioning previous stories, Nolan builds

Billy's life story on the kind of diligent research and hard-headed thinking matched only by the equally sound biographical work of Robert Utley.

Nolan encapsulates Billy's character in a few well-selected words. Billy's friends in Silver City and those such as the Coe cousins in Lincoln County remembered him "affectionately" as a boy with an "agile mind" and a person of "good humor." He was often "chipper" despite periodic doldrums and frequently displayed a "sense of mischief." Even Pat Garrett spoke of the Kid's positive attitude toward him when the sheriff was pursuing him or had him clapped in irons in the Lincoln jail. But there were the coldblooded parts of the Kid's character too. He willingly took part in—perhaps even led—the killings of Morton, Baker, and Brady. Among the "hotter heads" in the Regulators, the Kid, "urging reprisal," vindictively hunted Tunstall's killers. He also had a "perpetual grudge" against and verbally attacked John Chisum. He could live satisfactorily, and often did so, when he tried "getting off the hook." Frequently, Billy was likewise guilty of self-aggrandizing defensiveness, thinking more of himself than others. And on other occasions he could be trigger-happy. But Nolan never speaks of Billy as did the defense counsel Henry Waldo in Colonel Dudley's court of inquiry in 1879. The lawyer labeled Billy a degenerate criminal and a professional killer. There might be brutal, depraved sides to the Kid, offsetting his sunny qualities, but for Frederick Nolan they were never as negative as Waldo's description.

The increasingly popular approach of following a bifurcated Billy, paired with some kind of innovation in content or organization, typified two other books about the Kid appearing early in the twenty-first century. *Billy the Kid: The Endless Ride* (2007) by Michael Wallis displayed the veteran writer's innovation in a life-and-times biography. The second book by newcomer Mark Lee Gardner, *To Hell on a Fast Horse: Billy the Kid, Pat Garrett, and the Epic*

Chase to Justice in the Old West (2010), proved to be the only joint biography published thus far on Billy the Kid and Pat Garrett. Neither volume broke new ground, but both approached their topics differently from previous books on the Kid. Indeed these authors, like most biographers since the 1990s, perhaps realizing their stories carried no new information on Billy, chose a novel way of telling their story to grab more readers.

Wallis, a journalist by training, had turned out several books on such topics as Route 66, Pretty Boy Floyd, and the 101 Ranch before he turned to Billy. In *The Endless Ride*, he follows a new path in producing a life-and-times biography of the Kid, placing the young outlaw in the shifting sociocultural, economic, political, and legal contexts of his life. For example, the chapters on Wichita, Kansas, and Silver City and Lincoln, New Mexico, containing considerable background information, help to illuminate and enlarge Billy's life in those places.

Surprisingly, however, Wallis errs in what he says about recent interpretations of Billy the Kid. He writes that there "has never been much middle ground when it comes to judging Billy the Kid, just black and white with scant gray to calm the palette." His assessment is true enough for the period from 1881 to about the 1960, but in the half century since, it is in fact a grey Billy who has ridden through most books about him. As the present study has tried to show, biographies about Billy have increasingly depicted him not as an *either-or* character, all villain or hero, but as a *both-and* figure combining negative and positive actions. This bifurcated Billy appears clearly in the writings of such authors as William Keleher, Maurice Garland Fulton, Frederick Nolan, and Robert Utley.

Even Wallis himself creates a dual-sided Billy. He takes care to describe the Kid's friendships, his love of dance and music, his loyalty, and his sense of humor. But Wallis also portrays the Kid as an unbridled outlaw, depicting his rustling, thievery, and murdering in unsympathetic terms. Despite what Wallis says in his "Personal Introduction," his is a bifurcated Billy, both charismatic companion and lethal gunman.

Wallis's life-and-times approach sometimes works well but, on other occasions, weakens his otherwise well-written book. His discussions of physical and sociocultural settings enhance the comprehension of Billy. So do Wallis's comments about guns and his biographical information about Billy's followers and opponents. At the same time, Wallis often loses Billy in the swamps of those backgrounds. Pages of contextual information about dime novels, Buffalo Bill Cody, and showman P. T. Barnum are not closely connected to the Kid. Overall Wallis reads better as a book about Billy in his shifting milieus than as a closely focused biography of the Kid.

Mark Lee Gardner's joint biography of Billy and Pat Garrett, although not exhibiting large amounts of new information about the two figures, nonetheless provides a delightfully told story of these two notable characters. Gardner followed the now-familiar two-sided Billy. The Kid made bad decisions throughout his life, Gardner notes, even before he arrived in Lincoln County. He readily resorted to violence when his way was blocked or he was challenged. Clearly "he shot to kill." Billy had "reinforced a lifestyle of doing and taking what one pleased, regardless of the law." Along the way he had transformed from a young man desperate to find his way to a "full-fledged desperado." But Gardner's Billy is also a quick-thinking young man of grit, bravery, and courage. Gardner ends his biography by agreeing with Sallie Chisum's estimate of Billy: "There was good mixed with bad in Billy the Kid." Like his adversary Pat Garrett, Billy was "distinctly human," never entirely upstanding or villainous.

Gardner bases his story on the best recent sources in the writings of Nolan and Utley but also digs into obscure manuscript sources in New Mexico and national archives. The author's lively style and appealing anecdotes power his enticing narrative. In general the chapters on Billy the Kid are the most interesting and captivating of this book. In fact the closing chapters on Garrett's life from 1881 to his murder in 1908 drag when compared to the more dramatic sections on Billy's traumatic life.

This dual biographical approach casts another kind of light on Billy the Kid. In comparing the reactions of readers and viewers to Billy and Garrett after their violent deaths, Gardner illuminates a point that others have made briefly but in a less-revealing fashion. How is it that the Kid, achieving little of substance during his life, has become the subject of hundreds of biographical, historical, fictional, and cinematic treatments and that Garrett, the man who hunted and killed him in spectacular fashion, has been the focus of so few works of any kind. Even if Billy was a thief, outlaw, and killer, his romantic youth, daring escapades, and single-minded individualism continue to attract interested, even adoring fans. Garrett, on the other hand, is known primarily as "the man who killed Billy the Kid," not an achievement around which to build legends. Gardner's inviting book helps us to understand the differences between the lives and legends of Billy the Kid and Pat Garrett.

One of the most valuable studies to appear in the second decade of the twenty-first century is Kathleen Chamberlain's *In the Shadow of Billy the Kid: Susan McSween and the Lincoln County War* (2013). She addresses one of the missing pieces of the Lincoln County story by dealing with the role of women in the factional war, in this case through the life of Susan McSween, the wife of Alex. Chamberlain's sympathetic account furnishes the most thorough information thus far unearthed on the obscure early lives of Susan and Alex. The author devotes about half her book to Sue's challenging life during the Lincoln County conflicts from 1875 to 1878. And the closing chapters deal with Susan's

Kathleen P. Chamberlain, *In the Shadow of Billy the Kid: Susan McSween and the Lincoln County War*, 2013. This first-rate biography of Susan McSween illuminates the important story of the most significant woman, Susan McSween, in the Lincoln County War. Chamberlain's book is a model of diligent research and strong narration. Reproduction of book jacket courtesy of the University of New Mexico Press, Albuquerque.

rebound after her husband's death: her second marriage to George Barber; her rise to the Cattle Queen of New Mexico; and her final years of decline until her death in 1931 in the ghost-like town of White Oaks, New Mexico.

The thoroughly researched and smoothly written biography incisively details Sue McSween's personality and actions. Chamberlain illuminates Susan's challenges as one of the few Anglo women in a male-dominated, Hispanic, and isolated region. Nervous and uncertain at times, she nonetheless was courageous, ambitious, and driven to succeed. On other occasions, Susan betrayed her sharp tongue, vanity, and haughtiness. Chamberlain shows, however, that Lieutenant Colonel Nathan Dudley's scurrilous attacks on Susan's reputation, calling her a pushy, an overly ambitious, and a lewd woman, owed more to his wish to undermine her credibility as a critic of him than to fact and truth. In fact Sue's ambitions and actions made more than a few men in the region uncomfortable, and in defensive responses they frequently attacked her as immoral and dangerous.

Chamberlain also provides glimpses of Susan's attitudes toward Billy the Kid. Sue was not always consistent in her views, many of which emerged later in life. In August 1927 she gave interviewer J. Evetts Haley, the Texas writer and rancher, a glowing picture of Billy, characterizing him as ingratiating and helpful and "a perfect little gentleman." Two years later she painted an even more positive portrait to a group of visiting Boy Scouts: the Kid "was a very handsome young man, very polite and well mannered." She added, "He was always welcome in my home." But in a letter to Fulton written at about the same time she compared Billy to Jimmy Dolan, dismissing the Kid as a criminal and murderer.

Most importantly, Chamberlain's strong book succeeds in two memorable ways. First, she has given historians and readers the first study that centers on a woman in the Lincoln County War. Sue McSween saw the war through her home, her husband, and Lincoln's main street, not on horseback with a pistol in her hand. Second, Chamberlain's biography represents a model for the much-needed, full-length life stories of others, men and women, in Lincoln County and around Billy the Kid. These include Alex McSween, John Chisum, Lawrence G. Murphy, Jimmy Dolan, Warren Bristol, and William Rynerson. Altogether, this biography is a significant breakthrough in the study of the Lincoln County War.

Robert Utley, a leading authority on Billy the Kid, returned for one more book on the Kid and, in doing so, provided an account like no other previously published. Utley's achievement was one of a kind in *Wanted: The Outlaw Lives of Billy the Kid and Ned Kelly* (2015). No one thus far had written a book comparing one of the western demigods—Custer, Geronimo, Wyatt Earp, Jesse

James, or Calamity Jane, for example—with a legendary character from another country or culture. In this case, the comparable figure was Ned Kelly (1854–1880), the notorious bushranger of Australia.

Utley used his premier narrative talents to craft parallel life stories of the two legendary figures. Based on extensive research and careful conclusions, Utley's dual biography deals with the sites, persons, and occurrences that molded the stories of these two near-mythic heroes or villains. The final twenty pages furnish a compact comparison of Billy and Ned.

Ned Kelly fares better than Billy in Utley's narrative. In Utley's estimation, Kelly aimed for virtuous, if unreachable goals in his life and was a polite and generous man, a worthy leader, and "a man of quality." Billy, on the other hand, thought only of himself, was often impolite, loved only Sallie Chisum, reached out to no one but Hispanics, and had no larger goals than himself in mind. Because of these limitations, "almost no one [thought of Billy] as a hero."

Utley's low estimate of Billy might not please the Kid's fans. They are likely to mention the Kid's support for Tunstall and McSween, his willingness to testify for Governor Wallace, his romantic attachment to Paulita Maxwell and other young women, and his bright smile, cheerful outlook, and good humor, which appealed to many acquaintances.

Moving past these personality differences, Utley then compares the economic, social, and cultural similarities and disparities between the New Mexican and Victorian (Kelly's region of Australia) settings. Both areas were going through traumatic transformations, the gradual ending of the remote frontier in New Mexico, and the competition between the mainly English Squatters and the predominantly Irish Selectors in Victoria. Ned Kelly had close ties with his large Irish family, but Billy lost his supportive mother in his early teens, never connected well with his step father, and lacked parental guidance after the death of his mother. Both young men

were gunmen and suffered under poorly trained and preju-
diced law officers. Early on, both Ned and Billy became
thieves to benefit themselves but also, in Kelly's case, his
family and fellow Irish.

Finally, Utley compares the myths or legends that grew
up around Billy and Ned. The veteran author contends that
both outlaws spawned legends but that Billy's legends contained more myths than Ned's. Although generating some
essays and books, Kelly's legends have been captured in
many fewer novels, films, and books than the thousand or
more such accounts of Billy the Kid. In the end Utley concludes that neither young man played a significant role in
his nation's history, but their lively, adventurous, and controversial lives have captured the fascination of thousands
upon thousands of readers and viewers. Both have become
central and widely heralded folkloric heroes with reputations not likely to diminish or disappear in the future.

Two other authors, Gale Cooper and W. C. Jameson,
illustrated in their numerous books divergent interpretations of the Kid as well as conflicting views about who was
the real Billy the Kid. Both were prolific, opinionated writers who sparked a new round of controversies among Billy
followers. Both also dealt with legends surrounding Billy
the Kid but in far different ways and coming to vastly different conclusions.

Gale Cooper, an amateur historian with a doctoral degree
from the Harvard Medical School with specialties in forensic
psychiatry and murder-case consultation, has written more
pages about Billy the Kid than any other writer. And all her
books have appeared since 2008. In total she has written
seven books; none is brief; all overflow with diligent, new
research; and all advocate an uncompromising, pro–Billy
the Kid viewpoint.

Cooper's first work, published after nearly a decade of
extensive Billy research, was a novel entitled *Joy of the Birds*
(2008), later slightly expanded and retitled and republished

as *Billy and Paulita* (2012). A work of "docufiction," as Cooper defines it, the book sprawls to nearly 650 pages, covering Billy's life from his birth in New York City in 1859 until his death in 1881 in Fort Sumner. Cooper's fictional Billy is a freedom fighter seeing, enjoying, and mimicking the "joy of the birds." Although Billy's biological father, his brother Josie, and his stepfather William Antrim are abusive men or near-mad, Billy joys in his mother's love and his later support from Englishman John Tunstall, lawyer Alex McSween, Susan McSween, lawyer Ira Leonard, and Hispanic buddies like Yginio Salazar. His supporters have to buoy Billy's hopes, Cooper makes clear, because an evil, repulsive, and even-murderous empire, known as the Santa Fe Ring, sets out to destroy him. The chief villain in Cooper's novel is the unscrupulous Thomas Catron, a lawyer in Santa Fe, who works his dirty deeds through Lawrence G. Murphy and Jimmy Dolan in Lincoln town and through the legal shenanigans of Judge Warren Bristol and District Attorney William Rynerson. Eventually Pat Garrett, whom Cooper pictures as a traitorous former friend, sets up an ambush and kills Billy. But even as Billy moves toward his rendezvous with death, he discovers and enjoys several electric love-making trysts with Celsa Gutiérrez and a platonic and then full-bodied union with his true sweetheart, Paulita Maxwell. Cooper's division of the world into Billy's supporters and enemies would continue largely unchanged in her later works.

Cooper's next two books illustrate her delight in "cracking" hoaxes and revealing and dismissing "pretenders." In *MegaHoax: The Strange Plot to Exhume Billy the Kid and Become President* (2009), revised and expanded into *Cracking the Billy the Kid Case Hoax: The Strange Plot to Exhume Billy the Kid, Convict Sheriff Garrett of Murder, and Become President of the United States* (2013), Cooper takes on Sheriffs Tom Sullivan, Steve Sederwall, and Gary Graves, historian Paul Andrew Hutton, and even Governor

Bill Richardson as a cabal of self-interested men wanting to dig up Billy, Catherine McCarty Antrim, and others to prove whether Pat Garrett really killed the Kid or someone else. Cooper is convinced that she almost single-handedly stopped these "hoaxers." Linked to this case is another Cooper book, *Billy the Kid's Pretenders: Brushy Bill and John Miller* (2010), the story of two old-timers who claimed to be the real Billy the Kid and of the hoaxers who wanted to exhume them to prove whether they were the real thing. Cooper is convinced Governor Richardson supported these exhumers and hoaxers because the Billy stories would be good for New Mexico tourism and further his future run for the U.S. presidency.

Perhaps Cooper's most valuable book for Billy the Kid fans and researchers is *Billy the Kid's Writings, Words and Wit* (2011). The 574-page book reprints all of Billy's revealing letters, his testimonies at hearings, and other Billy documents. Making good use of the Lew Wallace collection in Indiana, Cooper provides copies of materials often unavailable to Billy readers and researchers. She has even uncovered a new "Billie" letter overlooked by nearly all previous researchers.

The longest of Cooper's books is the recent *Lost Pardon of Billy the Kid: An Analysis Factoring in the Santa Fe Ring, Governor Lew Wallace's Dilemma, and a Territory in Rebellion* (2017). The nearly thousand-page book extensively covers the pardon Lew Wallace promised Billy but never fulfilled and a dozen other contextual subjects dealing with Wallace, the Kid, and territorial New Mexico. The book's dedication clearly declares Cooper's perspective: "For Billy Bonney, who fought for justice and who deserved justice." The rambling volume furnishes near-exhaustive coverage of Governor Wallace's actions—or nonactions—and also thorough backgrounds on the political explosions rocking New Mexico in the 1870s and 1880s. Members of the Santa Fe Ring, clearly the "bad guys" of the story, too often were able to keep Wallace from carrying through on his promises to the Kid.

The least important of Cooper's books, the one least centered on Billy the Kid, is *The Nun Who Rode on "Billy the Kid": Sleuthing a Foisted Frontier Fable* (2017). Intrigued with but doubtful about Sister Blandina Segale's claim of her connections with Billy the Kid in her book *At the End of the Santa Fe Trail* (1932), Cooper set out to discover what was truth and hoax. She states her argument clearly and directly: Though Sister Blandina was being considered for sainthood, she had not told the truth in her book. In fact she had neither known nor met Billy the Kid as she claimed. Cooper surmises that the nun wanted perhaps to tell moral stories about helping Billy refrain from violence as models for others and to magnify her own image as a steady, sturdy sister on the far-southwestern American frontier.

There is much to praise in Cooper's books, especially the breadth of her research. She has dug deeply into primary sources including those in Lincoln County, Santa Fe, Washington, D.C., and the Lew Wallace collection in Indiana. Appended to all her books are extensive bibliographies of forty to ninety pages listing general sources as well as sources specific to individual books. Her expansive research allows Cooper to link an isolated southeastern New Mexican subject to happenings on the territorial and national levels. The author's diligent use of correspondence between officials in Santa Fe and Washington, D.C., also illuminates the pressures mounted from nearby and faraway centers of power on events unfolding in Lincoln County, New Mexico.

If Cooper's research is commendable, so is her thorough treatment of Billy and his short but active life. In nearly all her publications, Cooper provides clear discussions of Billy's actions and forceful interpretations of what readers should think about the Kid's ideas and actions. No one will miss Cooper's extraordinarily warm and positive depictions of Billy in her books. He is a hero too often treated as an outlaw and villain, a mistaken and misleading interpretation of the Kid in Cooper's view.

Cooper also furnishes more expansive coverage of several recent events surrounding Billy than other book-writers have provided. Hers works are the most extensive discussions of Kid pretenders Brushy Bill and John Miller, the hoaxers who wanted to "dig up" Billy and others to resolve the mysteries about his identity, and of Lew Wallace's central role in the promised pardon for the Kid. Cooper also reminds readers of the upheavals in Grant and Colfax Counties concurrent with the turmoil in Lincoln County and of how those rebellions give larger historical contexts and meanings for the Lincoln County War.

One wishes everything about Cooper's books could be stated positively. But her shortcomings unfortunately undermine several of the large strengths of her works. First, she is much too partisan, making Billy's side into heroes and sometimes near saints. On the other side Cooper depicts Catron, Murphy, Dolan, Bristol, and Rynerson as evil rascals with hardly a good bone in their bodies. Too often Cooper turns her stories into melodramas, with endless conflicts between white and black hats.

Second, this tendency to overly dramatize and take sides takes away from Cooper's portraits of Billy the Kid. It is true that at times he fought for many county residents suffering under the tyranny of the Santa Fe Ring and its cronies in Washington, D.C., and southern New Mexico. Although the Kid might be considered a freedom fighter, he was also a liar, a thief and rustler, and, to boot, a murderer. Perhaps Cooper wants to break clearly and cleanly from recent biographers and historians picturing a bifurcated Billy, part hero and villain; perhaps the interpretations of historians have been "too cautious," as Cooper asserts. But condensing Billy's times into a sensational scenario of good and bad guys reduces the complexity of Billy's character and his milieu. As he said several times to friends and acquaintances, he was ultimately looking out for himself, getting revenge on those who killed John Tunstall, and staying in Lincoln County to steal livestock for a living. Cooper is much too reluctant to see and acknowledge the darker sides of Billy. In that way her Billy the Kid is more akin to the Burns-created Billy as hero than the more recent two-sided Billy.

Finally, Cooper should produce better-written and –edited books to catch the attention of a wider audience. Thus far her self-published books contain too many errors in organization, presentation, diction, syntax, and facts to gain stronger marks from readers, specialists, and reviewers. She repeats information too often, is too self-congratulatory, and fills empty spaces of interpretation where evidence is lacking for her explicit conclusions. One hopes Cooper will see these shortcomings, correct and rein them in, and produce stronger books. The assistance from strong developmental and copy editors would be the place to start. Her diligent research and important findings deserve better editorial packaging.

W. C. Jameson is similar to Gale Cooper in several ways, but in others he differs markedly. Jameson is now the leading advocate of Brushy Billy Roberts as the authentic Billy the Kid. A prolific author with nearly a hundred books to his credit, Jameson is an authority on several life-after-death or life-beyond-the-grave stories such as those about John Wilkes Booth, Jesse James, and Butch Cassidy.

Most other writers have been satisfied to write one book about a Billy pretender. Among them are Helen Airy's unsuccessful championing of New Mexican John Miller as the authentic Billy the Kid in her *Whatever Happened to Billy the Kid* (1993). But W. C. Jameson is a relentless advocate for his pretender, William Henry Roberts. Beginning with *The Return of the Outlaw: Billy the Kid* (1998), coauthored with Frederic Bean, and through *Billy the Kid: Beyond the Grave* (2005), *Billy the Kid: The Lost Interviews* (2012), *Pat Garrett: The Man behind the Badge* (2016), and on most recently to *Cold Case: Billy the Kid—Investigating History's Mysteries* (2018), Jameson has told a similar story. Almost formula-like, it is based on the same evidence and reaches analogous conclusions.

That story can be briefly summarized. Jameson is convinced that Pat Garrett did not shoot and kill Billy the Kid. Instead his victim was a mysterious mixed-race young man named Billy Barlow, who was buried the next day in what since then has been called Billy's grave. The real Kid was William Henry "Brushy Bill" Roberts, a wandering westerner who went on to live in and around the West until his death in 1950.

Jameson builds his thesis on the unsolved mysteries surrounding Billy the Kid, especially those in conjunction with his death reported from Fort Sumner in July 1881. In support of Roberts's claim, Jameson asserts that the old man knew too much about the Billy the Kid and the Lincoln County War—in fact more than historians of the time, Jameson thought—to be a fraud. Following the earlier research of Sonnichsen and Morris in their pioneering book on Roberts, *Alias Billy the Kid* (1955), Jameson traces Brushy Bill's life from his Texas origins, through his many travels throughout the West and in Mexico, and on to his demise in Texas, where true believers in the town of Hico, have established a museum honoring Roberts as the genuine Billy the Kid. Jameson also deals with Roberts's attempt, at the urging of William Morrison, to gain from a New Mexico governor the pardon that Lew Wallace promised but never granted Billy.

Jameson deserves credit for his writing talents displayed in these books. His style is clear, straightforward, and fact filled. He tells an intriguing story as he traces the life of Brushy Billy Roberts hopping around the Southwest and other parts of the United States. And Jameson knows a good deal about the Lincoln County troubles, which he braids into his attractive narrative. One wishes Jameson's handling of the specifics of Billy's story, especially his early years and later actions, were as appealing as his storytelling power. Unfortunately, his employment of details about Billy leaves much to be desired.

Jameson focuses on several still unanswered questions surrounding Billy. Did Pat Garrett and John Poe tell the truth about the sheriff's killing the Kid? If so, why the conflicts between their stories? What about the bungled so-called coroner's reports, which, over time, appeared in two or three versions? What about the questions Fort Sumner residents raised about the identity of the young man Garrett shot? These and other conundrums push Jameson toward Roberts's story as being more acceptable than the one given by nearly all Billy the Kid specialists.

Jameson, however, is not willing to admit the large holes in Roberts's tale nor to deal with the questions critics have raised about his shaky story. Consider these queries that Jameson has not addressed satisfactorily: how should one react when a Roberts family member cites a Bible entry that Roberts was born in 1879, not 1859? What about Roberts's autobiographical comments not meshing with what is known of Billy's years in Indiana, Kansas, Arizona, and New Mexico? What about Roberts's claim that he did not kill anyone in his escape from the Lincoln jail when the shooting of deputies Bell and Olinger is fully documented? How is one to deal with Jameson's claim that Fort Sumner residents began to question whether Garrett shot Billy (Jameson names no one specifically) when Professor Robert Stahl shows that nearly thirty people saw Billy's corpse— and perhaps many more residents as well—when it was put on display the next day in a Fort Sumner saloon? How is it that none of Billy's fellow riders identified him as Brushy Bill Roberts rather than as Henry McCarty, Kid Antrim, or Billy Bonney?

On occasion Jameson's frustrations in not winning over more followers to his Roberts tale lead to larger problems.

A tone of anger invades many of his pages. He is upset that more readers, general and academic, have not accepted his arguments for Roberts's claim. Sometimes the anger leads to mistaken assumptions. He says on several occasions that historians and biographers have been following Pat Garrett's account too closely and for too long. As Jameson puts it, "The truth is, *virtually all works on Billy the Kid merely repeat in some form or another what Sheriff Pat Garrett, the alleged killer of the Kid, stated in his book in 1892.*" This statement is a major example of how uninformed and mistaken Jameson's assertions can be in his numerous books and articles. Historians and biographers, as this study has shown, have continually revised their stories about Billy the Kid. Walter Noble Burns traveled up a new path in 1926, and beginning in the 1950s and 1960s, the writings of William Keleher, Philip Rasch, and Maurice Garland Fulton moved in innovative directions. Even more so, the writings of Frederick Nolan and Robert Utley in the late twentieth century illustrate how far writers have moved away from the Garrett-Upson story published in 1882.

Why have not more Billy fans responded to Jameson's call to join the Brushy Bill Roberts bandwagon? There are probably two reasons: (1) Jameson and others supporting the pretenders have not been able to show that the life stories of their favorites can replace the facts about the life and death of the known Billy the Kid; and (2) their handling of the Kid's life is too incomplete and sometimes too wrong even for those wavering fans and readers to join the pretender march. But as Jameson's continuing publications and *Young Guns II* show, the story of Brushy Bill Roberts, despite its shaky evidence, is still alive for more than a few readers and viewers.

As historians and biographers continue to roll out numerous books and essays on the life and times of Billy the Kid, novelists have also been busy placing the Kid as a central figure in

From 1995 to the Present

their historical fiction. Not all are authentic history, however. In *Cost of Killing* (1996), Ralph W. Cotton often introduces mistaken "facts" and distortions. The historical Billy gets lost in an avalanche of intrigue, hidden gold, and romance. Overall Cotton hides the actual life of Billy to spin his own tale. Another novelist, John A. Aragon, promises much in *Billy the Kid's Last Ride* (2011) and then disappoints in the second part of his novel. A Janus-faced Billy, who by turns can be compassionate and passionate, then dangerously assertive and murderous, rides through the opening pages of Aragon's novel, but in the second half Aragon's work fails as historical fiction. He has Billy riding south into Mexico after his Lincoln jail escape and becoming involved in a horrendous shooting war among cowboys, Indians, and Mexican *ricos*. These closing chapters are beyond the novelist's grasp in his attempt to heighten the action of his novel.

At the same time, some of the best historical novels about Billy have appeared recently. One of these is Johnny D. Boggs's novel, *Law of the Land: The Trial of Billy the Kid* (2004). Most of what Boggs writes is sound history, following a good deal of the expanded information about Billy the Kid recently turned up by biographers and historians. Boggs does add imagined conversations and amplifies characters' temperaments, but these additions will strike most readers as complementing or reflecting history, not distorting or ignoring it. Boggs uses flashbacks to add historical information and, in doing so, remains faithful to the main tracks of the Kid's known history.

Law of the Land depicts the two-sided Billy. He can be loving, friendly, and gregarious with his mother, John Tunstall, and his pals. Conversely, Boggs's Lew Wallace sees Billy as an evil kid who becomes a turncoat. The talks between Ira Leonard, Billy's lawyer in his last few months, and Governor Wallace furnish images of the complex Billy, positive in the eyes of the lawyer and negative from the perspective of the governor.

Given Boggs's general dedication to historical accuracy, it is surprising to see his deviations from actual history when he depicts Billy's final weeks. For instance, Boggs has Pete Maxwell meeting with Pat Garrett in Roswell and telling the sheriff that Billy is hiding in Fort Sumner. The author also imagines Billy and Paulita making love in her Maxwell bedroom before the Kid leaves to retrieve meat for cooking, a decision that leads to his death at the hands of Pat Garrett. In addition Boggs departs clearly from what dependable sources say about events immediately after Billy's sudden death. Still, one comes away from this novel pleased with its generally solid history. A skilled writer, Boggs keeps his story open to general readers, remains true to nearly all historical facts, and provides a provocative and persuasive interpretation of a complex Billy the Kid ranging from friendly to mean depending on the situations surrounding him.

The largest challenge for historical novelists writing about Billy the Kid is the same as for biographers and historians: how does the writer tell a believable story about the Kid when so little is known about his first fourteen years and too little about his last seven. Part of the challenge is to fill in the spaces among the historical facts in convincing ways. Some reviewers have pointed to the previously discussed novels by Edwin Corle, Charles Neider, Amelia Bean, Elizabeth Fackler, and Johnny Boggs as the strongest fiction about the life of Billy the Kid .

Ron Hansen's recent novel *The Kid* (2016) surpasses all these earlier novels. It is a first-rate work, displaying carefully constructed, inviting combinations of historical accuracy, skillful scene-setting, and plausible interpretations of Billy. Hansen's work may be the most historically correct of any novel written about the Kid. Drawing thoroughly on important Billy books by Utley, Nolan, and several other historians, the novelist sticks close to the known facts of Billy's life. Readers see the conflicting theories about the outlaw's journey from his natal New York, through brief stays in Indiana, Kansas, and Colorado, and on to New Mexico in 1873. Most of the book deals with Billy's life in Silver City (1873–1875), Arizona (1875–1877), and Lincoln County (1877–1881).

Along the way Hansen nearly always constructs accurate scenes of Billy's presence in Silver City, Arizona, and Lincoln County. He shows Billy's love for his mother, his alienation from his stepfather, and his tendency to fall in with older, wayward men who lead him into thievery. More attention getting are Hansen's treatments of the major events in Lincoln County: the killing of Billy's friends, John Tunstall and Alex McSween; the Kid's participation in the murder of Sheriff Brady, bad Billy's worst offense; his rustling operations; and his other inexcusable killings.

Still Hansen gets a few things wrong or distorts the Kid's story beyond known facts. William Antrim, Billy's stepfather, was not a mean man, although he was distant and sometimes inattentive. Hansen overemphasizes Billy's amorous adventures and conquests, is too critical of Susan McSween, and mistakenly writes that Celsa Gutiérrez was both sister and cousin of Pat Garrett's wife. Few historians and biographers have claimed Yginio Salazar as Billy's cousin, but Hansen does. Finally, Billy did not tell Judge Bristol to go to "hell, hell, hell" at the end of his murder trial in Mesilla. That canard was scotched years ago.

From nearly the beginning Billy the Kid interpreters often pigeonholed him into opposite categories: Billy as villain or Billy as hero. Hansen provides a more provocative, appealing portrait: Billy the complex protagonist, who can be a murderer, thief, and liar while also being a carefree, joyous, and upbeat chum. In avoiding *either-or* and embracing *both-and* interpretations, the author furnishes a full-bodied picture of the controversial Billy.

Ron Hansen offers an engrossing story written in an appealing, straightforward manner. No reader will have trouble following Hansen's lucid and thoughtfully presented plot, characterizations, and ideas. In short Hansen's *The Kid* is an outstanding, top-drawer historical novel on one of the West's most-written-about characters. He proves more than any other novelist writing about the Kid that a work of fiction can be both a premier novel and accurate history. The most recent novel about Billy the Kid is also the best, an unusual case of serendipity.

Although numerous biographers and historians have produced important books and essays since the mid-1990s and even though several strong novels have been published in the same period, the few movies about Billy the Kid released since 1995 have generally been weak productions, rarely rising above mediocre at their best.

But some commentators miss a major point when their reactions to a movie—or a biography, history, or novel—are limited to the artistic shortcomings of the work. In these singular conclusions they fail to consider other salient ingredients needed in an interpretation of Billy the Kid: its attempts at historical accuracy; its treatment of character or personality; or its cultural commentary. Even though the artistry in a film or work of nonfiction or fiction falls far short of excellence, those products nonetheless ought to be assessed for their achievements—or lack thereof—in other areas. Such is the case with most films about the Kid released since the mid-1990s. None ranks among the best Billy films artistically, but these movies still remain valuable attempts at depicting the Kid and his times and thus are worthy of historical and critical evaluation.

Three such films are those directed by Christopher Forbes and starring Cody McCarver: *Billy the Kid* (2013), *The Last Days of Billy the Kid* (2017), and *Billy the Kid: Showdown in Lincoln County* (2017). The Forbes films provide bits of historical context, much of it jumbled, some inaccurate. All three movies depict Lincoln County and nearby areas in a civil war for political power and economic control. Brigham

Landon, resembling the historical figures of Lawrence G. Murphy and Jimmy Dolan, has Lincoln County under his unyielding and violent thumb. A coercive and trigger-happy merchant, Landon forces small ranchers and farmers to buy from his store and pay exorbitant prices. In *Billy the Kid: Showdown in Lincoln County,* John Tunstall enters the scene, establishes a competing store offering goods at lower prices, and is soon shot down by Landon's henchmen. Even though the handling of the fractious background provides worthy context, the details are so mixed up that they alienate historians.

The three movies also deal with Billy the Kid's family, furnishing details that biographers would both embrace and dismiss. In the trio of films, Cody McCarver, representing the best of the films' actors and starring in separate films as bounty hunters Leon Copper and Pat Harrett (Pat Garrett), is portrayed as William / Billy's biological father, sometimes newly discovered and acknowledged, sometimes on scene throughout the film. But this family connection is ahistorical because Billy's biological father has never been identified. None of the three films, however, mentions William Antrim, whom Billy knew and traveled with in Indiana and Kansas and who became his stepfather in New Mexico. In the first of the series, *Billy the Kid,* Billy's mother, Katherine (Catherine) Bonney, and the Kid reside in a two-story white colonial house in Dogma, New Mexico, when Billy's father suddenly appears as a bounty hunter. In truth Billy's mother had died from tuberculosis in Silver City several years before these conflicts in southeastern New Mexico. And in *The Last Days of Billy the Kid,* in which McCarver plays Pat Harrett, he eventually shoots his own son, as Billy's sister Lilly sings the catchy familiar tune "Billy Boy."

Billy, more often known as William in these films with Billy the Kid in their titles, fails here as a convincing historical or realistic figure. A complex, full-bodied Kid is too much for Christopher Bowman. Even though the films try to depict Billy as an innocent boy in his late teens who obeys his mother and then becomes a gunman, they are unsuccessful depictions of the Kid. Bowman cannot convincingly act out those conflicting tendencies. In *The Last Days of Billy the Kid,* Billy is smitten with saloon girl Emma, they quickly marry, and the happy couple flees to Mexico. When Emma is shot down by a woman bounty hunter, the anguished Billy returns to Lincoln County and quickly kills town leaders without reason but in a burst of frenzied anger. Those emotional moments call for superb acting; it is not found in these films. In their handling of historical backgrounds, Billy's family and Billy himself, the films' directors and actors are not equal to these demanding performances.

In his films, Forbes also tries to find more and larger roles for women. All three movies feature a One-Eyed Lilly. Played by Jezibell Anat, Lilly is part owner of a saloon in Lincoln. She hires innocent, fresh-faced girls to serve drinks and to "go upstairs" with men. These actresses unfortunately are the most amateurish of all the casts. One character is Emma, who captivates William (Billy). An astonishing oversight or omission is that none of these young women is Hispanic even though about 75 percent or more of Lincoln County residents were Hispanic in Billy's time. Not one of these young women is skilled enough in film acting to further the important roles of women in the Lincoln County story.

Overall the Forbes films detract from more than add to the cinematic Billy. Most of all, even though the director attempts to deal with Lincoln County history, the McCarty-Antrim-Bonney family, and Billy himself, the inadequacies of his actors, the rearranged and inauthentic history, and the episodic, awkward plots undermine the director's efforts to bring Billy to life. For example the close of *Billy the Kid: Showdown in Lincoln County* lacks clear meaning. It is neither linked to the previous plot nor completes the film with a tangible idea. A wandering "Traveler" says he has "an appointment" with Billy the Kid, but the reason is an enigma. And the film ends there.

Another film, *1313: Billy the Kid* (2012), illustrates the tendency of novelists and moviemakers to employ the name of Billy the Kid to attract attention to their fiction or films that contain little or nothing about the Kid. This film by David DeCoteau, the director of more than ninety low-budget movies, is part of the dozen or so in DeCoteau's *1313* series. Most of these films feature young men's athletic bodies and rarely include many women.

This film fits the usual formula of the *1313* series. The wounded Billy, recently escaped from the Lincoln County jail, stumbles into the isolated Hell's Heart, nearly a ghost town. He is quickly confronted with a series of conflicts, escalating mysteries, and then horrific events. The Kid gradually learns that the town is dominated by a mysterious group of "manitous," half-human and half-animal creatures, who devour humans, especially in the dark of night. Billy misbelieves the stories he hears and, then realizing he is dangerously wrong, changes his convictions and violently defeats his marauding opponents. It is a Western tale of suspense and horror.

Major shortcomings, like those in the Forbes films, limit the value of this Billy the Kid entry in the *1313* series. Low budget, overflowing with third-rate acting, and ahistorical in nearly every aspect, the movie falters, falls, and clearly fails. It even introduces Doc Holiday in the final scene, without an inkling of why he should appear. In short this film is not about the historical Billy the Kid, despite its promising title.

Films about Billy the Kid from the mid-1990s onward have been few in number and inferior in quality. Why? Some think the lasting popularity of the *Young Guns* in 1988 and *Young Guns II* in 1990 precluded more Kid movies in the next generation. Others are convinced that the social and cultural experiences of Americans in these decades have not encouraged other films on Billy.

But another fact may be an even more persuasive reason for the paucity of strong recent movies on the Kid. As more than one film specialist has noted, multifaceted figures—characters with conflicting sides to their personalities—are difficult to capture and keep before viewers in 90- to 120-minute films. Biographers and novelists can hold readers as they carefully delineate the ups and downs and the ins and outs of complicated characters such as Billy the Kid. This is not the case for filmmakers, the critics say. As one film producer put it, she needed a "thru-line" for her cinematic characters—that is, a continuing story line that gradually unfolds a protagonist's uniform character in a series of illuminating scenes. One cannot use a bifurcated Billy in such straight-line films because his gregarious, positive side, followed suddenly by his villainous acts, makes his divergent personality too complex and changeable for a unified movie plot. That two-way Billy has similarly vexed biographers and novelists in the past half century—but perhaps even more so film-makers.

Two recent controversial happenings reveal how much Billy the Kid still lurks as a dramatic backstory ready to burst on the scene even if new biographies, novels, and films are lessening in number.

In 2003 New Mexico county sheriffs and deputies Steve Sederwall, Tom Sullivan, and Gary Graves announced they were going to launch an alarming endeavor. They were setting out to prove—for all times—whether Billy the Kid shot J. W. Bell in the outlaw's escape from the Lincoln jail, whether Pat Garrett shot and killed Billy, and whether it was Billy or someone else buried in the Fort Sumner cemetery on 15 July 1881.

Gradually the startling endeavors gained momentum, and over time they became known as the "digging up Billy" episodes. The sheriffs, with support for a time from New Mexico governor Bill Richardson, some lawyers, and western historian Paul Andrew Hutton, moved ahead with their plan and added other items to their investigation. They would also exhume the remains of Billy's mother, Catherine Antrim, in Silver City and dig up the bones of Billy in Fort Sumner. Using the most up-to-date technology, they would compare the DNA of Catherine, Billy, and perhaps other figures involved in the burgeoning quest.

Hearing of the project in published stories in the *Albuquerque Journal* and the *New York Times,* Governor Richardson called in the sheriffs and a gaggle of reporters for a meeting in Santa Fe. The governor supported the project, he said, because it could "answer key questions that have lingered over 120 years surrounding the life and death" of Billy the Kid. And if the project encouraged tourism in the state, he "couldn't be happier."

The exhumation project stirred up immediate, stormy controversies. When Sederwall referred to the Kid as "saddle trash," he alienated large numbers of Billy advocates. A key Billy fan was amateur historian Gale Cooper, who immediately labeled the exhumers as "hoaxers," wrongly claiming later that Richardson used the case to advance his run for the presidency and that Hutton's role in the events represented the actions of a "bottom of the barrel" historian. Cooper set out on a crusade, first going through the courts, to block the project.

For more than ten years, the case roiled the courts and involved several lawyers, law firms, and journalists and other writers. The case even went international with a documentary movie, *A Requiem for Billy the Kid* (2006), narrated by Kris Kristofferson, and featuring Sederwall and Sullivan, and winning attention and accolades. And in addition to her indefatigable legal efforts, Cooper moved on to stop and penalize the "diggers" through her lengthy, blustery books: *MegaHoax* (2010) and *Billy the Kid's Pretenders* (2010). At first not getting all she wanted, Cooper thought that her challenge was lost and that "a pandemic virus, the Billy the Kid hoax . . . was about to infect the world."

But then unfolding events moved the contest in new directions. Officials in Fort Sumner and Silver City spoke out against the proposed exhumations. The whereabouts of Catherine Antrim's and Billy's bones could not be confirmed (Catherine's remains had been moved and Billy's possibly relocated by the flooding Pecos River), families of deceased relatives buried nearby objected to the exhumations, and the report of Billy's blood possibly being on an extant bench proved unsatisfactory.

On 15 May 2014, Cooper received a copy of a judicial decision that, she said later, allowed her to "crack" the Billy the Kid case and helped her to "win the Lincoln County War." The judge sided with Cooper and rewarded her lawyers and her with large sums of money for their efforts. Still dissatisfied, however, Cooper pushed on to achieve more; she want to completely shut down the hoaxers, which eventually happened. But Sederwall did not think he had "lost" the case. "I don't even give a shit," he claimed, then made a larger point about himself. According to one reporter, "he's just a guy who wants the truth, while scholars like Cooper will stop at nothing to control the history they're profiting from."

More important than the verbal fireworks of the opposing sides, however, were the implications of the eleven-year controversy for understanding the enduring popularity of Billy the Kid in history and popularity. The drama of the arguments and court cases revealed that nearly anything dealing with the Kid, his short life, and controversial actions could escalate into state, national, and international front-page stories. True, there were confusion, controversy, and

Saint Billy Bandit. Bob Boze Bell's appealing artwork depicts the two-way or bifurcated Billy the Kid portrayed in this volume. As this image makes clear, Billy was both positive and negative in his attitudes and actions. Illustration courtesy Bob Boze Bell.

contention, but Billy was again alive and well on the historical and cultural scene.

Similar electric notoriety flashed around Billy the Kid and possible photographs of him and provided still another example of the Kid's staying power in American culture. Soon after a tintype photograph of Billy, probably taken in 1879–1880, surfaced and circulated in the late nineteenth century, it gained wide credibility as an authentic portrait.

But three of the sections of the original four-part tintype—all the same image of the Kid—were gone several decades later. A handful of other possible photographs of Catherine Antrim or Billy surfaced in the twentieth century, but after some consideration all were dismissed. Questionable provenance and physical comparisons led to most of these rejections. Over the years the remaining copy of the tintype moved from Daniel Dedrick, to whom the Kid had gifted the photograph, and to relative Frank L. Upham, whose family loaned the tintype for exhibit by the Lincoln County Heritage Trust in 1986. Nine years later the photograph reverted to the Upham family.

Then a dramatic event drew more attention to the Kid and his photographs. In 2011 the Upham family put the authentic Billy photograph up for auction. William I. Koch, the noted conservative businessman, paid a record $2.3 million for the two-by-three-inch tintype, the highest price paid for any western memorabilia to date. The purchase set the scene for events soon to follow.

In 2010 collector Randy Guijarro had located and purchased several tintypes at a Fresno, California, flea market for two dollars. After a few days of examination Guijarro concluded he had bought a tintype photograph of Billy the Kid, other members of the Regulators, women including Sallie Chisum and Paulita Maxwell, and several children in a croquet-playing scene in front of a building in a southwestern setting.

Guijarro's sensational claim set off a firestorm of new attention to Billy the Kid, including several controversies and more investigation. Supporters of the collector were convinced that sufficient provenance, facial similarities, and recognizable backgrounds confirmed the authenticity of the croquet tintype claimed to be an image of Billy. Critics said the provenance lacked links to the Kid, that the Regulators were not in this area when the photograph was taken, and that the background building was not in existence in 1878.

But backers of Guijarro and the tintype gained support from National Geographic television network to help launch a show hosted by Kevin Costner and touting the photograph as real and now the second authenticated photograph of the Kid. The owner began to speak of the croquet tintype as being worth $5 million.

In the next few years other photographs were championed as authentic pictures of Billy the Kid. They stirred up similar contests contretemps in print and television media. None of the recently discovered photographs has satisfied serious collectors and academic specialists. Perhaps one museum owner spoke for collectors when he told this writer that those who supported the authenticity of new Billy photographs usually came from the ranks of collectors and museum operators. But he also thought Billy scholars were too skeptical of their claims and convinced of their own rightness. Perhaps he makes a valuable point, but he did not admit that collectors might be motivated to push for authenticity when they saw the possibility of millions of dollars from an auction sale on the horizon.

But again for our purposes, the emotional controversies surrounding these photographs are another proof of the enduring popularity of Billy the Kid. Whether in history or in legend, Billy still captures attention in newspaper headlines, television specials, and a variety of other popular media. Indeed the combined historical and legendary stories about Billy keep him before the widest of audiences.

Conclusion

Pondering the Life and Legends of Billy the Kid

We were walking down the main street of Lincoln, New Mexico. I was pondering how to tell the controversial Billy the Kid stories to my ten-year-old grandson, Adam. I wanted to give him a full-bodied story, not a one-sided one. He should hear about Billy's killings even as we walked in front of the jail building where Billy had killed two deputies to gain his freedom and when we strolled down the street where he and others were involved in the shooting of Sheriff Brady and Deputy Hindman. And as we passed where the McSween home had stood, I wondered how I might tell Adam about Billy's loyalties to the Regulators, Hispanics, and women and his resistance to his opponents.

My dilemmas on that day are similar to those that diligent historians, biographers, novelists, and moviemakers have faced in the roughly 150 years since Billy's name first appeared in print. At first faced with sensational tales without much supporting evidence, storytellers chose to depict Billy as an evil desperado. Those dark views of the Kid lasted for several decades. But reacting to these damning portraits, narrators after the mid-1920s chose to see Billy as heroic for the most part. Dissatisfied with these either-or interpretations, other interpreters, chose to tell both-and stories from the 1950s onward. This complex new Billy was a bifurcated young man whose personality often shifted back and forth from negative to positive actions. Most storytellers in the past half century have followed this more complicated picture, although a few writers depart from that dominant interpretation in describing Billy as more a villain or hero.

For those researchers and readers ambitious to find out more about the complete Billy the Kid narrative, large gaps in his story still exist in the literature. Historians and biographers know almost nothing of the first two-thirds of his life, with his name not appearing in print until 1873. And information about the next four years of the Kid's life remains very limited. Not until 1877 did he come directly on the scene in Arizona and New Mexico. Even after that, we know little about his daily life, his ideas, his thoughts. Those researchers willing to dig more deeply and broadly into available historical sources to examine Billy's life have several open fields before them.

Historians also need more information about the larger contexts of Billy's story. Full-length studies of Billy's important connections with Hispanics and women are still missing. The friendships and writings of Yginio Salazar, Juan Patrón, Miguel Otero Jr., Paco Anaya, and others merit much more attention. Hispanic supporters of The House and their enmity toward the Kid and the Regulators have received almost no inquiry by historians. Historian Kathleen Chamberlain shows what can be done with Billy and women in her superb biography of Susan McSween, *In the Shadow of Billy the Kid*, but the field still needs an extended study of Billy's connections with his mother, teacher Mary Richards, other New Mexico women such as Ma'am Jones, Ellen Casey, Lily Casey Klasner, and, of course, possible *novias* Sallie Chisum, Nasaria Leyba Yerbe, Abrana García, Celsa Gutiérrez, and Paulita Maxwell.

Too little is known about several of the Kid's opponents and supporters. The stories of Lawrence G. Murphy, Jimmy Dolan, Warren Bristol, and William Rynerson would add context to Billy stories. So would a biography of Alex

Conclusion

McSween, a large missing piece of the Lincoln County narrative.

Viewing Billy's position in larger western frameworks could also expand the meanings of his story. Richard Maxwell Brown provides a model for these contextual stories. In his insightful book, *No Duty to Retreat: Violence and Values in American History and Society,* he deftly shows how Billy and the Lincoln County happenings fit and did not fit into the larger patterns of frontier violence in U.S. history. Ambitious researchers could do the same by comparing Lincoln County experiences with those of other New Mexico counties and with other western territories. We still need more information on how federal policies crafted in Washington, D.C., shaped events in Lincoln County. Nor do we have insightful, meaningful comparisons of the rising legends of Billy the Kid with those enveloping other Old West luminaries such as Jesse James, Wild Bill Hickok, Wyatt Earp, and Calamity Jane. The field needs a full-blown study of the rise of western legends in the late nineteenth century and their evolution for more than a century.

These ponderings should lead to at least one solid conclusion: Billy the Kid will not disappear. Judging from events in the twenty-first century, not much new information about Billy has surfaced. But books, essays, novels, and, to a lesser extent, movies continue to appear. Controversies surrounding new exhumation efforts and photographs keep headlines buzzing. Hundreds of fans are members of the Billy the Kid Outlaw Gang, which continues to publish its widely circulated journal, *Outlaw Gazette,* and annual Billy the Kid gatherings draw sizable crowds to southeastern New Mexico locations. Stories about several Billy topics still garner headlines in major newspapers.

Historian Paul Andrew Hutton, drawing on the earlier words of Walter Noble Burns, once wrote about the Kid that he was a "dreamscape desperado" who "keeps riding across . . . our minds . . . free as a hawk. The outlaw of our dreams—forever free, forever young, forever riding." For nearly thirty years these words have been the most widely quoted and illuminating description of a charismatic Kid.

True enough, a bifurcated Billy will ride along the American and world imagination, challenging Jesse James and George Custer as the most-written-about character of the Old West. That Billy the Kid—part hero, part villain—will continue to entrance general readers, challenge scholars, and remain fodder for a wild variety of popular culture venues.

Essay on Sources

This book is based on a thorough examination of unpublished and published sources dealing with Billy the Kid. Full citations of sources listed in this section appear in the following bibliography. In this discussion the major published sources receive the most comment, but the bibliography lists many more valuable items including other manuscript sources.

ARCHIVES AND LIBRARIES

Four major libraries and archives contain the most important collections of manuscript materials pertaining to Billy the Kid. These are the Nita Stewart Haley Memorial Library and History Center in Midland, Texas, where the J. Evetts Haley and Robert N. Mullin collections are housed. Haley once planned to write a biography of the Kid and interviewed several old timers in southeastern New Mexico for the book he never wrote. Mullin, an oil executive and enthusiastic Billy fan, collected hundreds of important documents and photographs that he later deposited at the Haley Library.

The Special Collections at University of Arizona Libraries is also a major depository of Kid materials. Literary scholar Maurice Garland Fulton gathered information on Billy for several decades; those sources are now at the University of Arizona. So is a much smaller collection of revealing letters and other documents dealing with writer Walter Noble Burns and his significant book, *The Saga of Billy the Kid* (1926). A third and even smaller collection includes materials from medical doctor and missionary Taylor Ealy and his wife, Mary, in the Taylor F. Ealy Family Papers.

Two other collections of manuscript materials are particularly useful for scholars and writers. The New Mexico State Records Center and Archives in Santa Fe houses several useful collections. General files on Billy the Kid and Lincoln County are on deposit there, and researchers should also take note of biographer Victor Westphall's files dealing with Thomas Catron. Westphall's papers also include a typed copy of the Frank Warner Angel report so important for understanding the complex controversies in Lincoln County and other parts of the New Mexico Territory. Also located in this archive are Works Progress Administration (WPA) files of interviews with several persons involved in the Silver City and Lincoln County areas. General records of Lincoln County and those of the New Mexico Territorial Courts are also housed here.

At the University of New Mexico in Albuquerque, the Center for Southwest Research (CSWR) in the Zimmerman Library includes other important documents. Lou Blachly interviewed dozens of people who knew about the Kid; those interviews are archived in the CSWR. So is a smaller Taylor Ealy collection. More recently the Keleher family deposited in the CSWR the papers of lawyer and historian William A. Keleher, which are rich in materials he gathered for his New Mexico books. Dozens of photographs of pertinent New Mexico scenes and people are also found in this collection.

Several other libraries and archives contain materials pertinent for the Billy the Kid researcher. The Fray Angelico Chávez Library at the Palace of the Governors in Santa Fe houses some of the papers of Charles Siringo, writer and acquaintance of the Kid. The library also has a small William Bonney collection. In Lincoln, New Mexico, what used to be the Lincoln County Monument and now is the Lincoln County Historic Site, has hosted a very large and important collection of indefatigable researcher Philip Rasch and also a collection of revealing correspondence between W. A. Carrell and other Kid fans, but researchers should check before going to Lincoln because those collections have sometimes been unavailable or moved elsewhere. The Henn-Johnson Library and Local History Archives Foundation, located in an old adobe home just west of Lincoln, houses the Nora Johnson Henn and Alice Blakestad papers as well as other collections. The Lincoln County Archives in Carrizozo, New Mexico, contains a small collection of Lincoln County, Billy the Kid, and Pat Garrett materials, and a large collection of county newspapers. The Silver City Library has recently inherited from the Silver City Museum some of the Kid materials dealing with his years in Silver City. The Rio Grande Historical Collections in the New Mexico State University Library in Las Cruces has general sources on Billy the Kid and Lincoln County and houses an important collection gathered by Herman B. Weisner, a collection too often overlooked.

Finally, two other collections outside New Mexico should be noted. The National Archives in Washington, D.C., houses the reports that Frank Warner Angel gathered and wrote from his interviews in New Mexico. It also includes the proceedings of the revealing Dudley Court of Inquiry. Plus the National Archives maintains much of the correspondence of Presidents U. S. Grant, Rutherford B. Hayes, James A. Garfield, and their cabinet members and from their dealings with New Mexico. These materials have yet to be exhausted by Billy the Kid researchers. Finally, no one working on the Kid will want to overlook the large Lew Wallace Collections at the William Henry Smith Memorial Library at the Indiana Historical Society in Indianapolis and at the Lilly Library at Indiana University in Bloomington. Some of these materials have been microfilmed and are available in the Santa Fe New Mexico Records Center.

REFERENCE WORKS

Those researchers interested in checking for bibliographical listings of writings about Billy the Kid should begin with J. C. Dykes, *Billy the Kid: The Bibliography of a Legend* (1952). Dykes annotates more than four hundred articles and books and is particularly helpful on the early and obscure sources. More recently, Kathleen Chamberlain lists twice as many items in her unannotated bibliography, *Billy the Kid and the Lincoln County War: A Bibliography* (1997). The fullest recent bibliography, containing summary and evaluative annotations, is Richard W. Etulain, *Billy the Kid: A Reader's Guide* (2020). The several books by Frederick Nolan and Robert M. Utley (see titles below) all contain extensive bibliographical lists and footnotes overflowing with cited sources.

GENERAL BOOKS

The beginning place for those scholarly specialists and general readers wanting to know about Billy the Kid and Lincoln County are the numerous works of Frederick Nolan and Robert Utley. Nolan launched his long career as a Kid specialist with a book, *The Life and Death of John Henry Tunstall* (1965). Tunstall was the British rancher who was so supportive of Billy and whose murder escalated the Lincoln County War. Later Nolan produced the most comprehensive overview of the larger subject in *The Lincoln County War: A Documentary History* (1992, 2009). He has also written *The West of Billy the Kid* (1998). A fluent and prolific writer, Nolan infuses his works with an inviting literary style. These writings are also extraordinarily rich with hundreds of illuminating photographs.

Robert M. Utley is the most distinguished narrative historian of the American West in the late twentieth and early twenty-first centuries. An authority on the military and Native American history of the West, he has also authored four notable books on Lincoln County and Billy the Kid. His first volume, *Four Fighters of Lincoln County* (1986), focuses on the careers of Alexander McSween, Billy the Kid, Colonel Nathan A. M. Dudley, and Lew Wallace. The second, *High Noon in Lincoln: Violence on the Western Frontier* (1987), is an in-depth look at the most violent days of the Lincoln County War. The third, *Billy the Kid: A Short and Violent Life* (1989), is the best biography of the Kid written thus far. Utley also furnishes the only available study comparing Billy with a foreign outlaw, in this case Australian bushranger Ned Kelly, in *Wanted: The Outlaw Lives of Billy the Kid and Ned Kelly* (2015). Nolan and Utley have written and edited other books and penned dozens of essays, several of which are listed in the bibliography that follows.

Other biographies of Billy the Kid and general overviews of Lincoln County should not be overlooked. The first of these is Pat Garrett's *The Authentic Life of Billy, the Kid* (1882) parts of which were ghostwritten by the sheriff's friend, Marshall Ashmun "Ash" Upson, a journalist. This work must be used with caution, however. Part dime novel bluster, especially the opening chapters penned by Upson, the book nonetheless contains in the second half of the book Garrett's eyewitness account of the hunt for and killing of Billy the Kid. Charlie Siringo's *History of "Billy the Kid"* (1920) draws heavily on Garrett's book and a bit on Siringo's brief contact with the Kid. Two other strong researchers, lawyer William A. Keleher and Professor Maurice Garland Fulton, provided valuable overviews respectively in *Violence in Lincoln County, 1869–1881* (1957) and *History of the Lincoln County War* (1968, edited by Robert N. Mullin).

From the 1950s forward, new and thorough digging by Philip Rasch and Robert N. Mullin prepared the way for the later works by Nolan and Utley. The most recent general overview is Mark Lee Gardner's invitingly written dual biography, *To Hell on a Fast Horse: Billy the Kid, Pat Garrett, and the Epic Chase to Justice in the Old West* (2010).

Most of the general overviews provide helpful introductions to the later periods of the Kid's life that are discussed below.

The Early Years, 1859–1873

Nearly every biographer has tried without much luck to unravel the unsolved mysteries surrounding the Kid's first years up to 1873. The information that Philip Rasch, Robert Mullin, and several other historians assiduously dug up in the 1950s and 1960s remains the bedrock for most discussions of the Kid's first fourteen years. But unsolved mysteries confound searches for Billy's date and place of birth, the identity of his biological father, and the place(s) of his early residence.

Waldo E. Koop, in his brief study, *Billy the Kid: The Trail of a Kansas Legend* (1964), turned up most of what we know about the Kid's abbreviated stay in Wichita, Kansas, when he was known as Henry McCarty. Robert Mullin's *The Boyhood of Billy the Kid* (1967) summarizes the Kid's life up through his early years to the eve of the Lincoln County War.

Unfortunately, Donald Cline moves in wrong directions in *Billy the Kid: The Man behind the Legend* (1986) and *Antrim and Billy* (1990) and should not be followed.

The Middle Years in Silver City and Arizona, 1873–1877

Jerry (Richard) Weddle's *Antrim Is My Stepfather's Name: The Boyhood of Billy the Kid* (1993) remains by far the best account of Billy's life from his arrival in Silver City in early to mid-1873 to his gallop out of Arizona in early fall 1877. Weddle's superb notes provide other sources for these four years of the Kid's life. A handful of interviews with Silver City old-timers who claimed to know or know about Billy are included in Robert F. Kadlec, ed., *They "Knew" Billy the Kid* (1987).

The Lincoln County Years, 1877–1881

Any serious scholar should begin with Frederick Nolan's magisterial *Lincoln County War: A Documentary History* (1992, 2009) for this much written-about period of Billy's life. Nolan's other books and essays and Robert Utley's books and articles, especially the latter's *High Noon in Lincoln* (1987) and *Billy the Kid: A Short and Violent Life* (1989), are especially valuable accounts. Leon C. Metz provides the best source on the Lincoln County sheriff in his *Pat Garrett: The Story of a Western Lawman* (1974). John P. Wilson furnishes valuable comments on Lawrence G. Murphy and Jimmy Dolan in his thorough, balanced account, *Merchants, Guns, & Money: The Story of Lincoln County and Its Wars* (1987). Joel Jacobsen adds much detail on legal matters in his valuable *Such Men as Billy the Kid: The Lincoln County War Reconsidered* (1994).

Several biographies add valuable details to the Lincoln County story. See especially Kathleen P. Chamberlain's *In the Shadow of Billy the Kid: Susan McSween and the Lincoln*

County War (2013) and Paul L. Tsompanas, *Juan Patrón: A Fallen Star in the Days of Billy the Kid* (2013). Alex McSween, Lawrence G. Murphy, and Jimmy Dolan still await their biographers.

BILLY THE KID IN HISTORY AND LEGEND

The first step in sorting out the treatment of Billy the Kid in histories and legends is consulting Stephen Tatum's *Inventing Billy the Kid: Visions of the Outlaw in America, 1881–1981* (1982). His book links sociocultural changes in the United States to the shifting interpretations of Billy the Kid, including his reconstruction in histories and legends. Kent Ladd Steckmesser provides comparative perspectives on the evolving biographies and legends of Kit Carson, Wild Bill Hickok, George Armstrong Custer, and Billy the Kid in his still very useful book, *The Western Hero in History and Legend* (1965). Jon Tuska, in addition to including a brief biography, devotes chapters to fictional and cinematic treatments of Billy the Kid in his *Billy the Kid: His Life and Legend* (1994, 1997). It is regrettable that Tuska's book is marred by his excessive carping about the writings of Robert Utley as well as the works of several academic historians. Finally, Ramon Adams praises those books and essays that are factually correct in his estimation but devotes little attention to the artistic works of biographers and historians in his book evaluating historical accounts of the Kid, *A Fitting Death for Billy the Kid* (1960).

THE KID AND OTHER TOPICS

Western novelist Johnny D. Boggs contributes a first-rate study of Billy movies in *Billy the Kid on Film, 1911–2012* (2013). Paul Andrew Hutton has written several essays about the treatment of the Kid in film, nonfiction books, and popular culture. See especially his "Dreamscape Desperado" (1990) and "Silver Screen Desperado: Billy the Kid in Movies" (2007). Richard W. Etulain contributes an overview of the fictional Billys in "Billy the Kid among the Novelists" (2018) The extensive books of Gale Cooper deal with controversies surrounding Governor Lew Wallace's promise of a pardon to the Kid, controversial exhumation projects, and other topics.

Bibliography

MANUSCRIPTS

Fray Angélico Chávez Library, Palace of the Governors, Santa Fe,
  N.Mex.
  William Bonney Collection
  Charles Siringo Papers
Nita Stewart Haley Memorial Library and History Center, Midland,
  Tex.
  J. Evetts Haley Collection
  Robert N. Mullin Collection
Henn-Johnson Library and Local Archives Foundation, Lincoln,
  N.Mex.
  Nora John Henn Papers
  Alice Blakestad Papers
Historical Center for Southeast New Mexico, Roswell
  Sallie Chisum notebook
Indiana Historical Society, William Henry Smith Library, Indianapolis
  Lew Wallace Papers
Indiana University, Lilly Library, Bloomington
  Lew Wallace Manuscripts
Lincoln County Archives, Carrizozo, N.Mex.
  Billy the Kid and Pat Garrett Collections
  County newspapers

Bibliography

Lincoln County Collections, Lincoln, N.Mex.
W. A. Carrell Letters
Philip Rasch Collection
National Archives and Records Administration, Washington, D.C.
Frank W. Angel Report, The Death of John Tunstall, 44-4-8-3, General Records of the Justice Department, Record Group 60. (A complete typed copy is also in the Victor Westphall Collection in the New Mexico Records Center and Archives, Santa Fe.)
Dudley Court of Inquiry, CQ 1284, Records of the Office of the Judge Advocate General, Record Group 153. (For a published account, see Barron, Robert, later in the bibliography.)
U.S. Presidential Papers
New Mexico State Records Center and Archives, Santa Fe
Billy the Kid files
Lincoln County records
Lincoln County War History File, no. 20
Territorial Archives and Court Records
Victor Westphall Collection
WPA Files
Rio Grande Historical Collections, New Mexico State University, Las Cruces
Herman B. Weisner Papers
Silver City Library, N.Mex.
The library now houses most of the former Silver City Museum collections, save for Photographs.
University of Arizona Libraries, Special Collections, Tucson
Walter Noble Burns Collection
Taylor F. Ealy Family Collection
Maurice Garland Fulton Collection
University of New Mexico, Zimmerman Library, Center for Southwest Research, Albuquerque
Lou Blachly interviews
Taylor F. Ealy Papers
William A. Keleher Collections

NEWSPAPERS

Albuquerque (N.Mex.) Daily Journal
Albuquerque (N.Mex.) Review
Cimarron (N.Mex.) News & Press
Eco del Rio Grande (Las Cruces, N.Mex.)
Grant County Herald (Silver City, N.Mex.)

Las Cruces (N.Mex.) Thirty-Four
Las Vegas (N.Mex.) Daily Optic
Las Vegas (N.Mex.) Gazette
Lincoln County Leader (White Oaks, N.Mex.)
Mesilla (N.Mex.) News
Mesilla (N.Mex.) Valley Independent
New Southwest and Grant County Herald (Silver City, N.Mex.)
New York Sun
New York Times
Newman's Semi-Weekly (Las Cruces, N.Mex.)
Roswell (N.Mex.) Daily Record
Santa Fe Daily New Mexican
Santa Fe Weekly New Mexican
Silver City (N.Mex.) Enterprise
Silver City (N.Mex.) Mining Life

BOOK-LENGTH BIBLIOGRAPHIES, BIOGRAPHIES,
AND HISTORIES

Adams, Ramon. *Burs under the Saddle: A Second Look at Books and Histories of the West.* Norman: University of Oklahoma Press, 1964.
————. *More Burs under the Saddle.* Norman: University of Oklahoma Press, 1989.
————. *A Fitting Death for Billy the Kid.* Norman: University of Oklahoma Press,1960. Norman: University of Oklahoma Press, 1981.
————, comp. *Six Guns and Saddle Leather: A Bibliography of Books and Pamphlets on Western Outlaws and Lawmen.* Rev. and enl. ed. Norman: University of Oklahoma Press, 1969.
Airy, Helen. *Whatever Happened to Billy the Kid.* Santa Fe, N.Mex.: Sunstone Press, 1993.
Alexander, Bob. *Sheriff Harvey Whitehill: Silver City Stalwart.* Silver City, N.Mex.: High-Lonesome Books, 2005.
Anaya, A. P., and James H. Earle. *I Buried Billy.* College Station, Tex.: Creative Publishing, 1991.
Ball, Eve. *Ma'am Jones of the Pecos.* Tucson: University of Arizona Press, 1969.
Ball, Larry D. *Desert Lawmen: The High Sheriffs of New Mexico and Arizona, 1846–1912.* Albuquerque: University of New Mexico Press, 1992.
————. *The United States Marshals of New Mexico and Arizona Territories, 1846–1912.* Albuquerque: University of New Mexico Press, 1978.

Bibliography

Ballert, Marion, with Carl W. Breihan. *Billy the Kid: A Date with Destiny.* Seattle, Wash.: Hangman Press of Superior Publishing Company, 1970.

Barron, Robert M., ed. *Lieutenant Colonel N. A. M. Dudley Court of Inquiry, Fort Stanton, New Mexico.* 4 vols. El Paso, Tex.: Lincoln County War Series, 1995. Reprinted as *Court of Inquiry: Lieutenant Colonel N. A. M. Dudley, Fort Stanton, New Mexico, May-June-July 1879.* 2 vols. Edina, Minn.: Beaver's Pond Press, 2003.

Bell, Bob Boze. *The Illustrated Life and Times of Billy the Kid.* Cave Creek, Ariz.: Boze Books,1992. Published in 2d ed. Phoenix, Ariz.: Boze Books, 1996.

Bender, Norman J., ed. *Missionaries, Outlaws, and Indians: Taylor F. Ealy at Lincoln and Zuni, 1878–1881.* Albuquerque: University of New Mexico Press, 1984.

Billy the Kid: Las Vegas Newspaper Accounts of His Career. Waco, Tex.: W. W. Morrison, 1958.

Boggs, Johnny D. *Billy the Kid on Film, 1911–2012.* Jefferson, N.C.: McFarland and Company, 2013.

Branch, Louis Leon. *"Los Bilitos": The Story of "Billy the Kid" and His Gang.* New York: Carlton Press, 1980.

Brent, William. *The Complete and Factual Life of Billy the Kid.* New York: Frederick Fell, 1964.

Brown, Richard Maxwell. *No Duty to Retreat: Violence and Values in American History and Society.* New York: Oxford University Press, 1991.

Browning, James A. *The Western Reader's Guide: A Selected Bibliography of Nonfiction Magazines, 1953–91.* Stillwater, Okla.: Barbed Wire Press, 1992.

Burns, Walter Noble. *The Saga of Billy the Kid.* Garden City, N.Y.: Doubleday, Page, 1926.

Caffey, David L. *Chasing the Santa Fe Ring: Power and Privilege in Territorial New Mexico.* Albuquerque: University of New Mexico Press, 2014.

Caldwell, Clifford R. *Dead Right: The Lincoln County War.* Rev. 2d ed. Mountain Home, Tex.: n.p., 2008.

Chamberlain, Kathleen P. *In the Shadow of Billy the Kid: Susan McSween and the Lincoln County War.* Albuquerque: University of New Mexico Press, 2013.

———, comp. *Billy the Kid and the Lincoln County War: A Bibliography.* Occasional Papers, no. 13. Albuquerque: Center for the American West, University of New Mexico, 1997.

Bibliography

Cline, Donald. *Alias Billy the Kid: The Man behind the Legend*. Santa Fe, N.Mex.: Sunstone Press, 1986.

———. *Antrim and Billy*. College Station, Tex.: Creative Publishing, 1990.

Coe, George. *Frontier Fighter: The Autobiography of George Coe*. Albuquerque: University of New Mexico Press, 1934.

Cooper, Gale. *Billy the Kid's Pretenders: Brushy Bill and John Miller*. Albuquerque, N.Mex.: Gelcour Books, 2010.

———. *Billy the Kid's Writings, Words and Wit*. Albuquerque, N.Mex.: Gelcour Books, 2011.

———. *Cracking the Billy the Kid Case Hoax: The Strange Plot to Exhume Billy the Kid, Convict Pat Garrett of Murder, and Become President of the United States*. Albuquerque, N.Mex.: Gelcour Books, 2014.

———. *The Lost Pardon of Billy the Kid: An Analysis Factoring in the Santa Fe Ring, Governor Wallace's Dilemma, and a Territory in Rebellion*. Albuquerque, N.Mex.: Gelcour Books, 2017.

———. *MegaHoax: The Strange Plot to Exhume Billy the Kid and Become President*. Shelbyville, Ky.: Gelcour Books, 2009.

———. *The Nun Who Rode on "Billy the Kid": Sleuthing a Foisted Frontier Fable*. Albuquerque, N.Mex.: Gelcour Books, 2017.

Cramer, T. Dudley. *The Pecos Ranchers in the Lincoln County War*. Oakland, Calif.: Branding Iron Press, 1996.

Dworkin, Mark J. *American Mythmaker: Walter Noble Burns and the Legends of Billy the Kid, Wyatt Earp, and Joaquin Murrieta*. Norman: University of Oklahoma Press, 2015.

Dykes, Jeff C. *Billy the Kid: The Bibliography of a Legend*. Albuquerque: University of New Mexico Press, 1952.

Ealy, Ruth. *Water in a Thirsty Land*. Privately published, 1955.

Earle, James H., ed. *The Capture of Billy the Kid*. College Station, Tex.: Creative Publishing, 1988.

Edwards, Harold. *Goodbye Billy the Kid*. College Station, Tex.: Creative Publishing, 1996.

Etulain, Richard W. *Billy the Kid: A Reader's Guide*. Norman: University of Oklahoma Press, 2020.

———. *Re-imagining the Modern American West: A Century of Fiction, History, and Art*. Tucson: University of Arizona Press, 1996.

———. *Telling Western Stories: From Buffalo Bill to Larry McMurtry*. Albuquerque: University of New Mexico Press, 1999.

Fulton, Maurice Garland. *History of the Lincoln County War*. Ed. Robert N. Mullin. Tucson: University of Arizona Press, 1968.

Garcia, Elbert A. *Billy the Kid's Kid: The Hispanic Connection*. Santa Rosa, N.Mex.: Los Products Press, 1999.

Bibliography

Gardner, Mark Lee. *To Hell on a Fast Horse: Billy the Kid, Pat Garrett, and the Epic Chase to Justice in the Old West.* New York: William Morrow, 2010.

Garrett, Pat[trick] F. *The Authentic Life of Billy, the Kid, the Noted Desperado of the Southwest, Whose Deeds of Daring and Blood Made His Name a Terror in New Mexico, Arizona and Northern Mexico.* Santa Fe: New Mexican Printing and Publishing, 1882. Maurice Garland Fulton. New York: Macmillan, 1927. J. C. Dykes. Norman: University of Oklahoma Press, 1954. Frederick Nolan. Norman: University of Oklahoma Press, 2000.

Gilmore, Kay C. "Billy the Kid: The Growth of a Legend." Master's thesis, Kansas State University, 1966.

Haldane, Roberta K. *Gold-Mining Boomtown: People of White Oaks, Lincoln County, New Mexico.* Norman: Arthur H. Clark Company, 2012.

Hamlin, William Lee. *The True Story of Billy the Kid: A Tale of the Lincoln County War.* Caldwell, Idaho: Caxton Printers, 1959.

Hendron, J. W. *The Story of Billy the Kid: New Mexico's Number One Desperado.* Santa Fe, N.Mex.: Rydal, 1948.

Henn, Nora True. *Lincoln County and Its Wars.* Roswell, N.Mex.: Southwest Printers, 2017.

Hough, Emerson. *Story of the Cowboy.* New York: D. Appleton, 1897.

———. *Story of the Outlaw: A Study of the Western Desperado.* New York: Outing Publishing Co., 1907.

Hoyt, Henry F. *A Frontier Doctor.* Boston: Houghton Mifflin Company, 1929.

Hunner, Jon, comp. *A Selective Bibliography of New Mexico History.* Occasional Paper, no. 5. Albuquerque: Center for the American West, University of New Mexico, 1992.

Hunt, Frazier. *The Tragic Days of Billy the Kid.* New York: Hastings House Publishers, 1956.

Jameson, W. C. *Billy the Kid: Beyond the Grave.* Dallas, Tex.: Taylor Trade Publishing, 2005.

———. *Billy the Kid: The Lost Interviews.* Clearwater, Fla: Garlic Press Publishing, 2012.

———. *Cold Case: Billy the Kid: Investigating History's Mysteries.* Lanham, Md.: TwoDot, 2018.

———. *Pat Garrett: The Man behind the Badge.* Lanham, Md.: Taylor Trade Publishing, 2016.

———, and Frederic Bean. *The Return of the Outlaw: Billy the Kid.* Plano: Republic of Texas Press, 1998.

Jacobsen, Joel. *Such Men as Billy the Kid: The Lincoln County War Reconsidered*. Lincoln: University of Nebraska Press, 1994.

Jones, Daryl. *The Dime Novel Western*. Bowling Green, Ohio: The Popular Press, 1976.

Kadlec, Robert F., ed. *They "Knew" Billy the Kid: Interviews with Old-Time New Mexicans*. Santa Fe, N.Mex.: Ancient City Press, 1987.

Keleher, William A. *The Fabulous Frontier: Twelve New Mexico Items*. 1945. Albuquerque: University of New Mexico Press, 1962.

———. *Violence in Lincoln County, 1869–1881*. 1957. Albuquerque: University of New Mexico Press, 1982.

Klasner, Lily. *My Girlhood among Outlaws*. Ed. Eve Ball. Tucson: University of Arizona Press, 1972.

Koop, Waldo E. *Billy the Kid: The Trail of a Kansas Legend*. Kansas City, Kan.: Kansas City Westerners, 1965.

Lamar, Howard Roberts. *The Far Southwest, 1846–1912: A Territorial History*. New Haven, Conn.: Yale University Press, 1966.

———, ed. *The New Encyclopedia of the American West*. New Haven, Conn.: Yale University Press, 1998.

Larson, Robert W. *New Mexico's Quest for Statehood, 1846–1912*. Albuquerque: University of New Mexico Press, 1968.

Lavash, Donald R. *Sheriff William Brady: Tragic Hero of the Lincoln County War*. Santa Fe, N.Mex.: Sunstone Press, 1986.

McCarty, John L. *Maverick Town: The Story of Old Tascosa*. Norman: University of Oklahoma Press, 1946.

McCright, Grady E., and James H. Powell. *Disorder in Lincoln County: Frank Warner Angel's Reports*. Las Cruces, N.Mex.: Rio Grande Historical Collections, 1981.

———. *Jessie Evans: Lincoln County Badman*. College Station, Tex.: Creative Publishing, 1983.

Meadows, John P. *Pat Garrett and Billy the Kid as I Knew Them: Reminiscences of John P. Meadows*. Ed. John P. Wilson. Albuquerque: University of New Mexico Press, 2004.

Metz, Leon C. *Pat Garrett: The Story of a Western Lawman*. Norman: University of Oklahoma Press, 1974.

Morsberger, Robert E., and Katherine M. Morsberger. *Lew Wallace: Militant Romantic*. New York: McGraw-Hill, 1980.

Mullin, Robert N. *The Boyhood of Billy the Kid*. Southwestern Studies 5. Monograph no. 17. El Paso: Texas Western Press, 1967.

Nolan, Frederick W. *The Life and Death of John Henry Tunstall*. Albuquerque: University of New Mexico, 1965.

Bibliography

———. *The Lincoln County War: A Documentary History.* Norman: University of Oklahoma Press, 1992. Updated. Santa Fe, N.Mex.: Sunstone Press, 2009.

———. *The West of Billy the Kid.* Norman: University of Oklahoma Press, 1998.

———, ed. *The Billy the Kid Reader.* Norman: University of Oklahoma Press, 2007.

Otero, Miguel Antonio, Jr. *The Real Billy the Kid: With New Light on the Lincoln County War.* New York: Rufus Rockwell Wilson, 1936. Houston: Arte Público Press, 1998.

Poe, John. *The Death of Billy the Kid.* Intro. Maurice Garland Fulton. Boston: Houghton Mifflin, 1933.

Rasch, Philip J. *Gunsmoke in Lincoln County.* Ed. Robert K. DeArment. Laramie: University of Wyoming and National Association for Outlaw and Lawman History, 1997.

———. *Trailing Billy the Kid.* Ed. Robert K. DeArment. Laramie: University of Wyoming and National Association for Outlaw and Lawman History, 1995.

———. *Warriors of Lincoln County.* Ed. Robert K. DeArment. Laramie: University of Wyoming and National Association for Outlaw and Lawman History, 1998.

Reynolds, Bill. *Trouble in New Mexico: The Outlaws, Gunmen, Desperados, Murderers, and Lawmen for Fifty Turbulent Years.* 3 vols. Bakersfield, Calif.: by the author, 1994–1995.

Rickards, Colin. *The Gunfight at Blazer's Mill.* Southwestern Studies series. Monograph no. 40. El Paso: Texas Western Press, 1974.

Russell, Randy. *Billy the Kid: The Story, the Trial.* Lincoln, N.Mex.: Crystal Press, 1994.

Simmons, Marc. *Stalking Billy the Kid: Brief Sketches of a Short Life.* Santa Fe, N.Mex.: Sunstone Press, 2006.

Siringo, Charles A. *History of "Billy the Kid."* Santa Fe, N.Mex.: privately published, 1920. Albuquerque: University of New Mexico Press, 2000.

———. *A Lone Star Cowboy . . .* Santa Fe, N.Mex.: n.p., 1919.

———. *A Texas Cowboy; or, Fifteen Years on the Hurricane Deck of a Spanish Pony.* 1885. New York: Penguin Books, 2000.

Sonnichsen, C. L., and William V. Morrison. *Alias Billy the Kid.* Albuquerque: University of New Mexico Press, 1955.

Steckmesser, Kent L. *The Western Hero in History and Legend.* Norman: University of Oklahoma Press, 1965.

———. *Western Outlaws: The "Good Badman" in Fact, Film, and Folklore.* Claremont, Calif.: Regina Books, 1983.

Tatum, Stephen. *Inventing Billy the Kid: Visions of the Outlaw in America, 1881–1981*. Albuquerque: University of New Mexico Press, 1982.

Thorp, N. Howard, and Nel McCullough Clark. *Pardner of the Wind: Story of the Southwestern Cowboy*. Caldwell, Idaho: Caxton Printers, 1945.

Tsompanas, Paul L. *Juan Patrón: A Fallen Star in the Days of Billy the Kid*. [Richmond], [Va.]: Bell Isle Books, 2013.

Turk, David S. *Blackwater Draw: Three Lives, Billy the Kid, and the Murders That Started the Lincoln County War*. Santa Fe, N.Mex.: Sunstone Press, 2011.

Tuska, Jon. *Billy the Kid: A Bio-Bibliography*. Westport, Conn.: Greenwood Press, 1983. Reprinted as *Billy the Kid: A Handbook*. Lincoln: University of Nebraska Press, 1986. Revised as *Billy the Kid: His Life and Legend*. Albuquerque: University of New Mexico Press, 1997.

Utley, Robert M. *Billy the Kid: A Short and Violent Life*. Lincoln: University of Nebraska Press, 1989.

———. *Four Fighters of Lincoln County*. Albuquerque: University of New Mexico Press, 1986.

———. *High Noon in Lincoln: Violence on the Western Frontier*. Albuquerque: University of New Mexico Press, 1987.

———. *Wanted: The Outlaw Lives of Billy the Kid and Ned Kelly*. New Haven, Conn.: Yale University Press, 2015.

Wallis, Michael. *Billy the Kid: The Endless Ride*. New York: W. W. Norton and Company, 2007.

Weddle, Jerry (Richard). *Antrim is My Stepfather's Name: The Boyhood of Billy the Kid*. Tucson: Arizona Historical Society, 1993.

Westphall, Victor. *Thomas Benton Catron and His Era*. Tucson: University of Arizona Press, 1973.

Wilson, John P. *Merchants, Guns, & Money: The Story of Lincoln County and Its Wars*. Santa Fe: Museum of New Mexico Press, 1987.

DIME NOVELS

Cowdrick, J. C. *Silver-Mask, the Man of Mystery; or, the Cross of the Golden Keys*. Beadle's Half Dime Library, no. 360. New York: Beadle and Adams, 1884. Reprinted as *Billy, the Kid from Texas; or, Silver Mask's Clew*. Beadle Pocket Library, no 321. New York: Beadle and Adams, 1890. Reprinted as *Billy, the Kid from Frisco*. Beadle Pocket Library, 321. New York: Beadle and Adams, 1890.

Daggett, Thomas F. *Billy LeRoy, the Colorado Bandit; or, the King of American Highwaymen*. New York Police Gazette, 1881. Also appeared as *The Life and Deeds of Billy LeRoy, Alias the Kid, King of American Highwaymen*. New York: Richard K. Fox, 1883.

"The Dead Desperado, Adventures of Billy, the Kid, as Narrated by Himself." *Las Vegas (N.Mex.) Daily Optic*, 12–23 December 1881, parts 1–11. Reprinted in Bob L'Aloge, *The Code of the West*. Las Cruces, N.Mex.: B & J Publications, 1992, 1–31.

Doughty, Francis Worcester. *Old King Brady and "Billy the Kid," or, the Great Detective's Chase*. New York Detective Library, no. 411. New York: F[rank] Tousey, 1890.

Fable, Edmund, Jr. *The True Life of Billy the Kid; the Noted New Mexican Outlaw*. Denver, Colo.: Denver Publishing Company, 1881. Also published by the same publisher and in the same year as *Billy the Kid, the New Mexican Outlaw; or, the Bold Bandit of the West!* Denver, Colo.: Denver Publishing Company, 1881. Reprinted as *The True Life of Billy the Kid: The Noted New Mexican Outlaw*. College Station, Tex.: Creative Publishing Company, 1980.

Jenardo, Don [John Woodruff Lewis]. *The True Life of Billy the Kid*. Five Cent Wide Awake Library, no. 451. New York: F[rank] Tousey, 1881. Reprinted in Frederick Nolan, *The Billy the Kid Reader*. Norman: University of Oklahoma Press, 2007, 3–49.

The Life of Billy the Kid, a Juvenile Outlaw. Morrison's Sensational Series, no 3. New York: John W. Morrison, 1881.

One of the Kids. *The Cowboy's Career; or, the Daredevil Deeds of Billy the Kid, the Noted New Mexico Desperado*. Chicago: Belford, Clarke & Co., 1881.

NOVELS

Aragon, John A. *Billy the Kid's Last Ride: A Novel*. Santa Fe, N.Mex.: Sunstone Press, 2011.

Bean, Amelia. *Time for Outrage*. Garden City, N.Y.: Doubleday and Company, 1967.

Boggs, Johnny D. *Law of the Land: The Trial of Billy the Kid*. New York: Signet, 2004.

Braun, Matt. *Jury of Six*. New York: Pocket Books, 1980.

Coolidge, Dane. *War Paint*. New York: E. P. Dutton and Company, 1929.

Cooper, Gale. *Joy of the Birds*. Bloomington, Ind.: Author House, 2008. Revised and republished as *Billy and Paulita: A Novel*. Albuquerque, N.Mex.: Gelcour Books, 2012.

Corle, Edwin. *Billy the Kid*. Boston: Little, Brown and Company, 1953.

Cotton, Ralph W. *Cost of Killing*. New York: Pocket Books, 1996.

Bibliography

Fackler, Elizabeth. *Billy the Kid: The Legend of El Chivato.* New York: Forge, 1995.

Grey, Zane. *Nevada.* New York: Harper, 1928.

———. *Shadow on the Trail.* New York: Harper and Row, 1946.

Hansen, Ron. *The Kid: A Novel.* New York: Scribner, 2016.

Hough, Emerson. *Heart's Desire: The Story of a Contented Town, Peculiar Citizens, and Two Unfortunate Lovers; a Novel.* New York: Macmillan Company, 1905.

Lehman, Paul Evan. *Pistols on the Pecos.* New York: Avon, 1953.

Lewis, Preston. *The Demise of Billy the Kid.* New York: Bantam Books, 1994.

Mann, E. B. *Gamblin' Man.* New York: William Morrow and Company, 1934.

McGeeney, P. S. *Down at Stein's Pass.* Boston: Angel Guardian Press, 1909.

McMurtry, Larry. *Anything for Billy.* New York: Simon and Schuster, 1988.

Momaday, N. Scott. *The Ancient Child: A Novel.* New York: Doubleday, 1989.

Neider, Charles. *The Authentic Death of Hendry Jones.* New York: Harper and Brothers, 1956.

Nye, Nelson. *Pistols for Hire: A Tale of the Lincoln County War and the West's Most Desperate Outlaw, William (Billy the Kid) Bonney.* New York: Macmillan Company, 1941.

Ore, Rebecca [Rebecca B. Brown]. *The Illegal Rebirth of Billy the Kid.* New York: Tor Books, 1991.

Raine, William MacLeod. *The Fighting Tenderfoot.* New York: Doubleday, 1929.

Rhodes, Eugene Manlove. *Pasó por Aquí.* Boston: Houghton Mifflin, 1927.

Willoughby, Lee Davis [Jane Toombs]. *The Outlaws.* New York: Dell, 1984.

Whitlow, B. Duane. *Lincoln County Diary.* Santa Fe, N.Mex.: Sunstone Press, 1991.

ESSAYS AND BOOK CHAPTERS

Adler, Alfred. "Billy the Kid: A Case Study in Epic Origins." *Western Folklore* 10 (April 1951): 143–52.

Ball, Larry D. "Militia Posses: The Territorial Militia in Civil Law Enforcement in New Mexico Territory, 1877–1883." *New Mexico Historical Review* 55 (January 1980): 47–69.

Bibliography

Blazer, Paul A. "The Fight at Blazer's Mill: A Chapter in the Lincoln County War." *Arizona and the West* 6 (Autumn 1964): 203–10.

Brown, Richard Maxwell. "The Gunfighter: The Reality behind the Myth." *No Duty to Retreat: Violence and Values in American History and Society.* New York: Oxford University Press, 1991, 39–86.

Buffington, Ann. "Out of the Shadows: Women of Lincoln County." *True West* 47 (July 2000): 12–22.

Cain, Ellen Marie. "Testing Courage in New Mexico: Taylor Ealy and the Lincoln County War, 1878." *American Presbyterians* 11 (Spring 1994): 11–22.

Chamberlain, Kathleen P. "Billy the Kid, Susan McSween, Thomas Catron, and the Modernization of New Mexico." In *New Mexico Lives: Profiles and Historical Stories.* Ed. Richard W. Etulain. Albuquerque: University of New Mexico Press, 2002, 193–219.

———. "In the Shadow of Billy the Kid: Susan McSween and the Lincoln County War." *Montana: The Magazine of Western History* 55 (Winter 2005): 36–53.

Chapman, Arthur. "Billy the Kid: A Man All 'Bad.'" *Outing Magazine* 46 (1905): 73–77.

Cline, Donald. "Secret Life of Billy the Kid." *True West* 31 (April 1984): 12–17, 62.

———. "Tom Pickett: Friend of Billy the Kid." *True West* 44 (July 1997): 40–49.

DeMattos, Jack. "The Search for Billy the Kid's Roots" and "The Search for Billy the Kid's Roots Is Over." *Real West* 21 (November 1978): 12–19; 23 (January 1980): 20–25.

Edwards, Harold. "Barney Mason: In the Shadow of Pat Garrett and Billy the Kid." *Old West* 26 (Summer 1990): 14–19.

———. "From Prince to Knave to an Early Grave: The Story of Charlie Bowdre." *NOLA Quarterly* 19 (July-September 1995): 2–8.

Ellis, Bruce T., ed. "Lincoln County Postscript: Notes on Robert A. Widenmann by His Daughter Elsie Widenman." *New Mexico Historical Review* 50 (July 1975): 213–30.

Etulain, Richard W. "Billy the Kid among the Dime Novelists." *Outlaw Gazette* 30 (2017): 3–6.

———. "Billy the Kid among the Novelists." *New Mexico Historical Review* 93 (Winter 2018): 31–64.

———. "Billy the Kid: Thunder in the West." In *With Badges and Bullets: Lawmen and Outlaws in the Old West.* Ed. Richard W. Etulain and Glenda Riley. Golden, Colo.: Fulcrum Publishing, 1999, 123–38.

————. "The Ever-Present Billy the Kid: Protagonist of the Old West." *History News Network,* 19 August 2019.

————. Introduction to Walter Noble Burns. *Saga of Billy the Kid.* 1926. Albuquerque: University of New Mexico Press, 1999, ix-xvii.

————."Is There Anything Left to Say about Billy the Kid?" *Journal of the Wild West History Association* 11 (December 2018): 26–29.

————. "The Legendary, Mysterious Kid." *Wild West* 31 (February 2019): 38–43

Fergusson, Harvey. "Billy the Kid." *American Mercury* 5 (May 1925): 224–31.

Fleming, Elvis E. "Deputy J. B. 'Billy' Mathews: The Lincoln County War and Other Lives." *New Mexico Historical Review* 72 (July 1997): 239–56.

Fulton, Maurice Garland. "Billy the Kid in Life and Books." *New Mexico Folklore Record* 4 (1949–1950): 1–6.

Henry, O. "The Cabellero's Way." *Heart of the West.* New York: Doubleday, Page, 1904, 187–204. A short story.

Hinton, Harwood. "John Simpson Chisum, 1877–84." *New Mexico Historical Review* 31 (July 1956): 177–205; 31 (October 1956): 310–37; 32 (January 1957): 53–65.

Hough, Emerson. "Billy the Kid: The True Story of a Western 'Bad Man.'" *Everybody's Magazine* 5 (September 1901): 303–10.

Hutton, Paul Andrew. "Billy the Kid as Seen in the Movies." *Frontier Times* 57 (June 1985): 24–29.

————. "Billy the Kid's Final Escape." *Wild West* 28 (December 2015): 28–32.

————. "Dreamscape Desperado." *New Mexico Magazine* 68 (June 1990): 44–57.

————. "Silver Screen Desperado: Billy the Kid in the Movies." *New Mexico Historical Review* 82 (Spring 2007): 149–96.

————, and Jason Strykowski]. "Billy the Kid Filmography." *New Mexico Historical Review* 82 (Spring 2007): 197–219.

Jacobsen, Joel K. "An Excess of Law in Lincoln County: Thomas Catron, Samuel Axtell, and the Lincoln County War." *New Mexico Historical Review* 68 (April 1993): 133–51.

Jones, Oakah L. "Lew Wallace: Hoosier Governor of Territorial New Mexico, 1878–81." *New Mexico Historical Review* 60 (April 1985): 129–58.

Keleher, William A. "About John S. Chisum" and "Patrick Floyd Garrett." In *The Fabulous Frontier: Twelve New Mexico Items.* Albuquerque: University of New Mexico Press, 1962, 56–66, 67–101.

Kyle, Thomas G. "Computers, Billy the Kid, and Brushy Bill: The Verdict Is In." *True West* 37 (July 1990): 16–19.

Larson, Carole. "Billy the Kid and Pat Garrett." *Forgotten Frontier: The Story of Southeastern New Mexico*. Albuquerque: University of New Mexico Press, 1993, 153–85.

Lavash, Donald. "Thomas G. Yerby and Nasaria." *Outlaw Gazette* 5 (December 1992): 10–11.

Metz, Leon C. "The Death of Billy the Kid." *Wild West* 11 (August 1998): 30, 73.

Miller, Darlis A. "William Logan Rynerson in New Mexico, 1862–93." *New Mexico Historical Review* 48 (April 1973): 101–32.

———. "The Women of Lincoln County, 1860–1900." In *New Mexico Women: Intercultural Perspectives*. Ed. Joan M. Jensen and Darlis A. Miller. Albuquerque: University of New Mexico Press, 1986, 169–200.

Mills, William A. "Kid Brother." *Journal of the Wild West History Association* 12 (March 2019): 26–41.

Momaday, N. Scott. "The Strange and True Story of My Life with Billy the Kid." *American West* 22 (September–October 1985): 54–66.

Mullin, Robert N. "Here Lies John Kinney." *Journal of Arizona History* 14 (Autumn 1973): 223–42.

———, and Charles E. Welch Jr. "Billy the Kid: The Making of a Hero." *Western Folklore* 32 (April 1973): 104–11.

———, and Philip J. Rasch. "Dim Trails: The Pursuit of the McCarty Family." *New Mexico Folklore Record* 8 (1953–54): 6–11.

———, and Philip J. Rasch. "New Light on the Legend of Billy the Kid." *New Mexico Folklore Record* 2 (1952–1953): 1–5.

Nolan, Frederick W. "The Birth of an Outlaw." True West (17 May 2015). http://www.truewestmagazine.com/author/frederick-nolan.

———. "Bob Olinger: Blowhard or Badman?" *True West* 42 (February 1995): 14–21.

———. "Dick Brewer: The Unlikely Gunfighter." *NOLA Quarterly* 15 (July-September 1991): 19–27.

———. "'Dirty Dave' Rudabaugh, The Kid's Worst Friend." *Outlaw Gazette* 3 (December 1989): 7–13.

———. "First Blood: Another Look at the Killing of 'Windy Cahill.'" *Outlaw Gazette* 13 (November 2000): 2–4.

———. "The Hunting of Billy the Kid." *Wild West* 16 (June 2003): 38–44.

———. "The Men at Fort Stanton, Part One" and "The Men at Fort Stanton, Part Two." *NOLA Quarterly* 18 (July-September 1994): 5–12; 18 (October–December 1994): 29–41.

———. "The Private Life of Billy the Kid." *True West* 47 (July 2000): 33–39.

———. "The Search for Alexander McSween." *New Mexico Historical Review* 62 (July 1987): 287–301.

———. "She Taught the Kid a Lesson: The Life of Mary Richards." *True West* 53 (May 2006): 51–53.

O'Toole, Fintan. "The Many Stories of Billy the Kid." *New Yorker* (28 December 1998–4 January 1999): 86–98.

Page, Jake. "Was Billy the Kid a Superhero—or a Superscoundrel?" *Smithsonian* 21 (February 1991): 137–48.

Rasch, Philip J. "The Bonney Brothers." *Frontier Times* 39 (December 1964–January 1965): 43, 60–61. Reprinted in Rasch, *Trailing Billy the Kid* (1995), 110–15.

———. "Clues to the Puzzle of Billy the Kid." *English Westerners' Brand Book* 4 (December 1957–January 1958): 8–11. Reprinted in Rasch, *Trailing Billy the Kid* (1995), 53–58.

———. "Exit Axtell: Enter Wallace." *New Mexico Historical Review* 32 (July 1957): 231–45. Reprinted in Rasch, *Gunsmoke in Lincoln County* (1997), 193–207.

———. "Five Days of Battle." *Brand Book of the Denver Westerners* (1955). Reprinted in Rasch, *Gunsmoke in Lincoln County* (1997), 116–33.

———. "How the Lincoln County War Started." *True West* 9 (March–April 1962): 30–32, 48, 50.

———. "The Hunting of Billy the Kid." *English Westerners' Brand Book* 2 (January 1969): 1–10; 2 (April 1969): 11–12. Reprinted in Rasch, *Trailing Billy the Kid* (1995), 119–42.

———. "A Man Named Antrim." *Los Angeles Westerners' Brand Book* 6 (Summer 1956): 48–54. Reprinted in Rasch, *Trailing Billy the Kid* (1995), 38–45.

———. "The Murder of Huston I. Chapman." *The Los Angeles Westerners' Brand Book* 8 (1959): 69–82. Reprinted in Rasch, *Gunsmoke in Lincoln County* (1997), 243–59.

———. "Prelude to War: The Murder of John Henry Tunstall." *The Los Angeles Westerners' Brand Book* 7 (1957): 78–96. Reprinted in Rasch, *Gunsmoke in Lincoln County* (1997), 52–72.

———. "The Quest for Joseph Antrim." *Quarterly of the National Association and Center for Outlaw and Lawman History* 6 (July 1981): 13–17.

———. "The Rise of the House of Murphy." *Brand Book of the Denver Westerners* 12 (1956): 53–84. Reprinted in Rasch, *Gunsmoke in Lincoln County* (1997), 3–21.

———. "A Second Look at the Blazer's Mill Affair." *Frontier Times* (December 1963–January 1964). Reprinted in Rasch, *Gunsmoke in Lincoln County* (1997), 110–15.

———. "The Trials of Billy the Kid." *Real West* (November 1987): 32 ff. Reprinted in Rasch, *Trailing Billy the Kid,* 194–201.

———. "The Twenty-One Men He Put Bullets Through." *New Mexico Folklore Record* 9 (1954–1955): 8–14. Reprinted in Rasch, *Trailing Billy the Kid* (1995), 23–35.

———, and R. N. Mullin. "Dim Trails: The Pursuit of the McCarty Family." *New Mexico Folklore Record* 8 (1953–54): 6–11. Reprinted in Rasch, *Trailing Billy the Kid* (1995), 12–21.

———. "New Light on the Legend of Billy the Kid." *New Mexico Folklore Record* 7 (1952–1953): 1–5. Reprinted in Rasch, *Trailing Billy the Kid* (1995), 3–11.

Sanchez, Lynda A. "Recuerdos de Billy the Kid." *New Mexico Magazine* 59 (July 1981): 16–19, 68–71.

———. "They Loved Billy the Kid: To Them He Was 'Billito.'" *True West* 31 (January 1984): 12–16.

Sanderson, Wayne. "The Kid and the McCarty Name." *Wild West* (23 November 2016). www.historynet.com/kid-mccarty-name.htm.

Simmons, Marc. "Billy the Kid and the Lincoln County War." *American History Illustrated* 17 (June 1982): 40–44.

Slight, J. E. "Billy the Kid" and "The Lincoln County War: A Sequel to the Story of Billy the Kid." *Overland Monthly* 52 (July 1908): 46–51; (August 1908): 168–74.

Steckmesser, Kent Ladd. "Billy the Kid: A Short and Violent Life" and "Mr. Bonney and the Faking of History." In *Western Outlaws: The "Good Badman" in Fact, Film, and Folklore.* Claremont, Calif.: Regina, 1983, 79–92, 101–14.

Strykowski, Jason. "An Unholy Bargain in a Cursed Place: Lew Wallace, William Bonney, and New Mexico Territory, 1878–1881." *New Mexico Historical Review* 82 (Spring 2007): 237–58.

Theisen, Lee Scott. "The Fight in Lincoln, N.M., 1878: The Testimony of Two Negro Participants." *Arizona and the West* 12 (Summer 1970): 173–98.

———. "Frank Warner Angel's Notes on New Mexico Territory, 1878." *Arizona and the West* 18 (Winter 1976): 333–70.

Traylor, Ralph C. "Facts Regarding the Escape of Billy the Kid." *Frontier Times* 13 (July 1936): 506–13.

Turk, David S. "Billy the Kid & the U. S. Marshals Service." *Wild West* 19 (February 2007): 34–39.

Bibliography

Tuska, Jon. "Billy the Kid in Fiction" and "Billy the Kid in Film." In *Billy the Kid: His Life and Legend*. 1994. Albuquerque: University of New Mexico Press, 1997, 153–87, 189–226.

Utley, Robert M. "Billy the Kid and the Lincoln County War." *New Mexico Historical Review* 61 (April 1986): 93–120.

———. "The Final Days of Billy the Kid." *New Mexico Historical Review* 64 (October 1989): 401–26.

Weddle, Jerry (Richard). "Apprenticeship of an Outlaw: 'Billy the Kid' in Arizona." *Journal of Arizona History* 31 (Autumn 1990): 233–52.

Wilson, John P. "Building His Own Legend: Billy the Kid and the Media." *New Mexico Historical Review* 82 (Spring 2007): 221–35.

Woods, Walter. "Billy the Kid." In *The Great Train Robbery and Other Recent Melodramas*. Ed. Garrett H. Leverton. Princeton, N.J.: Princeton University Press, 1940, 197-255. A drama.

FILMS

(Chronological)

Billy the Kid, 1911 (Larry Trimble, director; Edith Storey as Billy the Kid; Julia Swayne Gordon as Billy's mother)

Billy the Bandit, 1916 (John Steppling, director; "Smiling Billy" Mason as Billy the Kid)

Billy the Kid, 1930 (King Vidor, director; Johnny Mack Brown as Billy the Kid)

Billy the Kid Returns, 1938 (Joseph Kane, director; Roy Rogers as Billy; Smiley Burnette as Frog Millhouse)

Billy the Kid Outlawed, 1940 (Sam Newfield, director; Bob Steele as Billy; Al St. John as Fuzzy Jones)

Billy the Kid in Texas, 1940 (Sam Newfield, director; Bob Steele as Billy; Al St. John as Fuzzy Jones)

Billy the Kid's Gun Justice, 1940 (Sam Newfield, director; Bob Steele as Billy the Kid; Al St. John as Fuzzy Jones)

Billy the Kid's Fighting Pals, 1941 (Sam Newfield, director; Bob Steele as Billy; Al St. John as Fuzzy Jones)

Billy the Kid, 1941 (David Miller, director; Robert Taylor as Billy; Brian Donlevy as Jim Sherwood; Mary Howard as Edith Keating)

Billy the Kid in Santa Fe, 1941 (Sam Newfield, director; Bob Steele as Billy; Al St. John as Fuzzy Jones; Rex Lease as Jeff)

Billy the Kid's Range War, 1941 (Sam Newfield, director; Bob Steele as Billy the Kid; Al St. John as Fuzzy Q. Jones; Carleton Young as Jeff)

Bibliography

Billy the Kid Wanted, 1941 (Sam Newfield, director; Buster Crabbe as Billy; Al St. John as Fuzzy Jones)

Billy the Kid's Round Up, 1941 (Sam Newfield, director; Buster Crabbe as Billy; Al St. John as Fuzzy Jones)

Billy the Kid Trapped, 1942 (Sam Newfield, director; Buster Crabbe as Billy; Al St. John as Fuzzy Jones)

Billy the Kid's Smoking Guns, 1942 (Sam Newfield, director; Buster Crabbe as Billy; Al St. John as Fuzzy Jones)

Law and Order, 1942 (Sam Newfield, director; Buster Crabbe as Billy; Al St. John as Fuzzy Jones)

Sheriff of Sage Valley, 1942 (Sam Newfield, director; Buster Crabbe as Billy; Al St. John as Fuzzy Jones)

West of Tombstone, 1942 (Howard Bretherton, director; Gordon DeMain as Billy/Wilfred Barnet)

The Mysterious Rider, 1942 (Sam Newfield, director; Buster Crabbe as Billy; Al St. John as Fuzzy Jones; Caroline Burke as Martha Kincaid)

The Kid Rides Again, 1943 (Sam Newfield, director; Buster Crabbe as Billy; Al St. John as Fuzzy Jones; Iris Meredith as Joan Ainsley)

The Outlaw, 1943 (Howard Hughes, director; Jack Beutel as Billy; Jane Russell as Rio McDonald; Thomas Mitchell as Pat Garrett; Walter Huston as Doc Holiday)

Fugitive of the Plains, 1943 (Sam Newfield, director; Buster Crabbe as Billy; Al St. John as Fuzzy Jones)

Western Cyclone, 1943 (Sam Newfield, director; Buster Crabbe as Billy; Al St. John as Fuzzy Jones; Marjorie Manners as Mary Arnold)

The Renegade, 1943 (Sam Newfield, director; Buster Crabbe as Billy; Al St. John as Fuzzy Jones)

Cattle Stampede, 1943 (Sam Newfield, director; Buster Crabbe as Billy; Al St. John as Fuzzy Jones)

Blazing Frontier, 1943 (Sam Newfield, director; Buster Crabbe as Billy; Al St. John as Fuzzy Jones)

Alias Billy the Kid, 1946 (Thomas Carr, director; Sunset Carson as Sunset Carson; Peggy Stewart as Ann Marshall)

Return of the Badmen, 1948 (Ran Enright, director; Dean White as Billy; Randolph Scott as Vance; Robert Ryan as Sundance Kid; Lex Barker as Emmett Dalton)

Four Faces West, 1948 (Alfred E. Green, director; Joel McCrea as Ross McEwen; Charles Bickford as Pat Garrett; Joseph Calleia as Monte Marquez; Frances Dee as Fay Hollister)

Son of Billy the Kid, 1949 (Ray Taylor, director; William Perrott as Billy; Al St. John as Fuzzy Jones; Lash LaRue as Marshal Jack Garrett)

Bibliography

The Kid from Texas, 1950 (Kurt Neumann, director; Audie Murphy as Billy; Gale Storm as Irene Kain; Will Geer as O'Fallon; Frank Wilcox as Pat Garrett)

I Shot Billy the Kid, 1950 (William A. Berke, director; Don "Red" Barry as Billy; Robert Lowery as Pat Garrett)

Captive of Billy the Kid, 1952 (Fred C. Bannon, director; Allan Lane as Marshal "Rocky" Lane; Penny Edwards as Nancy McCreary)

The Law vs. Billy the Kid, 1954 (William Castle, director; Scott Brady as Billy; James Griffith as Pat Garrett; Betta St. John as Nita Maxwell)

The Boy from Oklahoma, 1954 (Michael Curtiz, director; Will Rogers Jr. as Sheriff Tom Brewster; Tyler MacDuff as Billy; Nancy Olson as Katie Branningan)

Strange Lady in Town, 1955 (Mervyn LeRoy as director; Greer Garson as Dr. Julia Winslow Garth; Nick Adams as Billy; Dana Andrews as Rourke O'Brien)

Last of the Desperados, 1955 (Sam Newfield, director; James Craig as Pat Garrett; Jim Davis as John Poe; Bob Steele as Charlie Bowdre)

The Parson and The Outlaw, 1957 (Oliver Drake, director; Anthony Dexter as Billy; Sonny Tufts as Jack Slade; Charles "Buddy" Rogers as Reverend Jones)

Badman's Country, 1958 (Fred F. Sears, director; George Montgomery as Pat Garrett; Neville Brand as Butch Cassidy; Buster Crabbe as Wyatt Earp)

The Left Handed Gun, 1958 (Arthur Penn, director; Paul Newman as Billy; Lita Milan as Celsa; John Dehner as Pat Garrett)

One-Eyed Jacks, 1961 (Marlon Brando, director; Marlon Brando as Rio; Karl Malden as Dad Longworth; Pina Pellicer as Louisa; Katy Jurado as Maria; Slim Pickens as Lon Dedrick; Ben Johnson as Bob Amory)

A Bullet for Billy the Kid, 1963 (Rafael Baledon, director; Gaston Sands as Billy; Steve Brodie as Judd)

Deadwood '76, 1965 (James Landis, director; Arch Hall Jr. as Billy/Billy May; Richard Dix as Wild Bill Hickok; Melissa Morgan as Poker Kate)

The Outlaws Is Coming! 1965 (Norman Maurer, director; Larry Fine, Moe Howard, Joe DeRita as the Three Stooges; Johnny Ginger as Billy the Kid; Nancy Kovack as Annie Oakley)

Billy the Kid vs. Dracula, 1966 (William Beaudine, director; John Carradine as Count Dracula; Chuck Courtney as Billy the Kid)

Chisum, 1970 (Andrew V. McLaglen, director; John Wayne as John Chisum; Geoffrey Deuel as Billy; Glenn Corbett as Pat Garrett; Lynda Day as Susan McSween; Pamela McMyler as Sallie Chisum)

Bibliography

The Last Movie, 1971 (Dennis Hopper, director; Dennis Hopper as Kansas; Dean Stockwell as Billy; Stella Garcia as Maria; Rod Cameron as Pat Garrett)

Dirty Little Billy, 1972 (Stan Dragoti, director; Michael J. Pollard as Billy; Richard Evans as Goldie)

Pat Garrett and Billy the Kid, 1973 (Sam Peckinpah, director; Kris Kristofferson as Billy; James Coburn as Pat Garrett; Jason Robards Jr. as Lew Wallace; Katy Jurado as Mrs. Baker; Rita Coolidge as Maria; Bob Dylan as Alias)

Young Guns, 1988 (Christopher Cain, director; Emilio Estevez as Billy; Kiefer Sutherland as Doc Scurlock; Jack Palance as Lawrence Murphy; Lou Diamond Phillips as Jose Chavez y Chavez; Charlie Sheen as Dick Brewer)

Bill and Ted's Excellent Adventure, 1989 (Stephen Herek, director; Dan Schor as Billy; Alex Winter as Bill S. Peterson, Esq.; Keanu Reeves as Ted Logan)

Young Guns II, 1990 (Geoff Murphy, director; Emilio Estevez as Billy; Kiefer Sutherland as Doc Scurlock; James Coburn as John Chisum; Lou Diamond Phillips as Jose Chavez y Chavez)

1313: Billy the Kid, 2012 (David DeCoteau, director; Brandon Thornton as Billy; Jason Zahodnik as Whitecastle; Chelsea Rae Bernier as Lollie)

Billy the Kid, 2013 (Christopher Forbes, director; Christopher Bowman as William Bonney/Billy; Kimberly Campbell as Katherine [Catherine] Bonney [McCarty, Antrim]); Cody McCarver as Leon Copper)

The Last Days of Billy the Kid, 2017 (Christopher Forbes, director; Jason Cash as Billy; Cody McCarver as Pat Harrett; Jezibell Anat as One-Eyed Lilly)

Billy the Kid: Showdown in Lincoln County, 2017 (Christopher Forbes, director; Christopher Bowman as William Bonney/Billy; Cody McCarver as Leon Copper; Jezibell Anat as One-Eyed Lilly

Index

References to illustrations appear in italic type.

Index

Bail, John D., 176

bailes (dances), 31, 152

Baker, Frank, 95–96

Barber, Sue McSween, 116, 264–65, 295. *See also* McSween, Susan

Barlow, Billy, 260, 368

Bean, Amelia, 333–34

Bell, Bob Boze, 181, *381*

Bell, James W., 178–81

Bernstein, Morris, 129

Big Kill, the, 119–25, 204–6

Billy and Paulita (Cooper), 362–63

Billy LeRoy, the Colorado Bandit; or, the King of the American Highwaymen (Daggett), 228–30

Billy the Kid, *2*, 123–31, 137–40, 149–54, 158–59; biographical books and essays about, 242–49, 255–82, 308–27, 351–70; and family, 1–10, *25*, 23–30, 190–92; in dime novels, 227–38; in fiction, 249–54, 282–92, 333–41, 370–74; in films, 292–307, 341–50, 374–78; in Fort Sumner, 151–54, 161, 167, 184–88; and Hispanics, 112, 182–84, 188, 202; historiography of, 326–33; legends about, 160–70, 177, 281–82; and Lew Wallace, 146–48, 166, 172–73, 177–78, 209–10; in Lincoln town, 111–12, 123–25, 148–50, 178–81, 207; and Pat Garrett, 157–58, 160–64, 183–88, 218–19; in photographs, *2*, 381–83; trial of, 175–77; and women, 36,

191–92, 200, 202, 215–17. *See also* Antrim, Henry H.; Bonney, William (Billy) H.; and McCarty, Henry

Billy the Kid (movie, 1911), 293

Billy the Kid (movie, 1930), *285*, 294–96

Billy the Kid (movie, 1941), 297–98

Billy the Kid (movie, 2013), 374–77

Billy the Kid (Wood), 252

Billy the Kid: A Novel (Corle), 289–90

Billy the Kid: A Short and Violent Life (Utley), 101, *324*, 323–26

Billy the Kid: Showdown in Lincoln County, 374–77

Billy the Kid: The Bibliography of a Legend (Dykes), 327, 392

Billy the Kid: The Endless Ride (Wallis), 355–57

Billy the Kid: The Legend of El Chivato (Fackler), 340–41

Billy the Kid: The Life and Legend (Tuska), 331–33

Billy the Kid: The Trail of a Kansas Legend (Koop), 311–12

Billy the Kid Returns, 296–97

Billy the Kid's Last Ride (Aragon), 371

Billy the Kid's Pretenders: Brushy Bill and John Miller (Cooper), 364, 380

Billy the Kid's Writings: Words and Wit (Cooper), 364

Blazer, Joseph (Dr.), 101, 204

Blazer's Mill, *102*, 101–4

Boggs, Johnny D., 303–4, 371–72, 396

Index

Index

Index

Index

427

Index